CW00801381

The Essential Saker

from the trenches of the emerging multipolar world

The Saker

Nimble Pluribus
the post-imperialism library

Nimble Books LLC
1521 Martha Avenue
Ann Arbor, MI, USA 48103
http://www.NimbleBooks.com
wfz@nimblebooks.com
+1.734-646-6277

Printed in the United States of America
ISBN-13: 978-1-60888-058-4

♾ The paper used in this publication meets the minimum requirements of the American National Standard for Information Sciences—Permanence of Paper for Printed Library Materials, ANSI Z39.48-1992. The paper is acid-free and lignin-free.

For Ak., Anna, Claude, Fred, Jv., Pepe, Scott And Tatiana Who Believed In Me

Contents

ABOUT THE AUTHOR

The Saker was born in a military family of "White" Russian refugees in western Europe where he lived most of his life. After completing two college degrees in the USA, he returned to Europe were he worked as a military analyst until he lost his career due to his vocal opposition to the western-sponsored wars in Chechnia, Croatia, Bosnia and Kosovo. After re-training as a software engineer, he moved to the Florida where he now lives with his wife, a veterinarian, and their three children. When he does not blog or help his wife at work, the likes to explore the Florida wilderness on foot, mountain bike and kayak or play acoustic jazz guitar.

ABOUT THE SAKER'S BLOGS

The Saker is the founder of the Saker Community of Blogs, **the only such international and multi-lingual community of blogs**. It now features:

- **8** blogs (Main, French, Russian, Oceanian, Latin American, Italian, German, Serbian) written in
- 7 languages (English, Russian, French, German, Spanish, Italian and Serbian) on
- 4 continents (North and South America, Europe, Asia, Oceania) with
- 4 YouTube Channels (Main, Oceania, French, Italian)

The main blog alone gets well over **one million pageviews per month**. The community is composed of about **100 volunteers including professional translators** and it collaborates with all the main English-language blogs about Russia and the Ukraine. Articles from the Saker blog are picked up by **Russia Insider**, the **Asia Times**, **Information Clearing House** and many others news sources and our work has been quoted by **Paul Craig Roberts**, **Sheikh Imran Hosein**, **Pepe Escobar** and many others.

FOREWORD BY PEPE ESCOBAR

Is it a bird? Is it a Sukhoi? Is it a (digital) submarine?

Once in a long while across the vast spectrum of the surveilled, monopolized, sanitized by (alleged) common sense/copyright/control/ conformism Net, an unidentified digital object (UDO) catches our fancy and leads us to dream.

A UDO breaks on through what is already a mode of life, surveillance, production and organization, and crosses over to the other side.

This instance of poetic justice is even more appealing when we're talking about a state of the art submarine crossing a digital desert.

Well, the UDO in question happens to view himself as a submarine. But actually, he's the bird.

Don't you know about the bird?—as The Trashmen immortalized it in 1963. *The bird is the word.* And the bird with the word's got to be The Saker.

When I first came across The Saker, in one of those endless white nights prowling the Net, I loved it as much as The Trashmen forever changing the face of rock 'n' roll. The Saker was changing the Net forever as far as serious discussion of Russia was concerned.

This was the real deal; a Russian possessing a fine intellect, living in the underbelly of the Empire of Chaos, speaking from the heart, way beyond Left or Right, not to mention the middle. A post-everything Pre-Socratic, a neo-Diogenes searching for truth in the wasteland of the Russia versus The West manufactured crisis. And, crucially, a man of integrity.

Or, in his own words, "disrespectful of social dogmas and norms, oppositional and defiant towards authority, rebellious and aggressive by nature, deeply contrarian on an almost knee-jerk level, libertarian in outlook." What's not to like?

All that fully exposed via his own, inimitable style: straight from the heart marinated in intellectual acuity. As a running commentary on the Burroughs intuition of language as a virus from outer space, here was a UDO spreading a very powerful virus into the Russian demonization hydra.

The audience for this running epic was just there to be captured. So it was a pleasure to see how a one-man-blog steered by an anonymous incarnating a bird ended up morphing into a global community, in myriad languages, helped by tens of volunteers, in less than one year.

The bird? Sukhoi? submarine? has been relentless in deconstructing the Full Spectrum War launched by the usual suspects on Russia and Vladimir Putin.

This collection packs the punch of some certified classics, such as the ground-breaking Saker series on Russia and Islam.

By October 2103, even before the demented acceleration of both the Ukraine and Syria crises, The Saker penned a cracker destined for Net legend: his piece *1993-2013: is the twenty years long "pas de deux" of Russia and the USA coming to an end?*

He was already among the very, very few who unmasked the strategic demonization campaign against Russia, depicted as a threat to the West.

He dove deeper into the fundamental distinction in Russia between those he describes as "Eurasian Sovereignists" versus the "Atlantic Integrationists." Or, to simplify it, the "Putin people" versus the "Medvedev people."

And he was probably the only one to point out how the US under Obama had become so similar to the USSR under Brezhnev.

It's impossible not to admire the trademark Russian passion for ideas—and their almost religious reverence for major cultural icons. And then there's Russian genius.

When discussing the Russian national genius, Bakunin emphasized the sense of social justice and spirit of solidarity shared by Russians. So he was right to define Russians as insurgents—because they instinctively harbor a sense of justice. No wonder the Pentagon is so paranoid about Russia.

And we must, once again, rely on Dostoyevsky. He emphasized how the Russian sense of solidarity was not about the glorification of the individual; it was about a community linked around a moral exigency and the idea that social justice is absolutely fundamental.

So what the bird? Sukhoi? submarine is fighting for, one article at a time, is justice in a—geopolitical—world gone amok. No wonder, for so many of us, he's a cherished soul mate. So let's get into the game. Time to fly. Or, evoking Eliot, *to scuttle across the floors of silent seas* – like a silent submarine.

Pepe Escobar

Paris, October 2015

PREFACE

This volume is a collection of various articles and essays I wrote for my blog (initially at http://vineyardsaker.blogspot.com and later at http://thesaker.is) between 2007 and 2015. For many years my blog had very few readers, in the hundreds, at best, and most of my writing I, frankly, did for myself. For me, as a former military analyst, it was a much needed psychotherapy: I could write whatever I wanted, whenever I wanted and in whatever style I wanted. I did not have to look over my shoulder to check whether some boss would approve of what I wrote, I did not have to worry about offending somebody's political sensitivities, and I could basically write the way I speak: off the cuff and with no preparations. Looking back, I see that there were many advantages to this: the writing was spontaneous, informal, sometimes funny and always fast. But now that these articles have turned into a book, they bring with themselves a lot of weaknesses: not just poor grammar and ever-present typos, but also superficial fact-checking, sources given as links (including 'dead' ones) and references to missing images or videos. My heroic editor and Director of Research, Scott, did a fantastic job of cleaning up a very messy collection of essays, but there is only so much that could be done without a total re-write. So, dear reader, *caveat emptor*: the book you will be reading is, to put it mildly, not up to academic standards. My hope is that for some of you this might actually turn out to be a plus rather than an annoyance. To the others, I present my apologies.

The second admission that I need to make is that over the years I did change some of my views, sometimes radically. For example, I will freely admit that in the early 2000s I was deeply suspicious of Vladimir Putin. It also took be a long while to change my initially negative view of Ramzan Kadyrov and Bashar al-Assad. Heck – it took me 7 years to finally accept the truth about 9/11! Some will no doubt ridicule me for these changes of heart, but I personally see them simply as a proof that even when I make mistakes I am willing to be proven wrong by facts, a good thing, I think. So please pay close attention to the date indicated at the bottom of each article.

There are two things for which I do not make any apologies whatsoever: everything I wrote I did from the prospective of a Russian and Orthodox point of view. And when I say Russian, I do not mean "Soviet", but a mix of pre-1917 and post-2000 Russian worldviews. And by "Orthodox", I mean a traditionalist, Patristic, "original/ancient Christian" point of view which has its roots in the faith "*which the Lord gave, was preached by the Apostles, and was preserved by the Fathers. On this was the Church founded; and if anyone departs from this, he neither is nor any longer ought to be called a Christian*" (St. Athanasius) and not the bizarre "post-Christian Christianity" which nowadays passes for the real thing and for which I have no use and, for that matter, no patience. Thus my values are most definitely not the ones you will find anywhere near any form of "mainstream"—not political and not religious.

Last, but not least, I want to thank all those who made not only this book, but also the blog possible: my family, of course, but also the wonderful Saker Community including, translators, editors, team leaders, sponsors, moderators, commentators, writers, transcribers, video technicians, correspondents, IT specialists, webmasters, graphic designers, researchers, lawyers, donors, and simply friends who helped me day after day even in the most difficult circumstances and many of whom have since become my friends. There are no words to adequately express my deepest feelings of gratitude towards all of you!

The Saker

Introduction: "Submarines in the desert" *(as my deepest gratitude* to you)

I have been thinking about writing this post for several months now. But in a world where everything coming from the heart is misconstrued as some form of posturing, I was frankly afraid to do so. Also, writing that kind of stuff is not what bloggers do, much less so those who try to run a halfway credible blog. And yet, every time I got a kind email, a letter or even a gift, I felt that I have to write this. God knows I am opening myself up for even more misrepresentations as usual, but I think it is well worth it. My spiritual father always used to say "*one soul is more precious than the entire universe.*"

So I dedicate this post to that one soul.

Introduction

My life has been one of ups and downs. Early on, after a pretty nasty childhood, it went up, rather rapidly. Then came the "fall from (pseudo-) grace" and I lost my career. It is still too early to go into all the details, but let's just say that I used to be associated with a "three letter outfit" whose existence was not well known by the general public and which has since been disbanded. In my field, I got to the proverbial 'top' pretty early on, but soon the war in Bosnia began to open my eyes to many things I had never suspected before. Then I found out about two things which got me blacklisted in my own, putatively democratic, country: I found out that a group of people had uselessly been murdered as a result of the criminal incompetence of their superiors and I found out that one guy had taken a long jail sentence while all this superiors had managed to walk away from a crime they all had committed. And even though I never went public, or even told my closest friends about it (to protect them), I was blacklisted and prevented from ever working again.

In those dark days my wonderful wife was always trying to tell me that it was not my fault, that I had never done anything wrong, that I was paying the price for being a person of integrity and that I had proven many times over how good I was in my field. I always used to bitterly reply to her that I was like a "submarine in a desert": maybe very good at "something somewhere", but useless in my current environment (I always used to visualize a *Akula*-class SSN stranded smack in the middle of the Sahara desert—what a sight that would be! I wish somebody would use a Photoshop-like software to create that pic). What I have found out since, is that our planet is covered with deserts and that there are many, many submarines in them, all yearning for the vastness of an ocean.

Modest beginnings at first

I came to the USA in 2002 with **only** one desire: to leave my past on the other side of the ocean and to disappear, to become an anonymous "nobody" who would be left alone. More than anything else, I needed time to recover, to lick my wounds and to spend time with the only people who had stood by my side without ever doubting me: my wife and my kids.

The French have a very good saying: "*chassez le naturel et il revient au galop.*" which can roughly be translated as "try to suppress your nature, and it will come back with a vengeance." This is what happened to me. While in 2002 I had promised myself to never analyze anything more complicated that a fiction book, by 2007 I suddenly decided to start a blog. This blog. My goal? Very, very primitive: to write whatever the hell I wanted. I had spent so many years writing for "big people" who had very narrow limits of what they were willing to read that I decided to indulge in the joy of writing whatever I wanted with no concern or regard for anybody's opinion. I had an itch to scratch I decided to scratch it.

You can still parse the archives of 2007 or 2008 and you will see that I really was making **no** efforts to reach anybody, make a difference or become popular. A short and ill-fated contact with Antiwar.com (which ended up in disaster),[1] gave me a few more readers but my readership was still tiny.

My choice of topics did not help. Years before, I had literally "bumped" into the topic of Hezbollah and, my curiosity piqued, I spent a decade studying this movement and its amazing leader. By 2007 I was an unrepentant Hezbollah groupie and Nasrallah fanboy and most of the blog dealt with the Middle East. The other topic was Russia, simply because this was the country my family came from and which I had professionally analyzed for years. As for the Ukraine[2], I don't think that I ever mentioned it at all. While I was disgusted with the ignorance and hatefulness of Ukrainian nationalists, I did not care about the Ukraine: "let them soak in their own 'independent' and yet pathetic and clearly sinking statelet if they want—I have more inspiring things to look at" was my philosophy at the time. Sure, I kept an eye on events there, but to me this reminded me of Russia in 1993—I was disgusted with all the actors and with the entire situation. Besides, what could happen there which would be worthy of interest?

And sure enough, life proved me wrong (-: again :-)

The big wars of 2013

First, there was Syria and the Russian role in stopping Uncle Sam. Oh yes, there were the political efforts of the Russian diplomats, and they were "bad" enough. But less noticed what the fact that Russia sent a hastily assembled but capable naval task force to the Syrian coast. Not a task

---

[1] Reflections on the Antiwar.com debacle: http://thesaker.is/reflections-on-the-antiwar-com-debacle/

[2] Writing "Ukraine" makes no sense from the linguistic point of view *and* it is a rather crude attempt to obfuscate that the word "Ukraine" means "borderland" or "frontier" which, in turn, begs the question "borderland" or "frontier" of what? Since the answer is "Russia," "the" has to be dropped.

force big enough to fight the US Navy, but a task force capable of providing a full view of the skies over and beyond Syria to the Syrian military. In other words, for the first time the US could not achieve a surprise attack on Syria, not with cruise missiles, not with airpower. Worse, Russia, Iran and Hezbollah embarked on a covert and overt program of material and technical assistance for Syria which ended up defeating the Wahhabi insurgency. The AngloZionists (more on this in Part IV) were absolutely **livid**. So to teach Putin and those damn Russkies a good lesson, they blew up the Ukraine and, again, Putin did two things they had never expected and which they could never forgive: he did send forces to Crimea but he did not do so in Novorussia: there he helped covertly. There was no doubt possible: Russia had committed the "Crime of Crimes" of openly defying the will of our planetary overlords. The Empire's response was predictable: a full-spectrum "war" on Russia and Putin, albeit not an overtly military one (yet).

For me and my blog, the consequence of this mega-crisis was immediate: the readership literally exploded and, at the suggestion of others (it was not even my idea!), more Saker blogs suddenly began popping up. From a unknown one-man anonymous blog the Saker blog morphed into a global community, and that over less than one year.

[Sidebar: I often fell like a war profiteer. The worse the situation in the Ukraine, the more readers I get, the calmer, the less. On a really quiet day I get as little as 20,000 hits, on a really bad day, up to 69,000. I estimate my more or less regular readership at no more than 30,000.]

I am outlining all this to truthfully explain to you that this was never the plan for me. Not only was this completely unplanned, it even took me by surprise. In fact, I was so surprised that I could not honestly make sense of it. Think of it.

Here is a one-man blog, written by some anonymous dude with a silly alias, who repeatedly engages in all sorts of crimethink (like the day when I wrote—to a mainly Arab readership—that I believed that Hamas ought to unconditionally release Gilad Shalit,[3] LOL!) who is neither from the Left, nor from the right, whose writing is chock-full of typos and, frankly, very poorly written sentences—and yet this blog suddenly takes off like a rocket. And you can tell by my writing style that I don't even take myself too seriously. But so what in the world has happened here?

Sure, I am a decent analyst, I know Russian and a few other languages, I have studied Russia for all my life and the Middle East for, well, a little over a decade. This is not bad, but hardly a reason for such a success.

Then I understood:

It was never about me, but always about you.

Along with more daily visitors, I began receiving more and more emails and letters. And presents. Often very touching ones. Just look at the absolutely beautiful drawing of a Saker Falcon I got yesterday (thanks SO MUCH "S.T."! I will frame and posted it on my wall).

People who had never met me and who really knew nothing about me were literally pouring kindness over me. Most emails and letter centered on political issues, but a big minority were expressing much deeper feelings such as gratitude and a desire to morally support. I was amazed, really. Then my readers began suggesting that I should place a donation button on the blog. Many may not believe me here, but that idea had never even crossed my mind. Eventually, I did (God knows I needed the money) and to my absolute amazement people began donating. Why? Why would anybody in our cynical word filled with crooks donate some hard earned and always scarce money to a guy he/she has never met? Was that just because I was posting materials about Syria or the Ukraine? Or my oh-so-good analyses? Hardly.

And then there was also the rage. Many, many letters were literally oozing with rage. Rage against the government, its media, the Empire, the lies and the dishonesty. Rage at having been lied to. Rage at the hu-

---

[3] Why Hamas should release Gilad Shalit http://thesaker.is/why-hamas-should-release-gilad-shalit/

miliation of being treated like a serf or a slave. Rage at our dysfunctional and self-destructive society. Before that, I had no idea that so many people were so mad.

The most gut-wrenching letters were often from US servicemen. They often began with "I consider myself a patriotic American and I love my country which I served for many years in the military but ..." and here it inevitably turned into a painful admission that this country was led by evil crooks, occupied by parasites, owned by a 1% of SOBs whom everybody else despises. And you would simply not believe the kind of stuff these correspondents, including former servicemen, would write about Putin. It was amazing—I regularly joke that if given a chance to run, Putin might be elected as President of the US of A.

[Sidebar: By the way, I will not post these letters here. Not even excepts. First, I want to protect the trust of those who wrote to me. Second, some of these letters are so amazing and moving that I will inevitably be accused of making them up. So I will simply forgo presenting any "proof" for my statements. Believe me or not—makes no difference to me. And if you don't—then I guess that yours is not the soul I dedicate this post to anyway.]

So there I was trying to figure out—why such an outpouring of kindness for a total stranger (and an anonymous one at that!) and such an outpouring of rage against the society we live in. And then, I think that I figured it out.

The deserts are filled with submarines (but they are breaking free!)

That's it. I had mistakenly believed that I was the only one feeling like a submarine in a desert, but in reality the deserts of our society were filled with people who felt completely alienated. Several times in the past I posted here the beautiful song by David Rovics "We are everywhere"[4]

[4]David Rovics We Are Everywhere https://soundcloud.com/davidrovics/we-are-everywhere

because with each passing month I began to realize that he was **literally right**—we are, indeed, everywhere.

What society had done to me—made me completely powerless—it has also done to you. And just the way it had made me feel like a single lonely nutcase, it made you feel like you were the only one. I most sincerely believe that the real reason for the success of this blog, its global community, its vibrant discussions and the amazing outpouring of kindness toward me is in the following simple fact: I inadvertently made it possible for many thousands of people to realize that they were **not** alone, **not** crazy, **not** wrong but that quite literally "we are everywhere"!

The second thing that I did, again quite inadvertently, is to empower those who felt powerless to do something, to make a change, to really have an impact.

Our societies are designed to make us feel like prison inmates, serfs or slaves. We all know that voting is a useless joke, that our rulers don't give a damn about us, that political dissent is frowned on when it is real, that revolts are crushed in violence, that pluralism is viciously repressed by the prevailing ideology, that our schools brainwash and stupidify our kids and turn them against us, that the home brainwashing appliances like the Idiot Tube, the radio or the papers are here to do only three things: entertain us, get our money and zombify us. We know that, but we feel powerless to do anything about it.

By asking for help in my work on the blog and, especially, by allowing for what I call "spontaneous self-organization" (something which I had directly taken from how the Debian Linux software community functions) I had given those who shared my goals a readily available means to take action. And I have to say that the result exceeded my expectations by many orders of magnitude (and made me realize that some "amateurs" are at least as good as, or better, than "pros"). Treat people with respect, give them a chance, and they will do miracles for you!

[Sidebar: if you are interested in how big complex projects can self-organize, please read—online—chapter 2.4 "The Debian Community" pp 46-57 in this[5] book. Of course, I did not deliberately try to copy the Debian model, but I did apply the "just do it" principle and I let each Saker Blog self-organize in a completely independent manner. I also see my own role in the Saker community as one of a "benevolent dictator," another free software phenomenon, though, so far, I have only had to act in this capacity once.]

Thanks to my inadvertently stumbling into the fantastic and yet untapped potential of so many good people our community began to grow almost spontaneously (several Saker Blog Team Leaders have also expressed to me the same amazement I was feeling).

Suddenly many "submarines" had found their oceans to show what they were really capable off!

Do you know about the Asch conformity experiment? [If not, take a quick look here[6] before reading on]. Well, I think that my oppositional-defiant personality inadvertently crashed at least part of the gigantic Asch conformity experiment our society has become. I was calling it as I was seeing it and to hell with the consequences (I had so few readers anyways...) Then, in 2010 I decided to really give a good kick into the sandcastle of our delusions and posted an article entitled "Why am I not hearing the endless rumble of jaws dropping to the floor?"[7] In this post I basically repeated something which anybody could verify and which was undeniable: the National Institute of Standards and Technology (NIST) had, by **direct implication**, admitted that WTC7 had been brought down

---

[5] The Debian System http://www.e-reading.club/bookreader.php/138757/Krafft_-_The_Debian_System._Concepts_and_Techniques..pdf

[6] Asch conformity experiments https://en.wikipedia.org/wiki/Asch_conformity_experiments

[7] Why am I not hearing the endless rumble of jaws dropping to the floor?! (UPDATED!) http://thesaker.is/why-am-i-not-hearing-the-endless-rumble-of-jaws-dropping-to-the-floor-updated/

by controlled demolition. Furthermore, and contrary to popular belief, NIST has simply **no** explanation **at all** for how the WTC1 and WTC2 had fallen. And yet, this amazing fact was completely obfuscated by the collective Asch experiment being imposed on us. But the reality is that the 9/11 issue is just a tip of an iceberg. Our entire society is one big, long and never ending Asch experiment and most of us, at least on some level, know about it. We all feel what the "Matrix" series calls the feeling like a "splinter in our mind."

I suppose that for types like myself (disrespectful of social dogmas and norms, oppositional and defiant toward authority, rebellious and aggressive by nature, deeply contrarian on an almost knee-jerk level, libertarian in outlook) the outcome of the tension between what I feel and what I am told to feel results in a long battle against the established order and dominant ideology (no wonder another two of my favorite songs of David Rovics are "*Burn it down*"[8] and "*We will shut them down*"[9]). But once a bad guy like myself decided to yank the splinter out of my mind—others decided to give it a try too and that is how it all began.

My gratitude to you

And here is what I wanted to say through all of the above: I **know** that I personally do not deserve such kindness and gratitude. In reality, the very fact that **you** have shown me so much kindness also shows that you are truly the one deserving gratitude and praise. I am just the very very lucky one—you are the kind and generous one. And, please believe me, this has nothing to do with me engaging in some kind of false modesty—I truly believe it, this is the conclusion I have come to from **your** letter and **your** emails.

In conclusion, I want to share a special song with all those of your who have "poured out their souls to me" (Russian expression). It is from

---

[8] David Rovics Burn It Down https://soundcloud.com/davidrovics/burn-it-down

[9] David Rovics Shut Them Down http://www.soundclick.com/player/single_player.cfm?songid=759278&q=hi&newref=1

the Russian bard Vladimir Vyssotskii and it is called "*Song of the Earth*"[10]:

Here are the lyrics (translated by George Tokarev)[11]

Is the earth, as they say, burnt and dried?
Will a seed, as they say, never sprout?
Has the earth, as they say, really died?
No! It's taken a lengthy time-out!

Mother Earth will forever give birth,
Its maternity isn't a fiction!
Don't believe that they burnt down the earth,
No! It's blackened from grief and affliction.

Trenches, running like scars back and forth...
Bleeding guts black shell-craters expose...
They are open nerves of the earth,
Which unearthly unhappiness knows.

It will stand wars and grief - any thing!
It's not crippled, though booted and looted...
Don't believe that the earth doesn't sing,
That it's quieted down, diluted!

No, it's singing as loud as it can
From a trench, from a wound, from a hole!
Since the earth is the soul of Man,
Boots cannot trample down the soul!

---

[10] V.Vysotsky Песня о земле."Кто сказал: Все сгорело дотла..." https://www.youtube.com/watch?v=t5PlgV5IaE8

[11] Vladimir Vyssotskii Song about the Earth http://www.wysotsky.com/1033.htm?569

This last sentence, "boot cannot trample down the soul!" speaks, I believe, not only of physical boots, though these are also meant, but also about psychological, ideological, social boots who, no less than the real thing, try hard to trample down on our souls.

Remember the last sentence of Orwell's 1984? "He loved Big Brother." I always absolutely hated that sentence. Yes, for the purpose of the book, this was the correct ending being, as it was, a warning. But I always though "hell, no I will always hate Big Brother", "boots cannot trample down souls."

What you all, my friends, have proven to me is that there are many of us who will not love Big Brother and that Big Brother has not trampled down our souls. Twenty years ago I used to feel like the most lonely man on the planet. Now, thanks to you, I feel like we are everywhere and I have friend, free fellow humans, all over the planet.

And for that you have my eternal and most heartfelt gratitude,

The Saker

November 13, 2014

PART I: RUSSIA AND ISLAM

RUSSIA AND ISLAM, PART ONE: INTRODUCTION AND DEFINITIONS

Today, I am beginning a series of articles on the very complex topic of Russia and Islam, a topic which is mostly overlooked in the West or, when it is mentioned at all, is often completely misunderstood. I have been researching this fascinating topic for many months already and there is so much to say about it that I have decided to write a series of installments, each one covering one specific aspect of this topic. The nature of the current relationship and interaction between Russia and Islam is a very complex one, with spiritual, political, social, economic, historical and geostrategic aspects. Without already jumping to my conclusions, I will say that the dialectical relationship between Russia and Islam is, I believe, currently undergoing some profound and very dynamic changes which makes it impossible to confidently predict its future.

But first, it is important to stress here that Russia and Islam are not mutually opposite or mutually exclusive concepts. While relatively few ethnic Russians are Muslims, Russia has always been a multi-ethnic state, even when it was just a relatively small principality centered on the city of Kiev.

The word "Russian" in English is used to express two very different Russian concepts: the word "Russkii" means "Russian" as in "part of the Russian ethnicity or culture" and the words "Rossiiskii" which means "part of the country of Russia." Likewise, when Russians speak of "Russkie" they mean the Russian ethnicity whereas when they speak of "Rossiiskie" they refer to the nation-state, to a geographical area. Take for instance the current Minister of Defense of Russia, Sergei Shoigu. He is an ethnic Tuvan through his father (and an ethnic Russian by his mother). If we ignore his maternal lineage, we could say that he is not an ethic Russian ("Russkii") but he is a Russian national ("Rossiiskii"). By the way, Shoigu is not an Orthodox Christian, as most ethnic Russians, but a Buddhist. Likewise, Russia's Minister of Internal Affairs between 2003 and 2011 was Rachid Nurgaliev, an ethnic Tatar, who was born as a Muslim but who eventually converted to the Orthodox faith. Again, he would be considered as a "Rossiianin" (Russian national) but not as a "Russkii."

So while relatively few ethnic Russians are Muslims, there have always been many other (non-Russian) ethnic groups included in the Russian nation, including many Muslims, and these ethnic groups have often played a crucial role in Russian history. From the Vikings who founded the Kievian Rus', to the (mostly Muslim) Mongols who helped Saint Alexander Nevsky defeat the Teutonic Knights of the Papist Northern Crusaders, to the two Chechen special forces battalions who spearheaded the Russian counter-offensive against the Georgian Army in the 08.08.08 war—non-Russians have always played an important role in Russia's history and the existence of a fully legitimate historical "Russian Islam" cannot be denied. Put differently, if "Russkii Islam" is really a minor, almost private, phenomenon, "Rossiiskii Islam" is an phenomenon present throughout the 1000+ years of Russian history and an integral part of Russia's identity.

This is particular important to keep in mind when one hears the misinformed opinions of those who would have Russia as a part of the so-called "Western Christendom." Let's make something clear, the most frequent and meaningful form of interaction the Russian nation has had with western Christianity was war. And every single one of these wars was a defensive war against a Western aggression.

It is true that a good part of the Russian Imperial nobility, which was often of Germanic ethnic extraction, and almost totally composed of active members of the Freemasonry, wanted Russia to become part of the Western civilization. However, this has always been a fashion only among wealthy elites, the already very westernized classes, what Marx would call the "superstructure" of Russia. The Russian Orthodox masses, however, were culturally far closer to their Muslim or Buddhist neighbors than to the westernized elites who took over the reins of power in the 18th century under Tsar Peter I.

While before the 18th century nobody would seriously claim that Russia was part of the Western civilization, after the 18th century there has been an almost continuous effort made by certain members of the Russian upper classes to "modernize" Russia, which really meant "westernizing" it. From Tsar Peter I, to the Decembrist[12] Freemasons, to the Kerensky regime, to the Yeltsin years, Russian "Westernizers" never gave up their struggle to turn Russia into a Western state. I would even claim that the entire Soviet experiment was also an attempt to westernize Russia, albeit not along the usual Papist or Masonic models, but along a Marxist one. What **all** these models have in common is a visceral dislike for the real Russian culture and spirituality, and an obsessive desire to "turn Russia into Poland." The perfect expression for this disdain/hatred for the Russian culture and nation can be found in the following words of Napoleon who said : *"Grattez le Russe, et vous trouverez le Tartare"* (scratch a Russian and you find a Tartar). Coming from the "Masonic Emperor" who used the sanctuaries of the Russian Orthodox Churches as stables for his horses and who, out of spite, attempted to blow up the entire Kremlin, these words reveal the roots of his real aversion for the Russian people.

In contrast, 500 years before the (mostly Muslim) Mongols who invaded Russia usually treated the Russian Church and the Orthodox clergy with utmost respect. Sure, they did not hesitate to burn down a monastery and kill everybody inside, but only if the monastery was used by Russian insurgents in their struggle against the invaders. And yes, some Mongols did force Russian princes to walk through their pagan "purification fire," but these were not Muslim, but pagans. The undeniable fact is that when Russians were subjected to the Muslim yoke it was always far less cruel and barbaric than what the Papist, Masonic or Nazi

[12] Decembrist revolt https://en.wikipedia.org/wiki/Decembrist_revolt

invaders did every time they attempted to invade and subdue Russia. This is why there is no real anti-Islamic current in the Russian popular culture, at least not before the Soviet era which, unfortunately, fundamentally upset a delicate balance that had been reached before 1917.

In the past, westernizing forces saw themselves as "Europeans," as opposed to "Asians," and it is quite remarkable to see how these westernizing forces have become anti-Muslim nowadays (more about that later). While they wholeheartedly support the freedom to organize so-called "Gay pride" parades or the actions of the "Pussy Riot" group, these westernizing forces are categorically opposed to the right of young Muslim girls to wear a scarf on their heads while in school.

Frankly, I do not want to spend any more time discussing the pro-Western forces in Russia mainly because they really have been weakened to the point of representing less than 1 or 2 percent of the population by now. I have to mention these forces here, mostly as a leftover from almost 300 years of unsuccessful attempts to westernize Russia, but this is not were the "interesting stuff" is happening nowadays. Nowadays, it is the heated debates about Islam inside and among the various anti-Western or "patriotic" groups which is so interesting, and this will be the topic of a future installment. But next, we will need to look at the current spiritual condition of the majority of the Russian people.

February 16, 2013

RUSSIA AND ISLAM, PART TWO: RUSSIAN ORTHODOXY

Most people assume that Russia is a Christian Orthodox country and that the Russian Orthodox Church is the spiritual leader of the Russian people. This is a very superficial view and, I would even say, a fundamentally mistaken one. To explain what I mean by this, I will have to explain something absolutely crucial and yet something most fundamentally misunderstood by the vast majority of people, including many Russians. **The Russian Orthodox Church as an institution and the Orthodox spirituality of the Russian people have been severely persecuted since at least 300 years ago.** So crucial is this phenomenon that I will need to make a short historical digression into the history of Russia.

From the moment Russia was baptized into Christianity by Saint Vladimir in 988 to the 17th century rule of Tsar Aleksei Mikhailovich, the Orthodox Church was the organic core of the Russian civilization. In the words of Alexander Solzhenitsyn[13]:

> In its past, Russia did know a time when the social ideal was not fame, or riches, or material success, but a pious way of life. Russia was then steeped in an Orthodox Christianity which remained true to the Church of the first centuries. The Orthodoxy of that time knew how to safeguard its people under the yoke of a foreign occupation that lasted more than two centuries, while at the same time fending off iniquitous blows from the swords of Western crusaders. During those centuries the Orthodox faith in our country became part of the very pattern of thought and the personality of our people, the forms of daily life, the work calendar, the priorities in every undertaking, the organization of the week and of the year. Faith was the shaping and unifying force of the nation.

[13] Orthodox America: "Men Have Forgotten God" – The Templeon Address http://www.roca.org/OA/36/36h.htm

The 17th century, however, saw an abrupt and violent change to this state of affairs. Again, in the words of Solzhenitsyn:

> But in the 17th century Russian Orthodoxy was gravely weakened by an internal schism. In the 18th, the country was shaken by Peter's forcibly imposed transformations, which favored the economy, the state, and the military at the expense of the religious spirit and national life. And along with this lopsided Petrine enlightenment, Russia felt the first whiff of secularism; its subtle poisons permeated the educated classes in the course of the 19th century and opened the path to Marxism. By the time of the Revolution, faith had virtually disappeared in Russian educated circles; and among the uneducated, its health was threatened.

By the time Tsar Nicholas II inherited the throne in 1896 the Russian society was suffering from a deep spiritual crisis: most of the ruling class was highly secularized if not completely materialistic, almost every single aristocratic family had joined the Freemasonry, while the rest of the country, still mostly composed of peasants, was nominally Christian Orthodox, but not in the deep way the Russian nation had been before the 17th century.

Russian Tsars often ended up being real persecutors of the Russian Orthodox Church, in particular those upon whom the Russian aristocracy and the West bestowed the title of "Great." Peter I, the so-called "Great," decapitated the Russian Orthodox Church by abolishing the title of Patriarch from the head of the Church and replacing him by "Synod" run by a layman bureaucrat with the rank of "Chief Procurator" who did not even have to be Orthodox himself. De facto and de jure in 1700 the Russian Orthodox Church became a state institution, like a ministry. Under Catherine I, also called the "Great," monastic were persecuted with such viciousness that it was actually illegal for them to possess even a single sheet of paper in their monastic cell, lest they write something against the regime.

Other Tsars (such as Alexander II, or Alexander III) were far more respectful of the Church and Tsar Nicholas II, who was a deeply religious and pious man, even restored the autonomy of the Church by allowing it to elect a new Patriarch.

And yet, by and large, the Russian Orthodox Church underwent a process of quasi-continuous weakening under the combined effects of overt persecutions and more subtle secularization from the 17th to the 20th century.

In the 20th century during the reign of Tsar Nicholas II, Russian Orthodoxy saw a short but amazing rebirth immediately followed by a mass persecution under the Bolshevik rule whose viciousness and scale was previously unheard of in the history of the Church. Again, in the worlds of Solzhenitsyn:

> The world had never before known a godlessness as organized, militarized, and tenaciously malevolent as that practiced by Marxism. Within the philosophical system of Marx and Lenin, and at the heart of their psychology, hatred of God is the principal driving force, more fundamental than all their political and economic pretensions. Militant atheism is not merely incidental or marginal to Communist policy; it is not a side effect, but the central pivot. The 1920's in the USSR witnessed an uninterrupted procession of victims and martyrs among the Orthodox clergy. Two metropolitans were shot, one of whom, Veniamin of Petrograd,[14] had been elected by the popular vote of his diocese. Patriarch Tikhon[15] himself passed through the hands of the Cheka-GPU and then died under suspicious circumstances. Scores of archbishops and bishops perished. Tens of thousands of priests, monks, and nuns, pressured by the Chekists to renounce the Word of God, were tortured, shot in cellars, sent to camps, exiled to the desolate tundra of the far North, or turned out into the streets in

---

[14] Benjamin (Kazansky) of Petrograd http://http://orthodoxwiki.org/Benjamin_%28Kazansky%29_of_Petrograd

[15] Tikhon of Moscow http://orthodoxwiki.org/Tikhon_of_Moscow

> their old age without food or shelter. All these Christian martyrs went unswervingly to their deaths for the faith; instances of apostasy were few and far between. For tens of millions of laymen access to the Church was blocked, and they were forbidden to bring up their children in the Faith: religious parents were wrenched from their children and thrown into prison, while the children were turned from the faith by threats and lies...

This is a complex and tragic history which I cannot discuss in any details here so I will insist on only one important consequence of these events: the Russian Orthodox Church eventually split into at least four distinct groups:

a) The "official" or "state" Orthodox Church, which eventually became the Moscow Patriarchate. Largely composed of modernist clergymen, this "official" Soviet Church not only denied the reality of the persecution of Christians in Russia, it often *actively collaborated with these persecutions* (by denouncing "subversive" clergymen, for example).

b) The "*Josephites*" composed of the followers of Metropolitan Joseph of Petrograd[16]; they openly refused to submit the Church to Bolshevik regime and were eventually martyred for their stance. Some joined the following group:

c) The "*Catacomb Church.*" This was an illegal, underground, organization, led by secret bishops, which rejected the right of the Bolsheviks to take over the Church and which went into deep hiding, practically disappearing from public view.

d) The "*Russian Orthodox Church Abroad*": composed of exiles, this was an organization created by Metropolitan Anthony of Kiev[17] who, with the blessing of Patriarch Tikhon, united around itself most of the Orthodox Russians who had fled the Soviet Union.

---

[16] Joseph (Petrovykh) of Petrograd http://orthodoxwiki.org/Joseph_%28Petrovykh%29_of_Petrograd

[17] Anthony (Khrapovitsky) of Kiev http://orthodoxwiki.org/Anthony_%28Khrapovitsky%29_of_Kiev

It is important to stress here that even though the Josephites, the Catacomb Church and the Church Abroad did have very few practical means to communicate with each other, they were all in communion with each other and recognized each other as legitimate branches of the One Russian Orthodox Church, although each one in unique and specific circumstances. Not so with the first entity, the official "Soviet" Church which was denounced by all three groups as at the very least illegal and possibly even as the satanic tool of the Bolsheviks.

Why is all this so important?

Because the current official "Russian Orthodox Church of the Moscow Patriarchate" is a direct descendant of this first group, which was unanimously rejected by literally tens of thousands of saints who were martyred for their faith by the Bolshevik regime. In patristic theological terms, the Moscow Patriarchate and its members are "**lapsed**," i.e., those who did not have the courage to resist the persecutors of the Church and who therefore severed their communion to the Church. The fact that they created an ecclesiastical entity in conditions prohibited by canon law makes them "**schismatics.**" The fact that they developed a specific teaching ("Sergianism"[18]: the idea that the Church can be "saved" by way of compromise with evil) to justify such actions makes them "heretics" (please note that in a theological discourse terms like "**heretic**" are not insults, but simply indicators of a specific spiritual condition/status).

The above is an **extremely superficial and even simplistic mini-overview** of a long an extremely complex topic and I ask for the understanding of those who know about this and who might be appalled at how much I have **not** discussed here. I am aware of that, but this is simply not the time and place to write a halfway decent history of Russian Orthodoxy in the 20th century. The only other historical detail I will add here is that during WORLD WAR II, Stalin did very substantially ease

[18] Sergianism as an Ecclesiological heresy, by Vladimir Moss http://www.roac-suzdal.narod.ru/sergianism.htm

some of the worst persecutions against the Church and that these persecutions did, in part, resume under Khrushchev. Again, I apologize for the extreme "shorthand" of the outline above, and I ask that you take only the following two important concepts with you:

a) Russian Orthodoxy has been continuously weakened for the past 300+ years

b) The organization currently officially representing Russian Orthodoxy has major legitimacy issues and is often viewed with deep suspicion, even by very religious people.

I now need to say a few words about the modern "Moscow Patriarchate" as it is today, over two decades since the end of any anti-religious persecutions.

First, it is by far the most "Soviet" institution of the Russian polity. Or, to put it in other words, it is by far the least reformed "leftover" of the Soviet era. To make things worse, it is also currently run by a notoriously corrupt individual, "Patriarch" Kirill I, a sly and utterly dishonest individual, known for his shady business dealing and for his rabid adherence to the so-called "Ecumenical Movement"[19] (a heresy from the Orthodox point of view). To top it all off, there is some pretty good evidence that Kirill I might be a secret Papist Cardinal, something called a "*cardinale in pectore*"[20] which, if true, is probably used against him by the Russian security services to make sure that he does whatever the Kremlin says.

For all its faults, the Moscow Patriarchate fulfils an extremely important role for the Russian state: that of ideological substitute for the now officially abandoned Marxist ideology.

One often can hear the statement that about 70% of Russians are Orthodox Christians. This is wrong and highly misleading. According to data published in Wikipedia,[21] about 40% of Russians are Orthodox

---

[19]Ecumenism https://en.wikipedia.org/wiki/Ecumenism#Ecumenical_movement

[20] *In pectore* https://en.wikipedia.org/wiki/In_pectore

[21] Religion in Russia https://en.wikipedia.org/wiki/Religion_in_Russia

Christians. Better. But what does that really mean? Mostly that these Russians identify with the Russian Orthodox traditions, that they try to live by Christians ethics and that they refer to themselves as "Orthodox." But if we take the figures published annually by the Moscow city authorities on the attendance of the single most important religious service in the Orthodox tradition—Easter (called "Paskha" in Russian) we see that only about 1% of Muscovites actually attended it. What about the remaining 39%?!

It is impossible to come by one "true" figure, but I would estimate that *no more than 5% of the Russian population could be considered as "deeply/ consciously, religious."* And yet, the Moscow Patriarchate plays a crucial role in the Kremlin's power structure: not only does it provide a substitute for the now defunct Marxist ideology, it serve as a "patriotic education" organization, it offers a series of well-recognized symbols (beautiful churches, religious singing, icons, crosses, etc.) which can all be used a **national** symbols (rather than spiritual symbols). Those national symbols are recognized, if not necessarily fully endorsed, by far more than the 40+ percent of Russians which are nominally Orthodox. To paraphrase the American expression "to rally around the flag," Russians are nowadays encouraged to "rally around the cross" even if on a deep internal level they don't really understand, or care, what the symbol of the Cross really means in Orthodox Christianity.

Let me give you an example of what all this ends up looking like. Read the transcript of the speech which Vladimir Putin made at the Council of Bishops of the Moscow Patriarchate.[22] It is all about patriotism, patriotism and more patriotism. Not a single word in all this is devoted to spiritual topics. Not **one**. This speech could have been made to an assembly of officials of an ideological department of the Communist Partyof the Soviet Union (CPSU).

[22] Vladimir Putin met with delegates to the Russian Orthodox Church's Bishops' Council http://en.kremlin.ru/events/president/news/17409

For the Moscow Patriarchate, this tight collaboration with the Kremlin also has an immense advantage: it grants it a legitimacy which history so unambiguously denies it. While there are still remnants of the Catacomb Church in Russia, and while outside Russia there still is an Orthodox Church Abroad,[23] these organizations are tiny compared to the huge Moscow Patriarchate, with its 100+ bishops, 26,000+ parishes and 100,000,000+ official members. And when any of these small groups succeeds in gathering the funds to open a small parish somewhere in Russia, the Moscow Patriarchate can always count on the local riot police to expel them and "return" the building to the Moscow Patriarchate.

I apologize once again for the extreme degree of over-simplification I had to settle for to write this (already too long!) overview. What I have done is mention what I believe are essential background factors which must be kept in mind when looking into the topic of Russia and Islam.

In particular, it has to be clearly understood that the official Orthodox Church, the Moscow Patriarchate, is not an important factor at all in the dialectical relationship between the Russian society and Islam, if only because inside the Russian society the status of the Orthodox faith is an extremely weakened one. In other words, the topic of "Russia and Islam" should not be confused with the topic "Orthodox Christianity and Islam." In many ways, **modern Russia is neo-Orthodox, para-Orthodox or even post-Orthodox but most definitely not truly Orthodox**.

This, however, begs the obvious question: if the dominant ethos of the Russian society is not Marxist any more, and if it is not really Orthodox Christian either, than what is it? Other than being predominantly *anti-Western* or *anti-capitalist*, what does the Russian society today stand *for*

---

[23] Synod of Bishops Russia's Orthodox Church Abroad http://sinod.ruschurchabroad.org/engindex.htm

(as opposed to against) and how does Russian society react to the values offered by Islam. This will be the topic of the next installment of this series.

February 18, 2013

RUSSIA AND ISLAM, PART THREE: INTERNAL RUSSIAN POLITICS

In the first two installments of this series on Russia and Islam we have seen that the reasons why neither the modern European civilizational model nor the traditional Orthodox faith can, at this point in time, provide a viable and positive source of ideological or spiritual inspiration for post-Soviet Russia. While in the past three hundred years the ideologically dominant philosophical and political paradigm has been the "westernizing" one, the absolute disasters which inevitably resulted from any "liberals" coming to power in Russia (Kerensky, Yeltsin), combined with the West's betrayal of all its promises made to Gorbachev (NATO would not move East) has finally resulted in a collapse of this model. The vast majority of Russians today would agree on the following basic ideas:

a) The West is no friend to Russia, never was, never will be, and the only way to deal with it is from a position of strength.

b) Russia needs a strong government led by a strong leader.

c) Russian "liberals" (in the modern Russian use of the word) are a small degenerate group of US-worshiping intellectuals who hate Russia.

d) Russia has to be a "social state" and the "pure" capitalist model is both morally wrong and fundamentally unsustainable, as shown by the current financial crisis.

e) The democratic system is a fraud used by the rich for their own interests.

So far so good, but what is the alternative?

Historically, there used to be a traditionalist model which said that Russia needed to be an Christian Orthodox country, where the highest secular power needed to be vested in a Tsar, whose power must be kept in check by a powerful and autonomous Church, and where the people's will would be expressed in a *Zemskii Sobor*, a "Council of the Land," something like a Parliament with a primarily consultative function. This idea was expressed by philosophers and writers such as Khomiakov, Tikhomirov, Rozanov, Solonevich, Iliin, Solzhenitsyn, Ogurtsov and many others.

With many caveats and disclaimers, I would say that this would be the Russian Orthodox version of the type of regime we see today in the Islamic Republic of Iran. Not a theocracy, of course, but a regime in which the fundamental structure, nature, function and goal of the state is to uphold spiritual values. A regime with a strong democratic component, but whose popular will can, when needed, be vetoed by the highest spiritual authorities. I would call such a system a "directed democracy," in which the tactical decisions are left to the will of the majority of the people, but whose strategic direction is set and cannot be replaced by another one.

The big difference between Russia and Iran is that in Iran the Islamic model is clearly fully endorsed by a strong majority of the population. In contrast, in Russia even most nominally Orthodox Christians would have great reservations about attempting to establish such a "Orthodox Republic." It's hard to come by any credible figure, but my personal gut feeling is that no more than 10% of Russians would feel comfortable with such a proposition. In other words, the idea of the establishment of an "Orthodox Republic" would probably be opposed by 90% of the people.

I personally deplore this state of affairs, if only because this is the model which I believe would be best for Russia, but politics being the science of the possible, it makes no sense to stubbornly latch on an impossibility.

Then what? What are the other options?

The currently "visible" choice of political parties is both reflective of the main currents in society and, at the same time, rather misleading. Let's look at what these parties are:

1) "United Russia." Putin's party. I would describe it as moderately patriotic (but not nationalistic), definitely committed to a strong Russia, "social" in economic terms, "independent" in international relations.

2) The "Liberal-Democratic Party of Russia." Led by Vladimir Zhironovski, it is vehemently anti-Communist and anti-Soviet, nationalistic in a buffoon-like manner, also "social" in economic terms, plain crazy in international relations.

3) The Communist Party of Russia. Lead by Gennadii Ziuganov, this is a pathetically reactionary party which openly claims to be the successor of the former CPSU, it is led by a "boar" like politician who could be sitting right next to Brezhnev or Chernenko. It has no real vision, except for nostalgia for the USSR.

4) "Just Russia." Lead by Sergei Mironov, a former paratrooper turned Social Democrat, it is a moderately "left center" version of "United Russia," it's a "nice" party which will never make any real difference.

5) All the pro-US parties which could not even make it into the Duma, and whose protests and demonstrations rapidly fizzled out. They are fundamentally irrelevant.

What does all this mean in reality?

There is only one party in Russia—the "United Russia" party of Putin and Medvedev. Both the Liberal Democrats and the Communists are just here to provide a safety valve function for the unhappy. While these parties do absorb a big chunk of the people who oppose Putin and United Russia, in the Duma these parties always end up voting with the Kremlin. This is also pretty much true for "Just Russia", which is so small anyway, that it does not really matter. The other useful function of the Liberal Democrats and the Communist, is that it keeps the "crazies" away from the Kremlin. The hysterical nationalists and the nostalgic Communists are absorbed by these two parties and that makes them instantly irrelevant.

I feel that it is important to stress here that there are smart, well-educated and articulate nationalists and communists who do **NOT** belong to the Liberal-Democratic or Communist parties. I am thinking of nationalists like Dmitri Rogozin (who is currently the Deputy Premier of Russian government in charge of defense and space industry) or Stalinists such as Nikolai Starikov (the head of the Union of Citizens of Russia). Frankly, smart people say away from these two parties.

The reality is that there is only one game in town: United Russia and its non-party "All-Russia People's Front," created by Putin as a political movement for new ideas. Everything else is pretty much a way of making the system look "democratic" and legitimate.

Let's sum it all up.

Russia is a multi-ethnic country which currently lack any kind of unifying ideology or spirituality, led by a single group of people whose ideology can be summed up by mix or pragmatism, patriotism, modern socialism, and multilateralism in international relations. Most importantly, Modern Russia is neither the Imperial Russia of pre-1917 nor is it the Soviet Union and it would be fundamentally wrong to seek parallels in the past to understand the current nature of the relationship of Russia and Islam.

This is a big temptation, into which the vast majority of Western observers always falls: to seek parallels between current events and past events. While it is true that an understanding of the past if often the key to the understanding of the present, in the case of Russia and Islam this is not an appropriate approach. For example, to compare the wars in Chechnya under Yeltsin and then Putin, to the way Stalin dealt with Chechens or to the way Russia invaded the Caucasus under Alexander I can only fundamentally mislead, bring to wholly inapplicable parallels, and result in deeply mistaken conclusions.

Modern Russia does not have a clear definition of itself. Lacking that type of definition, it is unable to articulate some kind of consensual view on what Islam means for Russia.

Some Russians see in Islam a very dangerous enemy, others see Islam as a natural ally. This is all made even more complicated by the fact that Islam itself is hardly a unified phenomenon and that each time we think of Islam we need to be specific on what type and even what aspect of Islam we are talking about.

For Russia, Islam represents a mix of risks and opportunities in many aspects, including spiritual, political, social, economic, historical and geostrategic aspects. To be fully understood, the topic of "Russia and Islam" needs to be looked at in each and every one of these aspects and what we will see then is that there are different "currents" inside Russia who very much disagree with each other on whether Islam is a risk or an opportunity in every single one of these aspects. So rather than to speak of "risks and opportunities," I will refer to the spiritual, political, social, economic, historical and geostrategic "challenges" which Islam represents for Russia. This will be the topic of the next installment.

February 20, 2013

Russia and Islam, part four: "Islam" as a threat

The first thing to which I would like to draw your attention to is that in the title *Russia and Islam, part four: "Islam" as a threat* I put the word "Islam" in quotation marks. This is very important, as most of the issues I will be discussing today are not directly linked to Islam at all. However, *in the minds of many Russians,* these issues are linked to Islam and it is therefore simply impossible to analyze the topic of "Russia and Islam" without taking a long hard look at the connection which a lot of Russians make between some issues (with no direct relationship to Islam) and Islam itself.

The use of words can be very tricky in this context. Take the word "Muslim," what does it really mean? In Bosnia, the word "Muslim" was really used to describe a "non-Orthodox and non-Catholic Bosnian" since both Croats and Serbs often were natives of Bosnia and since Bosnian-Croats, Bosnian-Serbs and Bosnian Muslims are all of the exact same ethnic stock (hence the fallacy of speaking of "ethnic cleansing" in the Bosnian context). Later, the rather inept term "Bosniac" was coined, as opposed to "Bosnian" because to use "Muslim" or "Bosnian" just made no sense. Regardless, by fiat of some politicians, what used to be called "Muslim" became "Bosniac" overnight.

Likewise, in Ireland, the "troubles" were supposed to oppose Catholics and Protestants, but did the IRA or the Ulster Volunteers really care about the Papacy or Martin Luther? Did these denominations really play a relevant role in this conflict?

This is hardly a new issue. In the past, both the Russian Empire and the Ottoman Empire *assimilated religious groups to ethnic minorities* hence the Karaites in Russia were not considered as Jews while the Orthodox Patriarch of Constantinople was referred to by the Ottomans as "*Millet-Bashi*" or "ethnarc." In modern France there is a "problem" of the

Muslim immigration and its effects on the suburbs of many French cities. But taking a closer look at these (mostly Algerian) immigrants one could legitimately wonder to what degree this is an "Islamic" problem. This confusion between "Islam" (as a faith, a religion), "Muslim" (used as *both* a sign of *religious* and, often, *ethnic* affiliation) is as frequent in modern Russia as it is in France. Keeping all these caveats in mind, let's look at the type of issues which makes many Russians see "Islam" (in quotation marks) as a threat.

1) Immigration and crime

Ever since the dissolution of the former Soviet Union there has been a steady flow of immigrants from some former Soviet republics (Azerbaijan, Tajikistan, etc.) toward big Russian cities. In parallel to that, a large number of immigrants from the Caucasus (Chechens, Dagestani, etc.) also emigrated to central parts of Russia. The combination of these to migratory flow resulted in a vast increase of immigrants in every major Russia city. As is so often the case, while some of these immigrants came looking for a job, there were enough criminal elements among them to strongly tie the issue of immigration and crime to each other. Typically, these immigrants from the south were composed of a mix of four groups:

a) Law-abiding and hardworking workers, often ruthlessly exploited and treated as quasi-slaves by their local employers.

b) Arrogant and very poorly educated young men who, while not necessarily criminals, act in highly provocative and offensive manners.

c) Petty thugs who combine an official job with petty criminal activities.

d) Hardened criminals who are deeply involved in drugs, prostitution, illegal casinos, etc.

Typically, the first group is bigger than the second which, in turn, is bigger than the third, while the fourth group is the smallest of all. And yet, that explosive combination achieves in Russia exactly the same effect as it does in France: it associates crime and immigration in the mind of many, if not most, people.

Furthermore, since most of these immigrants come from historically Muslim countries and since many of them consider themselves as Muslims, many Russians experience their first or most frequent interaction with putative "Muslims" in a criminal situation. As for the fact that in the vast majority of these cases these "Muslim thugs" know absolutely nothing about Islam is not at all apparent, in particular from a Russian point of view.

The French author and philosopher Alain Soral, who is very actively engaged in efforts to reconcile and unite all French citizens against the NWO, including Christians and Muslims, speaks of "*Islamo-racaille*" ("Islamo-scum"): young loud thugs, wearing "rapper-gangsta" gear, with NYC baseball-hats and who speak of Allah and Kufars while driving around in sports cars—often high or drunk—looking for somebody to rob, rape or abuse. As Soral points out—these people are not exactly the type you would see coming out of a mosque and the very same is true of Russia. Still, it is undeniable that many Russians still make the association "Islam" <-> crime.

2) Wahhabism—internal

The wars in Chechnya and the Islamic terrorism in Dagestan and many other part of Russia have had a huge impact upon the Russian public opinion. The two was in Chechnya, in particular, and resulted in a deep aversion for the Chechen insurgents and any other Islamic terrorist group which could be described as "Wahhabi." Initially, the combined propaganda tsunami of the Western corporate media and the Russian "liberal" media left people confused as to what was really going on, but soon the horrible events on the ground become impossible to suppress: the Chechen insurgents combined the very worst of the Wahhabi extremism with the worst of Chechen thuggery. Thousands of people were summarily executed, women raped, Russian soldiers and even civilians were tortured to death, crucified, skinned alive, raped and beheaded. Hostages were kidnapped from all over southern Russia and a slave market was working each day in downtown Grozny. And all these horrors were committed by bearded men, brandishing green and black flags embroidered with *suras* of the Koran, and to the constant screams of *Allahu Akbar*. And since the Chechen insurgents loved to use their cell phones to videotape their atrocities, a steady stream of blood-curling videos made it to the Russian TV and Internet sites. By 2000 the Russian public opinion was ripe to give no quarter to any Islamic terrorist or anybody supporting them.

To make things worse, the Chechen insurgency had the support of the vast majority of the Muslim world which, just as in Bosnia or Kosovo, automatically sided with the "Muslim" party no matter what (I call this the "My *Umma*— right or wrong" position). That knee-jerk support for the Muslim side, even if it is largely composed of Wahhabi terrorists and criminals, put a big stain on the image of Islam in Russia and gave a lot of weight to the "conflict of civilizations" paradigm which the West and its supporters in Russia wanted to impose upon the Russian public opinion.

If under Yeltsin the Russian state proved completely incapable of taking any kind of measures to deal with this situation, under Putin things changed extremely rapidly as shown by the 2nd Chechen War which basically crushed the insurgency. Subsequently, the combined efforts of a completely re-vamped Russian security establishment and the coming to power of Akhmad and, later, Ramzan Kadyrov completely changed the situation. Grozny was rebuilt in a record time, and Chechnya became of the of safest republics of the entire Caucasus (at the expense of Dagestan where the situation got worse). The cost in human lives and suffering was absolutely horrendous, both for Russians (almost all those who survived left Chechnya) and for Chechens who died in huge numbers. The main scar left by this war though is that Russia has become a society with zero tolerance for any form of Wahhabism and the Russian people have fully endorsed what I call the "Putin doctrine" of dealing with Wahhabis:

"change your ways or expect to be annihilated." This, by the way, applies to both individuals and ethnic groups: against a Wahhabi enemy the Russian people will support the harshest possible military methods of warfare, something which a lot of Muslim communities are acutely aware of (more about that later).

In Chechnya itself, Ramzan Kadyrov instituted an even harsher anti-Wahhabi policy than in the rest of Russia. During the 2nd Chechen War, foreign mercenaries and preachers were interrogated and then summarily executed by both Russian and Chechen forces and ever since Saudi, Yemeni or Pakistani preachers are simply barred from entering Chechnya.

Contrary to the predictions of most "experts," the Kremlin did successfully deal with the situation in Chechnya, but one inevitable side effect of this success was that a lot of the Wahhabi extremists were flushed out of Chechnya into neighboring Dagestan and even the rest of Russia. And that second problem is far from solved. While the USA and the UK have now toned down their pro-Chechen rhetoric, the Saudis are still pushing Wahhabi Islam into Russia, although in a more discreet manner.

First, they train preachers in Saudi Arabia and send them back to Russia. Then these preachers form small communities, often inside mosques, were the faithful are recruited for social and religious activities. During that phase, the candidates for the next step are carefully investigated, vetted and selected for the next phase: the establishment of weapons caches, safe houses, training grounds, and the like. Eventually, the new recruits are used to attack police stations, banks, murder traditional (anti-Wahhabi) clergymen, and opposing mafia gangs. Russian security services have observed that sequence in Dagestan, Kazan or Stavropol (regions with large Muslim minorities), but also in Saint Petersburg, a city with a very small and very traditionalist Muslim population. So far, the security services have managed to stay one step ahead, but this is far from over and that kind of penetration efforts can last a very long time.

One of the crucial aspects of this dynamic is the reaction of the local, traditional, Muslim spiritual leaders. First, as I have mentioned above, no Russian Muslims want to have a "2nd Chechen War" happen in their own town or region, because they have no doubts whatsoever about the outcome of such a situation. Second, traditional Muslim spiritual leaders are themselves the first victims of the Wahhabi infiltrators who often begin their "active" phase of operations by murdering the local imams. Third, Muslims in Russia are often very rapidly disillusioned with the Saudi version of Islam which declares as "un-Islamic" many customs and traditions which are at the core of the cultural identity of many Muslim groups in Russia. Fourth, for all the thugs from the Caucasus behaving in obnoxious and vulgar manners in Central Russia, the fact is that the Muslim communities these young people come from are often very conservative and peaceful and that the older generation deeply disapproves of the kind of behavior which, in their opinion, brings shame upon their people. Fifth, one should not underestimate the legacy of the Soviet period which promoted both secularism and modernism and which has left a strong mark on the local elites. These elites are both outraged and horrified when they are told by Wahhabi preachers that they have to completely abandon their way of life and begin living according to medieval precepts. Finally, there is an inherent tension between any form of nationalism and the Saudi style Wahhabism being imported to Russia. This tension is one of the key elements which turned the Kadyrov clan against the various Wahhabi warlords in Chechnya which were viewed by the more nationalist Chechen leaders as arrogant foreigners who were enemies of the Chechen ancestral traditions. For all these reasons, there is a lot of push-back on the part of the local Muslim communities and Muslim leaders against the type of Wahhabi style Islam the Saudis have been trying to export to Russia.

3) Wahhabism—external

Wahhabism is not only an internal threat for Russia, it is also a major external threat. According to Russian analysts, the Obama administration has brought with itself a fundamentally new set of imperialist policies which are now being implemented. During the Bush era, the USA exercised direct control, mostly by means of military interventions, over the Middle East and Africa. This "direct" approach is the way the Jewish lobby and the neocons believed that the USA should maintain its global empire. Obama represents a very different type of constituency (old "Anglo" money) which is vehemently opposed to the neocons and which will agree to pay lip service to the Israel-firsters but, in reality, places US strategic interests far ahead of any Zionist priorities. In practical terms, this means that the Obama administration will withdraw as many US troops as possible and relinquish the direct control over contested regions, and that it will secure its domination over a country or region by means of chaos. **This is a policy of indirect imperial control.**

After all, why invade and occupy a country, thereby losing US blood and money, when one can use proxies to create a situation of absolute chaos inside that country? In the best of cases, chaos leads to a Libyan-style "regime change" and in the worst case, a civil war like the one taking place in Syria. But in either case, undesirable heads of state like Gaddafi or Assad have been "de-fanged" and their countries removed from any possible anti-US alliance. As for the "good guys" of the day (say Abdullah in Jordan or Hamad in Bahrain), they are protected from the surrounding chaos at very limited costs.

According to Russian analysts, **the Wahhabi and "al-Qaeda" types are the foot soldiers of this new US imperial policy**. The US simply "injects" them in any society it wants to subvert and then it sits on the sidelines without much else to do than to send in special forces to assist here and there, depending on the needs of the moment. In this situation, the

CIA agent is the puppeteer and the Wahhabi crazy is the puppet, whether it is aware of that or not.

The big fear of Russian analysts is that this US strategy will be used to remove Assad and then that it will be used against Iran. True, Syria has a large Sunni population, whereas Iran is predominantly Shia, whom the Wahhabis hate with a special seething loathing. Still, Iran does have small Kurdish, Turkmen and Balochi (Sunni) minorities which, combined with pro-Western "Gucci revolutionaries" of the upper classes can pose a real risk to the regime. And, if not, there is always the option of triggering a war between Iran and some Sunni country. Most Russians analysts believe that Iran is strong enough to resist such attempts at destabilizing it, but they remain very attentive to the situation because they agree that if Iran was to be engulfed into some form of US-sponsored chaos this would directly affect the southern regions of Russia.

Some analysts also see this US "indirect" or "control through chaos" strategy as a "win-win" for the USA even if their Wahhabi proxies are defeated. They ask a simple question: what will happen if Assad convincingly wins the war in Syria? Where **will the Wahhabis go next?** Back to Mali, which they temporarily left to avoid engaging the French? Or into Algeria, to start a civil war there? Or maybe into Kosovo or even southern France? And what if these Wahhabis decided to "test the waters" in Kazakhstan?

This type of concerns brings some Russian security specialists to actually see a positive aspect to the war in Syria. Simply put—Assad is killing a lot of al-Qaeda types and every Wahhabi crazy killed in Syria is one less candidate for a transfer to another holy war in another part of the world.

We now can clearly distinguish the rationale behind the Russian policy not to threaten to shut down NATO supply lines over Russia, regardless of the amount of obnoxious and hostile pronouncements and actions from the US side: the Russians want the Americans to remain in Afghanistan as long as possible to give time to Russia and its allies like Tajikistan to prepare for a Taliban regime back in power in Kabul. In the meantime,

Russia is strengthening its powerful 201 Russian Military Base (ex-201 Motor Rifle Division) in Tajikistan and providing technical assistance to the Tajik Border Guards.

As part of the recent reforms of the Russian Armed Forces the entire Russian military has been reorganized into four Strategic Commands, each capable of independently waging a regional defensive war independently by directly controlling practically all the military forces and resources in its area. It is interesting to note that while the Southern Strategic Command is the smallest one in size, it is by far the most combat ready. If there is anything which the 08.08.08 war with Georgia has convincingly shown, it is the lightning speed at which the 58th Army and the Black Sea Fleet were ready to go to war (and that even though it took the Kremlin quite some time to finally react). It is quite clear that following the Russian successes in Chechnya and Georgia Moscow is most definitely not letting its guard down and that it will remain ready to engage in a wide spectrum of military operations ranging from local clashes to a full-scale regional war.

4) Islam through the prism of the "clash of civilizations"

This aspect of the "Islamic threat" is fundamentally different from all the other ones as it is predicated on a thesis which is never really tested, but only proclaimed: that there is a "clash of civilizations[24]" taking place between, roughly, "Christian Europe" on one side and the "Eastern" or "Arab" Islam on the other. Never mind the fact that Europe has lost almost all signs of Christianity many years ago, never mind that Islam is neither primarily "Eastern" nor primarily "Arab," never mind that Islam includes very different civilizations (from Morocco to Indonesia) and never mind that no Muslim or Islamic "civilization" has attacked any Western interests for a very long time. By the way, proponents of this theory will include a theocratic and racist country such as Israel in the

[24] Clash of Civilizations https://en.wikipedia.org/wiki/Clash_of_Civilizations

"Western," if not "Christian European," camp while ignoring the key role Muslim Turkey plays in NATO. Simply put—this view is 100% ideology, no facts are needed. And yet, there are quite a few groups in Russia which are happy to promote this worldview:

a) **The Communists**. In the bad old Soviet mentality, Islam is, as any other religion, an ideological enemy. If Ziuganov & Co. do not speak of "opium of the people" it is because they are afraid to antagonize their Orthodox Christian members, in particular since nowadays being "Orthodox" gives you "patriotic" credentials. But being Muslim gives you exactly "zero" credentials with the Communists. If anything, they would be inclined to see Islam and Muslims as agents for foreign interests.

b) **Zionists**: contrary to the popular belief, there are still plenty of Zionists in Russia, including in the media, and they never miss the opportunity to fan the flames of Islamophobia. One of their favorite tricks is to always and deliberately conflate all forms of Islam, with the deeds of any "Muslim" whether actually religious or not and draw the conclusion that "Islam is our common moral enemy." For these people, Russia and Israel are natural allies against the common Islamic foe, and even Iran is not to be trusted. Needless to say, the Israelis go out of their way to court these circles and promote an image of "you had the Chechens, we have the Palestinians."

c) **Russian neo-Nazi racists**: this is really a small group, but an extremely vocal one. These are the famous Russian skinheads who feel that they are defending the "White Race" when they beat up a Tadjk in the subway. Some of them claim to be Orthodox, though a majority like to seek their roots into some distant "pagan Russia" populated by blue eyed White warriors. These groups exist mostly on the Internet, but they sometimes gather in remote places to "train" for the "conflict to come."

Recently a group of real Russian patriots got together and began quietly investigating these groups. It turns out that the most vocal and racist of them all usually had IP numbers in the USA, Canada and Israel. Russian security services strongly suspect that these groups are quietly supported by US and other Western intelligences services to create ethnic tensions in Russia. Unsurprisingly, since Putin came to power most leaders of these groups have landed in jail, or are hiding abroad.

d) **Roman Catholics and Orthodox Ecumenists**: both of these groups share a common belief: whatever "minor" differences they "might" have had in the past, Orthodox Russia belongs with the "Christian West," if only because both are "threatened" by a "common enemy." These people carefully avoid ever mentioning the undeniable fact that Russia has always chosen Asia over Europe or Islam over the Papacy, if only because of all the wars of conquest which were waged by the West against Russia. This group has no traction in the masses of people, but it has some following in the pro-US circles in the big cities.

Individually, these groups are not very powerful, with the notable exception of the Zionist one. And they do not officially work together. But if there are no signs of a conspiracy, there is an objective collusion between these groups when it comes to demonize Islam in all its forms, even the most moderate ones. This, in turn, means that there is a minority of the Russian population which will always view Islam as a threat, no matter what.

The good news is that these groups are counter-balanced by far more influential forces which see Islam as a potential (if not yet actual) natural ally of Russia. This will be the topic of the next installment.

February 26, 2013

RUSSIA AND ISLAM, PART FIVE: "ISLAM" AS AN ALLY

> "**Russia has become the first enemy of Islam and** Muslims because it has stood against the Syrian people; more than 30,000 Syrians have been killed by the weapons supplied by Russia."
>
> *Yusuf al-Qaradawi*[25]

Reading the words of al-Qaradawi,[26] who is arguably one of the most influential Muslim clerics on the planet whose TV show is followed by 60 million Muslims, one might wonder how anybody could ever think of Islam as an ally of Russia. But then, reading the rest of the article which quoted him, we see that he also "*called on pilgrims to pray for topple (sic) of Bashar al-Assad, elimination of Syrian army, Iran, Hezbollah, China and Russia.*" If we think of the logic of his own words, the list of enemies he names, and if we consider that he believes that Russia is the worst of them, does that not indicate that Russia must therefore be the main force behind of the others, behind Syria, Iran, Hezbollah and China? If so, then unless we assume that the Russians are irrational, we can probably conclude that Russia sees Syria, Iran, Hezbollah and China as allies which, of course, it does. And since Syria, Iran and Hezbollah are most definitely Muslim, this clearly shows two fundamental things: there are many different brands of "Islam" out there (Hassan Nasrallah would definitely not agree with al-Qaradawi's point of view) *and some of these brands of Islam are already objective allies of Russia.* So, once again, we need to set aside the vast category of "Islam" and look a little deeper into what has been going on inside the Muslim world.

---

[25] Sunni supreme spiritual leader Sheikh Qaradawi calls Russia Muslims' No1 enemy http://sputniknews.com/voiceofrussia/2012_10_18/Sheikh-Yusuf-al-Qaradawi-called-Russia-as-the-enemy-of-the-Muslim-world/

[26] Yusuf al-Qaradawi https://en.wikipedia.org/wiki/Yusuf_al-Qaradawi

The following is a self-evident truism:

The Muslim world is not a united, coherent, entity with a common goal, ideology or ethos. While some Muslims want to entertain that fiction, and *while all Islamophobes are more than happy to support and propagate such claims*, they are patently false. While all Muslims share certain common beliefs, this list is extremely short. In fact, all that is required to convert to Islam is a single heartfelt recitation of the Sahhadah: "there is no god but God, Muhammad is the messenger of God." Everything else is left to the interpretation of the various of various sects and schools of jurisprudence. This is why all the usual generalizations about Islam are so misleading—they ignore the immense diversity of Islam, from Morocco to Indonesia, from Saudi Wahhabism to Kazakh Sufism.

And yet, some generalizations can be made, even if accompanied by various disclaimers and caveats.

The first is that the richest segment of the Muslim world is definitely the one of the type of Sunni Islam found around the Persian Gulf, in particular the one represented by the Saudi type of Wahhabism. This Saudi brand of Islam combines three separate elements into one explosive mix: **a primitive but extremely aggressive ideology, immense disposable income and a militant dedication to proselytism and expansion.**

Second, Sunni Muslims are all potential targets of Saudi/Wahhabi indoctrination and recruitment efforts. This does not mean that all Sunnis will turn into al-Qaeda types, but that Saudi/Wahhabi recruitment efforts have already been successful in pretty much all Sunni groups, regardless of geography or tradition. Conversely, this also means that for traditional Sunni Islam the brand of Wahhabism the Saudis are spreading is a most dangerous foe.

Third, the United States have to be credited with the following: they took a local, largely irrelevant, sect and, with the complicity of the House of Saud, they literally federated all the Wahhabi crazies worldwide into if not one organization, then at least one movement. While the USA initially wanted to organize the resistance against the Soviet invasion of Afghanistan, they have since always commanded, if not always controlled, these movements worldwide, and they still are doing so today. From the US and Turkish "black flights" in Bosnia, to the arming of the Kosovo Liberation Army (KLA) in Kosovo, to 9/11, to the uprisings in Libya and Syria, the United States have always directed the Wahhabi crazies toward the enemies of the US global Empire.

Fourth, in contrast to the rest of the Islamic world, the Shia have always been a determined opponent of Wahhabi Islam and the US Empire. Conversely, this also means that for the US Empire and the Wahhabi crazies, the Shia are at the top of their enemy list and that they will spare no efforts in weakening, subverting or destroying any Shia movement or country. Remarkably, so far they have failed and that in itself is a testimony to the formidable intelligence, courage and resilience of the Shia people.

What does that mean for Russia?

While there are some circles which fully subscribe to the "clash of civilization" theory and who consider Islam as a threat (see in my previous installment[27] the "Islam through the prism of the "clash of civilizations" section), there are also several influential groups who very much see Islam as a natural ally:

a) **Orthodox patriots**: best represented by the views of the well-known journalist Maksim Shevchenko,[28] these are Russians nationals who as patriots, but not Russian nationalists, believe that Russia has a vocation to be an multi-ethnic country and civilization and who, as Orthodox Christians, believe that traditional Islam shares most, if not all, of the key values of Orthodox Christianity. Shevchenko, who is a long-time Orthodox activist, is also a specialist in the Caucasus region who has extensive contacts in the various Muslim communities in Russia. Unlike the

---

[27] Russia and Islam, part four: "Islam" as a threat http://thesaker.is/russia-and-islam-part-four-islam-as-a-threat/

[28] Maxim Shevchenko https://en.wikipedia.org/wiki/Maksim_Leonardovich_Shevchenko

"Orthodox Ecumenists," Shevchenko has no interest at all in finding some theological common ground with Islam, for him the value of Islam is in what it stands for culturally and politically. The fundamental belief of Shevchenko and those who support his ideas is that traditional Islam is the natural ally of Orthodox Christianity and the Russian civilization in its struggle against both Western imperialism and Wahhabi extremism. Needless to say, Russian Islamophobes absolutely despise Shevchenko and they regularly spread rumors about his (totally fictional) conversion to Islam.

b) **The security services**: Russian security services have enough analysts and experts to fully realize the potential of an Orthodox-Muslim alliance against their common enemies. It is not a coincidence that a former KGB officer like Putin put so much efforts in supporting the Kadyrov clan in Chechnya. There is an old tradition in the Russian security services to seek alliances with some Muslim movements against common enemies. From the long-standing alliance of the et Гла́вное разве́дывательное управле́ние, Glavnoye razvedyvatel'noye upravleniye (GRU) with Ahmad Shah Massoud, to the Слу́жба вне́шней разве́дки, Sluzhba vneshney razvedki (SVR) support for Assad, to the Федеральная служба безопасности Российской Федерации (ФСБ); Federal'naya sluzhba bezopasnosti Rossiyskoy Federatsi (FSB) support for Akhmad and Ramzan Kadyrov—the Russian security services have always sought allies in the Muslim world. They have always done that due to a mix of pragmatic considerations and real admiration for their counterparts (I can personally attest to the real and sincere admiration in which Massoud was held by commanders of the Kaskad/Vympel Spetsnaz force). Putin has personally stated many time that the traditional Muslim communities can count on the absolute support of the Russian state and that this support for traditional Russian Islam is a key strategic objective of the Russian state.

c) **Orthodox traditionalists**: Some of the dresses which would be considered traditional Orthodox dresses in modern Russia are very similar to what many Muslim women would wear? Now compare that with the kind of civilization model the various Pussy Riots, Gay Pride parades and other LGBT[29] movements present. The fact is that traditional Islamic and traditional Christian Orthodox ethics are very similar, and that they stand for the same values: traditional families, moderate patriotism, social responsibility, modesty, sobriety, charity, honor and respect for traditions including for other traditions. At a time when most Russian TV stations are spewing a constant stream of immorality, materialism and outright filth, Orthodox Christians look with understanding and admiration at those Muslim families who raise their children with respect for the elders and the traditions they represent.

Recently, there have been a few high-visibility scandals around the issue of whether Muslim girls should be wearing a scarf over their heads in public schools. Just like in France, some Russians felt threatened by such religious displays, in particular in the southern regions of Russia were immigration is a big problem, but interestingly the traditionalist Orthodox commentators sided with the Muslim girls saying that they are actually giving a good example to Russian Orthodox girls too. It is a fact that before the Bolshevik Revolution almost all rural Russian women wore a headscarf which is very much a traditional Russian way of dressing (those doubting this are welcome to check any Russian matryoshka[30] doll).

d) **The Russian foreign policy establishment**, while not necessarily as pro-Islamic as the Russian security services, is also largely convinced of the importance of supporting countries such as Syria and, in particular, Iran, which most Russian diplomats see as a key Russian ally in the Middle East. There also is, however, a strong pro-Western minority in the Russian foreign service which does believe that Iran has to submit to the orders of the UNSC even in cases where the UNSC takes decisions which are highly unfavorable to Russia. This is also the group which pre-

---

[29] LGBT https://en.wikipedia.org/wiki/LGBT

[30] Matryoshka doll https://en.wikipedia.org/wiki/Matryoshka_doll

vailed at the time when Russia betrayed Gaddafi and did not veto a resolution which was clearly designed to allow a US/NATO aggression on Libya (Russia also betrayed Iran on several occasions at the UNSC). Still, the prevailing thought, in particular since Putin's return to power, is that Iran is an important ally that Russia must support.

The Russian state, as a whole, is not a unitary actor. In fact, there is a lot of very intense infighting taking place right now, and there is strong evidence that at least two clans, one associated with Medvedev and one associated with Putin, are now in the midst of a covert war against each other. This topic, and what that means for Islam, will be the subject of the next installment of this series.

March 2, 2013

RUSSIA AND ISLAM, PART SIX: THE KREMLIN

This is a topic which I have been most hesitant to cover for many reasons, including the fact that my views on this topic have come to change, and that they did so not as a result of the discovery of indisputable facts, but under the combined action of much "in between the lines" readings of events, many indirect events pointing in the same direction, combined with a very strong, but inevitably subjective, gut feeling. To state my thesis bluntly, I have come to the conclusion that for many years already there have been several interest groups fighting against each other in the Kremlin and that one group has decided to break cover and engage in a quiet but still visible attack against the other. As a result of that, a profound revolution has now begun in Russia and that the next four to five years will see either huge changes or a major power struggle inside the Kremlin.

The Muslim world and the "Islamic factor" inside Russia play little or no role in this struggle, but the result of this struggle will define Russian policies both toward Muslims inside Russia and toward the Middle East and the rest of the world. This is why I have decided to address this issue now.

In the past, I was of the opinion that Putin and Medvedev were the representatives of the same interest group which could be loosely described as a mix of security services and big money. I credited this group with very skillfully deceiving the US-controlled regime of Yeltsin and his Jewish oligarchs only to systematically crush it as soon as Putin came to power. I still believe that this model is fundamentally correct, but I now also have come to realize that it has a deeper dimension which I have missed in the past.

First, I used to see the events of 1999-2000 as basically a victory of the "Putin people" against the Jewish oligarchy (which it was) and against US interests. The latter is not so simple. Yes, when Putin came to power he did basically "decapitate" the top figures of the oligarchy, but he simply did not have the means to change the system which the oligarchs and their US sponsors put in place. **The people were changed, the system remained fundamentally the same.** Berezovsky and Gusinsky fled Russia, Khodorkovsky was offered a much deserved trip to tree-logging camp in Siberia, but the system these guys had built stayed: the media toned down some of its most obnoxious propaganda (in particular on Chechnya), the "New Russian" millionaires stopped trying to simply buy the Duma (like Khodorkovsky had), the various separatists groups decided to keep a low profile, and the Russian mob decided to be more careful in its actions. But the basic laws, the Constitution, the system of government, all remained pretty much unchanged. Furthermore, inside the "Putin people" there were some who very much wanted to deepen the integration of Russia into the West and its US-controlled international system. Some were clearly CIA/MI6 paid agents of influence, others did that because they truly believed that this was the best course for Russia. This type of people were often seen "near" Medvedev, "near" both physically and ideologically. The 1990s also left a lot of these people in key positions in various government agencies, media groups and business interests. No less important than who was "in" the power circles at the time is who was kept away. Some extremely popular figures were sent far away from the centers of power. This is well illustrated by the case of Dmitri Rogozin sent to Brussels.

So what we have witnessed between 2000 and 2012 is a grand balancing act, a compromise, between at the very least two interest groups: I will call the first one the "**Atlantic integrationists**" and the second one the "**Eurasian Sovereignists.**" The first groups wants Russia to be a respected strategic partner to the West while the second group aims at the creation of a multipolar world in which no one country or alliance would hold supreme power.

Just as the late 1990s the "Putin & Medvedev" people succeeded in outwitting the Jewish oligarchy, in the past couple of years the "Putin" people have, apparently, succeeded in outmaneuvering the "Medvedev" camp. I very much doubt that the people around Medvedev realized what they were doing when they let Putin run for president, officially under the argument that his popularity was higher than Medvedev's (which is true). They probably were told that another six years of compromise and continuity were ahead, but in reality Putin has fundamentally changed the course of Russia since he came to power again.

In the past, cracks between the two camps had already appeared over a number of issues, including the S-300 sale to Iran, the UNSC resolution or the response to the 08.08.08 war against Georgia, but these differences were always settled under the fundamental fact that the role of the president and the one of head of Government ("Prime Minister") were clearly defined and each had to remain within his own sphere of competence. Medvedev made the point himself when he publicly declared that the decision not to veto the UNSC resolution on Libya allowing a US/NATO war was his personal one and that he personally instructed the Ministry of Foreign Affairs. In contrast, Putin denounced this decision in no uncertain terms, but could do nothing about it. Every time Medvedev and Putin butted heads over something, Medvedev's popularity sagged while Putin's rose.

This conflict came to a head around the person of Anatoly Serdyukov, the former, and now disgraced, Defense Minister. I will skip all the well-known details about how Serdyukov was caught, but I will state one obvious fact: neither the journalists who "uncovered" Serdyukov's indiscretions, nor the Investigative Committee which opened an investigation could have done so without the direct approval of the Presidential Administration. Just like Obama had to "clear" (read: instigate) the Petraeus scandal to get rid of a powerful figure and replace him with a loyal ally, so did Putin really instigate the downfall of Serdyukov. Let me add here that the widely held belief that Serdyukov was Putin's man is based on nothing but journalistic clichés and is irrelevant anyway. If, like I think, Serdyukov was imposed upon Putin by the "Atlantic integrationists," then Putin would inevitably be considered as co-responsible of Serdyukov's actions regardless of whether Putin wanted Serdyukov in the first place, or not. And that made it very difficult for Putin to do something against "his" protégé.

The reason why I am focusing so much on Serdyukov is because in the Russian political system, the Minister of Defense is something of a mini-president: he runs what is truly a mini-state inside the bigger state, it is both highly autonomous and extremely powerful. As a result, the position of Minister of Defense is one of the most powerful ones in Russia. I find it also very plausible that the "Atlantic integrationists" could have agreed to have Putin as a president, provided that Medvedev is #2 and Serdyukov #3. Medvedev is still #2, but Serdyukov has been ejected and disgraced, and his successor, Sergey Shoigu, is his polar opposite in almost every conceivable aspect.

As soon as Shoigu took over the Ministry of Defense, he summarily kicked out Serdyukov's Chief of General Staff, General Makarov (a person of exceptional mediocrity), and replaced him with a highly talented and immensely respected combat officer, General Valerii Gerasimov who, in turn, brought back a long list of respected and highly competent generals to key positions in the armed forces. Shoigu also immediately reversed some of the worst excesses of the so-called "Serdyukov's reforms" in many fields including military education, medicine, command and control, etc.

Predictably, and unlike Serdyukov, Shoigu has excellent relations with key personalities like Dmitri Rogozin, Vice-premier of Russian government in charge of defense industry, and Sergei Ivanov, Chief of Staff Presidential Administration of Russia (both of which are suspected by many observers to have played a key role in the downfall of Serdyukov).

There are also other signs of a potential shift in the top echelons of power in Russia. More and more observers are speculating that Putin's

All-Russia People's Front[31] is being developed not only as a movement to generate new ideas, which is what it was supposed to be, but as a tool to influence and, if needed, replace *the United Russia*[32] party which is seen as too much under the control of the "Atlantic integrationists." Again, this is speculation, but there are more and more well-informed observers who are predicting that Medvedev might not remain as head of government all too long. My personal take on that his that I get the feeling that Medvedev is a decent man, but of small political stature, who can be trusted to administer and manage, but without much of a vision. Surrounded by powerful visionaries like Putin, Shoigu or Rogozin, he will do as he is told. But yes, if he does not, he will probably be ejected fairly soon.

Before turning to the next aspect of this process, I would like to introduce a thesis here which I rejected for a long while, but which I ended up accepting as true.

There is no doubt that in 1991 the Soviet Union lost the Cold War: the country was split into fifteen separate pieces, the entire polity was brought down and the state practically ceased functioning, and all the wealth of the country was brought under the control of Western interests and their proxies (Jewish oligarchs), Poverty literally exploded, as did the mortality rate; NATO pushed forward its forces right up to the border of the Russian Federation, and American "advisors" literally created the new Russian state, the constitution, the system of government and most laws. Now here is the key concept I want to submit: for all its external appearances of independence, **the Russian Federation between 1991 and 2000 became a US colony, a US dependent territory, something similar to the status of Iraq following the withdrawal of most Ameri-**

---

[31] All-Russia People's Front party https://en.wikipedia.org/wiki/People%27s_Front_for_Russia

[32] United Russia party https://en.wikipedia.org/wiki/United_Russia

can forces or the status of, say, Poland or maybe Romania during the Soviet era.

Anyone who has any doubts about this needs to carefully study the events of 1993 when the comparatively legitimate Parliament of Russia was shot at by tanks with the full "support" (read: under the control of), the USA acting through its embassy in Moscow which during those days literally became the command post for the entire crackdown on the opposition. I personally was present in Moscow during these events, and I had first-rate information about what was really going on at the time. I can, for example, attest to the following two facts: a) the number of victims was *grossly under reported* and b) the scope in time and space of the repression was also *grossly under reported.* The true figures of casualties are close to 5000 (five thousand) people and it took 5-6 days of combat in the entire Moscow metropolitan area (including areas outside the city proper) to eventually crush the opposition (I personally witnessed an intense firefight right under the windows of my apartment on the evening of the 5th day after the assault).

This entire bloodbath was directed and coordinated by the USA via its embassy in Moscow and most of the atrocities were not committed by government forces in uniform, but by hired guns in plainclothes (including mobsters and Beitar squads) and without any legal authority. Does that not remind you of another capital? Yes, of course, that could have been Baghdad. Predictably the entire Western corporate press presented these events as a victory of democracy and freedom against the dark forces of revanchism, nationalism and communism.

If we accept the thesis that Russia was de facto a US-controlled territory until 2000, we can then immediately understand the next key implication: **the coming to power of Putin did not, in itself, magically change this reality**. Think of other examples like Saddam Hussein or Noriega who used to be loyal US puppets who eventually decided to take a more independent course? Did their countries change overnight? Of course not. The difference with Russia is, of course, that the US did not have the means to wage war on Russia, much less so occupy it and install another puppet regime. Even the terminally weakened and dysfunctional Russian state of the 1993-1999 years still had the means to transform all US major cites into a rubble of radioactive ashes. And yet, the Russian state could not even get together enough regiments to deal with the Chechen insurgency. All that the Russians could send to deal with the Chechen insurgency was a limited amount of so-called "mixed regiment" (сводный полк—really mixed "battalions"), a mishmash of hastily clobbered together subunits which often had no military training at all. Thus, by the time Putin came to power Russia has a quasi-dead state fully controlled by the USA.

And yet, Putin achieved some kind of miracle. First he skillfully crushed the Chechen insurgency. Then, he ejected the Jewish oligarchs which resulted in an immediate change in the tone of the media coverage of the war in Chechnya. Then he began to reassemble the state piece by piece and while rebuilding what he called the "verticality of power," meaning that he re-subordinated the various regions of Russia to the central government: mobsters were ejected from the gubernatorial seats they had purchased, the regions began to pay taxes to the Federal government (most had stopped) and Presidential envoys were sent out to restore order in the regions. If all this was a bitter pill to swallow for the British who had been deeply involved in breaking up Russia into many smaller pieces, it was really no big deal for the Americans who, at the time, and more pressing issues to deal with: the neocons had just successfully pulled off 9/11 and the Global War On Terror (GWOT) was in full swing. Besides, externally, Russia was playing it all very nice, actually helping the USA in Afghanistan. Logically, while the press in the UK was frantically cooking up all sorts of hysterically anti-Russian propaganda, the US press did not care very much.

I don't think that the Americans really liked Putin, but they probably saw him as a reliable partner that they could keep in check and who would not give them too much grief. Sure, he prevented the final break up of Russia, but every good thing has an end and it would have been unrealistic by 2000 to expect another decade of Yeltsin-like chaos and collapse. Besides, it's not like Russia really had tossed off the American yoke: the system which the USA had created was still in place and there is only that much that Putin could legally do.

So between 2000 and 2012 Putin and Medvedev began a very gradual step-by-step process of internal reconstruction. In foreign relations Russia did a lot of zig-zagging, sometimes acting in a way mildly irritating to the Americans, but always subservient when things got really important.

And then the USA did two truly dumb things: feeling buoyed by a sense of omnipotence and imperial hubris, the Americans let Georgia attack Russian forces in Ossetia and then they fully sided with the aggressor. That, combined with the maniacal insistence on deploying an anti-missile system around Russia, resulted in a wave of anti-American anger in Russia which Putin fully exploited. The Americans probably figured that, sure Medvedev was better, but Putin they had already seen in power, and it was no biggie—they could handle him too. Except that "Putin 2.0" was quite a different one from the original version.

There had been a warning sign which the West dismissed as just a political speech: Putin's speech at the 2007 *Munich Conference on Security Policy*[33] in which he unambiguously stated that the USA's planetary empire was the number one cause of all the world's major problems:

> The history of humanity certainly has gone through unipolar periods and seen aspirations to world supremacy. And what hasn't happened in world history?
>
> However, what is a unipolar world? However one might embellish this term, at the end of the day it refers to one type

[33] Vladimir Putin: Speech and the Following Discussion at the Munich Conference on Security Policy http://archive.kremlin.ru/eng/speeches/2007/02/10/0138_type82912type82914type82917type84779_118123.shtml

> of situation, namely one center of authority, one center of force, one center of decision-making.
>
> It is a world in which there is one master, one sovereign. And at the end of the day this is pernicious not only for all those within this system, but also for the sovereign itself because it destroys itself from within.
>
> And this certainly has nothing in common with democracy. Because, as you know, democracy is the power of the majority in light of the interests and opinions of the minority.
>
> Incidentally, Russia—we—are constantly being taught about democracy. But for some reason those who teach us do not want to learn themselves.
>
> I consider that the unipolar model is not only unacceptable but also impossible in today's world. And this is not only because if there was individual leadership in today's—and precisely in today's—world, then the military, political and economic resources would not suffice. What is even more important is that the model itself is flawed because at its basis there is and can be no moral foundations for modern civilization.

This speech with its unusually candid type of language did create an initial moment of shock, but it was soon dismissed and forgotten. The Western reaction was basically "*fine, you don't like us, but watcha gonna do about it*?!" and a shrug.

What Putin did about it is continue to systematically strengthen the state, launching the economy on a multi-year boom which even overcame the 2008 crisis, and slowly educating the people inside Russia on a new concept: "sovereignization" (суверенизация).

Sovereignization is a powerful concept because it combines a diagnostic (we are not really sovereign) with a goal (we need to become sovereign). It is not directed against anybody, but anybody openly opposing it immediately looks bad (how can anybody legitimately oppose sovereignization?). Furthermore, by introducing the concept of sovereignization, Putin pushed the people to ask key questions which had never been asked in the past: if we are not sovereign, why not? How did it happen that we are not sovereign? And who is really sovereign then? And what about those who oppose sovereignization, whose interests are they defending?

By the time the Americans realized that the genie had been let out of the bottle it was literally too late: by a single conceptual push the entire political discourse in Russia had been altered from a state of catatonic stupor to a potentially very dangerous cocktail of opinions.

And this time Putin did not stop at words: he also passed laws demanding that any foreign-financed NGO sign-up as a "foreign agent" and that any government employee with money or real estate abroad either justify its origin or resign. And these are just test runs, the big stuff is all ahead: Putin now wants to change the laws regulating the activities of the mass media, he plans to implement new legislation making it possible to incorporate major industries inside Russia (currently they are all incorporated aboard), he intends to change the taxation system of major foreign multinationals and, eventually and inevitably, he will have to initiate a revision of the Russian Constitution. Step by step, Putin is now using his power to change the system, cutting off each instrument of foreign control over Russia one after the other. Last, but not least, Putin has now openly embarked on a process to establish a new **Common Eurasian Economic Realm** (Единое Евразийское Экономическое Пространство) with any former Soviet republic willing to join (Belarus and Kazakhstan are already in) which will eventually become a new **Eurasian Union** (Евразийский Союз). This, of course, is utterly unacceptable to the USA, which is why Hillary Clinton took the unprecedented step to openly announce[34] that the USA would do everything in its power to either prevent this outcome or, at the very least, to delay it:

> "There is a move to re-Sovietize the region. It's not going to be called that. It's going to be called customs union, it will

[34] Clinton fears efforts to "re-Sovietize" in Europe http://news.yahoo.com/clinton-fears-efforts-sovietize-europe-111645250--politics.html

> be called Eurasian Union and all of that. But let's make no mistake about it. We know what the goal is and we are trying to figure out effective ways to slow down or prevent it."

This time around, however, it was Russia's turn to say "*fine, you don't like us, but watcha gonna do about it?!.*"

The fact of the matter is that there is precious little the USA can do about it. Oh sure, the US did raise a big stink about "stolen elections," the Pussy Riot movement, the Congress passed the *Magnitsky Act,*[35] and Hillary made her threats. But all that was way too little and way too late, by the time the Americans came to realize that they had yet another major problem on their hands, there was nothing much they could do about it.

This is not to say that there is nothing that they will do about it in the years to come. First and foremost, we can expect a surge in the number of terrorist attacks in the Caucasus and the rest of Russia. If Chechnya seems to be safe, at least for the time being, the situation in the neighboring republic of Dagestan is still very dangerous. Second, we can expect the anti-Putin propaganda to reach new heights. Third, the US CIA and the British MI6 will return to their Cold War practices of covertly funding and directing a dissident movement. Finally, and if all else fails, the West might try to find some crazy "lone gunman" to get rid of Putin himself.

Putin and his "Eurasian Sovereignists" supporters are probably not a majority of the people at this time. Yes, they are in key positions of power and they can use what is euphemistically called the "administrative resource" (административный ресурс—the power of the state bureaucracy) to promote their agenda, but they will have to deal with a Russian intelligentsia which is still fiercely anti-Putin and with a media which is even more hostile to any idea of sovereignization. And yet, as long as Putin does not engage into any excesses, it will be awfully hard for the

---

[35]Text of the Sergei Magnitsky Rule of Law Accountability Act of 2012 https://www.govtrack.us/congress/bills/112/s1039/text

media to openly trash a political program aiming at the sovereignization of the Russian nation. This is why when Putin repeatedly referred to this idea in his Message to the Federal Assembly[36] the media either ignored it, or played it down. And yet, gradually, this topic is becoming more and more common in the Russian political discourse, led by the very active Russian Internet (known as RuNet).

At this moment Putin has a very strong control of the state apparatus and most key positions in the Kremlin are in the hands of his allies. The state itself is in halfway decent condition, still plagued by corruption and a legal system designed to make it ineffective, it will work when needed, but it is still far from being a well-oiled machine. The Russian economy is doing pretty well, in particular compared to others, but it is still very heavy, often ineffective, and most revenue is still channeled abroad. Likewise, the Russian society is mostly happy that the 1990s are over, but the vast majority of people still are faced with many difficulties and hope for a better future. Finally, the Russian armed forces have suffered a great deal under Serdyukov, but they are already definitely capable of dealing with any realistically imaginable conflict and they are gradually working on restoring their full-spectrum deterrent capability. In this context, Putin's chances are overall good, but this is far from a done deal and it would be very naive to underestimate all the potential responses the US Empire could come up with to deal with this emerging threat to its domination.

The time frame to see what will happen is relatively short, four to six years max. If by the end of his term Putin does not succeed in his sovereignization program then all bets are off for Russia and since all parties, including the "Atlantic integrationists," realize that, the struggle inside the Kremlin is likely to only heat up. We can be sure that the next

---

[36]Vladimir Putin: Annual Presidential Address to the Federal Assembly http://en.kremlin.ru/events/president/news/17118

months and years will see a lot of political upheavals in Russia, possibly beginning by an open fallout between Putin and Medvedev.

And Islam in all that?

As I wrote above, neither the Muslim world nor the "Islamic factor" inside Russia are going to have any influence on the outcome of this struggle. At the most, the USA and their "Atlantic integrationists" allies will use Islamic terrorists to destabilize Russia. But as long as the state remains organized and solid, no amount of terrorism will be sufficient to truly influence the course of events. Besides, a resurgence of Islamic terrorism in Russia might have the exactly opposite effect: it might convince even more Russians that they need a powerful and independent regime to protect the country.

However, the outcome of this struggle might have a deep effect not only on the "Islamic factor" inside Russia, but on the Muslim world in general: "Atlantic integrationists" **are by and large anti-Muslim and pro-Israeli; they want to integrate Russia into a Western system of security as opposed to a Islamic one**. To one degree or another, "Atlantic integrationists" are always the proponents of the "clash of civilizations" paradigm. In contrast, the **"Eurasian Sovereignists," while not all necessarily pro-Islamic in any way, are all for a multipolar world and they have no problem at all with the idea that one of these poles of power would be an Islamic one**. In other words, **the only circumstance when "Eurasian Sovereignists" see a threat in Islam is when Islam is used by the US Empire as a tool to destabilize those countries who dare resist the USA**. From this point of view there is an "Islam" in Bosnia, in Kosovo or in Chechnya which is a clear enemy of Russia, but there is an Islam in Iran, Lebanon or Kadyrov's Chechnya which is an objective ally of Russia. It is characteristic that the **"Atlantic integrationists" always see Israel as Russia's natural ally in the Middle East while the "Eurasian Sovereignists" always name Iran.**

As long as these two forces continue to fight each other for the control of the Kremlin and Russia the Russian policies toward Islam inside Russia and the Muslim world will be inconsistent, at times indecisive, and therefore only moderately predictable. My personal sense is that Putin and his "Eurasian Sovereignists" are currently in a much stronger position than their opponents and that is definitely good news for the Arab and Muslim world, in particular for Syria. This process is far from over and it would be unwise to make too many predictions about what Russia might do, or to count on Russia to do the "right thing" just because logic would indicate that it should. The appalling example of Russia essentially giving the US/NATO a green light at the UNSC to invade Libya should serve as a reminder that Russia is still not a truly sovereign and that it cannot be counted on the always resist the USA's immense power.

March 9, 2013

RUSSIA AND ISLAM, PART SEVEN: THE WEATHERMAN'S COP OUT

In the bad old days when I used to do analysis for a living, I had a boss which always insisted that I offer him several possible outcomes. He wanted me to tell him, "either X or Y could happen, but if not, then Z is a definite possibility." In his mind, by covering all the possible outcomes our department's "analysis" would never be wrong, and he would ways been seen as "systematic" and "competent" by his bosses. I always hated that. From my point of view, this is exactly what the local weatherman does when he predicts "a hot mostly sunny day, with some clouds and possible afternoons showers with local thunderstorms." This, of course, describes almost "any" day in Florida, but this is hardly an acceptable cop out for an analyst who, I strongly believe, should be paid not to list all the possibilities, but to make a prediction based on his knowledge and expertise. I still believe that the difference between a real expert and an ignorant "pundit" is that the former has the skills to make the right call, and yet I am about to do exactly what I dislike pundits so much for: I will mention possible events, some general trends, but without making any firm prediction. And I will do that for exactly the same reasons as the pundits: I am simply unable to confidently predict what will actually happen.

I can, however, draw a few basic conclusions from the preceding installments, the most important one is that Russia is in a state of high instability and of constant change.

To illustrate what I mean by that, I have written two descriptions of modern Russia which appear to be contradictory or even mutually exclusive, but which both contain more than a few factual truths.

Russia version one:

Russia is: a country which is in the process of finally breaking off from the Western domination which, depending on whom you ask, began in the 17th century, February 1917, November 1917 or 1991. Between 1991 and 2000 the entire political system was re-designed according to US orders (all key ministries at the time were literally crowded with US "advisors" who basically told their subservient Russian "Ministers" "do this, sign that"). As for the Russian economy, it was totally controlled by the Jewish oligarchs which basically plundered it sharing the proceeds with their US patrons. As soon as Putin came to power he embarked on a massive program to get rid of US "advisors" and Jewish oligarchs and that, of course, earned him the eternal hatred of the West. As part of this national liberation process, Putin has also given the full support of the state to the main traditional/historical religions of Russia, which in practical terms means Christian Orthodoxy and Islam (nominally about 40% and 7% of the population respectively, only a much smaller proportion of which are truly religious). Pro-Western religions (Papism, Protestantism and Judaism taken together account for less than 0.5% of the population). Likewise, there are no pro-Western political parties in the Russian Duma, not because of any "stolen" elections, but simply because these parties could not even make the needed 5% to get a single representative. In other words, it is reasonable to assume that only about 5% of the population of Russia has any sympathies with the Western cultural, economic, political or societal model and 95% of Russians clearly want another course for their country.

The example of Chechnya has proven that the combined efforts of local traditional Muslim forces and of the Federal authorities are capable of dealing even with the worst forms of Wahhabi extremism. As a result of this, patriotic (but not nationalist) Russians and Muslims are joining forces against a common enemy: the Anglo intelligence services (CIA/MI6 & co.) and their proxies, the Wahhabi preachers and guerrillas.

The re-election of Vladimir Putin to the presidency has now triggered a deepening and acceleration of the movement initiated under his presidency during his first terms: following US advisors and Jewish oligarchs, it is now the turn of the proponents of the "*Atlantic integrationist*[37]" viewpoint to be given the boot: the process which began with the now disgraced ex-Minister of Defense Serdyukov might well end with a dismissal of Premier Medvedev who, in many ways, is the lead representative of this "Atlantic integrationist" worldview. Should that happen, and should the "*Eurasian Sovereignists*[38]" gain full control over Russia's foreign policy, this will result is a major shift of Russian policies toward Iran whom the Eurasian sovereignists always cite as the natural ally of Russia in the Middle East.

Along a revamping of relations with Iran, Russian foreign policy priorities will be, in order of importance, the establishment of a Eurasian Union, the deepening of the political collaboration with the Shanghai Cooperation Organization (SCO) member countries and the BRICS, in particular China and India. While Russia will continue to see the EU as an important economic partner, it will keep this relationship purely on an economically mutually beneficial basis with only "symbolic shows of togetherness." In the Middle East, Russia will continue to staunchly support Iran and Syria with all available means short of overt military intervention.

Russia number two:

Historically, Russia has always been an objective ally of Western imperialism, and this is unlikely to change in the foreseeable future. The main reason why Putin gave the boot to US advisors and Jewish oligarchs has little to do with some deeply-felt political beliefs and has everything to do with a typically Russian power struggle inside the Kremlin. The various factions in the Kremlin are now skillfully impersonating a conflict between pro-Western and nationalistic groups. This purely rhetori-

---

[37] Russia and Islam, part six: the Kremlin http://thesaker.is/russia-and-islam-part-six-the-kremlin/

[38] ditto

cal propaganda campaign makes it possible for the Russian elites to remain in power. Once we realize that elites are only interested in one thing—their own power and wealth—we also can easily predict their view of the West. For these Russian elites the West is primarily a source of more wealth and power, a giant which can be played against your opponents, an overlord which will let you share in the spoils of the vicious exploitation of Russia and its people as long has the West's interests are not truly threatened. Thus, it is equally obvious that the Kremlin will never openly challenge the West, much less do something which could truly trigger a determined response from the West.

Take the example of Chechnya: this conflict was "resolved" only when the West, busy with 9/11 and the GWOT, gave the "green light" to the Russian forces to butcher the Chechen people and install their own puppet-thug Kadyrov. The Russians have learned that simple lesson: as long as the West considers you "their SOB" then you are free to do pretty much anything at home but if you decide to take an independent course, you end up like Noriega, Saddam, Gaddafi and Assad (this threat was openly made by demonstrators during the recent color-coded revolution attempt in Russia).

Yes, most of the highly visible Jewish oligarchs have been exiled and one, Khodorkovsky, is in jail. But what does really mean? That these oligarchs, tired of a their decade long pillaging of Russia, have decided to follow the example of a satiated tick, and simply fell off from their host, to go and happily digest their orgy of blood in a friendlier place: Israel, the UK or somewhere else in Europe. Every departing Jewish oligarch has now been replaced with another, equally predatory and cynical, oligarch (either Jewish or Russian). The system of predatory bloodsucking of Russia and its people is still very much in place and is unlikely to ever change.

As for religions—they are practically irrelevant to Russia. Each religious denomination in Russia has a traditionalist wing which is too small to ever make a difference, while the rest of the country is populated by people who are either wholly lukewarm or even hostile to any religion. The Orthodox propaganda finds some followers in Russia only because it provides for a "patriotic" substitute for the now discredited Marxism-Leninism. As for the Wahhabi propaganda, the only reason why it is popular in some nominally Muslim ethnicities is because it gives a cachet of religious legitimacy to what could only be referred to as the basic thuggery of some ethnic groups which have lived from crime and robbery for centuries.

As for Russian foreign policy, it will continue to be a bizarre mix of petty grandstanding and grand collaboration with the USA and whoever has enough power to pressure the Russian elites. The only "natural ally" of Russia in the Middle-East is Israel, if only because both countries are run by pragmatic thugs who skillfully impersonate nationalists. The Russian mob and the Jewish mafia are, for all practical purposes, one and the same phenomenon, and they have never ceased working together for their mutual benefit. Religion or ethnicity are irrelevant for these people whose only loyalty is to themselves.

So which version of Russia do you prefer? Which one do you believe is correct?

Personally, it is pretty clear that I think that version number one is the correct overall description of what is taking place. I cannot deny, however, that version two still has a lot of factual basis behind it. In fact, version two is very much the version which "Atlantic integrationists" are instinctively comfortable with. And as long as the "Atlantic integrationists" will remain a powerful segment of Russian society Russia number two will remain a reality, at least in part.

What does that mean for Muslims in Russia and abroad?

From a pragmatic point of view, there is really very little Muslims can do to affect the processes currently taking place in Russia. Inside Russia Muslims have no other option than to support the regime in power for a very basic reason: any "success" of Wahhabi Islam in Russia will inevitably turn into a total disaster for all the Muslims affected by it. First, because Wahhabi Islam is a direct threat to the traditions and culture of Muslims in Russia. Second because, unlike what happened during the first Chechen war, Russia now has all the means to crush any separatist or extremist movement at any stage of its development, ranging from effective counter-intelligence work to the engagement of fully armed and trained units and formations in a spectrum of operations ranging from counter-insurgency to combined arms operations. Yes, there still are Wahhabi terrorist attacks in Dagestan and southern Russia, and there are Wahhabi preachers still involved in all kinds of murders of traditionalist Muslims, primarily in the region of Kazan but also in other parts of Russia. The primarily reason why this is still taking place is that the nuisance of these attacks is below the "reaction threshold" of the main Russian "power ministries" (State Security, Defense) and are dealt with mostly by the Ministry of Internal Affairs (sometimes assisted by *local* elements of State Security). After all, the murder of a few policemen or clerics is hardly a reason to justify the involvement of special forces or the military—the regular cops and courts should learn how to deal with this. But should the situation get out of control then the "Federals" will show up and deal with it, rapidly and ruthlessly.

Outside Russia, Muslims are all more or less stuck into doing more of the same. Iran, Syria and Hezbollah can only keep hoping that Putin's Russia will be a better ally or partner than Medvedev's, while the bulk of the rest of the Islamic countries does not need to give Russia much thought at all, if only because pretty much all of the Muslim countries on the planet besides Iran and Syria are now firmly under the control of Uncle Sam who, of course, will tell them what to think, say or do.

The main paradox

I wrote this series of articles on the topic of Russia and Islam because I saw both of these categories as a part of what I would call the global resistance against the West's imperialism. And most of my discussion has been focused on trying to see whether Russia would ever turn into a consistent part of this resistance or not. And my conclusion is, in this respect, a very hopeful one because I very much believe that Russia will not only turn into a consistent part of this resistance, but because I even see it as the most important and powerful actor in this movement (what other major country today has a population with only 5% of pro-Western elements and sits on top of a booming economy?). In contrast, it appears to me that most of the Islamic *Ummah* is now firmly in the hands of the West, either openly (Jordan, Morocco, Indonesia, etc.) or through its Wahhabi proxies (Qatar, Libya, Pakistan, etc.). In this context, the differences between the Egyptian *Ikhwan*, the "Syrian" FSA, the Palestinian Hamas, the Albanian thugs in Kosovo or the al-Qaeda constellation make very little difference to me. Fundamentally, they all, I repeat "ALL," have been co-opted and are controlled by the USA, at least to a degree sufficient to be manipulated and used as proxies. Thus, from the Russian point of view, they are all potential, if not actual, enemies at least as much, if not more, then the regime of Saakashvili in Georgia or the Latvian and Estonian nationalists.

As far as I can tell, the Shia are the only Muslims still resisting the West's imperialism. And when I look at the actions of the Iraqi government, I cannot even say that all Shia resist, as even nominally Shia politicians can be found among Western collaborators. Finally, just one thought about what could have happened in Iran if the Gucci Revolution of Rafsanjani & Co. would have toppled the Islamic Republic immediately tells me that even the Shia world is not nearly as stable and contradictions-free as I wish it was.

Personalizing ideas

I will now do something else which is usually a bad idea. I will speak of people rather than ideas. But I will do this only to illustrate a simple point. My belief is that Vladimir Putin, Ayatollah Khamenei and Hassan Nasrallah are, or at the very least, should be, natural allies. By extension, I would say that what these three people individually stand for should naturally bring them to support each other and join their efforts. The question is whether these political leaders will survive long enough to join forces.

My focus on "Russia and Islam" was probably flawed from the outset since it looked primarily at two high-level concepts whereas the most interesting developments are happening at a deeper, sub-national, level. Still, if my prediction about Russia proves to be correct, resistance in Russia to the West will soon go from sub-national to national, and if by that time the Islamic Republic is still in power in Iran, and I believe that it will be, the potential of a Russian-Iranian alliance could become truly immense, in particular if it is supported by other countries elsewhere (Venezuela at the OPEC or China at the BRICS). Such an alliance could not only save Syria, but also protect Lebanon—via Hezbollah—from a foreign takeover.

This last segment concludes my series on Russia and Islam. I am sorry that I was unable to give some kind of confident and optimistic prediction. My hope is that at the very least I might have contributed to the dispelling of some myths and clichés, an admittedly far more modest goal. For example, if I have succeeded in showing that while Russia and France both struggle with seemingly similar problems (immigration, extremism, crime, separatism, etc.) they are doing so in very different contexts and one should not think of Russia as some kind of "bigger France in the East." Muslims, in particular, should refrain from transposing Western realities to a fundamentally non-Western context.

My only confident prediction is that Russia in 10 years will be dramatically different from the Russia of today. Whether that will be for the better or the worse is, unfortunately, not something I can predict with confidence, though my personal and very strong feeling is that it will be for the better, and possibly even for the much better.

As always, time will show.

March 20, 2013

RUSSIA AND ISLAM, PART EIGHT: WORKING TOGETHER, A BASIC "HOW-TO"

Today I am going to look into the topic of Orthodox and Muslim co-operation, suggest one possible approach to this issue and give a practical example were this could be done immediately and with great benefit for all the parties involved. I consider this post today as the eighth installment of my "Russia and Islam" series and I suggest that those who have not read it take a look at it before proceeding (see preceding chapters for parts one,[39] two,[40] three,[41] four,[42] five,[43] six,[44] and seven[45]). For reasons obvious to anybody who has read these series, I will limit my scope to the topic of cooperation between Orthodox Christians and non-Wahhabi Muslims. As an Orthodox Christian myself I do not believe that any co-operation is possible between the Orthodox Church and the Papacy or the Reformed/Protestant denominations, nor do I believe that there is anything to discuss with Wahhabis. So when I will speak of "Christian" below this will strictly refer to Orthodox Christians and "Muslim" will refer to any Muslim except Wahhabis.

---

[39] Russia and Islam, part one: introduction and definitions http://thesaker.is/russia-and-islam-part-one-introduction-and-definitions/

[40] Russia and Islam, part two: Russian Orthodoxy http://thesaker.is/russia-and-islam-part-two-russian-orthodoxy/

[41] Russia and Islam, part three: internal Russian politics http://thesaker.is/russia-and-islam-part-three-internal-russian-politics/

[42]Russia and Islam, part four: "Islam" as a threat http://thesaker.is/russia-and-islam-part-four-islam-as-a-threat/

[43] Russia and Islam, part five: "Islam" as an ally http://thesaker.is/russia-and-islam-part-five-islam-as-an-ally/

[44] Russia and Islam, part six: the Kremlin http://thesaker.is/russia-and-islam-part-six-the-kremlin/

[45] Russia and Islam, part seven: the weatherman's cop out http://thesaker.is/russia-and-islam-part-seven-the-weathermans-cop-out/

The fundamentally misguided yet typical approach:

Having had many opportunities to exchange views with Muslims from different countries and having also heard Christian and Muslim religious figures engaged in various debates, dialogs and discussions, I can describe the typical scenario by which such dialogs are conducted.

Typically, both sides try to establish a list of all the issues Islam and Christianity agree upon. These include that God is love, that the Mother of Jesus was a virgin, that the Antichrist will come before the end of time, that Moses was a great prophet, that angels are the messengers of God and many other things. Added to this list of topics of agreement are usually statements about how Christians and Muslims have lived in peace side by side and how this should continue today. This is a well-meaning and polite way to engage in a dialog, but this is also a fundamentally misguided one for the simple reason that it overlooks absolutely fundamental theological and historical problems. Let's take these one by one.

Irreconcilable theological differences between Christianity and Islam

The highest most sacred dogmatic formulation of Christianity is the so-called "Credo" or "Symbol of Faith."[46] Literally *every letter down to the smallest "I"*[47]of this text is, from the Christian point of view, the most sacred and perfect dogmatic formulation, backed by the full authority of the two Ecumenical Councils which proclaimed it and all the subsequent Councils which upheld it. In simple terms—the Symbol of Faith is absolutely non-negotiable, non-re-definable, non-re-interpretable, you cannot take anything away from it, and you cannot add anything to it. You can either accept it as is, *in toto*, or reject it.

The fact is that Muslim would have many problems with this text, but one part in particular is absolutely unacceptable to any Muslim:

---

[46]Nicene-Constantinopolitan Creed http://orthodoxwiki.org/Symbol_of_Faith

[47] One Iota: Homoiousios and Homoousios http://xefer.com//2002/10/iota

> And in one Lord Jesus Christ, the Son of God, the Only-begotten, Begotten of the Father before all ages, Light of Light, Very God of Very God, Begotten, not made; **of one essence with the Father**, by whom all things were made

This part clearly and unambiguously affirms that Jesus Christ was not only the Son of God but actually God Himself. This is expressed by the English formulation "of one essence with the Father" (ὁμοούσιον τῷ Πατρί in Greek with the key term *homousios* meaning "consubstantial"). This is "THE" core belief of Christianity: that Jesus was *Theanthropos*, the God-Man or God incarnate. This belief is categorically unacceptable to Islam which says that Christ was a prophet and by essence a "normal" human being.

For Islam, the very definition of what it is to be a Muslim is found in the so-called "*Shahada*"[48] or testimony/witness. This is the famous statement by which a Muslim attests and proclaims that "There is no god but God, Muhammad is the messenger of God." One can often also hear this phrased as "There is no god but Allah, Muhammad is His prophet."

Now without even going into the issue of whether Christians can agree or not that "Allah" is the appropriate name for God (some do, some don't—this is really irrelevant here), it's the second part which is crucial here: Christianity does not recognize Muhammad as a prophet at all. In fact, technically speaking, Christianity would most likely classify Muhammad as a heretic (if only because of his rejection of the "Symbol of Faith"). Saint John of Damascus even called him a 'false prophet'. Simply put: there is no way a Christian can accept the "Shahada" without giving up his Christianity just as there is no way for a Muslim to accept the "Symbol of Faith" without giving up his Islam.

So why bother?

Would it not make much more sense to accept that there are fundamental and irreconcilable differences between Christianity and Islam and

[48] Shahada https://en.wikipedia.org/wiki/Shahada

simply give up all that useless quest for points of theological agreement? Who cares if we agree on the secondary if we categorically disagree on the primary? I am all in favor of Christians studying Islam and for Muslims studying Christianity (in fact, I urge them both to do so!), and I think that it is important that the faithful of these religions talk to each other and explain their points of view as long as this is not presented as some kind of quest for a common theological stance. **Differences should be studied and explained, not obfuscated, minimized or overlooked.**

The next divisive issue is the historical record.

Christians and Muslims—friends or foes? What does history show?

Another well-meaning and fundamentally mistaken approach often seen in dialogs between Christians and Muslims is the attempt to present the history of relations between these two faiths as a long uninterrupted love-fest. This is factually wrong and naive to the extreme.

First, both Muslims and Christians are human beings, imperfect and sinful human beings (both religions agree on that). Second, and just to make things worse, both Islam and Christianity have, at times, been official state religions, meaning that states acted in the name of their religion. As a result, there have been plenty of moments in history where Christians and Muslims fought each other. Yes, it is true that Muslims and Christians often did live in peace side by side, but unless one is a total bigot and ignoramus, it is simply impossible to ignore the fact that Christians and Muslims also waged war, persecuted and mistreated each other, sometimes viciously.

So what?

What needs to be established not whether Christians and Muslims did wrong each other in the past, but whether they **can** live in peace. And the answer to that is a resounding "yes!" I know, some naysayer will immediately object that both Christianity and Islam have an mixed record of interpretation of whether converting the other to your religion is a religious duty or not. The point here is not whether some Christians or Muslims do (or did) believe that they have to convert each other at all cost, but whether there are those who do not believe so. As long as this is a possibility compatible with one's faith this is sufficient.

I think that history, and plenty of statements from religious figures on both sides, prove that this is possible—and that there is a preponderance of evidence to show that—that both Christians and Muslims can accept that the decision to be a Muslim or a Christian should be freely taken inside each person's heart without compulsion or even interference. The fact that it is possible to interpret Christianity and Islam differently is irrelevant as long as it is also possible to accept such a basic stance on religious choices.

Yes, I know that in Islam apostasy is a capital crime, but I also know that over the centuries Muslims have also chosen to not enforce this. It is not for me as an Orthodox Christian to dictate what Muslim leaders decide, but it is also clear to me that there are enough wise and pragmatic Muslim leaders out there to fully comprehend the consequences of a decision on their part to enforce the death penalty on somebody choosing to abandon Islam.

So where do we go from here?

It is very simply to get Christians and Muslims to feel hostility toward each other. First, make a few theological statements which are unacceptable to the other party, call the other a heretic or unbeliever, then mention a few bloody and contentious episodes in history and soon you will have a very nasty situation on your hands. This is as easy as it is sterile as nothing at all can come from that.

Thankfully, it is just as easy to accept that there are irreconcilable differences between the core beliefs of both religions and that each person should have the means to freely make a choice between these two faiths according to his conscience. As for history, it is a no-brainer to accept that both parties have, at times, done wrong to each other and that we are not responsible for what happened in the past, but only for what we make of our present and future.

Still, having dealt with our differences, we still should ask ourselves whether we have something in common, a common interest, or common values, which we might want to jointly defend. And we most definitely do: our ethics.

The common ground—ethics:

Any religion has two primarily components: what it believes in, what it proclaims, and then the rules of life, the "how-to" of daily existence which it mandates. In Christian terms there is the *doxa* (what you proclaim or glorify) and the *praxis* (how you live your spiritual life on a daily basis). These are the basic rules common to most religions: not to kill, not to steal, to live a life of modesty, to protect the weak, etc. When comparing Islam and Christianity one can find both differences and similarities between their praxis and ethics. The differences in praxis are not that important because they mostly affect the private lives of the faithful: Muslims will fast during the month of Ramadan, Christians during the four major fasts of the year and on Wednesdays and Fridays. So let them, who cares? They really do not bother each other and, in fact, they are typically respectful of each other's traditions. On ethics, however, the two religions mostly agree both on a social/corporate and individual level and, with one notable exception which I will discuss below, Christianity and Islam have very similar ideas of what is right and wrong and what society should stand for or pro-actively reject. Rather than making a long list of what Islam and Christianity agree on, I will simply introduce a new actor for comparison's sake: the "post-Christian secular West."

What does the post-Christian and secular West stand for today?

First and foremost, the post-Christian and secular West stands for the freedom of each person to choose his or her own system of belief, code of behavior, system of morals, lifestyles, etc. In other words, the post-Christian and secular West categorically rejects the notion that something called "The Truth" exists. From that it is logically inevitable to conclude that there really is no "right" or "wrong" at all. In fact, a core belief of the post-Christian and secular West is that "your freedom stops were mine begins"[49] (originally expressed as "*The right to swing my fist ends where the other man's nose begins*"). Ergo—as long as others are not affected by it, you can do whatever you want. Each person has his or her "truth" and what you consider right another person might consider wrong and vice versa.

Second, and as a direct consequence of the first point, the post-Christian and secular West places the well-being of the individual above the well-being of the community. This is perfectly expressed by the famous "*Life, Liberty and the pursuit of Happiness*"[50] phrase of the US Declaration of Independence which states that these are the inalienable right of each individual. The contrast with both Christianity and Islam could not have been greater since these religions consider that the real life is the Eternal Life, that the human being is called to be in obedience to God and that true happiness is spiritual and not earthly. In fact, while the West considers life as the highest value, Christianity and Islam welcome death and consider that dying in the name of God is a most desirable act of witness of God (*martis* in Greek has exactly the same meaning as *shahid* in Arabic: witness).

Finally, and as a direct consequence of the two points above, the only common value to all people in the post-Christian and secular West is, of course, money. Money is, literally, the only "common currency" of a society without any supreme values in which each person is free to define right and wrong as he/she wishes. This results in an inevitable monetization of everything, including the life of a human being.[51]

---

[49] Oliver Wendell Holmes, Jr. https://en.wikiquote.org/wiki/Oliver_Wendell_Holmes,_Jr.

[50] Life, Liberty and the pursuit of Happiness https://en.wikipedia.org/wiki/Life,_Liberty_and_the_pursuit_of_Happiness

[51] The Ford Pinto case: The Valuation Of Life As It Applies To The Negligence-Efficiency Argument http://users.wfu.edu/palmitar/Law&Valuation/Papers/1999/Leggett-pinto.html

This is really a very minimal system of values, but it is plenty enough to make it **the "anti-religion" par excellence**. In comparison to that, the differences between Orthodoxy and Islam suddenly appear tiny, almost irrelevant. Today, this is best exemplified in Russia where both Orthodox Christianity and Islam are under a direct multi-level attack by the determined efforts of the post-Christian and secular West which spares no effort to subvert and destroy the vales of these religions and replace them by Western "values" promoted in multi-billion dollar propaganda campaigns, including music, movies, books, fashion, TV, talk shows, stores, politicians, famous personalities, etc.

The recent and famous cases of Pussy Riot, and the supposed "right" of Russian homosexuals to organize "pride" parades in Moscow are the perfect examples of the kind of agenda the post-Christian and secular West is pushing nowadays. And although this is not reported in the Western corporate media, I can attest to the fact that Muslim leaders in Russia **all** perfectly understand that they are also under attack and that this is not just an "Orthodox problem."

So what could they do about it?

A perfect opportunity—the Russian Constitution

Russian politicians are not blind to what is going on and with the exception of a few pathologically naive or dishonest "liberals," they all understand that what is happening now is a clash of civilizations between the post-Christian and secular West and post-Soviet Russia. The fact that this clash of civilizations is not only ideological, but also political and even military (as the examples of the Euromaidan in the Ukraine and the deployment of the US anti-missile system in Eastern Europe shows) only makes these matters more urgent.

It just so happened that the Russian Constitution[52] is celebrating its 20th anniversary and that possible changes to that Constitution are being

---

[52] the Russian Constitution http://www.constitution.ru/en/10003000-01.htm

discussed in many part of Russian society. One of the most bizarre features of the current Russian Constitution is that it forbids the state from having any ideology. Article 13.2 of the current Constitution states that "*No ideology may be established as state or obligatory one.*" The roots of this rather strange paragraph can be traced to a mix of the general rejection of the old Soviet official Marxist-Leninist Communist ideology and a transparent attempt of the foreign "advisors" to the Yeltsin regime in 1993 to make darn sure that nothing "Russian" would find its place in the new Russian Constitution.

Some Russian Orthodox politicians have suggested that this paragraph 13.2 should be expunged, and that some formulation would have to be found to express the notion that Orthodoxy played a key historical role in the culture and system of values of modern Russia, that Orthodox values are the basis of the modern ideology of Russia. So far, no exact formulation has been suggested and there is even a debate whether such a phrase should be included in the Constitution itself or in its preamble.

Needless to say, even raising such a notion has resulted in an outraged reaction by the small but very vocal minority of pro-Western "liberal" politicians. More importantly, a lot of Russian Orthodox Christians also have deep reservations about the wisdom of such an amendment because it might alienate all the non-Orthodox people in Russia, which include not only Muslims or Buddhists, but a probably majority of agnostics. Muslim leaders have also expressed concern that this would officially place Islam in a 2nd-category religion status (even though that is exactly the status of Christian dhimmis[53] under Sharia law) and given Orthodoxy a senior, leading role.

I strongly believe that this is the perfect example when Christians and Muslims can easily find a common ground and unite forces: **why not simply recognize the special role of Orthodoxy and Islam in the historical formulation of the Russian culture, society and system of values?**

---

[53] Dhimmi https://en.wikipedia.org/wiki/Dhimmi

First, this happens to be historically correct. Not only were there a lot of Muslims among the Mongols who occupied Russia, in particular in the late period of occupation, but the expansion of the Russian state included many areas with a majority Muslim population who became citizens of the Russian Empire. Muslims have fought in defense of the Russian state and nation in many wars from the times of Saint Alexander Nevsky, to WORLD WAR II to the 08.08.08 war against Georgia. Last but most definitely not least, Akhmad Kadyrov and his son Ramzan Kadyrov have played an absolutely crucial role in kicking the Wahhabis out of Chechnya and thereby they not only saved the Chechen nation from what would have been an absolutely devastating Russian assault, but they also probably saved Russia from a very dangerous and bloody war in the Caucasus. The same can be said of the Dagestani men who for several days single-handedly fought the invading "Islamic International Brigade" of Shamil Basayev and Khattab from Chechnya in 1999 until the main Federal forces got involved. Modern Russia is, beyond any possible doubt, a multi-ethnic and multi-religious state whose well-being and prosperity depends in great part on the kind of Islam Russian Muslims will chose: the Islam of Ramzan Kadyrov or the "Islam" of Doku Umarov (the *shaitan* who fancies himself the "President of the Chechen Republic of Ichkeria and Emir of the Caucasus Emirate").

Second, by acknowledging the role of both Orthodox Christianity and Islam the proponents of this constitutional amendment would gain the support of what is by far the largest segment of the religions population: there are Buddhists, Papists, Protestants, Jews and other religious denominations in Russia, but they are tiny compared to the big two. Personally, I would also include Buddhists in this list of "culture forming" religious whose values are shaping Russian society if only because (unlike the other small(er) religions) they are truly indigenous to Russia whereas the other denominations are "foreign imports" which, of course, have the right to exist in Russia, but which have had exactly zero influence on the formation of the Russian national identity or system of values.

As for the nominally religious and mostly agnostic people, the mere fact that two (or three) religions are recognized in a special role should assuage their concerns about any one system of values or ideology becoming official at the expense of everybody else. After all, most people in Russia would agree that the ethics of Islam and Christianity have a lot in common. The only major societal and moral issue in which Orthodox Christianity and Islam really disagree on is the issue of capital punishment. But that is irrelevant since Russia has pledged a total moratorium on executions anyway (of all things, to join—what else?—the Council of Europe); besides a majority of Russians still remain in favor of the death penalty to the point that it might even be re-introduced in the future.

Conclusion

Contrary to what a lot of people seem to think, cooperation between Orthodox Christianity and Islam is actually very easy to achieve. Both sides have **to accept the fact of irreconcilable theological disagreements**, both sides have **to accept that they did wrong each other in the past**, and both sides have **to affirm the right of each person to freely chose his or her religion**, including the right to switch from one to another. So far that should be a no-brainer.

Next, Christian and Muslims need to define a set of civilizational issues that they fully agree on. Also a no-brainer.

Finally, both sides should systematically defend their cultural, social and civilizational values together, side by side. In fact, as long as their cultural, social and civilizational values are not in conflict with each other, Orthodox Christians and Muslims should defend the values of the other side on principle, as being "Russian" formative and foundational values. For example, Russian Orthodox Christians should defend the right of Muslim girls to wear a scarf in school and elsewhere. Not only because it is beautiful or because before Peter I **all** Russian woman always wore the exact same scarves not only in church, but **all day long**—but because the so-called "Islamic veil" is in no way a threat to Christianity: just look at an icon of the Mother of God.

Recently, an Orthodox church was burned down at night in Tatarstan by some Wahhabi thugs. The local Muslim community got together and donated all the money needed for a full reconstruction. Likewise, in Chechnya, Ramzan Kadyrov has personally overseen the reconstruction of many Russian churches destroyed in combat or by the Wahhabis and the local government has now allocated money for the construction of an Orthodox cathedral in the center of Grozny. In the meantime, the city authorities of Stavropol have ordered the destruction of two "illegal" mosques. That is in a city which has only one mosque—currently used as a museum, it's tiny anyway—and a Muslim population of anywhere 60,000 and 500,000 people (depends on who you ask and how you measure). The city authorities did promise to build a full Islamic Center (with mosque, school, hotel, etc.) which is great, but nothing has been done so far. Granted, the situation in Stavropol is particularly bad and it is complicated by many other factors such as the existence of nominally "Muslim" gangs of thugs and the hostility of the local popularization to what they perceive as the "Islamization" of their city and region. This is the exact type of case where the Federal authorities need to energetically intervene, as Putin has often done in such cases, and deal with this problem in what is referred to as "manual regime" (in contrast to the bureaucratic autopilot). Overall, so far, the record of Orthodox-Muslim cooperation is checkered.

If Orthodox Christians and Muslims could get together and jointly push for a change in the Russian Constitution this would not only get the job done, but it would herald a new era for Russia because it would send a strong signal to the local level in Russia (such as Stavropol) and abroad (Iran, Syria, Lebanon) that Russia has taken the fundamental decision to work with any Muslim party willing to do so on the basis of a few clearly defined, mutually accepted and simple principles.

A special word to any naysayers

I personally find all of the above really basic and self-evident. But having met the naysayers from both sides, I know that some of you will not be convinced. You "know" that Christians are imperialists never to be trusted or the Muslims are out to establish a "world Caliphate" on our dead bodies. Okay. Now let me ask you the question Americans kids like to challenge each other with: "*and what are you gonna do about it?!*" Expel all Muslims out of Russia and cut-off the Caucasus? Kill all of *kufars* and organize an Islamic Caliphate in Russia? Fight the righteous struggle against everybody and all fronts at the same time all on your own? Convince everybody to convert?

I don't think so.

In fact, by doing any of that all you're going to do is to do *exactly* what the Western political elites really want you to do! You do that any nobody will be more happy than the Tamir Pardo, Zbigniew Brzezinski and Hillary Clinton. Politics is the art of the possible and to aim at the impossible is simply one form of political suicide. Those who desperately want to pit Christians against Muslims will never achieve anything but delivering yet another blow against the very religion they claim to defend. In my experience, these people have a very poor and superficial religious education and typically no historical education at all. They mistake their hatred for the "other" for a God-pleasing religious zeal, and they act not so much out of love for their own religion, as out of hate for the religion of the other. These are the folks who simply cannot see, in the beautiful words of Alexander Solzhenitsyn[54] that:

> All attempts to find a way out of the plight of today's world are fruitless unless we redirect our consciousness, in repentance, to the Creator of all: without this, no exit will be illumined, and we shall seek it in vain. The resources we have set

[54] "Men Have Forgotten God" – The Templeon Address http://www.roca.org/OA/36/36h.htm

> aside for ourselves are too impoverished for the task. We must first recognize the horror perpetrated not by some outside force, not by class or national enemies, but within each of us individually, and within every society. This is especially true of a free and highly developed society, for here in particular we have surely brought everything upon ourselves, of our own free will. We ourselves, in our daily unthinking selfishness, are pulling tight that noose...

God-fearing and pious Muslims and Christians alike must realize and accept that humility and sincere repentance for our own sins is what God calls us to do and that seeking an external enemy to fear and hate is not profitable for our souls. Our diversity of beliefs has no other cause than our own sinfulness, which itself is a direct consequence of our *common* humanity, a humanity which we all share regardless of our beliefs. Having found and espoused the true faith does not necessarily make us better people at all, it only makes us more fortunate and privileged ones, and that privilege places a special burden upon us to show forgiveness and compassion toward our erring fellow human being. Finally, if our goal is really to convert the other one, the best way to do that is by our individual *example* of true piety, purity and love and not by "winning" a political struggle.

December 18, 2013

Replies to the comments posted under "Russia and Islam, part eight: working together, a basic "how-to"

Dear friends,

Thanks for your interesting comments! I will reply to some of the questions which you have put to me:

alizard said...

> "Another way to achieve a consensus and keeping the neutrality of paragraph 13.2, could be considered by looking at the example given lately by Croatia: Hold a referendum and intro-

> duce one or several new constitutional articles as safeguards from 'the plot against civilization.'"

The Saker replies:

Yes, very good idea. Besides, I really believe that the people need to be consulted much more often by means of referendums. At the very least, all crucial, civilizational and moral questions should be submitted to a popular vote.

Anonymous said…

> Such an outcome would throw the imperialists into a tizzy … I think the vast majority of Muslims would celebrate—But I have to say, I'm not sure, do you understand implications of this? A Russian recognition of Islamic in this context, while maybe political, would be a civilizational move—. Because it would rightfully, tie Russia to the "Islamic world"—not just as it is now, but real terms of the future of Russia.

The Saker replies:

Modern Russia is *already* tied to the "Islamic world" not only because of the relatively large minority of Muslims living in modern Russia, but because Russia—along with Belarus—is eventually going to form a Federation with Kazakhstan. Anybody believing that Russia is not tied to the Islamic world does just not understand the reality on the ground. My position is simple: Russia would be far better of being *proactive* in tying itself to the Islamic world than being passive because in the former case Russia can influence what kind of ties it wants to have and with which part. See, in my opinion, and no offense intended to anybody, the concept of the "Islamic world" is a nice fantasy, but not a reality. There is no "ummah" out there, there are only very many countries, civilizations and various branches of Islam and Russia should try to get closer to those (such as the traditional Sufis of Chechnya and Kazakhstan or the Shia in the Middle East) with whom it could form an alliance against the liver-eating psychos. Being deliberately tied to the Islamic world does not mean becoming an Islamic Republic or somehow losing the Orthodox roots of most Russians, it just means accepting a fact of history which presents both risks and opportunities and take action to maximize the latter.

Anonymous said...

Fortunately there are plenty decent agnostics and atheists. So there must be hope for us! But what keeps a secular person decent?

The Saker replies:

First, and this is really important, so please everybody pay attention here: **I consider that being an agnostic or an atheist is the normal and healthy reaction to exposure to false religions**. Furthermore, agnosticism and even militant atheism can have very different causes. It can be a reaction against the absurdity or even dishonesty of false religions, it can be the result of inexplicable suffering and, literally, "anger at God" (in which case, of course, it is neither agnosticism nor atheism), it can be because of high ideals and honesty which are repelled by the very much less than perfect behavior of those who claim to believe, it can be what I call "existential cowardice" it can be simply the result of a lukewarm indifference to this issue. In all this list, only the last two are reprehensible: existential cowards simply do not have the courage to cope with the possibility that there might be a God above them so they go into denial, while the lukewarm simply don't give a damn ("*So, because you are lukewarm, and neither hot nor cold, I will spit you out of my mouth*" Rev. 3:16). The other forms of agnosticism and atheism are really a form of honesty and intellectual integrity. Allow me a simple thought experiment to explain my point:

Let us assume that there are 100 religions out there, all different, all contradicting each other. Since, by definition, the Truth is One and since, by definition, two religions contradicting each other cannot be both right, we have only two possible situations:

a) **all** 100 religions are wrong, invented, man-made, delusions, etc.

or

b) **one** of them is "right" and the 99 others are wrong, invented, man-made, delusions, etc.

Therefore, unless you have been exposed to the putative "true" religion, *rejecting the 99 wrong ones is the correct thing to do.*

Now what if you have been exposed to the putative "real one" and don't feel in your heart that it is the true one? In that case, you follow your conscience (something which you should **always** do no matter the price to pay for it), and also reject it until and unless you change your mind. God and man always act in synergy and as long as you are at least open to the concept that there might be a true religion out there, even if you have not identified it yet, you are doing nothing wrong and you are living according to your conscience, that is already a rightful way to live you live.

That, however, does not solve the other problem you raise: what can keep a secular person decent? Logically? Nothing. Dostoevsky was quite right when he stated that "if there is no God all is permissible." There is, however, something the Fathers of the Church called the "law of the heart," a leftover awareness in each human being that there is a right and a wrong along with a nostalgia or a yearning to communicate with God. Of course, an atheist will deny that too.

Is there a logical reason to suppose that there might be a God and a true religion out there? Yes, I think that there is. If you really study the Old Testament you will realize that the ancient Jewish prophets really did predict the life of Christ with great accuracy.[55] As Augustine of Hippo wrote, "*the New Testament is hidden in the Old Testament, and the Old Testament is revealed in the New Testament.*"[56] Let me immediately say that the notion that the Old or New Testaments were retroactively changed to "fit the bill" is ludicrous: first, there is no historical record of

[55] Concordance of Messianic Prophesies http://fatheralexander.org/booklets/english/prophecies_christ.htm

[56] The Old Testament Regarding the Messiah http://fatheralexander.org/booklets/english/old_testament_messiah.htm

such a forgery and, second, knowing how sacred these books were for the faithful then, it would have been impossible to forge them without everybody immediately raising the alarm. In fact, there was one attempt at forging them, by the Jewish Masoretes who tried to forge the Old Testament after 70AD, but since their Masoretic forgery could be compared to the original Greek Septuagint, that forgery failed miserably. Having intellectually accepted the reality of the life of Christ accurately predicted centuries before His birth, you would have to conclude that this is indeed a "miraculous" events which points to His messiahship. After that, "all" you need to do is find out if any of the 100 religions out there is still following His teachings without changing them or adding to them.

I understand that faith is really not an intellectual process but a gift of God. But if your brain tells you that there might be more out there than an nonsensical existence without meaning or purpose and that pretty good probability that there is a God out there, then you can simply repeat in your heart the simple words of this prayer: "*Lord, I believe; help my unbelief!*" (Mark 9:24).

As long as you always follow your conscience and seek The Truth will all your heart, mind and will, you are living a righteous life.

Mindfriedo said...

> In Islam, a law of Allah cannot be changed by humans. Even though it may sound noble and logical at the time.(...) "what Allah has made halal I cannot make haram."

The Saker replies:

That is absolutely logical and self-evident: what has been revealed cannot be changed. One can only deny the reality of the revelation, but not demand that what has been revealed suddenly be changed to fit human desires. Not being a Muslim myself I don't find it appropriate for me to make suggestions about this issue other than saying that it might be a "show stopper" in Christian-Muslim relations. Beyond that, it is not for me to suggest alternative approaches.

Old auntie said…

> Defending cultural, social and civilizational values together: Fine.
>
> Doing this by changing the Russian constitution: Really?

The Saker replies:

I am not sure that this is the only way or even the best way. I just think that this is a nice opportunity.

Anonymous said…

> Excellent post. I wonder though why you dismiss RC and the Protestants.

The Saker replies:

I am in no way dismissing the Papacy or the Reformed denominations. I just don't believe that there is any possibility of collaboration with them. For 1000 years now, the so-called "Christian West" has used every possibility to destroy or subjugate the Orthodox Church and that hostility is still evident all over the modern "post-Christian West." I am not talking about individual people here, but the Western "Christian" denominations are all more or less rabidly anti-Orthodox and anti-Russian. It just makes no sense to deny that reality, at least not from the Orthodox point of view. Having spent over 1000 years on the receiving end of the "brotherly love" of Western Christian denominations we learned our lesson really well.

WizOz said…

> What one can certainly agree upon, is that the whole problem is a particularly tricky one. I have the feeling that asserting a special role for Islam in the formulation of the Russian culture, society, system of values can lead only to the relativization of religion. The more that I am not convinced that its role was that important in shaping the character of Russia.

The Saker replies:

Pre-1917 Russia was indeed almost exclusively a product of the Orthodox culture and, after Peter I, the Western Masonic elites. But that old Russia is gone forever, murdered by the commissars, killed by the Nazis and finished off by the "democrats." What we have today is a qualitatively different reality I call "post-Soviet Russia" and that modern, post-Soviet, Russia has been from day 1 (which I place roughly around the turn of the millennium) strongly influenced by Muslims who, while fewer in numbers than the Orthodox Christians, are far more socially and political active. Again, the example of Kadyrov and Chechnya immediately comes to my mind. Who does modern Russia owe more to, that lying crook "Patriarch" Kirill, or Akhmad and Ramzan Kadyrov?

WizOz said...

> Russia was the continuator of Byzance, her Tsar the defender of Orthodoxy and the protector of all Orthodox. Against that role all hell broke loose and we had the Revolution. Now the time to recover that role has come for Russia.

The Saker replies:

Yes, Russia had that potential, that calling, but nothing spiritual happens "automatically," it has to be struggled for in the spiritual battle between light and darkness. I am sure you know the prophecies as well as I do: "*Russia without a Czar is a stinking corpse*" said Saint Anatolii of Optino, "*God will have mercy on Russia and will lead through great sufferings toward glory if the Russian people repent*" said Saint Serafim of Sarov while Father Ioann of Kronstadt said "*if the Russian people do not repent the end of the world is near.*" Do you see the Russian people repenting today? Their indifference to the truth has made it possible for the Sergianists to occupy the holy churches of the Kremlin—is that not the "abomination of desolation" which occurred first in Jerusalem and later in Rome, Constantinople and now Moscow? Can you imagine what the millions of New Martyrs would say if they knew what kind of individual is occupying the seat of many holy patriarchs including Saint Patriarch Tikhon?

[Kirill Gundaev, besides being a well-known "clerical businessman" during the Gorbachev years, is also a "spiritual son" of Nikodim Rotov, a former KGB collaborator and a secret Papist who died in the hands of Pope John-Paul I; Gundaev is also a rabid ecumenist and, according to some well-informed sources of mine, there is indirect evidence—though no proof—that he is also a cardinal *in pectore*].

Alas, all the evidence shows that the Third Rome has lapsed just as the two first ones and "the one who restraints has been taken out" (точию *держяй ныне дондеже от среды будет*).

WizOz said…

> It won't go to convert the Muslims or the Buddhists. But it cannot "hide the light under the bushel" either. How do you bring "réconciliation" hiding the Truth?

The Saker replies:

You don't. *You clearly remove the topic from the conversation about collaboration* and you leave it for each individual to freely decide in his heart according to his conscience. There is a proper time and place for each thing, and both Muslims and Orthodox Christians claim that their faith is true. Let them both freely and unambiguously proclaim it and then, having done so, let them sit down together and deal with the immediate issues at hand. Both Christians and Muslims should be free to speak their mind freely anytime they want, but that does not mean that this is the only topic they can ever speak about. After all, when Saint Alexander Nevsky—who armies were full of Mongols—fought back the Teutonic Knights he did not constantly have theological disputes with the Shamanist and Muslim Mongols who fought on his side. I am in no way suggesting that either Muslims or Christians give up their faith, or that they accept that both are of "equal value" (stupid statement anyway), I am not advocating religious syncretism or some silly "ecumenical dialog of love." I am just saying that we can fight battles together against our common enemies and, when we come home, after the battle has been won, we can have terrific theological disputations and passionate religious and historical debates and we can try to prove to each other that we are in the right until we are blue in the face. But first, let's us deal with our common enemies.

Two brothers can live in one house, and defend that house together, without having to agree on every single issue.

December 22, 2013

PART II: RUSSIA AND THE UKRAINE

Ukraine's "civilizational choice"—a Pyrrhic victory for Russia?

The latest decision by the Yanukovych government to delay any decision about the possible signing of an association agreement with the European Union has been greeted by a mix of shock and outrage by the Western corporate press. Unanimously, it was decreed that this apparent reversal by Yanukovych himself was the result of Russian blackmail, ruthless power politics and even not-so-veiled threats. Finally, the media presented this latest development as a personal victory for Putin and a strategic victory for Russia. In yet another triumph of form over substance Western commentators offered lots of drama and hyperbole and very little explanations about what has really happened. I propose to set aside all the ideological hype and begin with a few basic reminders.

What is "The Ukraine" really?

The Ukraine in its current borders is a completely artificial entity created by the Soviet regime whose borders have no historical basis at all. In many ways, the Ukrainian SSR was a "mini-Soviet Union, only worse" whose population had suffered horrendously during most of the 20th century (and before). Furthermore, it is often overlooked that during the early Bolshevik regime, the Nazi occupation, the Soviet regime after WORLD WAR II and since independence after the fall of the Soviet Union the Ukraine has undergone a steady process of "West-Ukrainization": the language, political culture, and even national myths historically associated with the western Ukraine have been forced upon the rest of the country which has resulted in constant tensions between the generally pro-Western West and the generally pro-Russian East and South.

Finally, to say that the Ukrainian economy is in a deep crisis would be an understatement. Not only did the Ukraine inherit a lot of very heavy and outdated Soviet industry, it has been completely unable to use any of it to begin a truly local production of goods and services. The only segments of the Ukrainian economy which have done reasonably well are those providing goods and services for the much larger Russian economy. In the process, however, these better segments have either become completely dependent upon Russian investments, or have actually been acquired by Russian companies.

None of the above, however, is enough to explain the absolute disaster which has befallen the Ukraine since its independence. For that, we need to take a look at the Ukrainian political elites.

Who has been running the Ukraine since independence?

Formally, Presidents Kravchuk, Kuchma, Yushchenko and Yanukovych. In reality, however, since its independence the Ukraine has been in the iron grip of Ukrainian oligarchs. This is the single most important thing to keep in mind to understand the entire dynamic currently taking place between the EU, Russia and the Ukraine.

In Russia the Presidential regime defeated the oligarchs, in the Ukraine the oligarchs defeated the Presidential regime

In fact, the Ukrainian oligarchs are very similar to their Russian counterparts of the Yeltsin era. The tragedy of the Ukraine is that there has been no "Ukrainian Putin" and what could have happened in Russia without Putin did actually take place in the Ukraine. To say that the Ukrainian political elites are corrupt would be an understatement. The reality is much worse. All Ukrainian politicians are absolutely unprincipled political prostitutes who can be bought and sold and who have no personal values whatsoever. None. It is quite pathetic to read in the Western press that Yulia Tymoshenko is some kind of firebrand nationalist while Yanukovych is pro-Russian. This is laughable! Tymoshenko and Yanukovych and, frankly, all the rest of them (Klichko, Symonenko, etc.), are political chameleons who have changed their affiliations many times and who will gladly do so again. And just as the Russian people were essentially manipulated, powerless and apathetic under the regime of the Yeltsin's oligarchs, so are the Ukrainians today who are simply not given any decent person to vote for or support.

The Ukraine between the EU and the Russian-backed customs union

The reason why the association agreement between the EU and the Ukraine was presented by all the political parties (except the Communists) as a "civilizational choice," a "strategic decision," and an "inevitable step" is that it was highly beneficial to the Ukrainian oligarchy, which is absolutely terrified of Putin, and which wants to keep its current position of power at any cost. True, a majority of Western Ukrainians want to join the EU, but they never would have had the political clout and, frankly, the money to force Yanukovych and the Party of Region to initially appear to support this. No, the real center of gravity of the pro-EU activism can be found in the Ukrainian oligarchy and its discreet but powerful "friends" in the West—the very same forces who threw their full support behind Yeltsin between 1990 and 2000: the Anglo-Zionist Empire and its European vassal states.

In contrast, the opposition to this association agreement with the EU was mainly found in the small to medium business circles in the eastern Ukraine which is essentially dependent on Russia and who would have immediately collapsed into bankruptcy if Russia had reduced its investment in joint programs. Regardless, the way the Ukrainian elites dealt with this issue made public opinion basically irrelevant.

A "civilizational choice" made by a small corrupt elite?

In trying to convince the Ukrainian people to support the association with the EU the Ukrainian oligarchs and their Western supporters very skillfully "framed" the issue to such a degree as to make it unrecognizable and to make it impossible for the people to express their opinion. Think of it—if the choice between an association with the EU and a possible participation of the Ukraine into a customs union with Russia, Belarus,

Kazakhstan, Armenia and others was truly a "civilizational choice"—would a popular referendum not be the only proper way to make such a dramatic decision? Yet, in reality, the decision was made by one man only: Yanukovych. Furthermore, is it even correct to speak of a "civilizational choice"?

Most polls ask the Ukrainians if they want **to join the EU**, but that is not at all what is being offered to them. What is offered to them is only an **association with the EU**: a deal with was also offered to countries such as Chile, South Africa or Egypt.[57] This is not at all a first step toward a membership into the EU (Turkey signed such an association in 1964 and is still waiting; does anybody believe that Chile will join the EU?). As for the entry into a customs union with Russia, it still has to be negotiated so at this point it is impossible to know for sure what the final terms of such a union would be (though the general outline is pretty clear). And yet, poll after poll after poll, the same question is being asked: "do you want the Ukraine to join the EU?" Here is an example of this in Wikipedia[58]:

So what is really at stake here?

The short answer is that what is at stake here is the future of the Ukrainian oligarchy. The more complex answer is that what is at stake here is what the West can gain by co-opting the Ukrainian oligarchy into its sphere of influence. In practical terms this means that as long as the West agreed to keep the oligarchs in power it could gain many very real advantages from the Ukraine such as a market for EU goods, cheap labor, the possibility to deploy NATO forces in the Ukraine (without necessarily offering the Ukraine to join NATO) and, first and foremost, the rock-solid guarantee to be able to dictate its terms to the Ukrainian oligarchy

[57] European Union Association Agreement https://en.wikipedia.org/wiki/European_Union_Association_Agreement

[58] Ukraine–European Union relations https://en.wikipedia.org/wiki/Ukraine%E2%80%93European_Union_relations#European_Union_Association_Agreement

which would have no other option than to be hyper-compliant to any Western demands. Furthermore, the West very much sees this as a zero-sum game: what the West gets—Russia loses. While not catastrophic by any means, the severance of the current economic ties between Russia and the Ukraine would most definitely hurt Russia, at least in the short term. Furthermore, the West also believes that an association with the EU would prevent any further integration of Russia and the Ukraine. That is, I believe, probably true, simply because no real integration between the Ukraine and Russia is possible as long as the Ukrainian oligarchs remain in power.

The real objective of the Anglo-Zionist Empire in the Ukraine

Just before Barack Obama got rid of her, Hillary Clinton made an amazingly candid admission about the Empire's real goals in Eastern Europe (page 70). "We are trying to figure out effective ways to slow down or prevent [Russia] from [re-Sovietization].

Simple, direct and clear. Even the use of the expression "re-Sovietize" shows that Hillary and, frankly, most of the Western elites are still completely stuck in a Cold War paradigm in which every Russian move is necessarily an evil one and the West and Russia play a zero-sum game. *In the logic of these people, any loss for Russia is by definition a good and highly desirable outcome for the West.* What better way for the Empire is there to "slow down or prevent" any integration of Russia and the Ukraine than to offer the Ukrainian oligarchy an association deal with the EU which would cost the EU nothing and which would inevitably trigger a trade war between the Russia and the Ukraine?

Russian objectives in the Ukraine

Russian objectives in the Ukraine are pretty straightforward. First, Russia believes that a customs union with the Ukraine would be mutually beneficial. Second, Russia also hopes that, with time, such a mutually beneficial union would serve to deflate anti-Russian feelings (which are always stirred up by the Ukrainian political elites) and that, with time, the Ukraine could become a member of the future Eurasian Union. Third, judging by its bitter experience with Central European countries, the Baltic states and Georgia, Russia definitely hopes to prevent the Ukraine from becoming the next colony of the Anglo-Zionist Empire in Europe. Finally, a majority of Russians believe that the Russian and Ukrainian people are either one nation or, at least, two "brother nations" who share a common history and whose natural calling is to live in friendship and solidarity.

Are the Russian objectives in the Ukraine realistic?

Ironically, Russia faces exactly the same problem in the Ukraine as the Anglo-Zionist Empire: the Ukraine in its current borders is a completely artificial creation. Everybody pretty much agrees that the Western Ukraine and the eastern Ukraine have almost exclusively opposite goals. On all levels—language, economy, politics, history, culture—the western and eastern parts of the Ukraine are completely different. The center and the capital city of Kiev is a mix of both east and west while the south is really a unique cultural entity, different from the rest of the country and even more diverse than the rest of the country.

An armchair strategist might suggest that the "obvious" solution would be to break up the Ukraine into two or more parts and let each part choose, but this "solution" has two major problems: first, breaking up an artificial country is an extremely dangerous thing to do (remember Bosnia or Kosovo!) and, second, there is absolutely no way that the West and its Ukrainian nationalist puppets are ever going to accept such a "solution" (they even insist that the Crimean Peninsula must forever be considered a part of the Ukraine, even though it was only donated by Khrushchev to the Ukrainian Soviet Socialist Republic [SSR] in 1954!)

Furthermore, I believe that an even deeper analysis of the consequences of an integration of the Ukraine into Russia should be made before jumping to conclusions. If, indeed, the Ukraine is a "big Bosnia," does it make sense for Russia to want to bring this "big Bosnia" inside its otherwise very prosperous union with Belarus, Kazakhstan and others nations to the east? I do not argue against the argument that history clearly shows that the Ukraine, Belarus, Kazakhstan, and all parts of one historical and cultural body. What I am saying is that the Ukrainian part of that body is suffering from a very dangerous form of gangrene, and that I do not see how Russia and the rest of the (future) Eurasian Union could heal this member. While some segments of the Ukrainian economy do have an interesting potential for Russia, most of it is a disaster with no chance at all for reform.

Politically, the Ukraine is a slow-motion disaster where corrupt politicians fight with each other for the chance to get money and support from the local oligarchs and their Western patrons. Socially, the Ukraine is a ticking time-bomb which must explode, sooner or later, and while Russia can continue to bail out the Ukrainian economy with loan after loan after loan, this cannot go on forever.

Finally, the western Ukraine is a Petri dish of the worst kind of russophobic hysteria, often crossing into outright neo-Nazi propaganda, which will never accept any deal with the hated "Moskals" (Russians, or "Muscovyites" in the nationalist lexicon). The frightening fact is that in its current configuration the Ukraine is headed for disaster no matter who prevails, Yanukovych or the opposition. Just look at what the "liberals" and "democrats" achieved during the rule of Yeltsin's oligarchs: Russia's economy completely collapsed, the country almost broke up into many small parts, mafia dons ran the entire underground economy while Jewish oligarchs literally pillaged the wealth of Russia and relocated it abroad, while the media was busy feeding the Russian people absolute lies and nonsense. *Well, today, exactly the same type people are running the show in the Ukraine.*

The big difference

Looking back to what happened in the past 20 years or so it becomes immediately apparent why the Ukraine ended up in its current nightmare, while Russia, Belarus and Kazakhstan did so much better. The answer has three words: Nazarbaev, Putin, Lukashenko. I listed Nazarbaev first because he always was for an integration with Russia and its allies—Kazakhstan never really wanted its independence in the first place and it was literally pushed out by Yeltsin and his "democratic" allies Kravchuk and Shushkevich.[59] Putin only showed up on the political scene a full decade after Nazarbaev had tried to do his best to maintain a single post-Soviet country. As for Lukashenko, he is a complex and eccentric personality who follows a rather bizarre policy toward Russia: he wants to integrate Belarus with the very market-oriented Russia while keeping Belarus and its economy and society in a "neo-Soviet" condition.

For all their differences, Nazarbaev, Putin and Lukashenko have emerged as three powerful figures who did get their local oligarchs under control and who have thereby prevented their countries from becoming Anglo-Zionist colonies. In contrast, no real national leader has emerged in the Ukraine: every single Ukrainian politician is a joke and a puppet in the hands of private interests.

Ukraine's "civilizational choice"—a Pyrrhic victory for Russia?

At this moment in time, the Western media is trying to present Yanukovych's decision to delay any further negotiations on the association with the EU as a huge strategic victory for Putin and Russia. I personally disagree. While it is true that by this decision Yanukovych has delayed the collapse of the Ukrainian economy this is only a delaying tactic, nothing in substance has changed.

Furthermore, while it is vital for the Ukraine not to sever its current economic ties with Russia, this is not true for Russia, especially in the

---

[59] Belavezha Accords https://en.wikipedia.org/wiki/Belavezha_Accords

long run. Of course, an economic collapse of the Ukraine would be bad news for Russia too who really does not need its big neighbor to go down the "Bosnian scenario" lest Russia be pulled in, which it almost inevitably would.

But having avoided an immediate disaster in the Ukraine is hardly something I could call a "strategic victory" for Russia. One could make the case that the best option for Russia would be to take some huge scissors, make a deep cut along the current border between Russia and the Ukraine and relocate the latter somewhere in the middle of the Pacific Ocean. This not being an option, the next best thing would be to make it possible for the Ukraine to break up into its natural components and integrate the eastern Ukraine into the Eurasian Union. Alas, at this moment in time, this option is as impossible as the first one.

What is then left for Russia? What is the "least bad" option Russia can try to make the best of? Exactly what it is doing today: try to prevent a complete collapse of the Ukrainian economy while hoping for a "Ukrainian Putin" to eventually emerge. A "Ukrainian Putin" would be a real patriot whose first priority would be to get rid of the Ukrainian oligarchs, the second one would be to clearly indicate to the AngloZionists that they are no longer welcome in their capacity as colonial overlords, and third to try to get the best deal possible for the Ukrainian people in a future Eurasian Union.

So far, there is absolutely no sign of such a figure emerging in the Ukraine. So yes, Yanukovych's last minute change of mind is good news for the Ukraine and for Russia, but this is hardly a victory of any kind for Putin or Russia.

First, I would not put it past Yanukovych to change his mind yet again (the man has no principles or values to speak of). Second, we already see that the Empire is going absolutely apeshit with rage over this latest development and that the US and EU will spare no efforts to orchestrate yet another revolution in Kiev. Same thing for the Ukrainian opposition which now will get a huge influx of dollars from the West to create as much chaos as possible. As for the Ukrainian people, they will be given no option at all other than to express their opinion in opinion polls asking the wrong question.

Finally, as long as the current Ukrainian oligarchy remains in power, there will be no reason at all to hope for any meaningful improvements in the plight of the Ukraine and its people.

November 24, 2013

THE GATES OF HELL ARE OPENING FOR THE UKRAINE

(written specially for ***the Asia Times*** *)*

Just as I have predicted in my last piece[60] about the developments in the Ukraine, European politicians and Ukrainian opposition parties have gone into overdrive to attempt yet another color-coded revolution in Kiev. The normally demure and low-key Eurobureaucrats have suddenly found it themselves to castigate Russia with irate statements about "unacceptable Russian interference," while their own diplomats actually went on stage to encourage the (illegal) demonstrations in Kiev. As for the opposition, it used its formidable resources to bring people from all over the Ukraine, the Baltic states and Poland to Kiev to organize a mass rally and, just to make sure that enough people would show up, they began the rally with a free rock concert. Finally the united opposition parties have declared that they are creating a "united headquarters of the resistance" which will have as its first task to coordinate a Ukrainian-wide general strike.

Finally, the opposition, led by Yulia Tymoshenko from her jail, is now openly calling for the overthrow of the Yanukovych government and new elections.[61]

Very impressive.

And what about the "pro-Russian" Yanukovych government?

Just as I have predicted, it is already prepared to "zag" following its surprise "zig" of last week. All Yanukovych & Co. have done is to send Prime Minister Azarov to explain the latest change of mind of President

---

[60] Ukraine's "civilizational choice" – a Pyrrhic victory for Russia? http://thesaker.is/ukraines-civilizational-choice-a-pyrrhic-victory-for-russia/

[61] Ukraine: l'opposition appelle à renverser le pouvoir après les violences http://tempsreel.nouvelobs.com/topnews/20131130.AFP3768/ukraine-la-police-disperse-violemment-les-manifestants-a-kiev.html

Yanukovych on a TV talk show hosted by a notorious russophobic Jewish anchor "Savik Shuster" (his real name is "Shevelis Shusteris"[62]—he first worked for the CIA-created Radio Free Europe/Radio Liberty, then for Russian "democratic" media outlets before joining the "Ukrainian" TV following the "Orange Revolution" in Kiev. This true "cosmopolite" also holds Italian and Canadian citizenship, probably along with an Israeli one) where nobody listened to a word he had to say: for each economic figure Azarov mentioned in defense of his position, the nationalists responded with emotional slogans, promises of a bright tomorrow and the usual rabid anti-Russian rhetoric. Still, Azarov explained that he had decided to show up because he hoped that at least on TV they would let him speak (that same day the opposition in the Ukrainian Parliament simply shouted Azarov down thereby successfully preventing him from taking the floor to explain the government's decision).

Yanukovych himself hinted that all that had happened was a "temporary delay" and that the Ukraine might sign after all, just a "little later," maybe in spring.

Next, the government ordered their riot cops to clear the Maidan square in Kiev at 4AM, which was done with the usual level of wanton violence (on both sides). Azarov then denounced the government's own cops and announced that a special commission would be set up to investigate the violence and find out who was responsible (who else could it be besides him is unclear).

Finally, Yanukovych officially declared that he was "deeply outraged"[63] by the violence and that all Ukrainians were united by, I kid you not, "our choice of our common European future."

Absolutely pathetic, if you ask me.

---

[62] Savik Shuster https://en.wikipedia.org/wiki/Savik_Shuster

[63] Ukrainian President Yanukovych 'outraged' by violence http://www.bbc.com/news/world-europe-25171534

As for the so-called "Russian" folks of Donetsk, they organized an anti-EU and pro-Yanukovych rally were they displayed an immense sea of blue-yellow Ukrainian flags while playing Beethoven's "*Ode to Joy*" form is 9th symphony (probably unaware that this was the official Anthem of the EU).

The contrast between two parties to this dispute could hardly be bigger, I think. Let' compare them:

The Eurobureaucrats and the Ukrainian nationalists

The Eurobureaucrats and the Ukrainian nationalists are mad, really really mad. They feel like just one man suddenly changed his mind, reneged on all his previous promises and suddenly single-handedly stopped a process in which they had invested a huge amount of political capital. *And they are absolutely correct, this is exactly what happened.* Now the Eurobureaucrats and the Ukrainian nationalists are exactly in the same predicament: both feel extremely weak and both fear Russia, both sides are financially bankrupt and hope that a political victory will overshadow their economic failure, both sides hate Russia and feel that it is absolutely crucial to deny Russia any possible advantage (real or imaginary) it might gain from a union with the Ukraine. Yes, these are purely negative, hate-filled, feelings of inadequacy mixed with self-delusion about a much hoped for but forever unachievable greatness. But negative feelings, in particular nationalistic ones, can be very powerful, as Hitler has so clearly demonstrated the entire world.

The supposedly "pro-Russian" Eastern Ukrainians

They have **no** vision, **no** ideology, **no** identifiable future goal. All they can offer is a message which, in essence, says "we have no other choice than sell out to the rich Russians rather than to the poor European" or "all we can get from the EU is words, the Russians are offering money." True. But still extremely uninspiring, to say the least. Worse, this point of view reinforces, at least by implication, the key theses of the Eurobureaucrats and the Ukrainian nationalists: that this is a sell out to Russia and that the Russians are blackmailing and interfering whereas, in reality, the blackmail was totally on the EU side as clearly shown with the demand that Tymoshenko be freed (while Berlusconi in Europe is charged with exactly the same crime, so much for double standards).

And what about Russia in all that?

I am beginning to fear that this will all explode into a real and very dangerous crisis for Russia. First, I am assuming that the Eurobureaucrats and the Ukrainian nationalists will eventually prevail, and that Yanukovych will either fully complete his apparent "zag" and reverse his decision, or lose power. One way or another the Eurobureaucrats and the Ukrainian nationalists will, I think, prevail. There will be more joyful demonstrations, fireworks and celebrations in Kiev, along with lots of self-righteous back-slapping and high-fiving in Brussels, and then the gates of Hell will truly open for the Ukraine. Why?

Well simply because joining one *Titanic* at the hip with another one will save neither. The EU is sinking and so is the Ukraine. Neither has **any** real vision of how to stop this disaster and both sides are absolutely dead set on hiding to hide their bankruptcy by an increasingly strident and outright nasty political rhetoric. Needless to say, neither empty promises nor nationalistic slogans will feed anybody and the already dying Ukrainian economy will collapse at which point the Russian priority will have to change from supporting it to protecting Russia from the chaos happening just across its 2300km long and mostly completely unprotected border with the Ukraine. What are the risks for Russia?

The real risks for Russia

Being drawn into the inevitable chaos and violence that will flare up all over the Ukraine (including the Crimean Peninsula), stopping or, at least, safely managing a likely flow of refugees seeking physical and economic safety in Russia and protecting the Russian economy from the consequences of the collapse of Ukrainian economy. Russia will have to do all that while keeping its hands off the developing crisis inside the Ukraine as it is absolutely certain that the Eurobureaucrats and the Ukrainian nationalists will blame Russia for it all.

The best thing Russia could do in such a situation would be to leave the Ukrainians to their private slugfest and wait for one side or the other to prevail before trying to very carefully send out a few low-key political "feelers" to see if there is somebody across the border who has finally come to his/her senses and is capable and ready to seriously begin to re-built the Ukraine and its inevitable partnership with Russia and the rest of the Eurasian Union. As long as that does not happen Russia should stay out, as much as is possible.

Sarajevo on the Dnieper

Right now, all the signs are that the Ukraine is going down the "Bosnian road" and that things are going to get really ugly. The explosive brew we now see boiling in the Ukraine is exactly the same one which so viciously exploded in Bosnia: local nationalist backed by foreign imperialists who are absolutely determined to ignore any form of common sense, never mind a negotiated solution, to achieve their ideological goals. To most sensible and rational people my doom and gloom scenario might seem too pessimistic. I would encourage these skeptics to take a look at this well-known Polish joke:

A Pole walking along the road happens to spy a lamp. He picks it up, and as it is covered in rust he gives it quick rub. Out comes a genie. "I'm the genie of the lamp and I can grant you three wishes," the genie says. "OK," says the Pole. "I want the Chinese army to invade Poland." Odd choice, the genie thinks, but nevertheless he grants the wish, and the Chinese army comes all the way from China, invades, and goes back home. "Right, second wish. Maybe something more positive," says the genie. "No," replies the Pole, "I want the Chinese army to invade again." So the Chinese come all the way from China, lay waste to more of Poland, and then go home. "Listen," says the genie. "You have one last wish.

I can make Poland the most beautiful and prosperous place on earth." "If you don't mind, I want the Chinese army to invade one more time." So the Chinese army comes again, destroys what's left of Poland, and then goes home for the last time. "I don't understand," says the genie. "Why did you want the Chinese army to invade Poland three times?." "Well," replies the Pole, "they had to go through Russia six times."

This is the kind of "humor" a deep-seated inferiority complex combined with a compensatory strident nationalism can produce. Ask anybody who has ever met a Ukrainian nationalist and he will confirm to you—they make the Polish nationalists look outright mild-mannered and sober.

Needless to say, when the Ukraine explodes the Eurobureaucrats will look the other way and lock the borders of their respective countries as best they can while the leaders of the Ukrainian nationalists parties will cut and run to the West where they will get well-paid position in academia, various think tanks and NGOs. As for the people of the Ukraine, they will be left to fight each other against a background of hypocritical outpouring of crocodile tears from the so-called "international community?

Lasciate ogne speranza, voi ch'entrate?[64]

I sincerely hope that I am wrong and that some individual or movement will rise up from the current chaos to prevent the Ukraine from collapsing into the "Bosnian scenario" but, unfortunately, I don't see any sign of that happening. Ukrainian politicians—all of them—are a disgusting sight. Ditto for the EU politicians, by the way. At the very best they are boring, uninspiring if marginally competent. At their habitual worst, they are pathological liars, political prostitutes and delusional imbeciles which are too illiterate and too arrogant to ever see the writing on the wall, even when it is written in big, thick, block characters.

---

[64] Let all hope abandon, ye who enter here. Dante, *Inferno*

Full disclosure here: I am by training, by trade and by character a pessimist (have you ever met an optimistic military analyst?). For example, ever since I published my very first post on this blog I have been predicting a US and Israeli attack on Iran, and that still has not happened (worse, I **still** think that sooner or later the Israelis and their neocon *sayanim* colleague will provoke such a US attack, if need be by a false flag operation). So I have been wrong, very wrong, in the past and I fervently hope that I am wrong again. Alas, I see no facts or arguments even indirectly suggesting that there is another, hopefully better, scenario for the Ukraine in the future.

Does anybody else see any?

November 30, 2013

UKRAINIAN NATIONALISM—ITS ROOTS AND NATURE

First, a short introductory sitrep:

The least one could say is that over the past 2 days the events in the Ukraine moved fast, very, very fast. While I had intended to take 2 days off, I still kept an eye on the most recent development and jotted them down on my computer's note pad. Here is what I wrote down (sorry for the shorthand):

- Lukin did not sign
- S&P downgrades Ukraine from CCC+ to CCC
- Pogroms in Kiev
- Attacks on Russian nationals
- Burned buses (incl. Belarussian)
- Yanuk did not attend Kharkov congress
- Yanuk only cares about his security
- Yanuk's mansion was looted
- Kharkov congress 3000 delegates
- Phone threats to all political opponents
- Black Sea Fleet on high alert
- In the East local authorities take full control
- Two Yanuk minister arrested while trying to flee
- NOBODY WANTS A SPLIT UKRAINE NOT EVEN RUSSIA
- BUT ONLY YULIA CAN HOLD IT TOGETHER
- RADA discusses limiting Russian TV channels
- Region turncoats bought over and threatened
- Not referendum but force of arms will decide
- Hunger is a real risk
- 7'000'000 Russians in the Ukraine officially
- 50% of Ukrainians speak Russian

- 15'000 volunteers mobilized in Crimea
- Also on Sunday, US National Security Advisor Susan Rice warned Russia it would be a "grave mistake" to intervene militarily
- Acting President Oleksandr Turchynov 2005—Head of Ukraine Security Service (SBU)
- New regime says Ukraine needs 35 billion dollars
- Hunger now a real risk
- Russia recalls ambassador
- Russian language basically banned
- Appointed Mayor of Sevastopol replaced by Alexei Chaly, a Russian citizen, directly elected by the local people
- EU politicians claim they can offer 20 billion dollar to the Ukraine. How they will explain that to Greece is unclear

Wow! Clearly, things have gone far beyond the terms of the capitulation of Yanukovych to the insurgency so "brilliantly" mediated by the EU bureaucrats. Truly, a qualitative change in the terms of the conflict has happened and the country is now in a de facto situation of civil war. But first, in order to make sense of what is taking place, we need to take a look far back into the distant past, as far back as the 13th century.

Ukrainian nationalism—its roots and nature

PART ONE: a preliminary excursion in ancient history

1204—THE EASTERN CRUSADE OF POPE INNOCENT III

Most people mistakenly believe that the Crusades only happened in the Middle East and that they were only directed at Islam. This is false. In fact, while the official excuse for Western imperialism at that time was to free the city of Jerusalem from the "Muslim infidels" the Crusades also were aimed at either exterminating or converting the "Greek schismatics" i.e. the Orthodox Christians. The most notorious episode of this anti-Orthodox crusade is the sack of Constantinople by the Crusaders in

1204, during the 4th Crusade, in which the city was subjected to three days of absolutely grotesque pillaging, looting and massacres by the Western "Christians" who even looted and burned down Orthodox churches, monasteries and convents, raped nuns on church altars and even placed a prostitute on the Patriarchal throne. This outpouring of genocidal hatred was hardly a fluke, but it was one of the earliest manifestation of something which would become a central feature of the mind-set and ideology of the Latin Church.

There is, however, another no less important episode in the history of the Latin hatred for the Orthodox Church which is far less known.

1242—THE NORTHERN CRUSADES OF POPE GREGORY IX

Unlike his predecessor who directed his soldiers toward the Holy Land, Pope Gregory IX had a very different idea: he wanted to convert the "pagans" of the North and East of Europe to the "true faith." In his mind, Orthodox Russia was part of these "pagan lands" and Orthodox Christians were pagans too. His order to the Teutonic Knights (the spiritual successors of the Franks who had pillaged and destroyed Rome) was to either convert or kill all the pagans they would meet (this genocidal order was very similar to the one given by Ante Pavelic to his own forces against the Serbs during WORLD WAR II: convert, kill or expel). In most history books Pope Gregory IX has earned himself a name by instituting the Papal Inquisition (which has never been abolished, by the way), so it is of no surprise that this gentleman was in no mood to show any mercy to the "Greek schismatics." This time, however, the Pope's hordes were met by a formidable defender: Prince Alexander Nevsky.

SAINT ALEXANDER NEVSKY'S "CIVILIZATIONAL CHOICE"

Even before dealing with the Pope's Crusaders Alexander Nevsky had already had to repel an earlier invasion of Russia by the West—the attempt to invade northern Russia by the Swedish Kingdom—which he defeated 1240 at the famous battle of the Neva.[65] No less important, however, is the fact that Alexander Nevsky was unable to defeat Mongol invasion from the East, and so he was placed between what can only be called a civilizational choice: he understood that Russia could not fight the Papacy and the Mongols at the same time, so the choice was simple: to submit to one and to resist the other. But which one should he chose to submit Russia to?

Prince Alexander (who would later be glorified as a saint by the Russian Orthodox Church) was truly a deeply pious man who had a deep understanding of the Holy Scripture and who remembered the words of Christ when asked whether Jews should pay taxes to the Romans: "*Render therefore unto Caesar the things which are Caesar's; and unto God the things that are God's*" (Matt 22:21) and "*And fear not them which kill the body, but are not able to kill the soul: but rather fear him which is able to destroy both soul and body in hell*" (Matt 10:28).

Alexander, who was very well-informed of the policies of his enemies, knew that the sole goal of the Mongols was to extract taxes from the Russians, but that they had no desire to convert anybody or to persecute the Church. Quite to the contrary, the putatively "savage" Mongols respected the Church and its clergy and they never persecuted it. In contrast, the Crusaders were given the specific order to convert or murder all the Orthodox Christians they would encounter as the Latins had done many times before, and as they would do many times later. Thus Prince Alexander Nevsky chose to submit to the Mongol Khan and to fight the Crusaders whom he defeated at the famous *Battle of the Ice* in 1242.[66]

WESTERN RUSSIA OCCUPIED, FALL OF THE 2ND ROME, RISE OF MOSCOW

Having been defeated by Russia twice, Western leaders temporarily renounced their invasion plans, but the Russian victory clearly did not

---

[65] Battle of the Neva https://en.wikipedia.org/wiki/Battle_of_the_Neva

[66] Battle on the Ice https://en.wikipedia.org/wiki/Battle_on_the_Ice

endear the Russian people or culture to the Western elites. Predictably the next wave of invasions from the West began in the early 14th century and lasted until 1385 when the *Union of Krewo*[67] sealed the union of Poland and Lithuania. At that moment in time all of what would be called later "the Ukraine" was fully conquered by the Latins.

In 1453, the Fall of Rome in the East, in Constantinople, marked the end of the "2nd Rome" and the end of the Roman civilization, which had survived the Fall of Rome by a full one thousand years (the western Roman Empire fell in 476 AD; the eastern Roman Empire fell in 1453).

The Latins did attempt to submit the Orthodox world by a careful mix of threats and promises to assist Constantinople against the Ottomans at the so-called *False Union of Florance,*[68] but they had failed, and Constantinople eventually fell to armies of *Mehmet the Conqueror.*[69] Thus, Moscow became the "Third Rome," the last free Orthodox Christian Kingdom, the civilizational heir to the Roman civilization. Moscow would now become the focal point of the Papist hatred for Orthodox Christianity. The next Western strike would come in 1595 and it would be a truly devastating one.

1595—POPE CLEMENT VIII CONCEIVES THE UKRAINE

By the end of the 16th century, most of western Russia had been occupied by the Latins for two hundred years (14th-16th), as long as the Mongol Yoke on eastern Russia (13th-15th century). Predictably, the situation of the Orthodox Christian peasants under the Latin occupation was nothing short of terrible. For all practical purposes, it was enslaved,

---

[67] Union of Krewo https://en.wikipedia.org/wiki/Union_of_Krewo

[68] St. Mark of Ephesus and the False Union of Florence http://orthodoxinfo.com/ecumenism/stmark.aspx

[69] Mehmed the Conqueror https://en.wikipedia.org/wiki/Mehmed_the_Conqueror

as Israel Shahak explains in his seminal book *Jewish History, Jewish Religion:*[70]

> Due to many causes, medieval Poland lagged in its development behind countries like England and France; a strong feudal-type monarchy—yet without any parliamentary institutions—was formed there only in the 14th century, especially under Casimir the Great (1333-70). Immediately after his death, changes of dynasty and other factors led to a very rapid development of the power of the noble magnates, then also of the petty nobility, so that by 1572 the process of reduction of the king to a figurehead and exclusion of all other non-noble estates from political power was virtually complete. (...)

This process was accompanied by a debasement in the position of the Polish peasants (who had been free in the early Middle Ages) to the point of utter serfdom, hardly distinguishable from outright slavery and certainly the worst in Europe. The desire of noblemen in neighboring countries to enjoy the power of the Polish *pan* (noble) over his peasants (including the power of life and death without any right of appeal) was instrumental in the territorial expansion of Poland. The situation in the "eastern" lands of Poland (Byelorussia and the Ukraine)—colonized and settled by newly enserfed peasants—was worst of all.

Indeed, the local elites had been more than happy to apostatize and sell out to the Polish occupier to enjoy the privileges of slave-owning (before that Russia had never known serfdom!) while the enslaved peasants stubbornly held on to their faith (interestingly, this is also the period of history when Ukrainian Judeophobia was born—read Shahak for details). Something needed to be done to find a "solution" to this "problem" and, sure enough, a Pope (Clement VIII) found it: the forcible conversion of

[70] Professor Israel Shahak: Jewish History, Jewish Religion: The Weight of Three Thousand Years http://www.abbc.net/historia/shahak/english.htm

the local Orthodox Christians to the Latin church: the so-called *Union of Brest.*[71]

Thus began a long period of vicious persecution of the Orthodox peasantry by the combined efforts of the Polish nobility, their Jewish overseers and, especially, the Jesuits who justified any atrocity under the slogan "*ad majorem Dei gloriam*" (to the greater Glory of God).

One man, in particular, excelled in the persecution of Orthodox Christians: Josphat Kuntsevich (whose biography you can read about in this text: *The Vatican and Russia*[72]). Kuntsevich—who was eventually lynched by a mob of peasants—was buried in the Saint Peter basilica in Rome near, I kid you not, the relics of Saint Gregory the Theologian and Saint John Chrysostom (!). The Latins still refer to this mass murderer as "martyr for Christ" (see this typical Papist hagiography of Kuntsevich[73]) and he is still greatly respected and admired among modern Ukrainian nationalists. And I can see why—it is during these years of occupation and persecution that modern "Ukraine" was created, maybe not yet as a territory, but definitely as a cultural entity.

THE ETHNOGENESIS OF THE "UKRAINIAN NATION"

Nations, like individuals, are born, live and die. In fact, as Shlomo Sands so brilliantly demonstrated in his book *The Invention of the Jewish People*, nations are really invented, created. In fact, the 20th century has shown us many nations invented *ex nihilo*, out of nothing (in order to avoid offending somebody or getting sidetracked, I shall not give examples, but God knows there are many). A "nation" does not need to have deep historical and cultural roots, it does not need to have a legitimate historiography, in fact, all it takes to "create a nation" is a certain amount

---

[71] Union of Brest https://en.wikipedia.org/wiki/Union_of_Brest

[72] Deacon Herman Ivanov-Treenadzaty: The Vatican and Russia http://orthodoxinfo.com/ecumenism/vatican_russia.aspx

[73] St. Josaphat, Bishop and Martyr http://catholicharboroffaithandmorals.com/St.%20Josaphat.html

of people identifying themselves as a community—all the rest can be created/invented later. Thus the argument of some Russians that there is no such thing as a Ukrainian nation is fundamentally mistaken: if there are enough people identifying themselves as "Ukrainian," then a distinct "Ukrainian nation" exists. It does not matter at all that there is no trace of that nation in history, or that its founding myths are ridiculous, as long as a distinct common is shared by its members. And from that point of view, the existence of a Ukrainian nation fundamentally different from the Russian one is an undeniable reality. And that is the immense achievement of the Latin Church—it undeniably succeeded in its desire to cut-off the western Russians from their historical roots and to create a new nation: the Ukrainians.

As an aside, but an important one I think, I would note that the Mongols played a similarly crucial role in the creation of the modern Russian nation. After all, what are the "founding blocks" of the Russian culture? The culture of the Slavs before the Christianization of Russia in the 10th century? Yes, but minimally. The continuation of the Roman civilization after the Fall of the 2nd Rome? Yes, to some degree, but not crucially. The adoption of the Christian faith after the 10th century? Yes, definitely. But the Russian "state," which grew out of the rather small Grand Duchy of Moscow,[74] was definitely shaped by the Mongol culture and statecraft, not Byzantium or ancient Rus.

It would not be incorrect to say that ancient Kievan Rus[75] eventually gave birth to two distinct nations: a Ukrainian one, fathered by the Papist occupation, and a Russian one, fathered by the Mongol occupation. In that sense the russophobic statement of the Marquis de Custine[76] and Napoleon "*Grattez le Russe, et vous verrez un Tartare*" (scratch the Russian and you will find a Mongol beneath) is correct. Equally, however, I

---

[74] Grand Duchy of Moscow https://en.wikipedia.org/wiki/Grand_Duchy_of_Moscow

[75] Kievan Rus https://en.wikipedia.org/wiki/Kievan_Rus%27

[76] Marquis de Custine https://en.wikipedia.org/wiki/Marquis_de_Custine

would argue that one could say that "scratch the Ukrainian, and you will find the Papist beneath."

At this point I do not want to continue outlining the history of the Ukraine because I think I have made my point clear: **the Ukrainian nation is the product of the thousand-year-old hatred of Orthodox Christianity by the Papacy**. Just as modern rabbinical Judaism is really nothing more than an anti-Christianity, the modern Ukrainian national identity is basically centered on a rabid, absolutely irrational and paranoid hated and fear of Russia. That is not to say that all the people which live in the Ukraine partake in that hysterical russophobia, not at all, but the nationalist hard-core definitely does. And this point is so crucial that I felt that I had to make this long digression into ancient history to explain it.

I have to add one more thing: the Latin Church has undergone tremendous changes in the 20th century and even its Jesuits have long departed from the traditions and ideas of their predecessors of the Counter-Reformation. Though hatred of the Orthodox Christians and Russian still exists in some Latin circles, it has mostly been replaced by a desire to "incorporate" or swallow the Orthodox Church into the Papacy by means of the so-called "Ecumenical dialog." As for the rank and file Roman Catholic faithful—they simply have no idea at all about this history which, of course, is never taught to them

The Papacy's goal end is still the same—submission to the Pope. But the methods and emotions have changed: it used to be hatred and terror, now it's a "dialog of love." Among the Ukrainian nationalists and Uniats, however, the mind-set practically has not changed. From the likes of Stepan Bandera[77] to his modern successor, Dmytro Yarosh, leader of the Right Sector,[78] the Ukrainian nationalists have kept the murderous ha-

[77] Stepan Bandera https://en.wikipedia.org/wiki/Stepan_Bandera

[78] Right Sector https://en.wikipedia.org/wiki/Right_Sector

tred of Josphat Kuntsevich, hence some of the crazy statements these folks have made.

We now need to make a three centuries long jump in time and look at the roots of fascism and National Socialism in the early 20th century. We have to do this jump not because these centuries were not important for the Ukraine—they very much were—but for the sake of space and time. The key feature of the time period we will skip is basically the rise of the power of Russia, which became an Empire under Peter I, and the corresponding weakening of the Polish and Lithuanian states which ended up completely occupied by Russia on several occasion.

Part Two: Fascism, National Socialism and their different roots

We are typically taught that WORLD WAR II war saw the victory of the "Allied Powers[79]" against the "Axis powers."[80] While not incorrect, these categories are often confusing. For example, according to Wikipedia, France and Yugoslavia were part of the Allied Powers. That, of course, depends on which regime one considers as legitimate, the one of Pétain or de Gaulle or the one of Pavelic, Tito or Mikhailovich? Also—does it really make sense to lump the Soviet Union with the British Empire and the USA? What about Pétain, Hitler and Hirohito?

Well, they were allies, no doubt here, but they were very different entities and their alliance was mostly one against common enemies rather than the result of real kinship. This is particularly true of Hitler's allies in Europe: Mussolini, of course, but also Franco, Pétain or Pavlic. Indeed, while both Hitler and Mussolini were atheist (and even rabid anti-clericalist), Franco, Pétain and Pavelic were all devout Roman-Catholics. And if the Papacy never felt comfortable with the secularist, nationalist and socialist ideas of Hitler or Mussolini, it gave its full support to Franco, Pavelic and Pétain.

---

[79] Allies of World War II https://en.wikipedia.org/wiki/Allies_of_World_War_II

[80] Axis powers https://en.wikipedia.org/wiki/Axis_powers

Hitler and Mussolini were primarily the expression of the views and interests of the *petit bourgeois* and worker classes, while Franco, Pavelic and Pétain were very much an expression of the interests of the financial elites and nobility. In France, in particular, the Pétainist movement always had a very strong anti-1789 almost monarchist *ethos.* Deeply, of course, there was not much love lost between the atheist-populist and Papist-monarchist groups. But what did united is a common hatred for Jews, Bolsheviks, Russians, and Orthodox Christians in general combined with a profoundly reactionary ideology.

THE TWO DIFFERENT *DRANG NACH OSTEN*

Both the atheist-populist and the Papist-monarchists factions had in common a very strong "*Drang nach Osten*[81]" (yearning, desire, thrust for the East) and both saw themselves as *Kulturträger,* literally "carriers of civilization" to the savage barbarians of the East. Hitler's beef with the Soviet Union was, of course, the very high numbers of Jews in the Bolshevik Party (hence his talk of Judeo-Bolshevism) while the Papacy hated Jews, atheists and Orthodox Christians pretty much equally (Franco liked to speak of the "*conspiración judeo masonica pagada con el oro de Moscú*" or "Judeo-Masonic conspiracy paid for by Moscow's gold"). And while Hitler looked toward the East to provide land and slaves[82] for his Master Race,[83] the Papacy saw a fantastic opportunity to finally submit the "Photian schismatics[84]" to Rome: already on the eve of World War I, Pope Pius X (who was canonized in 1954) pronounced "*Russia is the greatest enemy Of the [Roman] Church*" and "*If Russia is victorious, then the schism is victorious*" (and keep in mind that according to Latin doctrine—these folks are infallible when speaking ex cathedra, in the name of the Church and on issues of faith). Thus these two originally very dif-

---

[81] Drang nach Osten https://en.wikipedia.org/wiki/Drang_nach_Osten

[82] Lebensraum https://en.wikipedia.org/wiki/Lebensraum

[83] Master race https://en.wikipedia.org/wiki/Master_race

[84] Photian schism https://en.wikipedia.org/wiki/Photian_schism

ferent movement joined forces and united against the arch-enemy: Russia (whether atheist, Jewish and Bolshevik or Russian and Orthodox—it did not matter to them). Needless to say, this toxic brew of hatred found an absolutely perfect Petri dish for its views among the Ukrainian nationalists, especially, in the Western Ukraine.

Again, for a lack of time and space I will not go into a history of the Organization of Ukrainian Nationalists,[85] Stepan Bandera[86] or the "Ukrainian" SS Division Galizien,[87] you can read about on the Internet. I will just say that these forces were among the most cruel and murderous of any in World War II. In fact, the most rabid atrocities of World War II were not committed by Hitler's forces, not even the SS, but by the forces fully inspired and supported by the Vatican: the Croatian Ustashe of Ante Pavelic and the Ukrainian nationalists.

Eventually, the Ustashe and the Banderovsty were defeated, but a lot of its members not only survived the war, but prospered in exile, mostly in the USA and Canada, where the Anglosphere kept them away from actual politics, but active enough to be "defrosted" should the need arise. And, sure enough, following the end of the Cold War, the Anglo-Zionist Empire saw an opportunity to subvert and weaken its enemies: the descendants of the Ustashe were tasked with breaking up Yugoslavia while the descendants of Bandera were tasked with breaking the Ukraine as far away from Russia as possible. In the same time, both in Yugoslavia and Russia, the AngloZionists directed another of its terrorist franchises—the Wahhabi international aka "al-Qaeda"—to join the Neo-Nazis and Papists in a common struggle against the Orthodox/Socialist Yugoslavia and Russia. We all know what happened to Yugoslavia after that.

PART THREE—the Ukraine—back to the future

[85] Organization of Ukrainian Nationalists https://en.wikipedia.org/wiki/Organization_of_Ukrainian_Nationalists

[86] Stepan Bandera https://en.wikipedia.org/wiki/Stepan_Bandera

[87] 14th Waffen Grenadier Division of the SS (1st Galician) https://en.wikipedia.org/wiki/14th_Waffen_Grenadier_Division_of_the_SS_(1st_Galician)

2014— THE BELLY IS STILL FERTILE FROM WHICH THE FOUL BEAST SPRANG

At this point in time I want to say a few things about the (now ex-) Ukrainian "opposition." During the past months, we were mostly told that it was represented by three men: Vitali Klitschko[88] and his Ukrainian Democratic Alliance for Reform (UDAR)[89] movement, Arseniy Yatsenyuk[90] and his Batkivshchyna Party,[91] and Oleh Tyahnybok,[92] notorious leader of the Freedom Party.[93] Of course, the real leader of the Batkivshchyna Party always was Yulia Tymoshenko,[94] but since she had been jailed by Viktor Yanukovych, she could not directly participate in the most recent events.

Most Western observers have neglected to ask the question whether any of these political figures really could control the demonstrators on the Maidan square. Furthermore, they also neglected to look into how a crowed armed mostly with stones, baseball bats, iron bars and Molotov cocktails had "suddenly" been replaced by a well-organized and well-armed force of what can only be called insurgents. The force which really packed the most strength and firepower, was not composed of members of the UDAR, Batkivshchyna or even Svoboda (Freedom Party)—the real owner of the Maidan and now of the rest of Kiev is the so-called Right Sector,[95] a terrorist organization headed by Dmytro Yarosh:

If the photo above looks like it might have been taken in Chechnya during the war, that is because it could have been: many Ukrainian nationalists fought on the side of the Wahhabis in Chechnya, often under

---

[88] Vitali Klitschko https://en.wikipedia.org/wiki/Vitali_Klitschko

[89] UDAR https://en.wikipedia.org/wiki/Ukrainian_Democratic_Alliance_for_Reform

[90] Arseniy Yatsenyuk https://en.wikipedia.org/wiki/Arseniy_Yatsenyuk

[91] All-Ukrainian Union "Fatherland" https://en.wikipedia.org/wiki/All-Ukrainian_Union_%22Fatherland%22

[92] Oleh Tyahnybok https://en.wikipedia.org/wiki/Oleh_Tyahnybok

[93] Svoboda party https://en.wikipedia.org/wiki/Svoboda_(political_party)

[94] Yulia Tymoshenko https://en.wikipedia.org/wiki/Yulia_Tymoshenko

[95] Right Sector https://en.wikipedia.org/wiki/Right_Sector

the banner of the UNA-UNSO[96] terrorist organization. They also fought in Georgia against Russia, hence the visit Saakashvili made twice to the Maidan square.

It would be logical to ask what percentage of the people of the Ukraine support Mr. Yarosh and his Right Sector. It is hard to tell, but probably a sizable but small minority. By most estimates, the most popular leaders of the new regime are Tymoshenko and Klitschko, followed by Tyahnybok—at least that was true before the revolution of last Sunday. But that is hardly relevant: most Chechens were not Wahhabis, most Croats were not Ustashe and most Kosovo Albanians were not KLA—that did not prevent these small but well-armed groups from having a decisive control over the events.

This places the new regime in a very difficult situation: either it complies with the agenda of the likes of Yarosh and his Right Sector, or it risks to be swiped away by an armed insurrection. Keep in mind that the Ukrainian military basically exists only on paper and that the police forces are in no condition to impose their authority on the extremists.

What is worse, the Presidency of Yushchenko has shown that the so-called "moderate" nationalists constantly kowtow to the extremists. Thus Yushchenko even made Bandera "hero of Ukraine" (the decision was later rescinded) and printed nice little stamps with his face. The problem with that is kind of seemingly innocuous action is in reality a rehabilitation of genocidal ideology and that it sends a truly terrifying and revolting message to the East Ukrainians and Russians in the Ukraine: we are back and we mean business.

It has mostly been overlooked, but a similar situation took place in Croatia at the moment of the breakup of Yugoslavia: the Croats, even the so-called "moderates," found nothing more intelligent to do than to immediately reintroduce the checkered flag of the Ustashe of Pavelic as a

---

[96] UNA-UNSO https://en.wikipedia.org/wiki/Ukrainian_National_Assembly_%E2%80%93_Ukrainian_People%27s_Self-Defence

"Croatian national symbol." To what degree this encouraged the Serbs in the Krajinas to take up arms is open to debate, but it certainly did not help.

The same thing is now also taking place in the Ukraine. Besides the yellow and blue flags of the western Ukraine, one can also see lots of black and red flags, the flag of the Banderovsty, along with all sorts of neo-Nazi symbols. And, again, it does not really matter how many Ukrainians are suffering from genocidal tendencies, what matters is how these flags are seen in the eastern Ukraine or by the 7 million Russians who live in the Ukraine.

The reaction to the coup in Kiev was immediate. My reaction to on video showing a mass rally in the city of Sevastopol was this:

> Notice the flags? Before the coup, the rallies in the east featured almost exclusively Ukrainian yellow and blue flags, now the flags are mostly Russian with a few interspersed Russian Navy flags: the people are either angry or frightened. Probably both. And the potential for violence therefore rapidly escalates.

Then I saw another video of an attempt by pro-regime activist to hold a demonstration in the city of Kerch. The angry crowd begins with screams of "go away!" and "Fascists!" but soon the cops lose control of the situation and a mob begins to assault the nationalist activists.[97]

Just as in Croatia and Bosnia, EU and US politicians have ignored (whether by stupidity or deliberately) that fear begets violence which, in turn, begets more fear, in an endless positive feedback loop which is almost impossible to stop.

SO WHERE DO WE GO FROM HERE?

Frankly, I had some hopes that Yulia Tymoshenko might still save the Ukraine. No, not because I like her, but because I recognize the strength

[97] Banderivets got beaten up in Crimea on February 22, 2014 В Крыму избили «бандеровцев» 22.02.2014 https://www.youtube.com/watch?v=wXDEDGgD2Oc

of her personality, especially when compared to the either terminally stupid (Tyahnybok, Klichko) or spineless (Yatsenyuk, Yanukovych) men in Ukrainian politics. As one Russian journalist put it yesterday: it's good to finally see a "real man" entering the Ukrainian political scene.

And indeed, for all her other faults, Yulia has three things going for her: she is very intelligent, she is strong willed and she is very popular. Or, at least, that was what she had going for her before Yanukovych threw her in jail. When I saw the footage of her appearance on the Maidan, on a wheel-chair, her face puffed up, sounding hysterical and completely unaware of the fact that she was surrounded by neo-Nazis I began having my doubts. Clearly, she had a very bad time in Yanukovych's dungeon. And to those who will say that she has every bit as corrupt as all the other oligarchs I would say this: while all the other oligarchs see power as a way to make money, Tymoshenko sees money as a way to seize power. There is a huge difference here.

Then, unlike Tyahnybok or Yarosh, Tymoshenko does not look genocidal, nor has she ever tried to play the role of a "modern Bandera." Then, unlike the typical Ukrainian neo-Nazis, Yulia is nominally Orthodox, not "Greek Catholic" (i.e. Latin). Not that I believe that any of them are particularly religions, no, but at least Tymoshenko was not raised with the kind of maniacal hatred for everything Russian in which "Greek Catholic" kids are typically raised.

Finally, Tymoshenko is definitely smart enough to understand that there is no way to keep the Ukraine as a unitary state if the neo-Nazis are de facto in power, whether directly through a number of "moderate" puppets.

So maybe I was naive, but I had some hope that Yulia could keep the Ukraine together. No, not because I am such a true supporter of the "independent Ukraine," but because I would find any solution preferable to a partition of the Ukraine which would inevitably become violent.

WHY IS VIOLENCE INEVITABLE?

Paradoxically, the main cause here is not the followers of Bandera. Some of them have, in fact, spoken in favor of a separation of the western Ukraine from the rest of the country. As far as I know, they are in the minority, but it is still interesting that at least some of them are aware that the notion of turning all of the Ukraine into Galicia[98] is simply ludicrous. Most nationalists are, however, dead set against any partition for two reasons. Prestige: they know that "their" Ukraine is, in reality, much smaller than the Ukraine inherited form the Soviet era. Money: they know that all the real wealth of the Ukraine is in the East. Last, but not least, the real puppet-masters of the Ukrainian nationalists (the US) want to deprive Russia of the wealth of the eastern Ukraine and of the Ukrainian Black Sea coast. So anybody expecting the nationalists to gracefully agree to a civil divorce between West and Southeast is day dreaming: it isn't happening, at least not by referendum or any other form of consultations.

History also teaches us that it is impossible to force two groups to coexist when the hate and fear each other, at least not without "a lot" of violence.

The situation in the East is as simple as it is stark: Yanukovych is politically dead. The party of regions has basically exploded and new politicians are popping up in Kharkov, in Sevastopol, and in other cities. Large self-defense forces are being organized locally and the population is basically ready to fight. Considering the circumstances, these are all positive developments. On the negative side there is the fact that the eastern oligarchs are still here, still ready to betray their own people for profit (just as the Ukrainian elites did during the Union of Brest) and that the local political forces are, by most accounts, being rather amateurishly orga-

[98] Galicia (Eastern Europe) https://en.wikipedia.org/wiki/Galicia_%28Eastern_Europe%29

nized. Finally, there is a great deal of uncertainty about what Russia really wants.

What about Russia in all this?

I think that Russia truly does want to avoid a civil war in the Ukraine and that it prefers a separate Ukraine to a partition. Why? Think of it:

For Russia a separate and independent Ukraine is first and foremost a way of avoiding being drawn into a civil war. If, say, Tymoshenko managed to suppress the neo-Nazis and negotiate some kind of *modus vivendi* between, on one hand, the western Ukraine and Kiev and, on the other, the Eastern and Southern Ukraine there is little doubt that she and Putin could find some peaceful and pragmatic way to coexist. Oh, I am not speaking about a love-fest, that is simply not going to happen, but at least some mutually beneficial, civil and pragmatic relations are imaginable. That would most definitely be the Kremlin's preferred option (which just goes to show how stupid and paranoid the Ukie nationalist—and Susan Rice[99]—are when they hallucinate about a Russian invasion of the Ukraine).

The other option is to have the nationalists take full control over all of the Ukraine. That seems extremely unlikely to me, but who knows? I have been disappointed with Ukie politicians enough to put the worst possible outcome past them. That would mean that the Russian-Ukrainian border would turn into something between the wall which separated the two parts of Germany during the Cold War or the DMZ between the two part of Korea. From a military point of view, not a problem at all. As I wrote in the past, even if NATO deploys troops in the Ukraine, which they would, that close to the Russian territory military assets basically turn into lucrative targets: Russia would deploy enough Iskanders to cover its target list and that's all. As for the Black Sea Fleet, it

[99] Good advice, wrong address: Russia responds to Susan Rice "no tanks to Ukraine" warning http://www.rt.com/news/russia-usa-rice-advice-450/

could either simply refuse to leave and see if NATO has the stomach to try to force it, or engage in the costly but possible fallback option of relocating to Novorossiysk[100] (admittedly, not a good option, but better than nothing). But, again, this is an exceedingly unlikely scenario.

Which leaves option three: the nationalist attempt to subdue the south and east and fail. The violence escalates and eventually Russia is drawn in. Now in purely military terms, Russia could very easily defeat any Ukie army which would attempt to fight it. As for NATO and the US—they don't have the means to deploy some "combined joint task force" to repel the Russian military in the Ukraine. So short of starting a mutually destructive nuclear war, they would have to accept the facts on the ground.

But just imagine the nightmare resulting from a Russian military operation in eastern Ukraine! It would be back to a new Cold War, but this time on steroids: Western politicians would scramble over each other to denounce, declare, threaten, condemn, proclaim, sanction, and pledge God knows what kind of nonsense. Hysterical russophobia will become the order of the day and the Anglo-Zionist Empire would finally find the kind of eternal enemy it has desperately been seeking for since the end of the First Cold War. If they got really ugly, and they probably would, China would most likely get involved too and we would have exactly the kind of planet the 1% plutocracy has been dreaming about for so many years: Oceania locked into a total war against Eurasia and Eastasia, just like Orwell predicted.

This is most definitely not what Russia—or China—need. And yet, this is a real risk if a civil war breaks out in the Ukraine. One "least bad" option to avoid such a scenario would be to make sure that the east and southern Ukrainians are strong enough to repel a nationalist invasion by themselves so that the Russian military can stay out of the conflict.

---

[100] Novorossiysk https://en.wikipedia.org/wiki/Novorossiysk

So there is the difficult judgment call the Kremlin needs to make: the Kremlin has to decide whether:

a) the Eastern and Southern Ukrainian people are disorganized, demoralized, made passive by the rule of corrupt oligarchs and basically unable to defend themselves.

or

b) the Eastern and Southern Ukrainian people are united, organized and determined enough to really make a stand and fight the neo-Nazis down to the last bullet.

In the first case, the Kremlin would have to basically protect the Russian borders and prepare to manage the large numbers of refugees which will inevitably cross the border.

In the second case, the Kremlin would have a strong incentive to assist the Eastern and Southern Ukrainians by all possible means short of an over and direct military intervention.

Both of these options are dangerous and none of them is preferable to a united Ukraine lead by a more or less rational leader. This is why, at least at the initial stage, I expect Russia to "really" support any halfway sane regime in Kiev in the hope to avoid a breakup of the Ukraine.

WHAT ABOUT THE US AND THE EU IN ALL THIS?

Well, as I recently wrote,[101] the US and the EU have very different objectives in the Ukraine: the EU wants a market for its goods and services, the US want to hurt Russia as much as possible. We have all seen the total lack of effectiveness of the EU bureaucrats and their naive attempts at finding a negotiated solution. The US foreign policy goal has the advantage of being simple yet clear: fuck Russia and fuck the EU! From the US point of view, the worse the situation becomes, the better it is for Uncle Sam. At the very least, this hurts Russia, at the very best, it gives the

[101] The geopolitics of the Ukrainian conflict: back to basics http://thesaker.is/the-geopolitics-of-the-ukrainian-conflict-back-to-basics/

US a wonderful pretext to "protect" Europe from the "resurgent Russian bear" while standing up for civilization, democracy and progress. A neo-con's wet dream…

And then, there is the "S factor": stupidity, plain and simple. What often seems to be the result of some Machiavellian plan cooked up in a deep basement of the White House, the CIA or the Pentagon is often a mind-blowing example of the truly phenomenal stupidity, ignorance, and arrogance of our leaders. They believe themselves to be so powerful as to be free from the need to understand a culture, a history or even a single foreign language. After all, if a US policy was to failed somewhere, the response could always be the same: fuck them! Fuck the Yugoslavs! Fuck the Serbs! Fuck the Iraqis! Fuck the Afghans! Fuck the Pakistanis! Fuck the Libyans, and the Egyptians, and the Palestinians, and fuck the Somalis, the Koreans, the Colombians and the Venezuelans and, of course, fuck the Canadians, the Mexicans, and the Africans, and, of course, fuck the Russians, fuck the Chinese, and fuck everybody else with it! No matter how stupid or how destructive a US policy toward another party it—it either works, or fuck them! Ms. Nuland's words could really become the State Departments or the CIA's official motto.

MY CONCLUSION? PESSIMISTIC, OF COURSE

Those reading my blog for a while already will not be surprised to see that, yet again, I have reached a very pessimistic conclusion: the future of the Ukraine looks absolutely terrible: the country is ruined, it has no economy, it is socially, culturally and politically nonviable, it will most likely be lead either by imbeciles or by racist maniacs and the biggest power on the planet will spare no efforts to add more fuel on the fire. Keep in mind that not a single Ukrainian politician has anything even remotely resembling a plan to resurrect the currently dead Ukrainian economy. The only and last chance for the Ukraine was to survive on the "Russian financial respirator"—but that has now been turned off, at least for the foreseeable future: the Ukies can have their Banderovite Revolution, but the Russians don't have to pay for it.

Last November I wrote a piece entitled *The gates of Hell are opening for the Ukraine*[102] in which I pretty much predicted what has happened since. I wrote:

I am assuming that the Eurobureaucrats and the Ukrainian nationalists will eventually prevail, and that Yanukovych will either fully complete his apparent "zag" and reverse his decision, or lose power. One way or another the Eurobureaucrats and the Ukrainian nationalists will, I think, prevail. There will be more joyful demonstrations, fireworks and celebrations in Kiev, along with lots of self-righteous back-slapping and high-fiving in Brussels, and then the gates of Hell will truly open for the Ukraine.

We are now at this point: the Ukraine has now crossed the gates of Hell and has fully entered in a long cycle of tragedy and violence. This is truly immensely sad. And the blame for what will happen next lies first and foremost with those forces who recklessly opened the Pandora's box of medieval and 20th century hatreds, and who encouraged the nationalist demon to strike yet again. and with those who stood by and did nothing: the US and EU politicians among whom not a single one could be found to speak the truth. May they all rot in Hell for what they have done!

February 24, 2014

---

[102] The gates of Hell are opening for the Ukraine http://thesaker.is/the-gates-of-hell-are-opening-for-the-ukraine/

FOLLOW UP TO MY POST ABOUT THE ROOTS AND NATURE OF UKRAINIAN NATIONALISM

Dear friends,

As I promised, I am now going to reply to some of your comments concerning my recent post about the roots and nature of Ukrainian nationalism.[103] First, I thought of replying to your comments one by one, and then I changed my mind. I think that there are some general and recurrent topics which I need to address because they are mentioned several times. That would save space and time and probably make the answers more coherent. Here are the topics that I have identified:

1) The Holodomor

2) Jews or Khazars and their role in the Ukraine

3) The proper way to refer to the Roman Catholic Church, Papacy, Latins

4) My "general lumping and implication of all Catholics in whatever happened in Russia"

There are probably more and I am more than willing to address them, but these four are the "biggies" which I would like to address today. Ok? Here we go then. First, I will address the first two topics together.

The Holodomor, Ukrainians, Russians and Jews

I am aware that these are controversial topics and I welcome the controversy about it. I welcome this controversy just as I welcome any historical revisionism because the very point of the study of history is to examine the clash of ideas, theories, different historiographies and interpretations. In my opinion, no topic should ever be off-limits or "dogma-

[103] Ukrainian nationalism – its roots and nature http://thesaker.is/ukrainian-nationalism-its-roots-and-nature/

tized." Everything should be questioned, analyzed over and over again, if only because we know that history is written almost exclusively by victors and because we also know that it is mostly written by some very specific social classes (Michael Parenti writes about that). Besides, even authors whose views can appear "heretical" can offer fantastic insights and analyses, such as the Russian Stalinist Nikolai Starikov, whose Stalinism I totally reject, but whose books I find absolutely fascinating (well, except for the one on Stalin, of course). Anyway, I wanted you to know my philosophy of history before giving you my understanding of the Holodomor.

On that topics, opinions vary from "it was a genocide of Ukrainians by Russians," to "it was a genocide of Ukrainians by Jews," to "it was a famine resulting from Western sanctions against the USSR" (Starikov), to "it was an attempt by the Bolshevik regime to eradicate Orthodoxy and national awareness" to "it's all a myth and it never happened."

Let me admit immediately that I am not at all sure that I know the truth about this. I have read a lot about it and I think that I have a decent understanding of the basic facts which very much narrow down the possible interpretations. Still, caveat emptor, I am not an expert on this topic. Having said that, I will offer this:

First, I am 99.9999% sure that it did happen. I know personally met people—totally non-political, simple people—who lived through that. There is no doubt in my mind at all that a massive famine happened in the Ukraine before the war.

Second, I am also certain that it was in no way a "Russian genocide of the Ukrainian" people for the following reasons:

1) The famine was not limited to the Ukraine, it also affected Russia.

2) Bolsheviks never had any Russian national identity.

3) Bolsheviks were almost all rather rabid Russophobes.

4) Most key Bolsheviks were not even Russian by ethnicity.

5) A type of Holodomor was first tried in Russia in 1918-1921: war communism.[104]

So it did happen, but "who done it?" then and why?

I think that this was a combination of factors:

a) Western sanctions (boycott on gold) did force the export of grains and foodstuffs.

b) Stalin did want to "industrialize the agriculture."

c) The Bolshevik regime deeply distrusted all peasants (Ukrainian or Russian) for their religiosity, patriotism and what the Bolsheviks would call "reactionary class consciousness."

So the regime did order the de-Kulakization and collectivization of the Soviet rural regions. Now, look at who was tasked with implementing this policies: mostly Soviet commissars. Those were mostly Jews (more about that later) and they spoke Russian among themselves.

Now consider the history of Ukrainian Jewish relations:

Most Jews appeared in the Ukraine during the Polish occupation when they were mostly used by the Polish invaders as overseers of the local peasantry on behalf of the Polish nobility. One of their function was to "oversee" the Orthodox churches. Needless to say, that resulted in a deep sense of hatred toward them from the local peasants. Later, after the Ukraine was freed from the Polish rule, many Jews (and even Poles) stayed. Their comparatively privileged social status and wealth earned them even more hate from the locals. Finally, keep in mind that all of Judaism at this time was rabidly anti-Christian and that the hate which Ukrainians felt toward Jews was nothing compared to the hatred all Jews felt for all Christians, including the local.

Eventually, the pendulum of history swung the other way and Jews began to suffer from more and more mistreatment at the hands of the locals which eventually resulted in mass emigration of Jews to the West. While Alexander Solzhenitsyn did conclusively prove in his book *200*

---

[104] War communism https://en.wikipedia.org/wiki/War_communism

years together (still not translated into English due to Jewish opposition to this publication) that the Russian state did try hard to stop the so-called "pogroms" (mainly because this resulted in a terrible anti-Russian campaign in the Western press), these pogroms did happen. They were organized by locals and some did claim many innocent lives. What is little known is that some of the worst pogroms did not happen under the "bloodthirsty and anti-Semitic Czarist regime" but during the civil war and after and that a lot of them were carried out not by White forces, but by nationalists, anarchists, various Marxists, etc. who saw Jews class enemies, petit bourgeois and foreign agents. Now, when the Bolshevik faction eventually seized control over the Ukraine, the pendulum swung the other way again.

Most Bolsheviks were Jews (which, btw, does **not** mean that most Jews were Bolsheviks!) especially the local commissars. They absolutely "hated" the Ukrainian peasantry and when the de-Kulakization and collectivization began, found a perfect opportunity to take revenge on their former oppressors. Hence the mind-boggling cruelty with which the Bolshevik commissars implemented the Kremlin's orders. Mind you, the pendulum swung back again during Hitler's invasion of the Ukraine: not only did the Nazis shoot most Jews and all commissars on sight, the local Ukrainians—whether nationalist or not—gladly used this opportunity to massacre, torture, and kill as many Jews as they could.

After the war, the pendulum of history swung—albeit with much less momentum—the other way again and Ukrainian "collaborators" were hunted down and shot, but when the Ukraine became independent in 1991, the pendulum swung back again—again with even less momentum—and now we see the role of a small but very vocal Jew-hating and neo-Nazi segment in the current events.

The only (relatively) good news is that this pendulum of hate has less and less momentum for a number of reasons: many Jews have emigrated, the Soviet education system was firmly anti-racist, modern neo-Nazis are becoming more pro-Jewish and pro-Israeli (see Brevik) and Jews now have the means (finance, media, etc.) to counteract anti-Jewish propaganda. But that hate is still there and it cannot be ignored.

Now on a superficial level, here is what the poorly educated Ukrainians understood: the order to de-Kulakize came from Moscow, the executioners spoke Russian and hated the locals, millions died. It was easy for the nationalists to spin this as "a genocide of Russians against the Ukrainians," especially since Jews had such a huge stake in concealing their role in these events. In politics it's never mind the truth as long as its serves a political purpose, and all the russophobes (neo-Nazis, Ukie nationalists, Jews, Anglos, etc.) turned that famine into a "Holodomor" with a capital "H"—almost as politically useful as the other "H" genocide: the one of Jews by the Nazis.

So that's my take on this one. Next, come the issues of, well, what shall I call it?

What shall I call it?

When I began this blog I used to refer to the so-called "Roman Catholics" as Papists. The reason for that was extremely simple and straightforward: the so-called "Roman Catholics" are neither Roman nor Catholic. I have covered the first part (not Romans) many times here, so will just post two links to a through explanation of this topic:

Franks, Romans, Feudalism, and Doctrine[105] *Part 1: An Interplay Between Theology and Society* by John S. Romanides

Introduction to Romanity, Romania, Roumeli[106] by John S. Romanides

The reason why the so-called "Catholics" are not Catholic is that the word Catholic has a precise meaning in Greek: it means both "universal" and "conciliar." The "Roman Catholic Church" wants to present itself as

---

[105] John S. Romanides: Franks, Romans, Feudalism, and Doctrine Part 1: An Interplay Between Theology and Society http://www.romanity.org/htm/rom.03.en.franks_romans_feudalism_and_doctrine.01.htm

[106] John S. Romanides: Introduction to Romanity, Romania, Roumeli http://www.romanity.org/htm/rom.16.en.romanity_romania_roumeli.01.htm

"universal" for purely propagandistic grounds. When it calls itself "the Church this" or "the Church that" it lays the claim to be The One Original Christian Church. That is, of course, false for two reasons:

a) The so-called "Catholic Church" did break off from the One United Christian Church (formally in 1054) and formed its own ecclesiastical entity.

b) The so-called "Catholic Church" introduced a host of dogmas which are in contradiction with the faith "*which the Lord gave, which was preached by the Apostles, and was preserved by the Fathers*" (Saint Athanasios) and "*which has been believed everywhere, always and by all*" (Saint Vincent). For example, the dogma of the Immaculate Conception of the Papal Infallibility were only adopted in the 19th century!)

From the point of view of the Church, the Orthodox Church, the Roman Catholics have been in heresy for almost one thousand years already precisely because they have departed from the tradition of the ancient Church and the Church Fathers and they began to introduce innovations which were in direct contradiction with the teachings of Christ and his apostles.

Also, conciliar means that the highest authority in the Church is vested upon the Church councils, especially the Ecumenical Councils. The Papists have de facto and *de jure* transferred the authority which the Church only granted to the councils to one man: the Pope. So it's either "Papist" or "Catholic"—not both.

So, as an Orthodox Christian, I cannot honestly call the so-called "Roman Catholics" Roman Catholics. I could call them "the Frankish heretics" but that nobody would understand. So I used the word "Papists." Why?

Because the root cause of all Papist heresies is in their re-definition of what the notion of Pope and their maniacal insistence that all of Christianity submit to him. Mind you, this is hardly a 19th century invention. Check out the kind of crazy notions of the Papacy the Franks introduced in the so-called "*Dictatus Papae.*"[107] And keep in mind that this is a 11th century document adopted only 20 years after the Franks left the Christian Church. And ever since, the Papists have been willing to compromise on anything and everything except this one "idée fixe": everybody has to submit to the Pope. So, I figured, why not call them by their own main value: the Papacy. Nope! I got many emails telling me that I was offending and alienating the Papists by calling them Papists. So I tried to find a better word.

First, I asked the folks who were offended by the expression "Papist" what they would suggest. Not a single one offered anything. I even considered "Western Christians" but I discarded that option because that would lump all the Protestant and Reformed Churches with the Papacy. Then I thought "Latins." After all, that is an expression used in history, so why not? I even contacted my thesis advisor (I am working on a "Master's Degree in Patristic Studies"—it's not called that but its close enough) who replied that both Latin and Papist were reasonable. But I "still" got objections that this was "offensive." So what was I to do?

The Arabs had it simple: they called the Papist "Franks" and the Orthodox "Romans." They still do. Sounds great to me, but who will understand anything if I begin by writing about the Frankish role in the education of Bandera?! Exactly—nobody.

So I am stuck between using a term which is historically false, logically false and basically misleading and using accurate terms which offend **precisely** due to their accuracy.

So you tell me—do you have a better suggestion?

OK, let's try that. For the rest of today's post, and only for today's post, I shall use the Arab terminology and speak of "Franks" when referring to the so-called Roman-Catholics.

BTW, if you think—like some do, they told me so—that I have an anti-Frankish obsession I will reply the following: did you ever noticed that

[107] Dictatus papae https://en.wikipedia.org/wiki/Dictatus_papae

I never speak of modern "Judaism" without calling it "rabbinical Judaism"? Why? Same thing!

Modern Judaism is not at all the religion of Abraham, Isaac and Jacob—it is the religion of Maimonides, Karo and Luria and its key characteristic is the role of rabbis. In fact, the correct name for modern Judaism should be "Phariseeism" (as all modern versions of rabbinical Judaism are the direct descendants of the Sect of the Pharisees described in the Gospels).

Me, personally, I would be quite happy to speak of Romans, Franks and Pharisees. But nobody would understand what I mean. Nobody. So I use "Orthodox Christians, Papists and Rabbinical Judaics" instead. There I get people deeply offended.

So, again, what shall I do?

May I maybe suggest that what causes the offense is not the words I use but the factual historical reality they accurately convey?

Next.

Blaming all the Franks for the actions of some

I think that in my post about the roots of Ukrainian nationalism I have been clear when I wrote:

Though hatred of the Orthodox Christians and Russian still exists in some Latin circles, it has mostly been replaced by a desire to "incorporate" or swallow the Orthodox Church into the Papacy by means of the so-called "Ecumenical dialog." As for the rank and file Roman Catholic faithful—they simply have no idea at all about this history which, of course, is never taught to them.

And yet, I still get accused of lumping good and decent Franks with the genocidal maniacs I describe in my historical description.

But is that really a fair accusation?

After all, one is not born a Frank (Ouch! there we go. This sentence makes no sense at face value since being a Frank refers to an ethnicity, so one is indeed born a Frank. So? Shall I write "one is not born a Latin" or "one is not born a Papist"?) Being a Frank is a choice, a choice which implies some kind of acceptance, if not endorsement, for history. The Franks tried to have it both ways, on one hand they did apologize for the sack on Constantinople,[108] on the other hand they have not only made saints out of some of the worst enemies of the Orthodox Church, they have even pursued the very same policies! Just look at the role of the Franks in the movements of Ante Pavelic, or Stepan Bandera, or in the Ukraine right now! They are **still** at it, though the rhetoric has changed. From being the "Photian schismatics, they now call us their "Orthodox brothers." Thanks for that, of course, but when will you pretty please stop trying to convert us or side with all our enemies?! And when will you stop making web pages like this[109] one about some of the genocidal maniacs who have persecuted us?

Still, I know that most Franks are totally ignorant of the history of their own Church and that they are quite shocked when they hear about it. But even these Franks cannot help but wonder "if we forgot about all that, why does this guy constantly bring it up?! This is long gone, past history, what is he trying to prove? What is his problem?!." To this, I would reply the following:

My dear Franks, what for you is past history is integral to our *ethos* and consciousness. We are not Orthodox because we like golden cupolas, beautiful icons and Byzantine church singing—we are Orthodox because we try to remember it all, not only dogmas and traditions, but also our history. This is why we read the *Lives of the Saints* on a daily basis—to remember our martyrs and be inspired to follow their example. Just like the Shia have the Ashura at the core of their spiritual life, we have to Gol-

---

[108] Eight hundred years after the Fourth Crusade, Pope John Paul II twice expressed sorrow for the events of the Fourth Crusade. https://en.wikipedia.org/wiki/Siege_of_Constantinople_%281204%29#Legacy

[109] St. Josaphat, Bishop and Martyr http://catholicharboroffaithandmorals.com/St.%20Josaphat.html

gotha and every single martyr which died for Christ and His Church at the core of our spiritual life.

Our Menaion[110] is full of the names and lives of our brothers which you have massacred *ad majorem Dei gloriam*, for us these events are not "long gone history"—they are both today and timeless and when you tell us to please stop bringing it all up, we feel that you are trying, yet again, to change who we are and silence the voices and witness of those who have massacred.

The ancient Church has **always** had her martyrs at the core of Her liturgical life: a martyr's relic is embedded in every single one of our church altars, every one of our antimensons[111] also contains a small relic. This also used to be the practice in the West—just read the Western Church Fathers—which for a full millennium also used to be part of the Universal Church (formally: 33AD-1054AD). Nowadays, of course, there is many more of you then there is of us, but tiny as we are, we still will continue to preserve the full memory of the Church as best we can and we will witness of the past even if you don't like it. As the Chinese say: "me so sorry!" Not.

In conclusion I will repeat what I wrote above: could it be that what causes the offense is not the events I describe but the factual historical reality they accurately convey?

Still—my offer stands: suggest to me a word to describe the Franks which would not automatically reinforce the Frankish propaganda and I will gladly use it.

Ok, that's it for today. I have done my best to fully address some of the points which were raised in the comments section. I apologize if I have missed some. Please feel free to repost them again here and I will make sure to address them.

Many thanks and kind regards,

---

110 Menaion https://en.wikipedia.org/wiki/Menaion

111 Antimins https://en.wikipedia.org/wiki/Antimins

The Saker

PS: yes, I know and I agree that Ashkenazim Jews are predominantly Khazars. But then, I cannot check for each "Jew" I mention whether he/she is Ashkenazim or Sephardim. Besides, can you imagine if from now on I add "Khazar" and "Sfardi" to "Frank," "Roman" and "Pharisee"?! LOL :-) Right now I honestly have no energy for that…

February 26, 2014

How the Ukrainian crisis will eventually bring down the Anglo-Zionist Empire

There are many theories out there about what exactly caused the collapse of the Soviet Union. Some say that it is Ronald Reagan with his Star Wars program. Others say that this is the war in Afghanistan or the Polish union Solidarnosc. Other popular theories include the failure of the Soviet economy, the drop in oil prices, the inability to produce consumer goods, the yearning of many Soviets for Western-style freedoms and incomes, national/ethnic problems, a hypertrophic military-industrial complex, a massive and corrupt bureaucracy, the corruption of the CPSU and its *nomenklatura*,[112] the personal treason of Mikhail Gorbachev and many other theories. While all of these factors did contribute to weaken the Soviet system, I do not believe that they brought it down, not even combined together. What really brought down the Soviet Union was something entirely different: an unbearable cognitive dissonance or, to put it more simply, an all-prevailing sense of total hypocrisy.

But before I make my case about the role of hypocrisy, let me first clarify why I don't believe that any other of the theories I listed above make sense: simply because the USSR survived much, **much**, harder times. Frankly, the entire period from 1917 through 1946 was much worse than anything which happened during Brezhnev's "stagnation" or after. And yet, not only did the Soviet Union survive, it almost single-handedly defeated the biggest military machine Europe ever created—Hitler's Wehrmacht—it also deterred the Anglosphere from its plans to attack it at the end of the war. Then it more or less won the "space race" (with the very notable exception of the race to the moon which the USSR

---

[112] Nomenklatura https://en.wikipedia.org/wiki/Nomenklatura

lost on 24th of October 1960),[113] built what was arguably the most powerful conventional military force on the planet while enjoying an internal economic boom. By any measurement, the USSR was a formidable power during a very long period.

But then something went very, very wrong.

Personally, I am inclined to blame Nikita Khrushchev who, in my opinion, was by far the worst leader the Soviet Union ever had.

Though this is controversial, I believe that Khrushchev and a clique of supporters murdered Stalin by poisoning him, and then engaged in a massive propaganda campaign to justify their action and legitimize their rule. It all began with Khrushchev's (in)famous "secret speech[114]" at the 20th CPSU Congress and it continued throughout most of Khrushchev's rule. Khrushchev, who personally hated Stalin, used every truth and untruth possible to literally demonize Stalin. Worse, Khrushchev objectively joined forces with the many Trotskyists worldwide who had been spreading the "Stalinism" myth for decades.

Let me immediately clarify that I am not at all an admirer of Stalin whom I consider to be a bloody tyrant and an absolutely ruthless, if personally charming, dictator. But I will say that Stalin was most definitely no worse than Lenin, Trotsky or Khrushchev and that as a statesman he was far more skilled than any other Soviet leader. As for Khrushchev himself, he was the protégé of Lazar Kaganovich,[115] one of the worst scumbags in Soviet history; he was also an eager participant in many bloody repressions, and generally a comprehensively immoral, unprincipled and outright evil person.

Anyway, with his anti-Stalin campaign Khrushchev basically told the Soviet people that what used to be white yesterday is henceforth to be considered black and that what was black is now white. On a deeper level,

[113] Nedelin catastrophe https://en.wikipedia.org/wiki/Nedelin_catastrophe

[114] On the Cult of Personality and Its Consequences https://en.wikipedia.org/wiki/On_the_Cult_of_Personality_and_Its_Consequences

[115] Lazar Kaganovich https://en.wikipedia.org/wiki/Lazar_Kaganovich

that also showed that the Soviet Union was ruled by complete hypocrites who had no personal beliefs and who stood for nothing except for their own power.

The poison of *disillusionment and cynicism* injected by Khrushchev and his clique acted slowly, but surely, and by the time Leonid Brezhnev came to power (1964) it had already discreetly permeated all of Soviet society. By the 1980 it was omnipresent at all the levels of society, from the lowest and poorest to the top party officials. I don't want to go into all the details, but I will say that the fact that almost nobody stood up to defend the Soviet system in 1991 and in 1993 is a direct result of that poison's erosion of the Soviet society. By the 1990s everybody knew that even if the ideals of communism were good (which some still did believe while some did not), the modern Soviet society was built on a gigantic lie which nobody was willing to fight for, never mind die for it.

That rot of disillusionment and cynicism is also what defined the 1990s and the "democratic nightmare" of the Yeltsin years. People now say that this was the time when "every young Russian boy wanted to become a Mafia Don and every Russian girl a prostitute"—not quite literally true, of course, but generally true nonetheless. It is only with the coming to power of Putin that this poison began to weaken and that the Russian society began to re-discover true ideals and a belief in values worth standing up for.

How does that all apply to the Anglo-Zionist Empire and the Ukraine?

It is quite obvious, really. I tend to agree with Alexander Mercouris, Mark Sleboda, and Mark Hackard[116] when they say that the USA, ruled by incompetent and poorly educated politicians (rather than by professional diplomats or real statesmen) probably expected Russia to roll over and accept a Banderastani regime in power in the Ukraine. And when Russia refused to accept that and pushed back, the AngloZionists made

---

[116] CrossTalk: Chicken Kiev? https://www.youtube.com/watch?v=LeEnTcbl5qM

their initial miscalculation even worse by dramatically increasing their rhetoric, and by insisting that black was white and white was black.

For the Anglo-Zionist a neo-Nazi armed insurgency which seizes power in contradiction with an agreement it had signed less than 24 hours before is a "legitimate representative of the Ukrainian people." The Banderists are philosemites and democrats, while the people in the eastern Ukraine are either Jew-hating extremists, or Russian agents. When the folks in the western Ukraine engage in a campaign of terror, murder and looting, that is an expression of democracy, when the people in the east seize SBU buildings it is terrorism. When Yanukovych was faced by protesters the US demanded that he not use any force at all, not even cops with sidearms; when the junta leader Yatsenyuk faces protesters, he is acting with praiseworthy restraint when he sends in tanks, artillery pieces, and combat aircraft. The referendum in Crimea is illegitimate because it was allegedly conducted at the point of a gun, while the proposed upcoming presidential election will be legitimate even though they will be organized and conducted by bone fide neo-Nazis and even though two candidates get assaulted and cannot campaign. I could continue to multiply the example here *ad nauseam*, but you get the point: what the AngloZionists are declaring *urbi et orbi* is basically that black is white, the earth is flat, 2+2=3, up is down, etc. They are doing exactly the same that what Khrushchev did in the USSR: they are showing their own people that they believe in nothing and stand for nothing except their own power.

Not that the American people need much convincing, I would add.

In my admittedly subjective opinion the level of disgust of most American people with the Federal government is already sky high. Sure, most people feel impotent and believe that there is nothing they can do about it. When they vote for peace, they get more war. When they vote for less taxes, they get more. When they vote for more civil rights, they get less. There is an entire generation of Americans out there which is as disillusioned and as disgusted with their own rulers as the Soviets were with their rulers in the 1970s and 1980s.

Interestingly, there is definitely a strong anti-regime movement of American patriots out there. These are folks who have the wisdom to differentiate between, on one hand, their country, their people, the ideals upon which the US society was originally built, and, on the other hand, regime in DC and the 1% of the population whose interests this regime works for. Amazing, no? The Soviet Union had its formal nomenklatura while the USA has its own, informal, one. About 1% of the population in each case.

You want more uncanny parallels? Sure! How about

1) A bloated military budget resulting in an ineffective military

2) A huge and ineffective intelligence community

3) A crumbling public infrastructure

4) A world record in the per capita ratio of incarcerated people (US GULag)[117]

5) A propaganda machine which nobody trusts any more

6) An internal dissident movement which the regime tries to keep silent

7) A systematic use of violence against the citizens

8) An increase in tensions between Federal and local authorities

9) An industry whose main exports are weapons and energy

10) A population fearful of being spied on by the internal security services

11) A systematic assimilation of dissent with espionage and terrorism

12) An all-prevailing paranoia about internal and external enemies

13) A financially catastrophic over-reach of the Empire across the planet

14) An awareness that the entire planet hates you

---

[117] *Glavnoe upravlenie ispravitel'notrudovykh lagereĭ*: chief administration of corrective labor camps

15) A subservient press corps of presstitutes who never dare to ask the real questions

16) A sky-high rate of substance abuse

17) A young generation which believes in nothing at all

18) An educational system in free fall (the Soviet one was much better, btw)

19) A disgust with politics by the general public

20) A massive and prevailing amount corruption on all levels of power

These are just a few examples which apply as much to the USSR of the 1980 as it does to the 2014 USA. There are also plenty of differences, of course, no need to list them here as they are quite obvious.

My main point is not that the USSR and USA are the exact same, but only that the similarities between the two are becoming uncanny and numerous.

In conclusion and to put things simply: what the AngloZionists are openly and publicly defending in the Ukraine is the polar opposite of what they are supposed to stand for. That is an extremely dangerous thing to do for any regime and the Anglo-Zionist Empire is no exception to that rule. Empires often crumble when their own people become disillusioned and disgusted with massive discrepancy between what the ruling elites say and what they do and as a result, it is not so much that the Empire is faced with formidable enemies as it is the fact that nobody is willing to stand up—never mind die—in defense of it. Just look at the following sentence:

(in the Ukraine) "Barack Obama and the Democratic Party stand for racism and Fascism"

Amazing, no? But it is true, even though this short sentence has enough tensions inside it to explode the brain of many Americans, especially Democrats. I put the "in the Ukraine" in brackets to provide the context but, of course, the context does not matter one bit. You cannot be for liberal policies at home and for fascism abroad. Nor can you be an anti-racist who supports racism, it don't matter one bit were that racism is located. Values truly held are applicable to all and everywhere. You cannot oppose torture in country *x* but favor it in country *y*. That is plain ridiculous. So let me restate the sentence above this time without the context in brackets:

"Barack Obama and the Democratic Party stand for racism and fascism."

Blows your mind, doesn't it?

And, of course, the very same can be said of McCain and his party:

"John McCain and the Republican Party stand for racism and fascism."

Still painful, no?

How about this one:

"The EU stands for racism and fascism."

Or, even better:

"The ADL and the Weisenthal Center stand for racism and fascism."

Or this one:

"Amnesty International and Human Rights Watch stand for racism and fascism."

Pretty amazing, no?

Now try combining any of the above with this one:

"Putin and Russia stand for democracy, freedom and human rights."

Ouch! That one would really hurt a lot of American and Europeans.

Of course, this is not how the events in the Ukraine, or any other event, is presented in the official public media and the zombified public discourse. But neither was that the case in the USSR. Still, not all people are stupidified zombies—though some, of course, are—and they do their own, quiet, little thinking in their own heads. Sometimes they toss ideas around with their friends. In the Soviet Union the "Petri dish" for politically incorrect discussion was usually the kitchen. In the USA it might be near the barbecue.

Of course, we are not going to see mass demonstrations in the streets of Washington DC, most people are going to keep this kind of "crime thoughts" private or for a small circle of trusted friends, but let me remind you all that since we are making comparisons between the USSR and the USA, there was no "occupy the Kremlin" movement in the USSR while the Occupy Wall Street movement in the USA was very large and widely spread across this huge country. Nor has there ever been a Soviet equivalent of the huge **1990 anti-WTO protests in Seattle.**[118] So the American public is nowhere nearly as passive as some think.

The Ukraine is far away from the USA, and only 1/6th of Americans can place it on a map. But the consequences of the very high-visibility involvement of the US regime and the Anglo-Zionist Empire will be dramatic, if delayed in time. Already nobody in his/her right might would give Obama his Nobel Peace Prize again. So even though the formidable Western propaganda machine is way more capable and sophisticated than anything Goebbels or Suslov could have dreamed about, it cannot hide reality forever.

This is why the Empire is so desperate for some kind of victory in the Ukraine. If it cannot be respected any more, it needs to be at least feared. But if the Ukraine explodes and Russia gets Crimea and the East (which appears increasingly likely) then the AngloZionists won't even be feared anymore. Once that happens, the life expectancy of the Empire will become very, very short. So yes, knowing the truth does make one free, and **the truth is the most powerful empire-buster ever invented**. It

---

[118] 1999 Seattle WTO protests https://en.wikipedia.org/wiki/1999_Seattle_WTO_protests

brought down the USSR and it will bring down the AngloZionists too. It is just a matter of time now.

April 22, 2014

ONE MORE ATTEMPT AT CLARIFYING MY POSITION ON RUSSIAN OPTIONS

The pitfalls and risks of expressing feelings in a blog.

My recent rant "*Please tell me my worst fears will not come true*[119]" was clearly very poorly written and my **subsequent attempt to clarify what I meant**[120] did little to improve the mess I apparently had created. To be honest, I never went to "blogger school" and I am painfully learning this trade by trial and error including a lot of errors. I naively had thought that putting enough caveats would make my intentions clear:

> "I will thus readily admit that I might be over-reacting."
> "My brain tells me one thing, but my gut tells me another."

How could I make it more clear that 1) I was speaking from the heart/gut and not making an analysis and 2) that I was fully aware that I was over-reacting? I don't know about others, but to me the admission of doubts and fears is never a sign of weakness. **Courage and strength is not denying doubts and fears, but acting rationally in spite of such feelings**. Maybe that is not done in the blogosphere, or maybe I did it on a clumsy way, but I did it the best I could and with as much honesty I could. I would have imagined that those who had called me a "Putin groupie" or "Kremlin shill" would have approved of my open admission that I truly trusted neither Putin nor the Kremlin, but somehow only those who were upset by that admission showed up. Oh well, another valuable lesson for me: expected a beating every time you show your feelings.

---

[119] Saker rant: Please tell me my worst fears will not come true! http://thesaker.is/saker-rant-please-tell-me-my-worst-fears-will-not-come-true/

[120] My rant tonight – okay, I will try to clarify further http://thesaker.is/my-rant-tonight-okay-i-will-try-to-clarify-further/

But the "killer sentence" which I should never have written as I did was this one: "Russia has to act now and use her armed forces to liberate Novorossiya. Not to do so would be a betrayal of the Russian people." That was a *cri du coeur* (cry from the heart) which overshadowed all the caveats before it. This being said, I categorically deny that I had a change of heart. Before Poroshensko's inauguration speech I saw a set of circumstances we can call "A" while after his inauguration speech I saw a new and different set of circumstances we can call "B." A change of heart would be to say that a the same set of circumstances warrants a change in policy. That is not what I wrote, but I have to admit that what I did write was highly misleading: pure emotion and distress and not a rational analysis.

I also know what triggered my reaction, and here I will place the blame on Putin, Lavrov, Zurabov (Russia's ambassador to Kiev) and Peskov (Putin spokesman). What triggered my panic attack was the totally lame and lukewarm reaction of Russia to a speech which was a real declaration of war not only on Novorossiya but also on Russia herself: not only was Poroshenko's speech filled with various anti-Russian statements echoing the worst, most ignorant and most ugly Right Sector propaganda, but he even clearly spelled out that he considered Crimea was Ukrainian: that was a threat on Russian land. And what was Russia's response? "Nothing." Zurabov just sat there and Putin and Lavrov stayed silent. I have no heard a single word of criticism coming out of official Moscow. That is what really freaked me out. That and the "terrible" timing of the decision to strengthen the border between Russia and Novorossiya. And I still think that **Russia's public policy committed a terrible "faux pas" by remaining silent in the face of such a public display of Nazi bigotry and arrogance.**

I have spent the last 24 hours reading many Russian articles written by very sharp analysts, I have carefully listen to all the main news shows, I have also taken the time to listen to some specialized shows (such as Igor Korotchenko's "GenShtab" on Voice of Russia) and I have come to the conclusion that Russia will not accept a Nazi regime in Kiev nor will Russia abandon Novorossiya. Frankly, this is bigger than Putin and we should not focus on personalities too much, even political giants like Putin. Why? Because even in the exceedingly unlikely possibility that Putin for some reason cave to the Empire, he would be committing political suicide, Juan is absolutely correct about that. I still think that Putin does want to do the right thing, but if not—then he will be forced to.

So what do I think (rather than feel) Russia should do?

I have to admit that there is one major argument against a direct Russian military intervention in Novorossiya: it is an undeniable fact that the people from Novorossiya themselves have not done enough for themselves. Yes, the self-defense forces of Novorossiya are heroes, and yes, they are fighting very well even though the force ratios in the favor of the Nazis is anywhere between 5:1 to 100:1 (depending on the day and location). But even though more people have heard Strelkov's appeal the numbers are still nowhere near where they should be. That is a fact that I cannot deny.

The argument that the (Novorossiya Defense Forces) NDF are under-equipped is being addressed right now. I have seen footage shown on Russian TV of sophisticated air-defense radars used by the NDF and I have it from several good sources that modern equipment is regularly showing up. I have heard that today three Ukrainian main battle tanks (MBTs) and at least one Multiple Rocket Launching System (MLRS) have been destroyed by the NDF. My feeling is that pretty soon the NDF will establish their own "no-fly" zone which the Ukies will not dare to penetrate very often (they have already lost "a lot" of their rotary and fixed wing aircraft). This no-fly zone will soon be followed by a "no drive" zone for Ukie armor (enforced by modern anti-tanks weapon systems). The problem of artillery can only be solved by providing the NDF with the means for counter-battery fire. That will be tricky, especially with long range artillery. But with no FACs on the ground or in the air, artillery strikes will not be very effective, even if still devastatingly deadly for the local civilian population. Snipers could be found and trained, I suppose (they can make the life of an artillery unit really miserable). Supplies, ammo dumps, and generally the logistics should be attacked and sabotaged. In other words, as soon as it has the means to do so the NDF has to go on the offensive.

Frankly, there should be a "principle of subsidiarity" of sorts at work here: before the Russians intervene the people of the Donbass have the moral duty to everything they can to defend themselves. Then, if needed, Russia should intervene to prevent a genocide in Novorossiya. But first the locals have to do more. What Russia can and should do is to provide military, technical and financial aid to Novorossiya, whether covertly or overtly (why can Russia not do exactly the same as what the USA is doing in Syria?) **My understanding is that Russia is already doing that**.

There is, however, something that Russia is not doing or, rather, there is something which Russia is doing and which she should stop doing: smiling at Poroshenko and sticking to this silly "our Ukrainian brothers" script: what is left of the Ukraine today is no more no less than a Nazi Banderastan and Russia should not even bother pretending that there is a love-fest between these two entities. No need to do anything provocative or hostile, just to stop pretending like Russia is oblivious to the kind of Banderastan is being built. As for Novorossiya Russia should openly support it in the name of anti-Nazism and provide it with technical, financial, political and informational support. As for the West, it is "already" acting as if Russia was heavily engaged in a full-scale support campaign for the breakaway regions—so why not do that anyway?!

Finally, the Russian should learn from their American counterparts and make the human rights issue a huge political stick. Russian diplomats should simply inundate the world media with protest about every single war crime, every single human right violation, ever single violation of the freedom of the press and every single case of corruption. Protest constantly, drown the Ukie Nazis with lawsuits on all levels, denounce them at every public events, etc. First that will take a toll on the regime in

Kiev and, second, it will show the anti-Nazi forces in the Ukraine that they are not abandoned.

There is a lot Russia can do besides using her armed forces.

Bottom line is this: my heart and my gut tell me that Russia should intervene now: impose a no-fly zone, open humanitarian corridors and destroy the Nazi death squads. And if that happens tomorrow morning I will be elated. But my brain has to accept that the most rational way to deal with this situation is to do everything **short** of an over military intervention. I will readily admit that I am torn and that I have not found a way to reconcile the two. There are better people out there that have done a much better job at that then I have, but I am not sure that I envy them.

One more issue: a US nuclear threat to Russia?

I have no doubt at all that this is nonsense and that the US is not contemplating such a threat or, even less so, such an attack. Why? Because it is absolutely and categorically impossible for the USA to strike Russia in such a manner which would prevent Russia from executing a retaliatory counter-strike. I have already written about this and just want to repeat it here: while there probably are some politicians who dream about such an option, the US military knows that this is absolutely impossible and nothing will change that in the foreseeable future. No matter what attack scenario you consider, Russia always will have the means to basically make the USA disappear as a society. Of course, the same is true for the USA which Russia cannot disarm in a first counter-force strike. Forget it! Really.

During the Cold War we have made a lot of very fancy simulations and the result has always been the same, and all the folks in command in the USA know that. Also, nothing has fundamentally changed since the late 1980s. Most of the current nuclear systems date from that period and while all sorts of progress has been made, it has not resulted in some kind of breakthrough, much less so one upon which anybody could waged the survival of the entire northern hemisphere of our planet. In fact, I would argue that the Russian nuclear forces today are both more survivable and more capable, especially the latest road-mobile ICBMs and the submarine launched ballistic missiles.

So one thing I can guarantee: there is no nuclear attack threat to Russia (and nor is there one to the USA, of course). As for a US tactical nuclear strike on a Russian force entering Novorossiya, it would have an absolutely catastrophic political effect on the Anglo-Zionist Empire, not to mention that nobody in the Ukraine will be grateful for this. Even if the US used a "cleaner" neutron bomb the political fallout with be huge, even inside the USA. As for Russia, it could even win this one by not retaliating in kind (remember, war is the pursuit of politics by other means). So forget about these rumors about a US nuclear threat to Russia, even if B-2s and USN ships are moved around. They are "showing the flag"—not threatening Russia.

I hope that this last effort of mine to fully clarify my position has been more successful than my previous one. I know that this blog is making a lot of people angry and that they will use this opportunity to again misrepresent what I wrote or try to ridicule me. Fine, let them. Frankly, I don't care much about their "opinion" nor am I competing in some kind of popularity contest. Besides. I am confident that most of you will recognize these efforts for what they are.

Enough about doubts and fears for now—tomorrow back to the regular daily work.

June 10, 2014

PART III: RUSSIA AND THE WEST

THE REAL MEANING OF THE SOUTH OSSETIAN WAR: RUSSIA STRIKES BACK

The amazing and tragic events in South Ossetia seem to baffle most Western experts. While a majority of them fall back on the 'safe' position of blaming Russia for everything others, particularly on the left, appear to be rather unsure of what to think of all this; many basically ignore the issue altogether. In contrast to the leftist blogosphere or to the free and independent press, the corporate media immediately understood that this was, yet again, a perfect opportunity to prove to its political and corporate masters what a loyal propaganda tool it is. While CNN basically used an 24/7 "open mike" policy toward Saakashvili, the rest of the US and European media uniformly bought into the US propaganda on the causes and effects of this conflict. This purely ideological approach to the unfolding crisis ended up blinding almost everyone to the real nature of what is going on.

Two speeches

The first sign that something radically new was happening could have been noticed in the tone, if not the words, of the TV address of President Medvedev to the Russian people on the day of the Georgian attack. Though his words were carefully chosen, and his statement short, one could clearly sense something new in the demeanor of this otherwise rather restrained, if not withdrawn, technocrat. What one could clearly perceive was Medvedev seething sense of deep anger.

The second, and even more amazing, speech which clearly showed what the Russians were thinking was the statement made by the Russian representative to the UN Security Council, Vitaly Churkin. His statement was an unscripted, spontaneous, and Churkin, while not agitated in any way, was clearly furious, disgusted and extremely determined. Against the background of the usually carefully scripted and mostly diplomatic (read: ambiguous) language of the UN, Churkin's words were packing a punch which only a Russian speaker listening to the original audio or video could fully appreciate.

Something important, something absolutely crucial, became clear that evening. The Russians were truly outraged and they were going to do something about it.

Within minutes of Churkin's speech the Russian blogosphere literally exploded with hundreds of posts expressing the same anger and the same resolve.

Why were exactly the Russians so outraged? Why did they sound far more angry about the death of ten or twelve peacekeepers than over the death of far more many Russian soldiers in Chechnya? Why was Russia, who had been willing to let the Ukraine, the birthplace of the Russian nation, go without so much as firing a single gunshot, why was Russia so upset about South Ossetia being invaded by Georgians?

The answer is, of course, that this is not at all about South Ossetia—it was all about Russia.

What exactly is 21st century "Russia" Anyway?

Russia, as it is today, is neither a continuation of the former Soviet Union nor, even less so, a continuation of the pre-1917 Orthodox Russia of Princes and Czars. Don't ever listen to anyone using these kind of historical references which are always used with one sole purpose: to conceal the ignorance of the person making them. They make for good clichés but for bad analysis.

Post-1991 Russia is essentially a new phenomenon which did come out, with great difficulty, from the ashes of the Soviet Union after a decade or more of utter chaos and collapse. To make a long story short, following the dissolution of the Soviet Union by the Soviet elites (there never was a "collapse of communism") and the breakup of the "Soviet pie" into many little "cakes," Russia found itself at the mercy of ruthless and totally corrupt leaders. The Yeltsin era really marks the lowest moment in the history of the Russian nation; not even World War II heaped such chaos and destruction upon the Russian nation as 9 years of "democracy": in a short time the former Soviet superpower was reduced to the state of a "failed nation." Two closely allied forces played a key role in this process, one inside, the so-called 'oligarchs' and one outside: the USA.

The Great Betrayal

Does anybody still remember the late eighties? How the West promised Gorbachev that if the Soviets withdrew their armed forces from Europe NATO would not expand? How the Russians were told that if they agreed to let the Republics of the Soviet Union go the West would assist Russia economically and politically? Probably not, this is old history now, something which people in the West just don't feel like reminiscing a lot about. It would be wrong to infer that, in contrast, the Russians spend their lives still fuming about these years and the lies they were told. In fact, they mostly don't. It's what followed the breakup of the Soviet Union which really bothers them.

Think about it. Not only did NATO expand to include almost all of Eastern Europe (one wonders what kind of contingencies still justify the existence of this alliance anyway?), but the West illegally attacked and dismembered the only country still friendly to Russia: Yugoslavia. US politicians love to say that they are "sending messages" and the bombing of Serbian enclaves in Croatia and Bosnia followed by the bombing of Kosovo, Serbia and Montenegro by NATO did "send a message" to Russia: "we hate your guts—screw you!" The message was received, loud and clear.

Then there was the war in Chechnya during which the West strongly backed what can only be called a nasty gang of bloodthirsty and crazed Wahhabis. Sure, September 11th brought a rather self-serving 180-degree reversal of this policy, but that was too little, too late.

And then there is all the rest of the long litany of ugly Western imperial policies: the radars and missiles in Eastern Europe, all the nonsense about the "KGB" killing Politkovskaya and Litvinenko, the whining about the "not-so-democratic" elections in Russia (never mind that any idiot in Russia knows that Putin and Medvedev had no need to rig the elections at all) combined with the support for the electoral farce in Georgia, the systematic refusal to negotiate "anything" with Russia (this is politely referred to as "assertiveness" or "unilateralism") and last, but not least, the obscene support for the aforementioned "oligarchs" (who do you think paid for the Politkovskaya and Litvinenko propaganda campaigns?)

The oligarchs can best be compared to "mercenary bloodsuckers" who, with the full support of the West, literally tried to bleed Russia dry of all its resources. And, for a while, they did a very good job. US political "advisors" flooded Moscow and provided all the aide and expertise needed to help these 'oligarchs' (almost all of them Jewish) to plunder Russia as fast as possible. What only very few people realized at the time was that there was a force which was quite cynically letting all this happen and waiting for the best time to strike back.

The Hidden Power—the "Putin people"

While the pinnacle of power in the Soviet Union was formally in the hands of the Politburo's Security Council, the real, deeper, power of the Soviet regime was in the hands of the Central Committee of the Soviet Union. Few people realize, even today, that the presumably almighty KGB had no rights whatsoever to even investigate a CC CPSU member. This created a paradoxical situation: while the intellectual elite of the Soviet Union was, without any doubt, concentrated in the KGB, the real political power was in the hands of the CPSU. This created a rift which greatly contributed to the so-called "stagnation" years under Brezhnev.

When the Soviet Union was dismembered in 1991 the KGB went down into something of a duck and cover mode, hunkering down while the political passions of the time, including a very real hatred of the KGB for its oppression of the Russian people, overwhelmed the political scene. Many KGB officers left the "*Kantora*" (nickname of the KGB among its employees) and joined the Russian mob and became "businessmen." Some retired and some skillfully re-entered the political life as either "patriots" or "democrats" (or both). One group of younger KGB officials, however, managed to quietly regroup and reorganize itself behind the scenes.

This group, mostly based in Leningrad, realized that there was no way the KGB and what it represented could become popular again unless the situation in Russia became truly chaotic and desperate. These KGB officers, mostly from the First Main Directorate (Первое главное управление, Pervoye glavnoye upravleniye, or PGU) which dealt with foreign intelligence rather than internal security, understood the West very well, and they knew who had put the oligarchs into power after 1991. Still, unlike their mostly hapless colleagues from the "internal" KGB, these PGU officers sat and waited for the right moment to make their move. This moment came in 2000 when they literally conned the overconfident oligarchs to accept Putin, a totally uncharismatic and dull bureaucrat, as a compromise candidate which would threaten nobody. The ploy worked and without firing a single shot the KGB men retook the reins of power back into their hands. They immediately proceeded to purge the society of any and all oligarchs which would not immediately submit to their rule: some were jailed (Khodorkovsky), others were exiled (Berezovsky) and others were killed (Dudaev & Co.).

The Western imperial overlords rapidly understood what had happened, but there was nothing they could do about it. In a very real sense, Dubya "lost" Russia. The Brits, desperately frustrated at having their entire network in Russia quietly dismembered, resorted to a rather futile propaganda campaign against the "KGB murders." Predictably, it failed to interest, much less so impress, anybody in Russia. In contrast, Washington decided to step up, this time very overtly, its international campaign to isolate and weaken Russia. More recently France, now headed by the neocons Sarkozy and Kouchner, also joined into the anti-Russian chorus, but this had no more effect than the British efforts.

It is important to understand here that the KGB people which managed to seize the power away from the oligarchs fully understood, from day one, that the oligarchs were agents of the West and that these officers had absolutely no illusions whatsoever left about the West, its role, methods and objectives. For them the West had proved beyond any doubt that the old Soviet KGB had been correct in calling the West "the enemy number one": the oligarchs were not anti-Soviet—they were anti-Russian.

Another thing to keep in mind is that while it is not incorrect to speak of the importance of the KGB (and, in particular of the PGU) in this struggle, it would be wrong to reduce it all to this one organization. There are plenty of signs that the much less known, but no less sophisticated and powerful, military intelligence agency, the GRU, has concluded a strategic alliance with the "Putin people"[121] and that these formerly rather antagonistic organizations are now working together toward a common goal. The "Putin people" (and I refer to Putin himself not as a leader, but only as a symbol, a figurehead) are really composed of a mix of younger generation Russian intelligence officers from various services who joined forces with key personalities in the military-industrial and petrochemical complexes. They represent a generational change even more than any one single corporate interest. And if there is one thing which must be understood about them is that they are genuinely immensely popular in Russia. How could that be otherwise since, after all, the "Putin people" performed nothing short of a miracle in the eight short years between 2000 and 2008.

---

[121] Putin's legacy and the new Russia http://thesaker.is/putins-legacy-and-the-new-russia/

Lastly, don't get too upset about the ominous sounding "KGB" letters. Remember—it's not your father's KGB at all. It's not about Stalin, the GULag, or dissidents (which were dealt with by only one Directorate, the 5th, of the KGB). Think of it more like something of a slightly militarized elite corporate club with alumni of the best Ivy League colleges, and let Hillary and McCain spew the nonsense about the "coldness of Putin's KGB eyes."

For all their bad aspects, of which there are quite a few, these new Russian rulers managed to bring Russia back, big time, and now they are in control.

The chicken coming home to roost

It is quiet amusing, at least for me, to hear how the US now threatens Russia with "long-term damage" in their relationship. Think about it: is there anything, anything at all, short of a nuclear war, which the USA could do to Russia which it has not already done? One crackpot at the Heritage Foundation is now seriously suggesting that the West should prevent Russia from hosting the Olympic games. Some threat! A marginally more realistic option is for the West to implement some kind of economic sanctions except this idea overlooks two simple facts: first, Russia does not need the West, but the West needs Russia (think Iran, think North Korea, think oil) and second, this ignores the fact that most of the planet has no interest whatsoever in cutting down economic ties with Russia.

The US, having already lost the wars in Afghanistan and Iraq, barely has the energy to contemplate a conflict with Iran, never mind trying to take on Russia. The EU, for all the buffoonery of its leaders, is totally dependent on Russian gas and has no military means to intervene in the conflict. Worse, any crisis in a petrochemically-rich region (such as the Caucasus) only makes Russia richer and the West poorer. The greenback is in free fall and the US economy is in a recession. Talk about a paper tiger …

In their seemingly incurable imperial hubris, the imperial overlords in the USA think that they can threaten Russia with a worsening of relations while in reality it is Russia which could threaten the West. The Russians won't threaten though; there is a basic tenet of Russian hardball play which says that one should never threaten, never promise and only take direct action. This is exactly what happened in Ossetia.

The Conflict In Ossetia: Just The First Battle In A Much Wider War

Russia and the USA are at war and they have been at war since 1991—this is the ugly little secret which the imperial rulers are trying hide and which most Russian understand. The conflict in Ossetia is just the first time Russia is actually "returning fire" not so much at the American puppets in Tbilisi or at the US and Israeli-trained Georgian forces, but at the US Empire itself. The Russian response is a "message" to the West: "we will fight back!"

The initial Western response to Russia's stance is predicable: the USA will step up its anti-Russian propaganda campaign, NATO will declare that it will incorporate the Ukraine and even possibly Georgia and Western politicians will solemnly declare that their military budgets need to go further up to deal with the "Russian threat to our friends and allies."

Will Russia be deterred by such threats? Not at all.

As mentioned earlier, Russia has little to fear from the West on the economic front. Not only that, but Russia has nothing to fear from the Western military power. How is that possible?

Sure, the USA is spending more on "defense" (read: aggression) than the rest of the world combined, but that is explained by the fact that the USA seeks world domination. Russia, in contrast, has no such ambitions at all. At the most, Russia wants to be capable of fighting a war right across its border. That, and the capability to deter the USA with its nuclear forces. All in all, a cheap and eminently achievable objective and one which Russia does not need to strain too much to reach. The USA cannot match such a minimalist approach because if it did renounce world domination it would immediately collapse economically and become a "normal" country like any other i.e. a country which cannot take on Russia. Thus the USA is in a lose-lose situation: it cannot threaten Russia and seek world domination, but it cannot give up world domination and hope to be able to threaten Russia.

Paradoxically, Russia can afford an arms race with the USA precisely because the USA are already spending themselves into bankruptcy with their bloated, over-priced and under-performing armed forces.

So why are the Russians angry?

The Russians, both the people in the Kremlin and the general population are so angry at the West because they (correctly) feel that the West hates them and has being waging a unilateral war against everything Russian since 1991. They are angry because the double standards and the hypocrisy of the West are simply too immense to fully comprehend. For example, it is mind-boggling that the US representative at the UNSC accused Russia of using "disproportionate" actions in Georgia when the USA found it legitimate to bomb all of Serbia and Montenegro during its aggression on Kosovo. Two decade of "we hate you" "messages" from the West have not fallen on deaf ears in Russia and now the feeling has become very mutual.

The current outraged Russian anger at the West is, I believe, of a comparable fundamental quality, if not magnitude, to the one the Russians felt against the Nazis in World War II. It is fueled by an acceptance that Russia itself is being attacked by an uncompromising and evil foe which cannot be dealt with anything other than force. Those of you who have seen Russian TV and movies recently can attest that they are literally filled with stories about World War II and how the Russian people had to accept the greatest of hardships to prevail; some will call it "propaganda," which it is in many aspects, but it is also the expression of a popular mind-set, of a mental mode which says that you have to fight to survive.

The ugly attack by Washington's Georgian puppet on the Russian peacekeepers combined with the absolutely amazing hypocrisy of the

Western media and politicians who all fully sided with the aggressor turned into something of a "last straw" for Russia. This seemingly marginal development, at least when assessed quantitatively ("what else is new?") ended up making a huge qualitative difference: it brought up a new Russian resolve to deal with, to use a favorite neocon expression, an existential threat represented by the Western Empire. It will take a long while for the West to realize what has really happened and the most obtuse of pundits and politicians will probably hang on to their usual self-righteous rhetoric forever, but historians will probably look back at the month of August 2008 as the moment when Russia decided to strike back at the Empire for the first time.

August 12, 2008

THE POWER STRUGGLE INSIDE THE KREMLIN IS GRADUALLY EMERGING INTO THE OPEN

> "At the present time, the situation in Russia is characterized by some of the new features that distinguish it from the preceding period. One of them is the end of the 'tandem era.'"
>
> *Evgenii Primakov*[122]

As I have already mentioned in a past article,[123] there really is no "true" opposition in Russia. Putin and Medvedev have very skillfully manipulated the various political forces to make sure that none of the parties represented in the Duma would ever actually have a chance to come to power. They did that primarily by quietly promoting the emergence and continuous presence of political leaders whose positive image is dwarfed by their "*negative image.*" Take, for example, Zhirinovsky. Yes, he usually gets something in the range of 10-15% of the people to vote for him. But when asked "for which politicians would you never ever vote for, regardless of the circumstances?" roughly 70-75% Russian immediately reply "Zhirinovsky." The fact is that the man is pretty much hated by all those who do not support him in the first place.

The figures for that old Communist dinosaur Zyuganov are only marginally better. Again, the Kremlin, in this case both Medvedev and Putin, has very skillfully manipulated the system to make the "United Russia" the "only game in town," the rest is just a "democratic" fig-leaf aimed at giving the illusion of pluralism.

There are definite advantages to this setup. For one thing, no US-paid for "color-coded" revolution is likely to happen in such circumstances.

---

[122] Примаков объявил о конце «эпохи тандема» http://www.forbes.ru/news/232038-primakov-obyavil-o-kontse-epohi-tandema

[123] Russia and Islam, part three: internal Russian politics http://thesaker.is/russia-and-islam-part-three-internal-russian-politics/

Second, everybody in Russia with money, power and ambition realizes that if you want to succeed you need to be with "United Russia" or risk facing the kind of problems which befell Khodorkovsky and his pro-Western allies. Thirdly, this type of setup guarantees a certain degree of stability and continuity. Simply put, if you do not have to worry about petty politics and elections, you can deal with the real business of running a country. And yet, there are also very real risks in this kind of set-up, in particular in the mid to long term.

First, a lot of people have already become disgusted with the inevitable arrogance of those who feel that their power in theirs forever and who can basically ignore the public opinion. Second, by eliminating real diversity in the Duma this setup only pushes the discontent into the street, hardly a desirable outcome.

One clumsy and utterly hapless manifestation of this kind of "relocation" of the dissatisfied from the Duma into the street can be seen in the demonstrations which took place between the Parliamentary and presidential elections last year. Yes, the "white bands" (i.e. US-style "color-coded") movement was a crazy mix of hardline leftists, hyper-conservatives, hyper-liberals, pro-US and rabidly nationalistic elements, but that is mainly true of the "political leaders and organizers" of these protests. But this "tree" should not hide the "forest" of the *many simply angry, frustrated and alienated Russians who took to the streets to express their deep dissatisfaction.* Yes, many more people were pro-Putin than anti-Putin, but that does not mean that there is not a large minority which is basically disgusted with the system in place.

Still, all these street demonstration never represented a real risk for the stability of Russia. As I said, this was a chaotic, disorganized, largely discredited movement which had nothing to offer, and no chance to ever even get into the Kremlin.

There is a far more dangerous phenomenon taking place which could present a real danger not only for Putin's rule but even for the stability of Russia: dissenting movements "INSIDE" the Party in power.

As I have mentioned in the past, there are clear signs of real tensions between Putin and Medvedev.[124] One of the most knowledgeable Russian politicians, Yevgeny Primakov,[125] (ex- Russian Foreign Minister, ex- Prime Minister of Russia, ex- Speaker of the Soviet of the Union of the Supreme Soviet of the Soviet Union, and ex- chief of intelligence service. Primakov is an academician and a member of the Presidium of the Russian Academy of Sciences) basically admitted to that in the quote at the top of this page. The "tandem" is over, now Putin and Medvedev are in semi-opposition to each other.

Following the sacking of Serdyukov, it is now the turn of the Minister of Education of Russia, Livanov, to be threatened with dismissal (for using crude language in front of a not-disconnected microphone). An increasing number of commentators are now speculating that Putin might use this opportunity to sack the entire government, including Medvedev.

There has even been a far more ominous development recently. A number of rather influential members of the "United Russia" (government) party have published a "*Manifesto of Russian Political Liberalism*" and, even more amazingly, they managed to publish it on the official website of the "United Russia" party! (original text here[126]).

Now, of course, this is Russia, not Luxembourg, so the authors had to put a lot of disclaimers and caveats about what exactly they meant when they spoke of "liberalism," a concept which is now totally discredited in Russia. Here is a typical Russian joke which illustrates the typical Russian view of liberals:

A new teacher comes into the class:

- My name is Abram Davidovich. I'm a liberal. And now all stand up and introduce yourself like I did …

- My name is Masha. I'm a liberal …

---

[124] Russian Defense Minister Serdiukov sacked – my version http://thesaker.is/russian-defense-minister-serdiukov-sacked-my-version/

[125] Yevgeny Primakov https://en.wikipedia.org/wiki/Yevgeny_Primakov

[126] Манифест российского политического либерализма http://er.ru/news/96408/

- My name is Petia, I'm a liberal ...

- My name is Little Johnny. I'm a Stalinist.

- Little Johnny, why are you a Stalinist?!

- My mom is a Stalinist, my dad is a Stalinist, my friends are Stalinists and I too am a Stalinist.

- Little Johnny, and if your mother was a whore, your father—a drug addict, your friends - homos, what would you be then in that case?!

- Then I would be a liberal.

Notice that the new teacher has a typically Jewish name, which illustrates the Russian belief that Jews are the prime proponents of the kind of "liberalism" folks like Berezovsky or Khodorkovsky incarnated in the 1990s.

Still, beyond the caveats and disclaimers, there is now a semi-official faction of the "United Russia" party which openly advocates some form of liberalism even though this is in direct contradiction with Putin's declared political objective stated in his article "Building justice: A social policy for Russia"[127] which began with the words "*Russia is a welfare/social state. We have a much higher level of social guarantees than other countries with similar productivity and per capita income levels.*" In Russia the concepts of "liberal" and "social" are mutually exclusive, yet high ranking members of the party "United Russia" are suddenly publishing an article in defense of liberalism.

The three authors, which include Valery Fadeev, editor-in-chief of the magazine "*Expert*,"[128] have signed their names and added the title "coordinator of the liberal platform."

In other words, the party "United Russia" now has an official "liberal platform" coordinated by three party bigshots. If that sounds like a direct challenge to Putin and his views it's because this is exactly what this is.

---

[127] Vladimir Putin: Building justice: A social policy for Russia http://thesaker.is/building-justice-a-social-policy-for-russia/

[128] Expert (magazine) https://en.wikipedia.org/wiki/Expert_%28magazine%29

To be fair, in this new struggle, it was the Putin camp which fired the first shots. First, the "*All-Russia People's Front*" created by Putin in 2011 as a "broad popular front of like-minded political forces" which would stand "above party lines" is now gradually turning into a "Putin Party," especially since Putin himself resigned from the leadership of "United Russia" when he was re-elected as president. Then Serdyukov was sacked. At this point, it was clear that Putin was getting rid of his too pro-Western competitors and what is taking place now is a struggle inside United Russia to resist Putin's policies.

Interestingly, the party United Russia is nowhere nearly as popular as Putin himself and, and this is even more important, there are far more Russians with a negative view of the party United Russia than there are with a negative view of Putin. All this only strengthens the fears of the Medvedev camp that Putin might turn the All-Russia People's Front[129] into a new party literally overnight, and that this party would have far more popular support than United Russia and its current leader Medvedev.

Until very recently, all was officially rosy and peaceful in the "tandem," and the supposed love-fest between Putin and Medvedev was still supposed to be in full swing. Today, however, yet another direct shot was taken by Putin at the Medvedev government.

In a carefully staged leak, Putin was recorded "off camera" scolding the government for its poor performance and openly threatening to dismiss it. Here is a translation of the key words spoken by Putin in the video of that so-called leak:

> How do we work? Quality of our work - negligible. Everything is done superficially. If this is how we work we will get friggin nothing done. But if we work more aggressively and professionally, then we will get things done. So let's raise the quality of our work. **Orders need to be executed. If they are**

[129] People's Front for Russia https://en.wikipedia.org/wiki/People%27s_Front_for_Russia

> **not then either I am not working effectively, or you are all not doing your jobs, and you all need to leave! I draw your attention to the fact that at this moment in time I am leaning toward the second option.** You need to understand that and not have any illusions.

Not much of a love-fest left here, don't you think?

The "leaked" video (as if anything at all can be leaked from a Russian government meeting!) showed up on the website of the Russian tabloid *Life News*[130] which triggered a tepid protest from Putin's press secretary, who declared it unethical to air a recoding made after Putin expressly requested that the cameras be switched off.

Right. As if anybody is duped.

Bottom line: the fight between Putin's "Eurasian Sovereignists" and Medvedev's "Atlantic integrationists" is heating up and becoming semi-official.

My personal sense is that Putin will probably end up sacking the entire government—including Medvedev—and form a new one led by a very different figure. A likely first priority of this new government will reverse the pro-capitalist course of the previous governments (which even included calls for a second wave of privatizations!) and will embark upon a much more social/socialist type of economic policies (including the nationalizations of even more large "strategic" companies). Polls show that a large majority of the Russian people do want to see big changes in the social sphere, including an improvement of the living standards of the lower-middle class, a group which so far has been excluded from the benefits generated for the higher social classes by the rapid growth of the Russian economy.

Needless to say, should any of that happen, it will trigger an even bigger wave of Putin-bashing by the Western political elites and their corporate media.

---

[130] Vladimir Putin threatens to dismiss the entire cabinet of ministers http://lifenews.ru/news/112845

Speaking of the West, the entire Russian press was incredulously commenting on the outright imbecilic attitude of the Western press during Putin's recent trip to Germany and Holland. At a time when the EU was in a deep, structural, crisis, when the war in Syria was showing no signs of ending, when issues such as immigration, terrorism or the planet's ecology should be at the forefront of the discussions between world leaders, the Western press only had one single topic which seemed to interest them: homosexuals and their so-called "right" to marriage. That, and the chicks from Femen who somehow managed to elude the otherwise all-seeing eye of the German security services and showed their breasts to Putin at the Hanover exhibition. To say that the Russian press was unimpressed would be an understatement. Frankly, most commentators are openly wondering whether the West has gone completely crazy.

As for the very few pro-US politicians left in Russia, they are terribly embarrassed to be associated in any way with the USA or the EU, and they are forced to retreat into arguments such as "yes, this is disgusting, but our country also has bad problems" which, I am sure you will agree, is not much of a platform to stand on.

The internal power struggle inside the Kremlin is clearly reaching a new, more overt, phase and it will have to come to some sort of resolution rather soon as the current situation is unsustainable, in particular at a moment in time when the situation in Syria is threatening to turn into yet another regional war. One could also say that now is the perfect time to get rid of unimaginative, tepid or otherwise confused political figures like Medvedev and his allies, and to make sure that the Russian state is run by one team united by a common vision.

Russia needs a government less preoccupied by pleasing the West, and more concerned with the desires and needs of the Russian people.

April 17, 2013

A NEW COLD WAR HAS BEGUN—LET US EMBRACE IT WITH RELIEF!

Considering the relative lull which seems to be taking place in the Ukraine, this might be a good time to look at the impact which the dramatic developments in the Ukraine have had upon the internal political scene in Russia and what that, in turn, could mean for the international (dis)order. In order to do that, I would like to begin by a short summary of a thesis which I have already mentioned in the past (**for a discussion** please see here.[131] here,[132] here[133] and here[134]):

Setting the Russian part of the stage

First, some bullet-style reminders on topics previously covered on this blog:

1. There is no real Parliamentary opposition in Russia. Oh, not at all because "Putin is a dictator" or because "Russia is not a democracy," but simply because Putin has brilliantly managed to either co-opt or defang any opposition. How? By using his personal authority and charisma to promote an agenda which the other parties could not openly oppose. Formally, opposition parties do, of course, still exist, but they completely lack credibility. This might eventually change with the new Law on Political Parties.

---

[131] Russia and Islam, part three: internal Russian politics http://thesaker.is/russia-and-islam-part-three-internal-russian-politics/

[132] Russia and Islam, part six: the Kremlin http://thesaker.is/russia-and-islam-part-six-the-kremlin/

[133] The power struggle inside the Kremlin is gradually emerging into the open http://thesaker.is/the-power-struggle-inside-the-kremlin-is-gradually-emerging-into-the-open/

[134] 1993-2013: is the twenty years long "pas de deux" of Russia and the USA coming to an end? http://thesaker.is/1993-2013-is-the-twenty-years-long-pas-de-deux-of-russia-and-the-usa-coming-to-an-end/

2. The only "hard" opposition to Putin in modern Russia are the various openly pro-US individuals (Nemtov, Novodvorskaia, etc.) and their associated movements and parties. At best, they represent something in the range of 5% (max!) of the population.

3. Putin did a "judo move" on his real opponents (more about them later) by using the strongly "presidential" Constitution adopted in 1993 to basically concentrate all the power in his hands.

4. The "real" "opposition" to Putin and his project can only be found "inside" the Kremlin, the "United Russia" party and some influential figures. I refer to this real opposition as the "**Atlantic Integrationists**" because their key aim is **to integrate Russia into the Anglo-Zionist worldwide power structure.**

5. The "real" power base of Putin is in the Russian people themselves who support him personally, the *All-Russian People's Front*,[135] and in the group which I call the "**Eurasian Sovereignists**" (ES) whose primary aims is to develop a new, multipolar, world order, **to break free from the current Anglo-Zionist controlled international financial system, to re-orient as much of the former USSR as possible toward an integration with the East**, and to develop the Russian North.

If I wanted to simplify things further, I would say that in 1999 the Atlantic Integrationists and the ES jointly made the push to put Putin into power to replace Yeltsin. The AI (roughly representing the interests of big money and big business) wanted a rather grey and dull bureaucrat like Putin (or so they thought!) to assure continuity and not rock the boat too much after Yeltsin's departure. The ES (roughly representing the interests of a certain elite of the former KGB, especially, its *First Chief Directorate*[136]) and Putin himself, brilliantly used the power given to him by the 1993 Constitution (adopted under Yeltsin and the AI!) to slowly but

[135] People's Front for Russia https://en.wikipedia.org/wiki/People%27s_Front_for_Russia

[136] First Chief Directorate https://en.wikipedia.org/wiki/First_Chief_Directorate

surely change the course of Russia from a total submission to, and colonization by, the USA to a process which Putin and his supporters call "**sovereignization**" i.e. national liberation. A long tug-of-war ensued, mainly behind the scenes, but with regular visible flare-ups such as the open clash between Putin and Medvedev on Iran and Libya, or the sacking of Kudrin by Medvedev (the two had been set on a collision course by Putin, of course). As a last over-simplification I would say that Medvedev represents the Atlantic Integrationists and Putin the Eurasian Sovereignists.

Again, I have very much over-simplified all of the above to keep this short, but if any of this is new to you, please do go and read the four previous articles I mention above, *including the comments.*

Setting the Ukrainian part of the stage

Until this winter the biggest difference between Russia and the Ukraine was that in Russia Putin had basically destroyed the old oligarchy, which was US- and Israeli- controlled, and replaced it with a new one, which was either supportive of the Kremlin or neutral. Putin's message to the Russian oligarchy was simple: "you can be rich, but don't compromise the welfare of the Russian nation or try to enter the political struggle." For those who might wonder why Putin did not eliminate the Russian oligarchy as a class, I would restate here that *everything* which Putin did since 1999 until now *was always* a compromise between his ES and the still very powerful AS. Putin could simply not directly challenge this very powerful, well-connected and wealthy group, so he had to proceed slowly and with caution, step by step.

In contrast to Russia, in the Ukraine the oligarchs realized what I would call "*the Khodorkovsky Dream*"—they basically bought everything: the entire economy, the totality of the mass media, the Parliament and, of course, the presidency. For the past 22 years, the Ukraine has been basically enslaved by a number of oligarchs who made a simple deal with the West: you support us, and we support you. As a result, the Western leaders and the corporate media did "not notice" that all the Ukrainian politicians were corrupt to the bone, including Yanukovich and Tymoshenko, that—unlike in Russia, contrary to the Anglo-Zionist propaganda—political disagreements in the Ukraine were often settled by assassinations, that the Ukrainian plutocracy was literally sucking the Ukraine dry of its wealth. Eventually, even the amazingly rich Ukraine ran out of resources and wealth to pillage and the crisis became obvious for all to see.

Besides the pillaging of resources and wealth, another major "achievement" of the Ukrainian oligarchs was the total subordination of the state and its instruments to their needs: for them the state itself became an instrument of power and influence. For example, the Ukrainian security service SBU (ex-KGB) spent all its time and resources involved in the internal power struggles between the various oligarchs and their power bases and, as a result, **the SBU has not caught one single foreign spy in 22 years**! To make things worse, the SBU was basically run from the local station of the US CIA. This wholesale destruction of the state apparatus itself played a key role in the events this winter and is still a central factor in the situation on the ground: for all practical purposes, there is no "Ukrainian state."

The Eurobureaucrats and Uncle Sam come waltzing in

It is against the background of this total collapse of the Ukraine as a state and a nation that the EU decided to make its move: it offered the Ukraine an association with the EU. Uncle Sam loved the idea, especially since it included a political chapter to conduct the Ukraine's foreign and security policy in agreement with the EU. This notion of a EU-run Ukraine also appealed to the USA which basically believed that the Ukraine was the key to Russia's putative imperial ambitions.[137] Besides, the White House knew that if the Ukraine was run by the EU, and the EU

[137] The geopolitics of the Ukrainian conflict: back to basics http://thesaker.is/the-geopolitics-of-the-ukrainian-conflict-back-to-basics/

run by the USA (which it has always been), then the Ukraine would be run from the USA. So, the West began dangling a big carrot in front of the Ukrainian people: "make a "civilizational choice"[138] and join the EU and become rich, wealthy, happy and healthy; as for Russia—it has nothing to say in this, the Ukraine is a sovereign state." For millions of impoverished and exploited Ukrainians, this was a dream come true: not only would they become wealthy and happy as the Europeans supposedly are (only in propaganda reports, but never mind), they would finally get rid of the corrupted clique in power. As for the Ukrainian oligarchs—they loved it too: they would get to continue exploiting the Ukraine and its people as long as they maintained an anti-Russian stance (which was easy enough—the Ukrainian oligarchs were literally terrified of Putin and, even more so, of the notion of a "Ukrainian Putin").

The big explosion

There is a saying which says that if your head is in the sand, your butt is in the air and, indeed, reality came back to bite the Ukrainians in the butt with exquisite vengeance: the country was broke, ruined, just weeks away from a default and the only place were money could be found to prevent the final collapse was Russia. The Russians, however, put a condition on their help: no association agreement with the EU, because Russia could not have an open market with the Ukraine while the Ukraine would open its market to EU goods and services (this was no "Machiavellian ploy" by Putin, but a basic and obvious necessity understandable to anybody with an "Economics 101" course under the belt). At this point, Yanukovych suddenly made a 180 turn which sincerely baffled many Ukrainians, turned to Moscow for help and all Hell broke loose: outraged Ukrainians took to the street and wanted to know why their dream of prosperity was denied to them.

---

[138] Ukraine's "civilizational choice" – a Pyrrhic victory for Russia? http://thesaker.is/ukraines-civilizational-choice-a-pyrrhic-victory-for-russia/

The USA also panicked—if Russia was allowed to rescue the Ukraine it would inevitably control it—"you paid for it, you own it" says the US logic. So the USA threw in its biggest weapon: the "Ukrainian Taliban" aka the "Right Sector," the Freedom Party (ex Social Nationalist Party) and its assorted neo-Nazi thugs. The sudden appearance of bona fide Banderites[139] and other neo-Nazis scared the Russian-speakers so badly that while the freaks in the new revolutionary regime in Kiev were busying themselves with banning Russian as an official language or decriminalizing Nazi propaganda, Crimea seceded and most of the Ukraine entered a period of complete chaos and lawlessness.

We all know what happened since, so there is no need to cover it again, and we can now look at these events from the point of view of Russian internal politics and their likely global impact.

The view from Moscow

The first thing to say here is that *Putin's popularity with the Russian public has soared to new heights: it currently stands at 71.6%* and that even though there has been little progress on the anti-corruption front, no progress at all in the much needed reform of the judicial system, and with a Russian economy going through some difficult times. Still, regardless of many unsolved problems facing Russia—Putin is currently simply impossible to attack, as he has positioned himself as the man who saved Crimea and, possible, even Russia (more about that below).

The second dramatic effect of the events in *the Ukraine is that is has further polarized the Russia society.* I am not saying that this is fair, but the fact is that Russian politicians now have two choices. They can position themselves either as:

1) True Russian patriots who support Putin, support the reintegration of Crimea, support the Russian policy of standing up to the West or,

[139] Stepan Bandera https://en.wikipedia.org/wiki/Stepan_Bandera

2) Russian "liberals," who are russophobic, bought and paid for by the US, who are nothing more than a *5th column*[140] (Putin used this term), pro-capitalist, pro-NATO and even pro-Nazi (remember, the West does now openly support Nazis in the Ukraine!)

Needless to say, all the Russian politicians scrambled over each other to show that they firmly belonged to Group One. Even Sergei Mironov, the head of the "Just Russia" Party and last "real" opposition leader inside the Duma, took the lead in helping Crimea (which got him on the US and EU sanctions list). Those who failed to do so are now dead meat.

The most credible of them all, Alexei Navalny,[141] the **only** opposition leader **not** associated with the Yeltsin regime of the 1990s, wrote an article in the NYT entitled "*How to punish Putin*"[142] in which he went as far as to make a list of names the US should punish. In the current political mood in Russia, this is nothing short of a political suicide and Navalny's political career is now ended. He might as well emigrate to the London or the USA.

But the biggest result of the crisis in the Ukraine was to put Russia and the USA on an **open** collision course. Seen from Russia this is what the West has done:

1) organized an illegal armed insurgency;

2) overthrown a legitimate (if corrupt) government;

3) supported neo-Nazis;

4) put anti-Russian policies over democratic values;

5) put anti-Russian policies over the right of self-determination;

6) refused to recognize the will of the Russian people in the Crimea;

7) refused to recognize the will of the Russian-speakers in the Ukraine;

8) sanctioned Russia symbolically only because it could not do more;

---

[140]Fifth column https://en.wikipedia.org/wiki/Fifth_column

[141] Alexei Navalny https://en.wikipedia.org/wiki/Alexei_Navalny

[142] Alexey A. Navalny: How to Punish Putin http://www.nytimes.com/2014/03/20/opinion/how-to-punish-putin.html?_r=0

9) failed to intervene militarily only because it feared Russia's military might;

10) strong-armed the world at the UN to condemn Russia.

Against this background—what chance do the Atlantic Integrationists have to get any support for their policies? None, of course. Not only that, but the sanctions used by the West have made it possible for Putin to do that which he could not have done before: scare Russians away from Western banks (either into off-shores or into Russian banks), create a Russian *SWIFT*[143]-like inter-bank pay system, shift more efforts into exporting gas to China and the rest of Asia, reduce the Russian participation in US-run bodies such as the G8 or NATO, force Russia to deploy more powerful military capabilities on its western borders (Iskanders[144] in Kaliningrad, Tu-22M3s[145] in Crimea), reduce Russian tourism abroad and send it to Russian regions and last, but not least, further reduce the Russian use of the US dollar.[146] All this is a dream come true for economists like Glazyev,[147] or politicians like Rogozin,[148] who have lobbied hard for such measures for many years, but whose advice Putin had to ignore lest the Atlantic Integrationists strike back. Now there is even some serious talk in Russia about withdrawing from many key military treaties (strategic nuclear, conventional, nuclear verification, etc.) or even the WTO (unlikely).

It now has become extremely easy for Putin to fire anybody on the grounds that this person is not effectively implementing the president's decisions. Now everybody knows that and *every single Atlantic Integrationist now runs the risk of being summarily dismissed.* In truth, it must be

---

143 Society for Worldwide Interbank Financial Telecommunication https://en.wikipedia.org/wiki/Society_for_Worldwide_Interbank_Financial_Telecommunication

144 9K720 Iskander https://en.wikipedia.org/wiki/9K720_Iskander

145 Tupolev Tu-22M https://en.wikipedia.org/wiki/Tupolev_Tu-22M

146 Putin Flushes the US Dollar: Russia's Gold Ruble Payments System Delinked from Dollar? http://www.informationclearinghouse.info/article38112.htm

147 Sergey Glazyev https://en.wikipedia.org/wiki/Sergey_Glazyev

148 Dmitry Rogozin https://en.wikipedia.org/wiki/Dmitry_Rogozin

said that Barack Obama has helped Putin immensely and that thanks to the truly insane US policy on the Ukraine the position of the (generally pro-US) Atlantic Integrationists has been undermined for many years to come.

A joke told for the first time on Russian TV by, of all people, the spokesman of the Russian Investigative Committee (a "Russian FBI" one could say), not exactly somebody noted for his humor, has become particularly popular these days. It goes like this:

Barack Obama boycotted the Olympics and did not attend the games in Sochi—and we brilliantly won and the Olympics and Para-Olympics. Thank you, Comrade Obama!

Obama then strongly supported extremists Kiev junta—and we miraculously regained Crimea. Thank you, Comrade Obama!

Obama imposed sanctions on our oligarchs—and now their money is not in the West but in Russia. Thank you, Comrade Obama!

Now, if we may, we have more wish: we would like to win the World Soccer Cup...

Jokes aside, there is much truth to this joke—the more the USA is trying to maximize the stakes and beat back Russia, the stronger Russia becomes and the stronger Putin becomes in Russia.

As for the poor few pro-US activists left in Russia, they are truly in a desperate situation: for years they had to fight off accusations of being associated with the horrors of the Yeltsin regime in the 1990s and now, to this terrible legacy, they can add the new burden of having to fight off accusations of being "pro-Banderastan." Frankly, they all might as well all pack and leave for the West, as in Russia they are finished.

What does that mean for the rest of the world?

I have often described the covert struggle between the Atlantic Integrationists and the Eurasian Sovereignists as "internal" or "behind the scenes," which was mainly true until now. The events in the Ukraine have now changed this and the kind of issues the "Eurasian Sovereignists" have been only alluding to in more or less oblique terms are now openly discussed on Russian TV: how to coexist with a hysterically russophobic and openly pro-Nazi West, how to decrease the Russian participation in, and dependence upon, the Anglo-Zionist controlled international financial system, what kind of measures to take to make sure that the US and NATO will never have a viable military option, how to deal with the "internal 5th column" inside Russia so as to avoid a "Maidan in Moscow," how to deal with the kind of US-sponsored subversive organizations (such as NED, Carnegie, etc.) who still operate in Russia, how to make sure that any rabidly anti-Russian government in Kiev is not allowed to survive economically and socially, etc. I would call that the "Nuland stance[149]" but applied not to the EU, but to the USA. Does that mean a new Cold War?

Yes, you betcha it does!

But I would immediately stress here that this new Cold War is entirely, 100%, the creation of the USA, and that all Russia has now done is accept the new reality it is operating in. Neither Putin nor anybody else in Russia wanted this new Cold War, but it has been unilaterally imposed upon them by the US and its EU colonies for the past 20 years or more. Think of this: **the true main reason why the US and EU are not imposing any meaningful sanctions on Russia is that they have already done so in the past and that there is nothing left to impose** short of sanctions which will hurt the West as much, or even more, than Russia. The same goes for the so-called "international image of Russia." Has anybody forgotten all the idiotic canards systematically and metrically promoted by the Western corporate media about Russia **before** the crisis in the

[149] "Fuck the EU": US diplomat Victoria Nuland's phone call leaked - video http://www.theguardian.com/world/video/2014/feb/07/eu-us-diplomat-victoria-nuland-phonecall-leaked-video

Ukraine? Here is a quick reminder taken from my past article on this topic:[150]

- Berezovsky as a "persecuted" businessman
- Politkovskaya "murdered by KGB goons"
- Khodorkovsky jailed for his love of "liberty"
- Russia's "aggression" against Georgia
- The Russian "genocidal" wars against the Chechen people
- "Pussy Riot" as "prisoners of conscience"
- Litvineko "murdered by Putin"
- Russian homosexuals "persecuted" and "mistreated" by the state
- Magnitsky and the subsequent "Magnitsky law"
- Snowden as a "traitor hiding in Russia"
- The "stolen elections" to the Duma and the presidency
- The "White Revolution" on the Bolotnaya square
- The "new Sakharov"—Alexei Navalny
- Russia's "support for Assad," the (Chemical) "Butcher of Damascus"
- The Russian constant "intervention" in Ukrainian affairs
- The "complete control" of the Kremlin over the Russian media

I would say that this list is already long enough, and that nobody in Russia needs to worry that anything the Kremlin does from now on will make it worse. Short of waging war on Russia, as they did on Iraq, Afghanistan, Pakistan, Bosnia, Croatia, Kosovo, Libya or Syria—the USA has pretty "maxed out" its anti-Russian policies, and the fact is they don't amount to much.

---

[150] 1993-2013: is the twenty years long "pas de deux" of Russia and the USA coming to an end? http://thesaker.is/1993-2013-is-the-twenty-years-long-pas-de-deux-of-russia-and-the-usa-coming-to-an-end/

So what do you call a little bit of something bad, but not enough to really hurt you. Nietzsche would call it a power boost. Modern medicine calls it an immunization. The choice of words does not matter, only the actual phenomenon does: the US and EU did inflict a considerable amount of pain on Russia, but not enough to break it and, as a direct consequence of that, Russia has received a powerful "anti-Anglo-Zionist immunization" which will make it far stronger than it was.

And that is good news for everybody.

For better or for worse, Russia is objectively the undisputed leader of the world resistance to the Anglo-Zionist Empire. Yes, the Chinese economy is much bigger, but China's military is not, and China is heavily dependent on Russia for energy, weapons and high-tech. I do think that China will inevitably take the lead in the struggle against the AngloZionist Empire, but this is still not the case today: China needs more time. Iran is most definitely the oldest and first country to dare to openly defy the AngloZionists (along with Cuba and the DPRK, but those are really weak), but Iran's ambitions are primarily regional (which, by the way, is a sign of wisdom on the part of the Iranian leadership). As for Hezbollah it is, in my opinion, the **moral** leader of the worldwide Resistance, not only by its truly phenomenal military achievements, but primarily by its willingness to stand completely alone, if needed. But being a moral beacon does not mean being able to globally challenge the Empire. Russia, China, Iran and Hezbollah form what I would call, to paraphrase Dubya,[151] the "Axis of Resistance to Empire" and Russia plays the key role inside this informal but strong alliance.

The other place where "it" is happening is, of course, Latin America, but the recent vote at the UN[152] has clearly shown that Bolivia, Venezuela, Nicaragua and Cuba are the only ones who already dare openly defy

[151] Axis of evil https://en.wikipedia.org/wiki/Axis_of_evil

[152] UN General Assembly declares Crimean vote invalid http://thesaker.is/un-general-assembly-declares-crimean-vote-invalid/

the US hegemony (and the regime in Venezuela is currently fighting for its survival). Thus, while Latin America has a huge potential, but it is far from being realized, at least at this point in time.

Conclusion

A New Cold War has been in the making since the very day the previous Cold War officially ended. Thus, **we can only welcome the new reality introduced by the crisis in the Ukraine: Russia has now openly accepted the US challenge and all the pretenses of some kind of US-Russian strategic partnership are long gone**. As for the EU, its role has been so shameful and disgraceful that Russia will treat it exactly as it deserves to be: a thoroughly submissive US protectorate with no policy or opinion of its own. Now that the pretense of "partnership" is finally being dropped, we can expect a much more assertive, if not confrontational, Russia on the international scene. Of course, I don't mean that Putin will start banging his shoe at the UN like (allegedly) Khrushchev did, nor will Putin threaten to "bury"[153] the West—Putin, Lavrov and Churkin are real statesmen and diplomats, and they will remain impeccably courteous—but you can expect many more "no" votes at the UN and many "we are so sorry" on many bilateral issues.

The big beneficiary of this new Cold War will be Iran, of course, but also China. Not only will Iran and China probably get the weapons they have been wanting so badly (S-300 and Su-35 respectively), China will get some very sweet deals on Russian energy prices (the Chinese are definitely smart enough to use this new situation without overplaying their hand—they will do it "just right"). Syria and Hezbollah will get more money, more weapons and more political support. Countries aspiring to eventually become members of the "Axis of Resistance to Empire" will get more financial and political aid (Cuba, Nicaragua, Bolivia and, especially, Venezuela need all the help they can get) as will more or less

[153] We will bury you https://en.wikipedia.org/wiki/We_will_bury_you

pragmatic countries who did not fully sell out to the USA (the BRICS[154] of course, but also smaller countries such as Argentina, Iraq, Afghanistan, Pakistan and all the others who abstained at the infamous UN vote recently).[155] One should also not underestimate the assistance China can render to these countries or all the benefits these countries can reap from cooperating with the other BRICS countries.

As for the EU, it will get the gas it pays for, and it will have to deal with the economic aftershocks of its involvement in the Ukrainian crisis: it will have to keep the Ukrainian economy afloat, barely above the waterline at best, and it will have to deal with the inevitable flood of economic refugees, and it will have the dubious pleasure of having to deal with the thorny problem of "Ukrainian Taliban" now running loose in their self-styled Banderastan. The EU will have to deal with all that under the high auspices of a USA which barely hides its contempt for Europe or, as was the case with Nuland, does not even bother hiding it any more. As for Uncle Sam—what he can't get, he burns down, and that is what he will end up doing with the rump-Ukraine aka "Banderastan": turn it into a larger Kosovo—a big pain for all its neighbors, but a place the US military machine can use as it wishes. Unlike Kosovo, however, rump-Ukraine will eventually fall apart, one way or another, but the fiction of a functioning state can be maintained for a long while, especially if there is a consensus in the plutocracies which run the West that form matters much more than substance and that as long as the appearance of a unitary Ukrainian state are there, all is well. Frankly, and no offense intended to any Ukie nationalist reading this, Uncle Sam has much bigger fish to fry than to deal with the problems of a "Kosovo v2" in Central Europe.

The trends I sketched out above are, of course, just general trends. There will be some "zigs" and some "zags" in this process, but barring

---

[154] BRICS https://en.wikipedia.org/wiki/BRICS

[155] UN General Assembly declares Crimean vote invalid http://thesaker.is/un-general-assembly-declares-crimean-vote-invalid/

some major and unforeseen event, this is where, I think, we are heading. Sure, there will be a presidential election held in grotesque conditions, a completely corrupted oligarch like Poroshenko[156] will buy himself a victory, while the US-backed regime in Kiev and the "Ukrainian Taliban" settle scores and murder each other. Russia will most likely not intervene militarily, unless the situation becomes really crazy, some form of US-Russian agreement is more likely, and the eastern Ukraine will try to find a way to make some money with Russia. The Crimea will see an unprecedented economic boom which will attract a lot of attention in the rump-Ukraine, which will be desperate to get some small portion of the financial windfall enjoyed by Crimea. As they say "money talks."

As for Obama, he will go down in history as the worst US president ever. Except the next one, of course.

April 2, 2014

---

[156] Petro Poroshenko https://en.wikipedia.org/wiki/Petro_Poroshenko

1993-2013: Is the Twenty Years Long "Pas de Deux" of Russia and the USA Coming to an End?

The latest tensions between the EU and Russia over Greenpeace's stunt in the Arctic with two of its activists scaling the Prirazlomnaya oil rig only confirmed a fact which nobody really bothers denying anymore: Western political and financial elites absolutely hate Vladimir Putin and they are appalled at Russia's behavior, both inside Russia and on the international scene. This tension was quite visible on the faces of Obama and Putin at the G8 summit in Lough Erne[157] where both leaders looked absolutely disgusted with each other. Things got even worse when Putin did something quite unheard of in the Russian diplomatic history: he publicly said that Kerry was dishonest and even called him a liar.[158]

While tensions have reached some sort of climax over the Syrian issue, problems between Russia and the USA are really nothing new. A quick look at the recent past will show that the Western corporate media has been engaged in a sustained strategic campaign to identify and exploit any possible weaknesses in the Russian "political armor" and to paint Russia like a very nasty, undemocratic and authoritarian country, in other words a threat to the West. Let me mention a few episodes of this Russia-bashing campaign (in no particular order):

- Berezovsky as a "persecuted" businessman
- Politkovskaya "murdered by KGB goons"
- Khodorkovsky jailed for his love of "liberty"
- Russia's "aggression" against Georgia
- The Russian "genocidal" wars against the Chechen people
- "Pussy Riot" as "prisoners of conscience"

[157] They really "HATE" each other! http://thesaker.is/they-really-hate-each-other/

[158] Putin calls Kerry a "liar" http://thesaker.is/putin-calls-kerry-a-liar/

- Litvinenko "murdered by Putin"
- Russian homosexuals "persecuted" and "mistreated" by the state
- Magnitsky and the subsequent "Magnitsky law"
- Snowden as a "traitor hiding in Russia"
- The "stolen elections" to the Duma and the presidency
- The "White Revolution" on the Bolotnaya square
- The "new Sakharov"—Alexei Navalny
- Russia's "support for Assad," the (Chemical) "Butcher of Damascus"
- The Russian constant "intervention" in Ukrainian affairs
- The "complete control" of the Kremlin over the Russian media

This list is far from complete, but its sufficient for our purposes. Let me also immediately add here that it is not my purpose today to debunk these allegations one by one. I have done so in this blog many times the past, so anybody interested can look this up. I will just state here one very important thing which I cannot prove, but of which I am absolutely certain: 90% or more of the Russian public believe that all these issues are absolute nonsense, completely overblown non-issues. Furthermore, most Russians believe that the so-called "democratic forces" which the Western elites support in Russia (Yabloko, Parnas, Golos, etc.) are basically agents of influence for the West paid for by the CIA, MI6, Soros and exiled Jewish oligarchs. What is certain is that besides these small liberal and democratic groups, nobody in Russia takes these accusations seriously. Most people see them exactly for what they are: a smear campaign.

In many ways, this is rather reminiscent of how things stood during the Cold War where the West used its immense propaganda resources to demonize the Soviet Union and to support anti-Soviet forces worldwide, including inside the USSR itself. I would argue that these efforts were, by and large, very successful and that by 1990s the vast majority of Soviets, including Russians, were rather disgusted with their leaders. So why the big difference today?

To answer that question, we need to look back at the processes which took place in Russia in the last 20 years or so because only a look at what happened during these two decades will allows us to get to the root of the current problem(s) between the USA and Russia.

When did the Soviet Union truly disappear?

The official date of the end of the Soviet Union is 26 December 1991, the day of the adoption by the Supreme Soviet of the Soviet Union of the Declaration № 142-H which officially recognized dissolution of the Soviet Union as a state and subject of international law. But that is a very superficial, formal, view of things. One could argue that even though the Soviet Union had shrunk to the size of the Russian Federation it still survived within these smaller borders. After all, the laws did not change overnight, neither did most of the bureaucracy, and even though the Communist Party itself had been banned following the August 1991 coup, the rest of the state apparatus still continued to exist.

For Yeltsin and his supporters this reality created a very difficult situation. Having banned the CPSU and dismantled the KGB, Yeltsin's liberals still faced a formidable adversary: the Supreme Soviet of the Russian Federation, the Parliament of the Russian Soviet Federative Socialist Republic, elected by the Congress of People's Deputies of the Russian Federation. Nobody had abolished this "very" Soviet institution which rapidly became the center of almost all of the anti-Yeltsin and pro-Soviet forces in the country. I cannot go in all the details of this legal nightmare, suffice to say that the Supreme Soviet presented itself as the "Russian Parliament" (which is not quite true) and that its members engaged in a systematic campaign to prevent Yeltsin to implement his "reforms" (in hindsight, one could say that they tried to prevent Yeltsin from ruining the country). One could say that the "new Russia" and the "old USSR" were fighting each other for the future of the country. Predictably, the

Supreme Soviet wanted a parliamentary democracy while Yeltsin and his liberals wanted a presidential democracy. The two sides presented what appeared to be a stark contrast to most Russians:

1) **The Russian President Yeltsin**: officially he represented Russia, as opposed to the Soviet Union; he presented himself as an anti-Communist and as a democrat (never mind that he himself had been a high ranking member of the CPSU and even a non-voting member to the Politburo!). Yeltsin was also clearly the darling of the West and he promised to integrate Russia into the western world.

2) **The Supreme Soviet**: headed by Ruslan Khasbulatov[159] with the support of the Vice President of Russia, Alexander Rutskoi,[160] the Supreme Soviet became the rallying point of all those who believed that the Soviet Union had been dissolved illegally (which is true), and against the will of the majority of its people (which is also true). Most, though not all, the supporters of the Supreme Soviet were if not outright Communists, then at least socialists and anti-capitalists. A good part of the rather disorganized Russian nationalist movement also supported the Supreme Soviet.

We all know what eventually happened: Yeltsin crushed the opposition in a huge bloodbath, far worse than what was reported in the Western (or even Russian) media. I write that with a high degree of confidence because I have personally received this information from a very good source: it so happens that I was in Moscow during those tragic days and that and I was in constant contact with a Colonel of a rather secretive special forces unit of the KGB called "Vympel" (more about that below) who told me that the internal KGB estimate of the number of people killed in the Moscow Oblast was close to 5,000 people. I can also personally attest that the combats lasted for far longer than the official narrative clams: I witnessed a very sustained machine gun battle right under my

[159] Ruslan Khasbulatov https://en.wikipedia.org/wiki/Ruslan_Khasbulatov

[160] Alexander Rutskoy https://en.wikipedia.org/wiki/Alexander_Rutskoy

windows *a full 5 days after the Supreme Soviet had surrendered.* I want to stress this here because I think that this illustrates an often overlooked reality: the so-called "constitutional crisis of 1993" was really a mini civil war for the fate of the Soviet Union and only by the end of this crisis did the Soviet Union really truly disappear.

In the days preceding the tank assault against the Supreme Soviet I had the opportunity to spend a lot of time with supporters of the president and the Supreme Soviet. I took the time to engage them in long conversations to try to find out for myself what each side stood for and whether I should side with either party. The conclusion I came to was a rather sad one: *both* sides were primarily composed of ex- (or not ex-) Communists, *both* sides claimed that they were defending democracy, and *both* sides accused each other of being Fascists. In reality both sides were in reality very much alike. I think that I was not the only person to feel that way in these days and I suspect that most of the people of Russia deeply felt this and ended up being really disgusted with all of the politicians involved.

I would like to share one more personal anecdote here: these tragic days were personally quite amazing for me. Here I was, a young man born in a family of rabidly anti-Soviet Russian émigrés, who had spent many years fighting the Soviet system and, especially, the KGB. And yet, ironically, I ended up spending most of my time in the company of a Colonel of a special forces unit of the KGB (how we met is a long story for another post). Even more amazing for me was the fact that for all our differences, we had the exact same reaction to the events taking place before our eyes. We both decided that we could not side with either party engaged in this conflict—both sides were equally repugnant to us. I was in his apartment when he received a call from the KGB headquarters ordering him to show up at a location downtown to prepare a special forces assault against the "White House" (that was the street nickname of the Russian Parliament building)—he refused to obey, told his bosses to get lost, and hung up. He was not alone in that decision: just as in 1991, neither the Russian paratroopers, nor the special forces agreed to shoot at their own people (others, supposedly "democratic" forces showed no such scruples). Instead of obeying his bosses orders, my new friend took the time to give me some very valuable advice about how to safely get a relative of mine out of Moscow without getting shot or detained (being a native Russian speaker with a foreign passport was not a very safe thing in these days).

I wanted to retell this story here because it shows something very important: by 1993 a vast majority of Russians, even exiled émigrés and KGB Special Forces Colonels, were deeply disgusted and fed up with **both** parties to this crisis. In a way, one could say that most Russians were waiting for a THIRD force to appear on the political scene.

From 1993 to 1999—a democratic nightmare

After the crushing of the opposition by Yeltsin's thugs, the gates of Hades truly opened for Russia: the entire country was taken over by various mafias and the vast natural resources were pillaged by (mostly Jewish) oligarchs. The so-called "privatization" of the Russian economy created both a new class of multi-millionaires and many tens of millions of very poor people who could barely survive. A huge crime wave overtook every city, the entire infrastructure of the country collapsed and many regions of Russia began actively planning their secession from the Russian Federation. Chechnya was allowed to secede from the Russian Federation after a grotesque and bloody war, which saw the Russian military backstabbed by the Kremlin. And throughout these truly hellish years, the Western elites gave their fullest support to Yeltsin and his oligarchs. The only exception to this love-fest was the political, economic and military support given by the Anglosphere to the Chechen insurgency. Eventually, what had to happen did happen: the country declared bankruptcy in 1998 by devaluing the ruble and defaulting on its debt. Though we will never know for sure, I firmly believe that by 1999 Russia was only a few steps away from completely disappearing as a country and as a nation.

The legacy left by the liberals/democrats

Having crushed the opposition in 1993, the Russian liberals acquired the complete freedom to write a new constitution which would perfectly suit their purpose, and with their typical short-sightedness they adopted a new Constitution which gave immense powers to the president and really very little to the new Parliament, the Russian Duma. They even went as far as abolishing the post of Vice President (they did not want another Rutskoi to sabotage their plans).

And yet, in the 1996 presidential elections the liberals almost lost it all. To their horror, the Communist Candidate Gennadi Zuiganov won most of the votes in the first round, which forced the liberals to do two things: first, of course, they falsified the officials results and, second, they passed an alliance with a rather popular Army General, Alexander Lebed. These two moves made it possible for them to declare that they had won the second round (even though in reality Ziuganov won). Here again, the West fully supported Yeltsin. Well, why not? Having given Yeltsin full support for his bloody crackdown on the supporters of the Supreme Soviet, why not also support Yeltsin in a stolen election, right? In for a dime, in for a dollar.

Yeltsin himself, however spent most of his time drinking himself to death and it soon became rather clear that he would not last very long. Panic seized the liberal camp which ended up committing a huge mistake: they allowed a little-known and rather unimpressive bureaucrat from Saint Petersburg to replace Yeltsin as Acting President: Vladimir Putin.

Putin was a quiet, low-key, competent bureaucrat, whose main quality appeared to be his lack of a strong personality, or so did the liberals think. And, boy, was that one big miscalculation!

As soon as he was appointed, Putin acted with lightning speed. He immediately surprised everybody by becoming personally involved in the Second Chechen War. Unlike his predecessor, Putin gave all the freedom to the military commanders to wage this war as they wanted. The Putin surprised everybody again when he made a truly historic deal with Ahmad Hadji Kadyrov to bring peace to Chechnya, even though the latter had been a leader of the insurgency during the first Chechen war.

Putin's popularity soared and he immediately used that to his advantage.

In an amazing twist of history, Putin used the Constitution developed and adopted by the Russian liberals to implement a very rapid series of crucial reforms and to eliminate the power basis of the liberals: the Jewish oligarchs (Berezovksy, Khorodkovsky, Fridman, Gusinsky, etc.). He also passed many laws destined to "strengthen the vertical power" which gave the Federal Center direct control over the local administrations. This, in turn, not only crushed many of the local mafias who had managed to corrupt and infiltrate the local authorities, it also rapidly stopped all the various secessionist movements inside Russia. Finally, he used what is called the "administrative resource" to create his United Russia party and to give it the full support from the state. The irony here is that *Putin would never have never succeeded in these efforts had the Russian liberals not created a hyper-Presidential Constitution which gave Putin the means to achieve his goals.* To paraphrase Lenin, I would say that the Russian liberals gave Putin the rope to hang them.

The West, of course, rapidly understood what was going on, but it was too late: the liberals had lost power forever (God willing!) and the country was clearly being taken over by a third, previously unseen, force.

Who really put Putin into power?

That is the $10,000 question. Formally, the official answer is straightforward: Yeltsin's entourage. Still, it is rather obvious that some other unidentified group of people managed to brilliantly con the liberals into letting the fox inside their hen house.

Now remember that the pro-Soviet forces were comprehensively defeated in 1993. So this was not the result of some nostalgic revanchists who wanted to resurrect the old Soviet Union. So no need to look to the this camp who, in fact, has mostly remained opposed to Putin to this day. So who else then?

It was an alliance of two forces, really: elements of the ex "PGU KGB SSSR" and a number of key industrial and financial leaders. Let's take then one by one:

The first force was the PGU KGB SSSR: the foreign intelligence branch of the Soviet KGB. It's official name was First Chief Directorate of the Committee of State Security of the USSR. This would be the rough equivalent of the British MI6. This was beyond any doubt the most elite part of the KGB, and also its most autonomous one (it even had its own headquarters in the south of Moscow). Though the PGU dealt with a number of issues, it was also very closely linked to, and interested by, the world of big business, in the USSR and abroad. Since the PGU had nothing to do with the KGB's most ugly activities such as the persecution of dissidents (that was the role of the 5th Directorate) and since it has little to do with internal security (that was the prerogative of the 2nd Chief Directorate), it was not high on the list of institutions to reform simply because it was not hated as much as the more visible part of the KGB.

The second force which put Putin in power was constituted by young people coming from key ministries of the former Soviet Union which dealt with industrial and financial issues and which hated Yeltsin's Jewish oligarchs. Unlike Yeltsin's oligarchs, these young leaders did not want to simply pillage all the resources of Russia and later retire in the US or Israel, but they did want Russia to become a powerful market economy integrated into the international financial system.

Later, the first group would turn into what I call the "Eurasian Sovereignists"[161] while the second one would become what I call "Atlantic Integrationists."[162] We could think of them as the "Putin people" and the "Medvedev people."

Lastly, it should not be overlooked that there is, of course, a third force which threw its full support behind this Putin-Medvedev tandem—the Russian people themselves who have, so far, always voted to keep them in power.

An absolutely brilliant formula but which has now outlived its shelf life

There is no doubt in my mind that the idea to create this "tandem" has been nothing short of brilliant: Putin would cater to the nationalists, Medvedev to the more liberally oriented folk. Putin would get the support of the "power ministries" (defense, security, intelligence) while Medvedev would get the support of the business community. Putin could scare the local authorities into compliance with the orders from the federal center, while Medvedev would make the US and EU feel good at Davos. Or, let's put it this way: who would be *against* the Putin & Medvedev duo? Diehard supporters of the Soviet Union, rabid xenophobic nationalists, rabid pro-US liberals and Jewish exiles. That's pretty much it, and that isn't much.

By the way—what do we see in today's opposition? A Communist Party catering to those nostalgic of the Soviet era, a Liberal-Democratic Party catering to the nationalists, and a pretty small "Just Russia" party whose sole purpose appear to be to take votes off the other two and coopt some of the rabid liberals. In other words, Medvedev and Putin have basically eliminated any type of credible opposition.

---

[161] Russia and Islam, part six: the Kremlin http://thesaker.is/russia-and-islam-part-six-the-kremlin/

[162] The power struggle inside the Kremlin is gradually emerging into the open http://thesaker.is/the-power-struggle-inside-the-kremlin-is-gradually-emerging-into-the-open/

As I have mentioned in past posts, there are now clear signs of serious tensions between the "Eurasian Sovereignists" and the "Atlantic Integrationists" to the point that Putin has now created his own movement (the "All-Russia People's Front,"[163] created by Putin in 2011; again, for background on that please see here[164] and here).[165]

Having looked at the complex processes which ended up creating the Putin presidency in Russia, we need to look at what took place in the USA during the same time period.

In the meantime—the US gets neoconned

Unlike the Soviet Union which basically disappeared from the map of our planet, the USA "won" the Cold War (this is not factually quite true, but this is how many Americans see it) and having become the last and only real superpower the US immediately embarked on a series of external wars to establish its "full-spectrum dominance" over the planet, especially after the events of 9/11 which deeply transformed the nature of the US society itself.

Still, the post 9/11 society has its roots in a far more distant past: the Reagan years.

During the Presidency of Ronald Reagan a group which later become known as the "neocons" made a strategic decision to take over the Republican Party, its affiliated institutions and think tanks. While in the past ex-Trotskyites had been more inclined to support the putatively more left-leaning Democratic Party, the "new and improved GOP" under Reagan offered the neocons some extremely attractive features:

1) Money: Reagan was an unconditional supporter of big business and the corporate world. His mantra "government is the problem" fitted per-

---

163 People's Front for Russia https://en.wikipedia.org/wiki/People%27s_Front_for_Russia

164 Russia and Islam, part six: the Kremlin http://thesaker.is/russia-and-islam-part-six-the-kremlin/

165 The power struggle inside the Kremlin is gradually emerging into the open http://thesaker.is/the-power-struggle-inside-the-kremlin-is-gradually-emerging-into-the-open/

fectly with the historical closeness of the neocons with the robber barons, mafia bosses and big bankers. For them, de-regulation meant freedom of action, something which was bound to make speculators and Wall Street wise guys immensely rich.

2) Violence: Reagan also firmly stood behind the US military-industrial complex and a policy of intervention in any country on the planet. That fascination with brute force and, let be honest here, terrorism also fitted the Trotskyite-neocon mind-set perfectly.

3) Illegality: Reagan did not care at all about the law, be it international law or domestic law. Sure, as long as the law happens to be advantageous to US or GOP interests, it was upheld with great ceremony. But if it didn't, the Reaganites would break it with no compunction whatsoever.

4) Arrogance: under Reagan, patriotism and feel-good imperial hubris reached a new height. More than ever before, the US saw itself as not only the "Leader of the Free World" protecting the planet against the "Evil Empire," but also as unique and superior to the rest of mankind (like in the Ford commercial of the 1980s: "*we're number one, second to none!*")

5) Systematic deception: under Reagan lying turned from an occasional if regular tactics used in politics to the key form of public communication: Reagan, and his administration, could say one thing and then deny it in the same breath. They could make promises which were clearly impossible to keep (Star Wars anybody?). They could solemnly take an oath and then break it (Iran-Contra). And, if confronted by proof of these lies, all Reagan had to do is to say: "well, no, I don't remember."

6) Messianism: not only did Reagan get a huge support basis among the various crazy religious denominations in the USA (including all of the Bible Belt), Reagan also promoted a weird kind of secular Messianism featuring a toxic mix of xenophobia bordering on racism with a narcissistic fascination with anything patriotic, no matter how stupid, bordering on self-worship.

So let's add it all up:

Money + violence + illegality + arrogance + deception + Messianism equals what?

Does that not all look very, very familiar? Is that not a perfect description of Zionism and Israel?

No wonder the neocons flocked in greater and greater number to this new GOP! Reagan's GOP was the perfect Petri dish for the Zionist bacteria to grow, and grow it really did. A lot.

I think that it would be reasonable to say that the USA underwent a two-decades-long process of "Zionisation" which culminated in the grand 9/11 false flag operation in which the PNAC-types basically used their access to the centers of power in the USA, Israel and the Kingdom of Saudi Arabia (KSA) to conjure up a new enemy—"Islamo-fascist terror"—which would not only justify a planetary war against "terrorism" (the GWOT), but also an unconditional support for Israel.

There were also losers in this evolution, primarily what I call the "old Anglo camp"[166] which basically lost control of most of its domestic political power and all of its foreign policy power: for the first time *a new course in foreign policy* [167] gradually began to take shape under the leadership of a group of people which would in time be identified as "Israel-Firsters." For a short time the old Anglos seemed to have retaken the reins of power—under George Bush Senior—only to immediately loose it again with the election of Bill Clinton. But the apogee of Ziocon power was only reached under the Presidency of George W. Bush who basically presided over a massive purge of Anglos from key positions in government (especially the Pentagon and the CIA). Predictably, having the folks

---

[166] Daddy - what's a "neocon"“?! Ethnic mafia wars is the USA http://vineyardsaker.blogspot.com/2007/05/daddy-whats-neocon-ethnic-mafia-wars-is.html

[167] How a medieval concept of ethnicity makes NATO commit yet another a dangerous blunder http://thesaker.is/how-a-medieval-concept-of-ethnicity-makes-nato-commit-yet-another-a-dangerous-blunder/

which Bush Senior called "the crazies in the basement"[168] actually in power rapidly brought the USA to the edge of a global collapse: externally the massive worldwide sympathy for the USA after 9/11 turned into a tsunami of loathing and resentment, while internally the country was faced with a massive banking crisis which almost resulted the imposition of martial law[169] over the USA.

In comes Barack Obama—"change we can believe in!"

The election of Barack Obama to the White House truly was a momentous historical event. Not only because a majority White population had elected a Black man to the highest office in the country (this was really mainly an expression of despair and of a deep yearning for change), but because after one of the most effective PR campaigns in history, the vast majority of Americans and many, if not most, people abroad, really, truly believed that Obama would make some deep, meaningful changes. The disillusion with Obama was as great as the hopes millions had in him. I personally feel that history will remember Obama not only as one of the worst Presidents in history, but also, and that is more important, as the last chance for the "system" to reform itself. That chance was missed. And while some, in utter disgust, described Obama as "Bush light," I think that his presidency can be better described as "more of the same, only worse."

Having said that, there is something which, to my absolute amazement, Obama's election did achieve: the removal of (most, but not all) neocons from (most, but not all) key positions of power and a re-orientation of (most, but not all) of US foreign policy in a more traditional "USA first" line, usually supported by the "old Anglo" interests. Sure, the neocons are still firmly in control of Congress and the US cor-

---

[168] Jim Silva: Prof. Strauss and the neocon takeover http://www.informationclearinghouse.info/article11811.htm

[169] Bailout push included threat of martial law the http://www.wnd.com/2008/10/77860/

porate media, but the Executive Branch is, at least for the time being, back under Anglo control (this is, of course, a generalization: Dick Cheney was neither Jewish nor Zionist, while Henry Kissinger can hardly be described as an "Anglo"). And even though Bibi Netanyahu got more standing ovations in Congress (29) than any US president, the attack on Iran he wanted so badly did not happen. Instead, Hillary and Petraeus got kicked out, and Chuck Hagel and John Kerry got in. That is hardly "change we can believe in," but at least this shows that the Likud is not controlling the White House any more.

Of course, this is far from over. If anything the current game of chicken played between the White House and Congress over the budget with its inherent risk of a US default shows that this conflict is far from settled.

The current real power matrix in the USA and Russia

We have shown that there two unofficial parties in Russia which are locked in a deadly conflict for power, the "Eurasian Sovereignists" and "Atlantic Integrationists." There are also two unofficial parties in the USA who are also locked in a deadly conflict for power: the neocons and the "old Anglos imperialists." I would argue that, at least for the time being, the "Eurasian Sovereignists" and the "old Anglos" have prevailed over their internal competitor, but that the Russian "Eurasian Sovereignists" are in a far stronger position that the American "old Anglos." There are two main reasons for that:

1) Russia has already had its economic collapse and default and

2) a majority of Russians fully support President Putin and his "Eurasian Sovereignist" policies.

In contrast, the USA is on the brink of an economic collapse and the 1% clique which is running the USA is absolutely hated and despised by most Americans.

After the immense and, really, heart-breaking disillusionment with Obama, more and more Americans are becoming convinced that changing the puppet in the White House is meaningless and that what the US really needs is *regime* change.

The USSR and the USA—back to the future?

It is quite amazing for those who remember the Soviet Union of the late 1980 how much the US under Obama has become similar to the USSR under Brezhnev: internally it is characterized by a general sense of disgust and alienation of the people triggered by the undeniable stagnation of a system rotten to its very core. A bloated military and police state with uniforms everywhere, while more and more people live in abject poverty. A public propaganda machine which, like in Orwell's 1984, constantly boasts of successes everywhere while everybody knows that these are all lies. Externally, the US is hopelessly overstretched and either hated and mocked abroad. Just as in the Soviet days, the US leaders are clearly afraid of their own people so they protect themselves by an immense and costly global network of spies and propagandists who are terrified of dissent and who see the main enemy in their own people.

Add to that a political system which far from co-opting the best of its citizens deeply alienates them while promoting the most immoral and corrupt ones into the positions of power. A booming prison-industrial complex and a military-industrial complex which the country simply cannot afford maintaining. A crumbling public infrastructure combined with a totally dysfunctional health care system in which only the wealthy and well-connected can get good treatment. And above it all, a terminally sclerotic public discourse, full of ideological clichés an completely disconnected from reality.

I will never forget the words of a Pakistani Ambassador to the UN Conference on Disarmament in Geneva in 1992 who, addressing an assembly of smug Western diplomats, said the following words: "*you seem to believe that you won the Cold War, but did you ever consider the possibility that what has really happened is that the internal contradictions of communism caught up with communism before the internal contradictions of capitalism could catch up with capitalism*?!" Needless to say, these prophetic words were greeted by a stunned silence and soon forgotten. But the man was, I believe, absolutely right: capitalism has now reached a crisis as deep as the one affecting the Soviet Union in the late 1980s and there is zero chance to reform or otherwise change it. Regime change is the only possible outcome.

The historical roots of the russophobia of the American elites

Having said all of the above, it's actually pretty simple to understand why Russia in general, and Putin in particular, elicits such a deep hatred from the Western plutocracy: having convinced themselves that they won the Cold War they are now facing the double disappointment of a rapidly recovering Russia, and a Western economic and political decline turning into what seems to be a slow and painful agony.

In their bitterness and spite, Western leaders overlook the fact that Russia has nothing to do with the West's current problems. Quite to the contrary, in fact: the main impact the collapse of the Soviet Union on the US-run international economic system was to prolong its existence by creating a new demand for US dollars in Eastern Europe and Russia (some economists—such as Nikolai Starikov— estimate that the collapse of the USSR gave an extra 10+ years of life to the US dollar).

In the past, Russia has been the historical arch-enemy of the British Empire. As for Jews—they have always harbored many grievances toward pre-revolutionary Tsarist Russia. The Revolution of 1917 brought a great deal of hope for many East-European Jews, but it was short-lived as Stalin defeated Trotsky and the Communist Party was purged from many of its Jewish members. Over and over again Russia has played a tragic role in the history of the Ashkenazi Jews and this, of course, has left a deep mark on the worldview of the neocons who are all deeply russophobic, even today. Somebody might object that many Jews are deeply grateful for the Soviet Army's liberation of Jews from the Nazi concentration camps or for the fact that the Soviet Union was the first country to recognize Israel. But in both cases, the country which is credited with these actions is the *Soviet Union* and not Russia which most Ashkenazi Jews still typically associate anti-Jewish policies and values.

It is thus not surprising that both the Anglo and the Jewish elites in the US would harbor an almost instinctive dislike for, and fear of, Russia, especially one perceived as resurgent or anti-American. And the fact is that they are not wrong in this perception: Russia is most definitely resurgent, and the vast majority of the Russian public opinion is vehemently anti-American, at least if by "America" we refer to the civilizational model or economic system.

Anti-American sentiment in Russia

Feelings about the USA underwent a dramatic change since the fall of the Soviet Union. In the 1980 the USA was not only rather popular, it was also deeply in fashion: Russian youth created many rock groups (some of them became immensely popular and still are popular today, such as the group DDT[170] from Saint Petersburg), American fashion and fast foods were the dream of every Russian teenager, while most intellectuals sincerely saw the US as "leader of the free world." Of course, the state propaganda of the USSR always wanted to present the USA as an aggressive imperialistic country, but that effort failed: most of the people were actually quite fond of the US. One of the most popular pop group of the 1990s (Nautilus Pompilius[171]) had a song with the following lyrics:

Good bye America, oh
Where I have never ever been
Farewell forever!
Take your banjo
And play for my departure

---

[170] DDT (band) https://en.wikipedia.org/wiki/DDT_%28band%29

[171] Nautilus Pompilius (band) https://en.wikipedia.org/wiki/Nautilus_Pompilius_%28band%29

la-la-la-la-la-la, la-la-la-la-la-la
Your worn out blue jeans
Became too tight for me
We've been taught for too long
To be in love with your forbidden fruits.

While there were exceptions to this rule, I would say that by the beginning of the 1990 most of the Russian people, especially the youth, had swallowed the US propaganda line hook and sinker—Russia was hopelessly pro-American.

The catastrophic collapse of the Soviet Union in 1991, and the West's total and unconditional backing for Yeltsin and his oligarchs changed that. Instead of trying to help Russia, the USA and the West used every single opportunity to weaken Russia externally (by taking all of Eastern Europe into NATO even though they had promised never to do so). Internally, they West supported the Jewish oligarchs who were literally sucking out wealth out of Russia live vampires suck blood, while supporting every imaginable form of separatism. By the end of the 1990s the words "democrat" and "liberal" became offensive curse words. This joke of the late 1990s about "little Johnny" the Stalinist recounted at page 172 is a good example of these feelings. Notice the association between being a liberal and Jews (Abram Davidovich is a typical Jewish name). Notice also the inclusion of the category "homosexual" in between a whore and drug addicts and remember that when evaluating the typical Russian reaction to the anti-Russian campaign waged by Western homosexual organizations.

The political effect of these feelings is rather obvious: in the last elections not a single pro-Western political party has even managed to get enough votes to make it into the Parliament. And no—this is not because Putin has outlawed them (as some propagandists in the West like to imagine). There are currently 57 political parties in Russia, and quite a few of them are pro-Western. And yet it is an undeniable fact that the percentage of Russians which are favorably inclined toward the USA and NATO/EU is roughly in the 5% range. I can also put it this way: every single political party represented in the Duma is deeply anti-American, even the very moderate "Just Russia."

Anti-Russian feelings in the USA?

Considering the never ending barrage of anti-Russian propaganda in the Western corporate media one could wonder how strong anti-Russian feelings are in the West. This is really hard to measure objectively, but as somebody born in Western Europe and who has lived a total of 15 years in the USA I would say that anti-Russian sentiment in the West is very rare, almost non-existent. In the USA there have always been strong anti-Communist feelings—there still are today—but somehow most Americans do make the difference between a political ideology that they don't really understand, but that they dislike anyway, and the people which in the past used to be associated with it.

US "politicians," of course, mostly hate Russia, but most Americans seem to harbor very few bad feelings and little apprehension about Russia or the Russian people. I explain that by a combination of factors.

First, since more and more people in the West realize that they are not living in a democracy, but in a plutocracy of the 1%, they tend to take the official propaganda line with more than a grain of salt (which, by the way, is exactly what was happening to most Soviet people in the 1980s). Furthermore, more and more people in the West who oppose the plutocratic imperial order which impoverishes and disenfranchises them into corporate serfs are quite sympathetic to Russia and Putin for "standing up to the bastards in Washington." But even more fundamentally, there is the fact that in a bizarre twist of history Russia today stands for the values of the West of yesterday: international law, pluralism, freedom of speech, social rights, anti-imperialism, opposition to intervention inside sovereign states, rejection of wars as a means to settle disputes, and so on.

In the case of the war in Syria, Russia's absolutely consistent stance in defense of international law has impressed many people in the USA and Europe and one can hear more and more praise for Putin from people who in the past has deep suspicions about him.

Russia, of course, is hardly a utopia or some kind of perfect society, far from it, but it has taken the fundamental decision to become a "normal" country, as opposed to being a global empire, and any normal country will agree to uphold the principles of the "West of yesterday," not only Russia. In fact, Russia is very un-exceptional in its pragmatic realization that to uphold these principles is not a matter of naive idealism, but a sound realistic policy goal. People in the West are told by their rulers and the corporate media that Putin in an evil ex-KGB dictator who is a danger for the US and its allies, but as soon as these people actually read or listen to what Putin actually says they find themselves in a great deal of agreement with him.

In another funny twist of history, while the Soviet population used to turn to the BBC, Voice of America or Radio Liberty for news and information, more and more people in the West are turning to Russia Today, Press TV, or TeleSUR to get their information. Hence the panicked reaction of Walter Isaacson, Chairman of the Broadcasting Board of Governors, the US outfit overseeing US media directed at foreign audiences, who declared that "*we can't allow ourselves to be out-communicated by our enemies. You've got Russia Today, Iran's Press TV, Venezuela's TeleSUR, and of course, China is launching an international broadcasting 24-hour news channel with correspondents around the world.*" Folks like Isaacson know that they are slowly but surely losing the informational battle for the control of the minds of the general public.

And now, with the entire Snowden affair, Russia is becoming the safe harbor for those political activists who are fleeing Uncle Sam's wrath. A quick search on the Internet will show you that more and more people are referring to Putin as the "leader of the Free World" while other are collecting signatures to have Obama give his Nobel Prize to Putin. Truly, for those like myself who have actually fought against the Soviet system it is absolutely amazing to see the 180 degree turn the world has taken since the 1980s.

Western elites—still stuck in the Cold War

If the world has radically changed in the last 20 years, the Western elites did not. Faced with a very frustrating reality they are desperately trying to re-fight the Cold War with the hope of re-winning it again. Hence the never ending cycle of Russia-bashing campaigns I mentioned at the beginning of this post. They try to re-brand Russia as the new Soviet Union, with oppressed minorities, jailed or murdered dissidents, little or no freedom of speech, a monolithic state controlled media and an all-seeing security apparatus overseeing it all. The problem, of course, is that they are 20 years late and that these accusations don't stick very well with the Western public opinion and get exactly "zero" traction inside Russia. In fact, every attempt at interfering inside Russian political affairs has been so inept and clumsy that it backfired every single time. From the absolutely futile attempts of the West to organize a color-coded revolution in the streets of Moscow to the totally counter-productive attempts to create some kind of crisis around homosexual human rights in Russia—every step taken by the Western propaganda machine has only strengthened Vladimir Putin and his the "Eurasian Sovereignists" at the expense of the "Atlantic Integrationist" faction inside the Kremlin.

There was a deep and poignant symbolism in the latest meeting of the 21 APEC[172] countries in Bali. Obama had to cancel his trip because of the US budget crisis while Putin was treated to a musically horrible but politically deeply significant rendition of "Happy birthday to you!" by a spontaneous choir composed of the leaders of the Pacific Rim countries. I can just imagine the rage of the White House when they saw "their" Pacific allies serenading Putin for his birthday!

---

[172] Asia-Pacific Economic Cooperation https://en.wikipedia.org/wiki/Asia-Pacific_Economic_Cooperation

Conclusion: "we are everywhere"

In one of his most beautiful songs, David Rovics sings the following words which I want to quite in full, as each line fully applies to the current situation:

When I say the hungry should have food
I speak for many
When I say no one should have seven homes
While some don't have any
Though I may find myself stranded in some strange place
With naught but a vapid stare
I remember the world and I know
We are everywhere
When I say the time for the rich, it will come
Let me count the ways
Victories or hints of the future
Havana, Caracas, Chiapas, Buenos Aires
How many people are wanting and waiting
And fighting for their share
They hide in their ivory towers
But we are everywhere
Religions and prisons and races
Borders and nations
FBI agents and congressmen
And corporate radio stations
They try to keep us apart, but we find each other
And the rulers are always aware
That they're a tiny minority
And we are everywhere
With every bomb that they drop, every home they destroy
Every land they invade
Comes a new generation from under the rubble

Saying "we are not afraid"
They will pretend we are few
But with each child that a billion mothers bear
Comes the next demonstration
That we are everywhere.

(you can listen to the song here[173])

These words are a beautiful expression for the hope which should inspire all those who are now opposing the US-Zionist Empire: we are everywhere, literally. On one side we have the 1%, the Anglo imperialists and the Ziocons, while on the other we have the rest of the planet, including potentially 99% of the American people. If it is true that at this moment in time Putin and his Eurasian Sovereignists are the most powerful and best organized faction of the worldwide resistance to the Empire, they are far from being central, or even less so, crucial, to it. Yes, Russia can, and will, play its role, but only as a *normal country* among many other normal countries, some small and economically weak like Ecuador, other huge and powerful like China. But even small Ecuador was "big enough" to grant refuge to Julian Assange while China seems to have asked Snowden to please leave. So Ecuador is not that small after all?

It would be naive to hope that this "de-imperialization" process of the USA could happen without violence. The French and British Empires collapsed against the bloody backdrop of World War II, while did the Nazi and Japanese Empires were crushed under a carpet of bombs. The Soviet Empire collapsed with comparatively fewer victims, and most of the violence which did take place during that process happened on the Soviet periphery. In Russia itself, the number of death of the mini civil war of 1993 was counted in the thousands and not in the millions. And by God's great mercy, not a single nuclear weapon was detonated anywhere.

---

[173] We Are Everywhere - David Rovics https://www.youtube.com/watch?v=n8j8BmgeYLA

So what will likely happen when the US-Ziocon Empire finally collapses under its own weight? Nobody can tell for sure, but we can at least hope that just as no major force appeared to rescue the Soviet Empire in 1991-1993, no major force will attempt to save the US Empire either. As David Rovics puts it so well, the big weakness of the 1% which rule the US-Ziocon Empire is that "*they are a tiny minority and we are everywhere.*"

In the past 20 years the US and Russia have followed diametrically opposed courses and their roles appears to have been reversed. That "pas de deux" is coming to some kind of end now. Objective circumstances have now again placed these two countries in opposition to each other, but this is solely due to the nature of the regime in Washington DC. Russian leaders could repeat the words of the English rapper Lowkey and declare "I'm *not anti-America, America is anti-me*!" and they could potentially be joined by 99% of Americans who, whether they already realize it or not, are also the victims of the US-Ziocon Empire.

In the meantime, the barrage of anti-Russian propaganda campaigns will continue unabated simply because this seems to have become a form of psychotherapy for a panicked and clueless Western plutocracy. And just as in all the previous cases, this propaganda campaign will have no effect at all.

It is my hope that next time we hear about whatever comes next after the current "Greenpeace" campaign you will keep all this in mind."

October 13, 2013

REMEMBERING THE IMPORTANT LESSONS OF THE COLD WAR

If anything the past 24 hours have proved, once again, that the US and NATO are opposed to any form of negotiations, confidence-building measures or any other type of negotiations with the Donbass and with Russia. Even though Putin tried really hard to sound accommodating and available for a negotiated solution, the US/NATO policy is clearly to provoke and confront Russia and its allies in every imaginable way. The same goes, of course, for the junta freaks whose forces have acted with special brutality during repressive operations in the city of Mariupol. As for the Anglo-Zionist Empire, it is organizing all sorts of military maneuvers in Poland, the Baltic states and elsewhere. Logically, many of you are coming to the conclusion that a war is becoming a very real possibility and I therefore want to repeat a few things yet again.

First, there is no military option for the AngloZionists in the Ukraine, at least not against Russia. This is primarily due to three fact things: geography, US over-reach and politics. Geography, it is much easier for Russia to move ground forces to the Ukraine than it is for the US/NATO, especially for heavy (mechanized, motor rifle, armored, tank) units. Second, simply too many US forces are committed elsewhere for the US to have a major war in against Russia in Eastern Europe. Third, for the time being the Western public is being deceived by the corporate media's reports about the "Russian paper tiger," but as soon as the real fighting starts both Europeans and Americans will suddenly wonder if it is worth dying for the Ukraine. Because if a shooting war between the USA and Russia really begins, we will all be at risk (see below).

Remember how the very same media promised that the poorly equipped, poorly trained, poorly commanded and poorly motivated Russian military could not crack the "tough nut" represented by the NATO-trained Georgian military?

Second, we have to remember that it is never possible to oppose two forces on paper and say that "A" is stronger than "B." Afghanistan and Iraq are perfect examples of the kind of misguided conclusions a self-deluding political leadership can reach when it begins to believe its own lies. So without committing the political "crime of crimes" and suggesting that the invincible US military is anything but invincible, let me suggest the following: if the Russian conventional forces were to be defeated you can be absolutely sure that Russia would have to engage its tactical nuclear capabilities at which point the situation would escalate into a well-known Cold War conundrum. The theory of deterrence suggests that you should reply at the same level, but not above, then your adversary's first move. So, a Russian tactical nuclear strike in, say, Poland or even the Ukraine would have to be met by a similar US strike. But where? Where is the Russian equivalent of Poland for the USA? Belarus? But that is much more like a Russian strike on Canada—really close to home. Kazakhstan? Ridiculous—too far. Obviously not Armenia. So where would the US retaliate? Against Russian forces in the Donbass, but that is right across the border. Maybe in Russia itself? But that would mean striking at the Russian territory proper. What will Russia do in this case—strike at Poland? Germany? The "equivalent" response would be to strike at the US mainland, of course, but that would be inviting a full-scale US retaliation, which would inevitably be followed by a Russian one. And since neither side can disarm the other in a counter-force disarming strike, we are talking about a nuclear world war à la Dr. Strangelove, with nuclear winter and all.

Some might find this kind of reasoning ridiculous, but anybody who has participated in the Cold War will tell you that the best minds in the USA and USSR were busy full time grappling with these issues. Can you guess what they concluded? That a nuclear won cannot be won. But that, in turn, means that no war opposing the USA to Russia can be won because **any war** of this kind will **inevitably** turn nuclear before the weaker sides surrenders. Let me put it to you in a somewhat silly but truthful way: the survival of the USA depends on Russia not losing a war. Yes, that's right. And the converse is also true: Russia's survival is contingent on the USA not being defeated either.

This is why Foreign Minister Lavrov has been repeating over and over again that *no one side can achieve security at the expense of the other and that security has to be collective and even mutual.* But was anybody listening to him across the Atlantic?

Of course, for the time being and for the foreseeable future, *this will only be true for a war directly opposing Russian and US military forces.* Proxy wars are okay, as are covert operations and wars against third parties. But for the time being, only Russia and the USA have the kind of full-spectrum nuclear capabilities that make them able to completely destroy the other side "no matter what." Let me explain.

It has often been said that the Russian and US nuclear forces have to be on high alert and that to avoid being destroyed in a counter-force (counter military) first strike they would have to launch on warning i.e., to launch while the other side's missiles are incoming and before they hit their targets. The fact is that both countries practice what is called "launch under attack" which is launching while some enemy missiles have already hit. But the truth is that both the USA and Russia could afford what is called "riding out the attack" completely and still have enough strategic nuclear weapons to destroy all the key population centers of the other side. This is due to their highly redundant strategic nuclear forces. The fact is that even if, say, the USA managed to destroy every single Russian bomber and every single Russia nuclear silo, and every single Russian strategic nuclear missile carrying submarine, even those in port (who can launch right from there if needed), Russia would still have enough road-mobile ICBMs to wipe off the USA as a country. The exact same can be said of a Russian first strike on the USA which, even if unrealistically successful would still expose Russia to a massive retaliation by USN strategic nuclear missile carrying submarines. And in the real world no first strike is 100% successful. Even 95% successful is not enough if the remaining 5% can still be shot back at you.

Civilians often complain that Russia and the USA have enough nuclear weapons to destroy the planet many times over as if that was a sign of insanity. In reality, it is exactly the opposite: it is because both Russia and the USA have the peacetime ability to destroy the planet several times over that in wartime neither side can have any hopes of achieving a first strike successful enough to avoid a massive retaliation. Yes, in the world of nukes, more is better, at least from the point of view of what is called "first strike stability."

This what sets Russia and the USA really apart: no other nuclear power has a nuclear force whose first strike survivability is as high as Russia and the USA; for the foreseeable future all other nuclear-weapons possessing powers are susceptible to a disarming first strike.

Let me give one more example of how nuclear warfare is counter-intuitive in many ways. We often hear of alert levels (DEFCONs[174] in the USA) and the assumption is that a lower level of defense alert is better. It is not. In fact, a higher alert level is better from the point of view of first strike stability. Here is why:

In complete peacetime (DEFCON 5), most bombers are sitting on the tarmac, most crews doing their training, most subs are moored in port and most critical personnel busy with normal daily tasks. This is exactly when these forces are the most vulnerable to a disarming first strike. At higher levels of alert, the crews will be recalled to their bases, at even higher levels they will be sitting in their planes with engines running and at the highest threat level the bombers will be airborne in prepared holding positions, submarines will be flushed out to sea, all personnel in wartime command posts and, in the USA, the president has his key aides either in the air in Air Force one or deep inside a bunker. In other words,

[174] DEFCON https://en.wikipedia.org/wiki/DEFCON

a higher degree of alert means much less vulnerability to a first strike and that, in turns, means more time to negotiate, find out what is really going on, more time to avoid a war.

What I am trying to illustrate here is that both Russia and the USA have developed a very sophisticated system to make it impossible for the other side to "win" a war. That system is still there today, in fact Putin has just invited the other heads of state of the Collective Security Treaty Organization (CSTO)[175] to be present during a large-scale test of the Russian strategic deterrence forces (not because of the Ukraine, this exercise was scheduled over a year ago).

In other words, this means that the US/NATO know that they cannot "win" a war against Russia, not a conventional one and not a nuclear one either. Those who claim otherwise have simply no idea what they are talking about.

Which leaves two possible explanations for the current behavior of the West, and neither of them is encouraging.

First, Obama, Merkel & Co. are lunatics, and they are hell-bent on starting World War III. I frankly cannot imagine that this is true.

Second, Obama, Merkel & Co are playing a reckless game of chicken with Putin hoping that he is bluffing and that Russia will accept a neo-Nazi run Banderastan which would be hysterically russophobic, a member of NATO and generally become an Anglo-Zionist puppet state like Poland or Latvia.

That, my friends, is not going to happen. This is why on March 1st of this year I wrote an *article warning that Russia was ready for war.*[176] And it has nothing to do with Putin, Russian imperialism or the kind of nonsense the Western corporate media is spewing and everything to do with

---

[175] Collective Security Treaty Organization https://en.wikipedia.org/wiki/Collective_Security_Treaty_Organization

[176] Obama just made things much, much worse in the Ukraine – now Russia is ready for war http://thesaker.is/obama-just-made-things-much-much-worse-in-the-ukraine-now-russia-is-ready-for-war/

the fact that the US wants to turn the Ukraine into an existential threat to Russia while keeping together by brute violence and terror a fictional country invented by the deranged minds of Western Popes and Jesuits which has no existence in reality and which would implode in less than 24 hours if left by itself.

What makes me believe that we are in a crisis potentially much more dangerous than the Cuban Missile Crisis is that at that time both the US and the USSR fully understood how serious the situation was and that the world had to be brought back from the brink of nuclear war. Today, when I listen to idiots like Obama, Kerry, Psaki & co. I am struck by how truly stupid and self-deluded these people are. Here they are playing not only with our existence, but even with theirs, and they still are acting as if Putin was some Somali war lord who needed to be frightened into submission. But if that tactic did not work with Somali warlords, why would they think that it will work with Putin?

I will want to force myself to believe that behind all these crazy and ignorant lunatics there are men in uniform who have been educated and trained during the Cold War and who still remember the many hours spent running all kinds of computer models which all came back with the same result over and over again: a victory is impossible and war was simply not an option.

It is also possible that the Empire wants to escalate the situation in the Ukraine enough to force a Russian intervention but not enough to have a shooting war. If so, that is a very risky strategy. I would even call it criminally reckless. It is one thing to engage in all sorts of macho saber-rattling with the DPRK, but quite another to try the same trick on a nuclear superpower. The scary fact is that the bloody Democrats already have such a record of utter recklessness. Do you remember when in 1995 Clinton sent in two US aircraft carriers into the Strait of Taiwan[177] in a cowboy-

[177] Third Taiwan Strait Crisis https://en.wikipedia.org/wiki/Third_Taiwan_Strait_Crisis

like show of macho force? At that time the Chinese wisely decided against responding to a stupid action by an equally stupid reaction, but what if this time around Obama decides to show how tough he really is and what if Putin feels that he is cornered and cannot back down?

It is scary to think that the fact that Russian and Chinese leaders are acting in a responsible way actually entices the US to act even more irresponsibly and recklessly but this does seems to be the case, especially when a Democrat is in the White House.

When is the last time you remember a US president taking upon himself to make a constructive proposal to avoid military action or a way? I honestly cannot recall such an instance.

In conclusion I can only repeat what I said so many times: there is no military option for the US/NATO against Russia. As for whether the Anglo-Zionist plutocracy of the 1% who rule over us has gone completely crazy—your guess is as good as mine.

May 8, 2014

Making sense of Obama's billion dollar hammer

You probably heard it by now: Obama has pledged a billion dollars to what my "beloved" BBC called[178] "*European security.*" The official name for this initiative is the "European Reassurance Initiative." You see, Obama and the BBC apparently believe that Europeans are really terrified and that they believe that the Russian tanks might roll into Warsaw, Athens, Rome or Lisbon at any time. The good news is that Uncle Sam is here to reassure them that he will let no such thing happen and that this additional one billion dollars will deter the Russian Bear.

Have you ever read something more ridiculous?

So what is really going on here?

There is a wonderful American expression which says that "*to a man with a hammer everything looks like a nail.*" Well, to Obama, the EU and the Ukraine sure do look like nails, because the only instrument the USA has used in its foreign policy for many decades now is a "hammer" composed of money and guns. But let's backtrack for a second.

I submit that the US policy in Europe is nothing short of a total failure. Not only has the US-instigated coup in the Ukraine turned into a full-spectrum disaster, but the latest elections in Europe clearly show that the European public is becoming more anti-EU and more anti-US. In fact, since the EU **is** nothing more than a US instrument of colonial domination over Europe, being anti-EU is being anti-US. Bernard Henri Levi, the hyper-Zionist clown who fancies himself a "philosopher" and who is the darling of the European elites, once said that "anti-Americanism is a metaphor for anti-Semitism." To paraphrase him I would say that "anti-Europeanism is a metaphor for anti-Americanism" (at least if by "Europe" we understand that trans-national horror known as the EU and not

[178] European Reassurance Initiative: Obama announces $1bn fund http://www.bbc.com/news/world-europe-27671691

the "Europe of the fatherlands" which de Gaulle, a true patriot of France and Europe, had called for). And the folks in DC understand that too, they are not stupid. Worse of all for them, time is running out and the situation on the ground is getting worse and worse not by the day, but by the hour. France, in particular, might explode literally any day.

But the real problem is not in Europe or in the Ukraine, it is in the USA. The US leadership, clearly intoxicated on imperial hubris and 1% class arrogance, has simply forgotten Bismarck's motto that "*politics is the art of the possible*" and this is why instead of seeking some kind of best possible compromise leading to the best possible outcome, they are holding on with a desperate death-grip to an *impossible* outcome: a Europe run by the EU and a unitary state of Banderastan on the border with Russia. That isn't going to happen, of course. In fact, the harder the US pushes for such an outcome, the less likely it is to ever become reality. No need to read Hegel to understand that—a quick look at the recent events in Europe clearly shows that the Anglo-Zionist imperial design for the Atlantic to the Ural (ATTU) zone is going nowhere and will end up in an embarrassing meltdown.

Faced with this prospect, the White House does what the French call "*fuite en avant*" ("fleeing forward" if you want, or "advancing even faster into the quicksands"). The Russians did not take the Ukrainian bait? Fine—we will pretend like they did anyway and "reassure" the Europeans by declaring[179] that "the security of America's European allies is sacrosanct" with enough gravitas to hopefully make them believe that they are really threatened. The neo-Nazi junta has just engaged in yet another massacre in the east? No problem, we will simply praise the regime for its restraint and "democratic nature." The EU leaders are having a panic attack over the latest elections? No problem either, we will just give them a one billion dollar bribe to show them that we will stand by them no

[179] European Reassurance Initiative: Obama announces $1bn fund http://www.bbc.com/news/world-europe-27671691

matter what and regardless of whom those pesky Europeans might vote for the next time around.

Because, of course, this is what this billion dollar is all about. It's just bribe money for the 1% in the US and the EU to be distributed among these plutocrats under the guise of "reassuring Europe." In reality, the "European Reassurance Initiative" only serves to reassure the European elites and the Eurobureaucrats as they are the only ones who will truly benefit from it. And were shall the money come from? Well, hell, Uncle Sam can just create it out of thin air with a few keystrokes on the right computer. And as long as the EU and the rest of the US-colonized planet continues to accept payments in dollars, they will be the ones really paying for this "EU plutocracy reassurance initiative."

You might retort that this is a stupid strategy which will only make things worse. And you would be right. But not in the **very short term,** which is really the only term which has ever mattered to capitalists anyway. Besides, money and guns are the only two "policy instruments" the US elites understand, so why not throw some money at the issue and hope that guns will make the Empire look stronger?

It is as pathetic, as it is immoral. The good news is that the Anglo-Zionist Empire is really sabotaging itself and that it does so faster and better than any outside power could ever dream of. And we are far from having seen the worst of it (just think of what a Hillary presidency would look like!)

As for the people of Novorossiya and Russia—they should keep their cool and realize that all this hot air blowing from the West is just that—hot air. Yes, sometimes they "sound" scary, but that only because American politicians are the masters of make believe and that they are running what Chris Hedges[180] so brilliantly called the "Empire of Illusions." No matter what they say, the reality on the ground, in the real world, is that

---

[180] Chris Hedges: *Empire of Illusion: The End of Literacy and the Triumph of Spectacle* http://www.amazon.com/Empire-Illusion-Literacy-Triumph-Spectacle/dp/1568586132/

Kiev does not have any military option in the Donbass, just like the Anglo-Zionist Empire has no military option against Russia. Yes, they can "pretend" like they have, but that does not make it so.

What we all should keep in mind is that neither money nor guns win wars. Yes, they are important factors, but they cannot decide an outcome. Willpower does. The Americans, by the way, are quite aware of that. The dumb ones really believe their own propaganda, but the smart ones know that the real purpose of the US "make believe propaganda" is not to really make it happen, but to demoralize the opponent and break down his will to resist. The danger of that is that the moment your opponent really understands that he will immediately understand something else too: that your bark is far bigger than your bite. This is what has happened with Hezbollah.

For years the Anglo-Zionist propaganda has presented the Israel Defense Force (IDF) as some kind of elite, almost invincible, force (which they never were, as anybody who has trained with them knows). And that myth of Israeli invincibility has literally paralyzed the entire Middle East until Hezbollah challenged it. As Robert Fisk reported in 2006 "while in the past the Lebanese would jump into their cars and drive north as soon as an Israeli attack was announced, now they would jump in their cars and drive south." That "switch" in the mind of the Lebanese is what really defeated the IDF in 2006, not some kind of Hezbollah super-weapon.

What does this mean for Novorossiya?

It means that the people of Novorossiya must truly believe in themselves and stop hoping for a Russian intervention which is not going to happen, at least at this moment in time. Let Obama shake his billion dollar hammer until he drops in exhaustion, but never let that distract you from a victory which is very much within your reach. Yes, the massacres in Odessa, Mariupol, Slaviansk, Kramatorsk, Donetsk and now Lugansk are disgusting atrocities which cannot be forgiven or forgotten, but they are not on the same scale as the horrors of World War II, and yet the Russian people eventually also won that war.

Lies and terror have the exact same purpose: to defeat the will of their target and we can expect a lot more lies and terror from the neo-Nazis in Kiev and from the Anglo-Zionist Empire. But if we take heed of Hezbollah's example in Lebanon and if we keep in mind that time is very much on our side, we will prevail, sooner rather than later.

June 3, 2014

THINKING THE UNTHINKABLE

Introduction

I have been putting off writing about this topic for a very long while. In fact, I wrote several articles trying to explain the self-evident truism that the US/NATO/EU does not have a military option in the Ukrainian war. First, in an article entitled **Remembering the Important Lessons of the Cold War**[181] I tried to explain that the reason the Cold War did not turn into a hot, shooting war is that both sides understood that they simply could never win, and that any escalation in strikes and counter-strikes could very rapidly lead to an intercontinental nuclear war, something which neither side was willing to risk.

In a piece entitled **Making Sense of Obama's Billion Dollar Hammer**[182] I tried to show that all the money the US will by pouring into "European security" is just a grandiose bribe for some European elites and that it had no real effect on the ground. A few days later I posted an article entitled **Why the US-Russian Nuclear Balance is as Solid as Ever**[183] in which I tried to dispel the myth prevalent in the West about the putative state of disrepair of the Russian military in general, and of the Russian nuclear forces in particular. Lastly, in a piece entitled **Short Reminder about US and Russian Nuclear Weapons**[184] I tried to show that in reality it was *the **US** nuclear forces who were in a state of disrepair.* And over and over again, in many comments, I tried to lay out the rea-

[181] Remembering the important lessons of the Cold War http://thesaker.is/remembering-the-important-lessons-of-the-cold-war/

[182] Making sense of Obama's billion dollar hammer http://thesaker.is/making-sense-of-obamas-billion-dollar-hammer/

[183] Why the US-Russian nuclear balance is as solid as ever http://thesaker.is/why-the-us-russian-nuclear-balance-is-as-solid-as-ever/

[184] Short reminder about US and Russian nuclear weapons http://thesaker.is/short-reminder-about-us-and-russian-nuclear-weapons/

sons for which I simply did not believe that the US/NATO/EU would dare to attack Russia.

In summary, I will say this: the US is not nearly as powerful as the US propaganda claims. Without going into long debates about what "victory" and "defeat" mean, I will just say that in my personal opinion the last time the US military fought well was in Korea, and even there it had to accept a draw. After that, it was all downhill. This is not the fault of the US solider, by the way, but by the fact that big money and politics got so heavily involved in the US military that they corrupted everything. This is most evident in the USAF which still has superb pilots, but who are given a terrible choice: either fly on good but old aircraft or fly on new but terrible ones (I believe that given the choice, most would chose the former). As for the European NATO allies, they are such a joke that they hardly deserve mention. They even look bad on a parade.

As for a military option in the Ukraine, it appears unthinkable to me not only because, frankly, I don't see a single military in the West capable of taking on the Russian military in full-scale battle, but also because geography powerfully argues against such a crazy idea (the very same geography which would make it impossible for Russia to try to invade Western or even Central Europe).

And yet, something in all this very logical reasoning felt wrong to me. A few days ago it finally hit me. What bothered me was

The American Duck

Among the many beautiful and witty expressions and neologisms Americans use, I always loved this one: *If it looks like a duck, swims like a duck, and quacks like a duck, then it probably is a duck.* This so-called "Duck test" is funny, but it is also a powerful logical method which ended up chewing at me day after day after day. Here I was, all sure and certain that the US/NATO/EU would never consider such a ludicrous notion as the one of an military attack on Russia or on Russian forces. But kept hearing the voice of the American Duck telling me: *look at what they are doing, what does that look like to you? Suspend your conclusions and just tell me what are you observing? Tell me, if they had decided to escalate to the point of a military confrontation with Russia, would they be doing things differently*? And a few days ago, I threw in the towel (at the duck, of course) and had to accept that while I did not know what they were thinking or what their intentions really were, it sure looked to me like the Western plutocrats had decided to escalate the crisis as high as possible.

In truth, I have to admit that when I studied the theory of deterrence in the 1980s my teachers always insisted that this theory of deterrence was predicated on what they called a "rational player." To put it simply—how do you deter a lunatic? Or a desperate man with nothing to lose? Or a person hell-bent on mutual destruction? The truth is, you cannot. *Deterrence assumes a rational actor making a logical decision about unacceptable costs.* As far as I know, nobody has ever developed a theory of deterrence applicable to a madman. When I initially wrote my pieces explaining why I believed that a US/NATO/EU attack was impossible a lot readers posted comments saying that while maybe the top US military command was still mainly composed of rational men, the US imperial elites had clearly gone crazy a long time ago and that they were so stuck in their arrogance, their imperial hubris, there delusion of invincibility and their knee-jerk and systematic use of violence that they could no more be considered as rational. At the time I replied that, yeah, sure, maybe, but what is the point of analyzing something crazy. How do you try to make sense of the suicidally insane?

And yet, this is what I propose to do today. I will try as best I can to try to place myself in the mind of these lunatics and see what they could try doing, and what the consequences of that would be. I will go through several possible plans that these crazies might have starting from the most limited one and then going up the insanity slope.

Plan one: a symbolic and limited intervention

This plan is already underway. We know that there are US military advisors in the Ukraine, including at least one general, we know that the Dutch and Australians will be sending in a lightly armed force to "protect" the investigators at the crash site of MH17 (although how a few men armed with assault rifles can protect anybody from Ukie artillery, tank or mortar fire is anybody's guess). Then there are all the reports of foreign mercenaries, mostly US and Polish, fighting with the Ukie death squads. There is also some good evidence that Poland is sending military equipment, including aircraft and, possibly, crews. Well, all of that is dumb and serves very little useful purpose, but that is what the West is so good at: pretending. If this plans stays at this level I would say that it is not very important. But, alas, there is a nastier possibility here:

Plan two: a tripwire force

This is just an extension of plan one: bring in a few men, and then have them killed. This would trigger the needed "popular outrage" (carefully fanned and reported by the corporate media) to force the Europeans to accept more US sanctions in Europe or even some kind of "EU-mandated" "peacekeeping force." Of course, if the Russians or the Novorossians do not take the bait and fail to kill the "observers," US/NATO false flag teams could easily do that. Just imagine what a heavy-mortar strike on a building with these OSCE observers would look like. The junta in Kiev would be more than happy to "invite" such a "peacekeeping" force into Novorossiya and since this would be an "invited" force, no UNSC resolution would be needed. Finally, such a "peacekeeping" force would be regularly reinforced and augmented until it could basically cover the flanks of the Ukies in their attacks against Novorossiya. This force would also assume the command and control of Ukie forces, something which the Ukies could greatly benefit from (their current command and control is a mess).

Plan One and Plan Two assume that Russian forces stay on the other side of the border and that the only opposition to such a deployment could come from the Novorossians. But what if the Russians decided to move into Novorossiya either to protect the locals or stop his limited US/NATO/EU "peacekeeping force"? Then the US/NATO/EU would have to take a dramatic escalatory step send in a much bigger force, more capable of defending itself.

Plan three: UPROFOR on the Dnieper?

This is the Yugoslav scenario. The West would send in something on the order of ten battalions which would each be given an area of responsibility for "peacekeeping." Then police forces would be also sent to "maintain law and order" and EU commissars would be sent in to "help" the local population "express their will" and "organize" a local government. Soon there would be some kind of EU-run election and all the Novorossian forces would be declared "bandits" from which the local population need to be "protected." Since Strelkov himself fought in Yugoslavia, as did many other Russians, I don't believe that the Russians or Novorossians would fall for this one. I think that Russia would express its opposition to such a plan and that if she was ignored, she would move in her own forces along the line of contact.

This might be the US/NATO/EU end goal: to create a Korea like "line of demarcation" which would isolate the Donetsk and Lugansk People's republics from the rest of Novorossiya and the rest of the Ukraine, this would mean getting plenty of Kosovo-like "Camp Bondsteels" all along the Russian border and it would make it looks like the "Wartime President of the One Indispensable Nation" "stopped the Russian Bear." Finally, it would create a perfect Cold War-like environment in which the Western one-percenters could continue to exploit the 99% while constantly scaring them with the "Russian threat."

Plan four: Operation Storm in Novorossiya and Crimea?

I would not put it past the folks in the Pentagon and Mons to try to pull off an "Operation Storm"[185] in Novorossiya and even possibly Crimea. That is the scenario Glazev fears: the US/NATO/EU would put enough forces inside the Ukraine to allow it to survive long enough to mobilize a sufficient number of men and equipment for a lightning fast attack in Novorossiya and even possibly Crimea. And, in theory, if we assume that Banderastan does not collapse under its own weight and the economic disaster, the Ukraine has the resources to mobilize far more men and equipment that the tiny People's Republics of Donestk and Lugansk or even Crimea. But that, again, assumes that Russia will let that happen, which she won't, so now we have to look at the really crazy plans:

Plan five: first "~~Desert~~ Steppe Shield" then "~~Desert~~ Steppe Storm"

That is a crazy notion: to do with Russia what the US did with Iraq. First, to place down a "protection force" in the Ukraine, isolate Russia, and then attack in a full-depth and full-scale determined attack. We are definitely talking about a continental war with a fantastic potential to turn into a world war. This plan would have be based on two crucial assumptions:

1) The US/NATO/EU conventional forces would be capable of defeating the Russian military.

2) If facing conventional defeat, Russia would not use nuclear weapons.

I think that both of these assumptions are deeply mistaken. The first one is based on a mix of propaganda, bean counting and ignorance. The propaganda is that Western militaries are very good. They are not. Most Western armies are a pathetic joke, and those who can fight well (the Brits, the Turks) are too little to matter. That leaves the US military

[185] Operation Storm https://en.wikipedia.org/wiki/Operation_Storm

which have capabilities far in excess of what its NATO allies can muster. Just as in World War II all the serious fighting had to be done by German units, in case of a World War III (or IV?) all the serious fighting would have to be done by Americans. The problem is that the Americans would have an extremely hard time bringing in enough forces to really make the difference. In any case, I have the biggest doubt about the current fighting capabilities of the US Army and Marine Corps. Faced with a Russian battalion defending its own soil I think that an equivalent USA/ Marine force would get slaughtered.

The "bean counting" is when you compare all the NATO APCs or tanks to the number available to the Russian military. The corporate media loves this kind of charts in which soldiers, APCs, tanks, aircraft and other gear are compared. Professional analysts never use them simply because they are meaningless. What matters is how much of that gear is actually available for battle, the kind of tactics used, the training and morale of the soldiers, the skills of their commanding officers, and stuff which is "never" mentioned: supplies, logistics, petroleum, lubricants, ammunition, lines of supply, medical standards, even food and weather. Bean counters simply never see that. But one could argue that the number of trucks is more important to a military than the number of tanks. Yet trucks are never counted. But yes, on paper NATO looks huge. Even though most NATO gear could not even survive your average Ukrainian road, never mind the winter.

But let us assume that the Hollywood image of the US military is true: invincible, best trained, best armed, with a fantastic morale, led by the very best of the best officers, it would easily defeat the primitive Russian military, armed with antiquated weapons and commanded by fat drunken generals. Okay, and then what? If is the official Russian nuclear deterrence doctrine that in this case Russia would use nuclear weapons. Since even in Hollywood movies nobody makes the claim that the US anti-missile systems could stop Iskanders, cruise missiles or even gravity bombs, we would have to accept that the invincible US force would be turned into radioactive particulates and, that, in turn, would leave the US president two terrible choices: a) take the loss and stop b) retaliate and the second option would have to include the location from where the strike came from: Russia proper. That, of course, would place the following choices for the Russian President: a) take the loss or b) strike at the continental United States. At this points nuclear mushrooms would start appearing all over the map.

Now please make no mistake: Russia can not only destroy Mons, the Pentagon and Cheyenne Mountain (just a matter of placing enough warheads on the right spot), but also every single major city in the United States. Sure, the USA can retaliate in kind, but what kind of consolation would that be for anybody left?

I cannot believe that the US deep state would truly, deliberately, want to start a planetary nuclear war. For one thing, US leaders are cowards and they will not want to take such a monumental decision. A far more likely version is that being stupid, arrogant and cowards they will stumble upon just that outcome. Here is how:

Plan six: American football's "Hail Mary"

In American football there is a specific pass which is used only when seconds are left on the clock and your teams is badly losing anyway. Basically it works like this: every single person who is not defending the quarterback rushes to the end zone, as do all the defenders, and the quarterback then just throws the ball straight into that zone with the very slim hope that one of his own players will catch it and score a touchdown. This is called a "Hail Mary"[186] for very good reason as only a miracle makes such a desperate plan work. Most of the time the ball is either fumbled or caught by the other team. But, very rarely, it works (as seen in the preceding footnote).

---

[186] Top 10 Hail Mary Plays All Time https://www.youtube.com/watch?v=ywcD94gqxQM

I can very much imagine a desperate Obama trying to show the American people that he "has hair on his chest" and that he is not going to let "regional power" challenge the "indispensable nation." So what he and, really, his administration risks doing is the following: to play a game of chicken[187] hoping against all odds that the Russian will yield. This is my worst nightmare and the worst possible assumption to make because Russia **cannot** yield.

In March of this year I issued a warning which I entitled "Obama just made things much, much worse in the Ukraine—now Russia is ready for war."[188] What prompted me to issue that warning was the fact that the Council of the Russian Federation has just unanimously passed a resolution allowing Putin to use Russian armed forces in the Ukraine. Since, this resolution has been repealed at Putin's request and for obvious political motives, but the mood, the determination is still there. In fact, I think that it has grown much stronger.

There has been much useless speculation about Putin, his motives and his strategy. This is way bigger than just Putin. If the US/NATO/EU really push too far, and that includes a genocide in Novorossiya, an attack on Crimea or an attack on Russian forces, Russia will go to war, Putin or no Putin. And Putin knows that. His real base of support is not in the Russian elites (who mostly fear him), but in the Russian people (with whom his current rating are higher than ever before). And Putin himself openly spoke about the "threats to Russian sovereignty" though he did add that because of the Russian nuclear forces there was, in his opinion, no immediate threat to the Russian territory.

If the US decides to play a game of chicken with Russia, then it will do the same thing as a car driver playing a game of chicken against an in-

---

[187] Chicken (game) https://en.wikipedia.org/wiki/Chicken_%28game%29

[188] Obama just made things much, much worse in the Ukraine – now Russia is ready for war http://thesaker.is/obama-just-made-things-much-much-worse-in-the-ukraine-now-russia-is-ready-for-war/

coming train: regardless of the train's driver, the train is on tracks and its momentum is too big: it **cannot** stop or veer away.

The problem is that the USA has a long record of making absolutely irresponsible statements which end up putting them into a corner from which they cannot bulge without losing face. Just look at the MH17 disaster: the Obama administration immediately rushed to blame the Russians for it, but what will it do when the evidence to the contrary comes out? What if Obama also draws a red line somewhere (it does not really matter where) and then **forces** Russia to cross it?

Sadly, I can imagine the USA declaring that the US/NATO will defend the Ukie airspace. I think that they are dumb enough to try to seize a Russian ship entering or leaving the Black Sea. Remember—these are the folks who hijacked the aircraft of Bolivian President Evo Morales to try to find Snowden on board. These are the folks who regularly kidnap Russian citizens worldwide (the last time the son of a well-known Russian member of Parliament who was kidnapped in the Maldives Islands). And, of course, these are the folks who did 9/11. Their arrogance knows no limits because they are profoundly evil sociopaths. For them the organization of false flag operations is a normal, standard, procedure. They almost triggered a war between the DPRK and South Korea by sinking a South Korean military vessel. They used chemical weapons in Syria not once, but several times. And the last time we had a Democrat in the White House, he was crazy enough to send two US aircraft carrier groups into the Strait of Taiwan to threaten China.[189]

My biggest fears

This is my biggest fear: some kind of desperate "Hail Mary" maneuver in which the US will try to convince Russia that "look, we are crazy enough to start this thing, so you better back off" not realizing that Rus-

[189] Third Taiwan Strait Crisis https://en.wikipedia.org/wiki/Third_Taiwan_Strait_Crisis#U.S._military_response

sia **cannot** back off. The other thing which really scares me is that during the Cuban Missile Crisis everybody was aware of the stakes and most people were truly terrified. Now, thanks to the propaganda of the corporate media, almost nobody is afraid and hardly anybody is paying attention. Russia and the USA are on a clear collision course and nobody cares! How come?

Because if 9/11 proved anything is that there are things which most people are simply unwilling to contemplate, no matter how close and real they are. It would only make sense that the *Empire of Illusion*[190] would be populated by a people in total denial. After all, illusion and denial usually go hand in hand.

Most of you, dear readers and friends, seem to be sharing with me a sense of total distrust in the sanity of our leaders. When I asked you whether you believed that the US/NATO were crazy enough to use military forces against Russia,[191] an overwhelming number of you answered that "yes" and a good part of you were even emphatically sure of that. Why? Because we all know how crazy and deluded our imperial overlords are. Crazy and deluded enough not to quality as "rational actor"? Crazy and deluded enough to play a game a chicken with a train? Crazy and deluded enough to risk the planet on "Hail Mary? Alas, I think that this is a very real possibility.

But what does Uncle Sam really want?

There is a gradual realization in Russia that for Uncle Sam this is not about the Ukraine. It is about Russia and, specifically, about *regime change in Russia.* A vast majority of Russian experts seem to believe that the US wants to overthrow Putin and that this entire war in the Ukraine is a means to achieve that. As a very cynical joke going around now says

---

[190] Chris Hedges: *Empire of Illusion: The End of Literacy and the Triumph of Spectacle* http://www.amazon.com/Empire-Illusion-Literacy-Triumph-Spectacle/dp/1568586132

[191] Could Glazev be right? Request for your comments http://thesaker.is/could-glazev-be-right-request-for-your-comments/

"Obama is willing to fight Putin down to the very last Ukrainian." I think that this is correct. The US hopes that one of the following will happen:

1) A Russian military intervention in Novorossiya which will allow the US to restart a Cold War v2 on steroid and which will also fully re-enslave Europe to the USA. Putin would then be blamed for falling in the US trap.

2) The creation of a US-run "Banderastan" in the Ukraine. That would "contain" and destabilize Russia. Again, Putin would be blamed for letting that happen.

3) A "nationalist Maidan" in Russia: this is what is behind the current Putin-bashing campaign in the blogosphere: to paint Putin as a weak and/or corrupt man, who traded Crimea for the Donbass (you know the tune—these folks even comment on this blog). These efforts are supported and, sometimes, even financed by Russian oligarchs who have a great deal of money involved in the EU and who really don't need the current tensions. Here Putin would be blamed for not doing enough.

In all three cases, Putin would risk a (patriotically) color-coded revolution which would, inevitably, bring either crazy rogue ruler or a clueless fossil to power (a la Zhirinovsky or Zuiganov) or, much better, a pro-American "liberal" (a la Medvedev). I think that all of these plans will fail.

Putin will not give Uncle Sam the intervention he wants. Instead, Russia continue to support the Resistance in Novorossiya until Banderastan goes "belly up," i.e. for another 30-60 days or so. As for the "nationalist Maidan," the Russian people see straight through this "black PR campaign" and their support for Putin is higher than it ever was. It's not Putin who does not want to intervene overtly in the Donbass, it is the Russian people. The attempts at stirring up anti-Putin by first stirring up anti-Strelkov feelings have completely failed and, in fact, they have backfired. A lot of these "hurray-patriots" are now overly called "useful idiots" for the CIA or even provocateurs.

Finally, while they are at this point in time only rumors, there seems to be more and more specialists of the opinion that MH17 was a deliberate false flag by the US. If the news that the Ukies did it ever becomes public, then the entire destabilization plan will go down the tubes. At this point, I would not put anything, no matter how crazy, past the US deep state.

And that is a very scary thought.

July 31, 2014

The Russian response to a double declaration of war

The context: a double declaration of war

Listening to Poroshenko a few days ago and then to Obama at the UNGA can leave no doubt whatsoever about the fact that the **Anglo-Zionist Empire is at war with Russia.** Yet many believe that the Russian response to this reality is inadequate. Likewise, there is a steady stream of accusations made against Putin about Russia's policy toward the crisis in the Ukraine. What I propose to do here is to offer a few basic reminders about Putin, his obligations, and his options.

First and foremost, Putin was never elected to be the world's policeman or savior, he was only elected to be President of Russia. Seems obvious, but yet many seem to assume that somehow Putin is morally obliged to do something to protect Syria, Novorossiya, or any other part of our harassed world. This is not so. Yes, Russia is the de facto leader of the BRICS and SCO countries, and Russia accepts that fact, but Putin has the moral and legal obligation to care for his own people first.

Second, Russia is now officially in the crosshairs of the Anglo-Zionist Empire which includes not only three nuclear countries (US, UK, FR) but also the most powerful military force (US+NATO) and the world's biggest economies (US+EU). I think that we can all agree that the threat posed by such an Empire is not trivial and that Russia is right in dealing with it very carefully.

Sniping at Putin and missing the point

Now, amazingly, many of those who accuse Putin of being a wimp, a sellout or a naive Pollyanna also claim that the West is preparing nuclear war on Russia. If that is really the case, this begs the question: if that is really the case, if there is a real risk of war, nuclear or not, is Putin not doing the right thing by **not** acting tough or threatening? Some would say that the West is bent on a war no matter what Putin does. Okay, fair enough, but in that case is his buying as much time as possible before the inevitable not the right thing to do?!

Third, on the issue of the USA vs. ISIL, several comments here accused Putin of backstabbing Assad because Russia supported the US resolution at the UNSC.

And what was Putin supposed to do?! Fly the Russian Air Force to Syria to protect the Syrian border? What about Assad? Did he scramble his own air force to try to stop the US or has he quietly made a deal: bomb "them" not us, and I shall protest and do nothing about it? Most obviously the latter.

In fact, Putin and Assad have exactly the same position: protest the unilateral nature of the strikes, demand a UN resolution, while quietly watching how Uncle Sam turned on his own progeny, and now tries to destroy them.

I would add that Lavrov quite logically stated that there are no "good terrorists." He knows that ISIL is nothing but a continuation of the US-created Syrian insurgency, itself a continuation of the US-created al-Qaeda. From a Russian point of view, the choice is simple: what is better, for the US to use its forces and men to kill crazed Wahhabis or have Assad do it? And if ISIL is successful in Iraq, how long before they come back to Chechnya? Or Crimea? Or Tatarstan? Why should any Russian or Syria soldier risk death when the USAF is willing to do that for them?

While there is a sweet irony in the fact that the US now has to bomb its own creation, let them do that. Even Assad was clearly forewarned and he obviously is quite happy about that.

Finally, UN or no UN, the US had already taken the decision to bomb ISIL. So what is the point of blocking a perfectly good UN resolution? That would be self-defeating. In fact, this resolution can even be used by Russia to prevent the US and UK from serving as a rear base for Wahhabi extremists (this resolution bans that, and we are talking about a mandatory, Chapter VII, UNSC resolution)

And yet, some still say that Putin threw Assad under the bus. How crazy and stupid can one get to have that kind of notion about warfare or politics? And if Putin wanted to toss Assad under the bus, why did he not do that last year?

Sincere frustration or intellectual dishonesty?

But that kind of nonsense about the Syria is absolutely dwarfed by the kind of truly crazy stuff some people post about Novorossiya. Here are my favorite ones. The author begins by quoting me:

> "This war has never been about Novorossiya, or about the Ukraine."

and then continues:

> That statement is too vacuous and convenient as a copout. Do you really mean to say that the thousands of people murdered by shelling, the thousands of young Ukrainian conscripts put through the meat grinder, the thousands of homes destroyed, the more than 1 million people who have turned into refugees… NONE of that has anything to do with Novorossiya and Ukraine? That this is only about Russia? Really, one would wish you'd refrain from making silly statements like that.

The only problem being, of course, that I never made it in the first place.

Of course, it is rather obvious that I meant that FOR THE ANGLO-ZIONIST EMPIRE the goal has never been the Ukraine or Novorossiya, but a war on Russia. All Russia did was to recognize this reality. Again, the words "*do you really mean to say that*" clearly show that the author is going to twist what I said, make yet another straw man, and then indignantly denounce me for being a monster who does not care about the Ukraine or Novorossiya (the rest of the comment was in the same vein:

indignant denunciations of statements I never made and conclusions I never reached).

I have already grown used to the truly remarkable level of dishonesty of the Putin-bashing crowd and by now I consider it par for the course. But I wanted to illustrate that one more time just to show that at least in certain cases an honest discussion is not the purpose at all. But I don't want to bring it all down to just a few dishonest and vociferous individuals. There are also many who are sincerely baffled, frustrated and even disappointed with Russia's apparent passivity. Here is an excerpt of an email I got this morning:

> I guess I was really hoping that perhaps Russia, China The BRICS would be a counter-force. What I fail to understand is why after all the demonization by the U.S and Europe doesn't Russia retaliate. The sanctions imposed by the West is hurting Russia and yet they still trade oil in euros/dollars and are bending over backward to accommodate Europe. I do not understand why they do not say lift all sanctions or no gas. China also says very little against the U.S, even though they fully understand that if Russian is weakened they are next on the list. As for all the talk of lifting the sanctions on Iran that is farcical as we all know Israel will never allow them to be lifted. So, why do China and Russia go along with the whole charade. Sometimes I wonder if we are all being played, and this is all one big game, which no chance of anything changing.

In this case the author correctly sees that Russia and China follow a very similar policy which sure looks like an attempt to appease the US. In contrast to the previous comment, here the author is both sincere and truly distressed.

In fact, I believe that what I am observing are three very different phenomena all manifesting themselves at the same time:

1) An organized Putin-bashing campaign initiated by US/UK government branches tasked with manipulating the social media.

2) A spontaneous Putin-bashing campaign led by certain Russian National-Bolshevik circles (Limonov, Dugin & Co.).

3) The expression of a **sincere** bafflement, distress and frustration by honest and well-intentioned people to whom the current Russian stance really makes no sense at all.

The rest of this post will be entirely dedicated to try to explain the Russian stance to those in this third group (any dialog with the two first ones just makes no sense).

Trying to make sense of an apparently illogical policy

In my introduction above I stated that what is taking place is a war on Russia, not hot war (yet?) and not quite an old-style Cold War. In essence, what the AngloZionists are doing is pretty clear and a lot of Russian commentators have already reached that conclusion: *the US are engaged into a war against Russia for which the US will fight to the last Ukrainian.* Thus, for the Empire, "success" **can never** be defined as an outcome in the Ukraine because, as I said previously, this war is not about the Ukraine. For the Empire "success" is a specific outcome **in Russia**: regime change. Let's us look at how the Empire plans to achieve this result.

The original plan was simplistic in a typically US neocon way: overthrow Yanukovych, get the Ukraine into the EU and NATO, politically move NATO to the Russian border and militarily move it into Crimea. That plan failed. Russia accepted Crimea and the Ukraine collapsed into a vicious civil war combined with a terminal economic crisis. Then the US neocons fell back to plan B.

Plan B was also simple: get Russia to intervene militarily in the Donbass and use that as a pretext for a full-scale Cold War v2 which would create 1950's style tensions between East and West, justify fear-induced policies in the West, and completely sever the growing economic ties between Russia and the EU. Except that plan also failed—Russia did not take the bait and instead of intervening directly in the Donbass, she began a massive covert operation to support the anti-Nazi forces in Novorossiya. The Russian plan worked, and the Junta Repression Forces (JRF) were soundly defeated by the Novorossian Armed Forces (NAF) even though the latter was suffering a huge deficit in firepower, armor, specialists and men (gradually, Russian covert aid turned all these around).

At this point in time the Anglo-Zionist plutocracy truly freaked out under the combined realization that their plan was falling apart and that there was nothing they could really do to rescue it (a military option was totally impossible as I explained it in the past).[192] They did try economic sanctions, but that only helped Putin to engage in long overdue reforms. But the worst part of it all was that each time the West expected Putin to do something, he did the exact opposite:

- Nobody expected that Putin would use military force in Crimea in a lightning-fast takeover operation which will go down in history as at least as amazing as Storm-333.[193]
- Everybody (including myself) expected Putin to send forces into Novorossiya. He did not.
- Nobody expected Russian counter-sanctions to hit the EU agricultural sector.
- Everybody expected that Putin would retaliate after the latest round of sanctions. He did not.

There is a pattern here and it is one basic to all martial arts: first, never signal your intentions, second use feints and third, hit when and where your opponent doesn't expect it.

Conversely, there are two things which are deeply ingrained in the Western political mind-set which Putin never does: he never threatens and he never postures. For example, while the US is basically at war with Russia, Russia will gladly support a US resolution on ISIL if it is to Rus-

---

[192] Thinking the unthinkable http://thesaker.is/thinking-the-unthinkable/

[193] Operation Storm-333 https://en.wikipedia.org/wiki/Operation_Storm-333

sia's advantage. And Russian diplomats will speak of "our American partners" or "our American friends" while, at the same time, **doing more than the rest of the planet combined to bring down the Anglo-Zionist Empire.**

A quick look at Putin's record

As I have written in the past, unlike some other bloggers and commentators, I am neither a psychic not a prophet and I cannot tell you what Putin thinks or what he will do tomorrow. But what I can tell you is that which Putin has already done in the past: (in no particular order)

- Broken the back of the Anglo-Zionist-backed oligarchy in Russia.
- Achieved a truly miraculous success in Chechnya (one which nobody, prophets included, had foreseen).
- Literally resurrected the Russian economy.
- Rebuilt the Russian military, security and intelligences forces.
- Severely disrupted the ability of foreign NGOs to subvert Russia.
- Done more for the de-dollarization of the planet than anybody before.
- Made Russia the clear leader of both BRICS and SCO.
- Openly challenged the informational monopoly of the Western propaganda machine (with projects like *Russia Today*).
- Stopped an imminent US/NATO strike on Syria by sending in a Russian Navy Expeditionary Force (which gave Syria a full radar coverage of the entire region).
- Made it possible for Assad to prevail in the Syrian civil war.
- Openly rejected the Western "universal civilizational model" and declared his support for another, a religion and tradition based one.

- Openly rejected a unipolar "New World Order" led by the AngloZionists and declared his support for a multipolar world order.
- Supported Assange (through RussiaToday) and protected Snowden
- Created and promoted a new alliance model between Christianity and Islam thus undermining the "clash of civilization" paradigm
- Booted the AngloZionists out of key locations in the Caucasus (Chechnya, Ossetia)
- Booted the AngloZionists out of key locations in Central Asia (Manas base in Kyrgyzstan)
- Gave Russia the means to defend her interest in the Arctic region, including military means.
- Established a full-spectrum strategic alliance with China which is at the core of both SCO and BRICS.
- Is currently passing laws barring foreign interests from controlling the Russian media.
- Gave Iran the means to develop a much needed civilian nuclear program.
- Is working with China to create a financial system fully separated from the current Anglo-Zionist controlled one (including trade in Rubles or Renminbi).
- Re-established Russian political and economic support for Cuba, Venezuela, Bolivia, Ecuador, Brazil, Nicaragua and Argentina.
- Very effectively deflated the pro-US color-coded revolution in Russia.
- Organized the "Voentorg" which armed the NAF.
- Gave refuge to hundreds of thousands of Ukrainian refugees.
- Sent in vitally needed humanitarian aid to Novorossia.

- Provided direct Russian fire support and possibly even air cover to NAF in key locations (the "southern cauldron" for example).
- Last but not least, he openly spoke of the need for Russia to "sovereignize" herself and to prevail over the pro-US 5th column.

and that list goes on and on. All I am trying to illustrate is that there is a very good reason for the Anglo-Zionist's hatred for Putin: his long record of very effectively fighting them. So unless we assume that Putin had a sudden change of heart or that he simply ran out of energy or courage, I submit that the notion that he suddenly made a 180 makes no sense. His current policies, however, do make sense, as I will try to explain now.

If you are a "Putin betrayed Novorossiya" person, please set that hypothesis aside for a moment, just for argument's sake and assume that Putin is both principled and logical. What could he be doing in the Ukraine? Can we make sense of what we observe?

Imperatives Russia cannot ignore

First, I consider the following sequence indisputable:

First, **Russia must prevail over the current Anglo-Zionist war against her**. What the Empire wants in Russia is regime change followed by complete absorption into the Western sphere of influence including a likely break up of Russia. What is threatened is the very existence of the Russian civilization.

Second, R**ussia will never be safe with a neo-Nazi russophobic regime in power in Kiev.** The Ukie nationalist freaks have proven that it is impossible to negotiate with them (they have broken literally every single agreement signed so far), their hatred for Russia is total (as shown with their constant references to the use of—hypothetical—nuclear weapons against Russia). Therefore,

Third, regime change in Kiev followed by a full de-Nazification is the only possible way for Russia to achieve her vital objectives.

Again, and at the risk of having my words twisted and misrepresented, I have to repeat here that Novorossiya is **not** what is at stake here. It's not even the future of the Ukraine. What is at stake here is a **planetary confrontation** (this is the one thesis of Dugin which I **fully** agree with). The future of the planet depends on the capability of the BRICS/SCO countries to replace the Anglo-Zionist Empire with a very different, multipolar, international order. Russia is crucial and indispensable in this effort (any such effort without Russia is doomed to fail), and the future of Russia is now decided by what Russia will do in the Ukraine. As for the future of the Ukraine, it largely depends on what will happen to Novorossiya, but not exclusively. In a paradoxical way, Novorossiya is more important to Russia than to the Ukraine. Here is why:

For the rest of the Ukraine, Novorossiya is lost. Forever. Not even a joint Putin-Obama effort could prevent that. In fact, the Ukies know that and this is why they make no effort to win the hearts and minds of the local population. If fact, I am convinced that the so-called "random" or "wanton" destruction of the Novorossian industrial, economic, scientific and cultural infrastructure has been intentional act of hateful vengeance similar to the way the AngloZionists always turn to killing civilians when they fail to overcome military forces (the examples of Yugoslavia and Lebanon come to mind). Of course, Moscow can probably force the local Novorossian political leaders to sign some kind of document accepting Kiev's sovereignty, but that will be a fiction, it is way too late for that. If not de jure, then de facto, Novorossiya is never going to accept Kiev's rule again and everybody knows that, in Kiev, in Novorossiya and in Russia.

What could *a* de facto but not *de jure* independence look like?

No Ukrainian military, national guard, oligarch battalion or SBU, full economic, cultural, religious, linguistic and educational independence, locally elected officials and local media, but all that with Ukie flags, no official independence status, no Novorossian Armed Forces (they will be called something like "regional security force" or even "police force") and no Novorossian currency (though the ruble—along with the dollar and euro—will be used on a daily basis). The top officials will have to be officially approved by Kiev (which Kiev will, of course, lest its impotence becomes visible). This will be a **temporary**, **transitional** and **unstable** arrangement, but it will be good enough to provide a face-saving way out to Kiev.

This said, I would argue that **both Kiev and Moscow have an interest in maintaining the fiction of a unitary Ukraine**. For Kiev this is a way to not appear completely defeated by the accursed Moskals. But what about Russia?

What if **you** were in Putin's place?

Ask yourself the following question: *if you were Putin* and your goal was regime change in Kiev, would you prefer Novorossiya to be part of the Ukraine or not? I would submit that having Novorossiya inside is much better for the following reasons:

1. It makes it part, even on a macro-level, of the Ukrainian processes, like national elections or national media.

2. It begs the comparison with the conditions in the rest of the Ukraine.

3. It makes it far easier to influence commerce, business, transportation, etc.

4. It creates an alternative (Nazi-free) political center to Kiev.

5. It makes it easier for Russian interests (of all kind) to penetrate into the Ukraine.

6. It removes the possibility to put up a Cold War-like "wall" or barrier on some geographical marker.

7. It removes the accusation that Russian wants to partition the Ukraine.

In other words, to keep Novorossiya *de jure*, nominally, part of the Ukraine is the best way to appear to be complying with Anglo-Zionist demands while subverting the Nazi junta in power. In a recent article[194] I outlined what Russia could do without incurring any major consequences:

1. Politically oppose the regime everywhere: UN, media, public opinion, etc.

2. Express political support for Novorossiya and any Ukrainian opposition. Continue the informational war (Russian media does a great job).

3. Prevent Novorossiya from falling (covert military aid).

4. Mercilessly keep up the economic pressure on the Ukraine.

5.Disrupt as much as possible the US-EU "axis of kindness."

6. Help Crimea and Novorossiya prosper economically and financially.

In other words—give the appearance of staying out *while very much staying in*.

What is the alternative anyway?

I already hear the chorus of indignant "hurray-patriots" (that is what these folks are called in Russia) accusing me of only seeing Novorossiya as a tool for Russian political goals and of ignoring the death and suffering endured by the people of Novorossiya. To this I will simply reply the following:

Does anybody seriously believe that an independent Novorossiya can live in even minimal peace and security **without** a regime change in Kiev? If Russia cannot afford a Nazi junta in power in Kiev, can Novorossiya?!

In general, the hurray-patriots are long on what should be done now and very short any kind of mid or long-term vision. Just like those who believe that Syria can be saved by sending in the Russian Air Force, the

---

[194] September 21 Ukraine and Russia mini-SITREP http://thesaker.is/september-21-ukraine-and-russia-mini-sitrep/

hurray-patriots believe that the crisis in the Ukraine can be solved by sending in tanks. They are a perfect example of the mind-set H. L. Mencken was referring to when he wrote "For every complex problem there is an answer that is clear, simple, and wrong."

The sad reality is that the mind-set behind such "simple" solutions is always the same one: never negotiate, never compromise, never look long term but only to the immediate future and use force in all cases.

But the facts are here: the US/NATO block is powerful, militarily, economically and politically and it can hurt Russia, especially over time. Furthermore, while Russia can easily defeat the Ukrainian military, this hardly would be a very meaningful "victory." Externally it would trigger a massive deterioration of the international political climate, while internally the Russians would have to suppress the Ukrainian nationalists (not all of them Nazi) by force. Could Russia do that? Again, the answer is that yes—but at what cost?

A good friend of mine was a Colonel in the KGB Special Forces unit called "Kaskad" (which later was renamed "Vympel"). One day he told me how his father, himself a special operator for the GRU, fought against Ukrainian insurgents from the end of World War II in 1945 up to 1958: that is thirteen years! It took Stalin and Khrushchev thirteen years to finally crush the Ukrainian nationalist insurgents. Does anybody in his or her right mind sincerely believe that modern Russia should repeat that policies and spend years hunting down Ukrainian insurgents again?

By the way, if the Ukrainian nationalists could fight the Soviet rule under Stalin and Khrushchev for a full 13 years after the end of the war—how is it that there is no visible anti-Nazi resistance in Zaporozhie, Dnepropetrovsk or Kharkov? Yes, Luganks and Donetsk did rise up and take arms, very successfully—but the rest of the Ukraine? If you were Putin, would you be confident that Russian forces liberating these cities would receive the same welcome that they did in Crimea?

And yet, the hurray-patriots keep pushing for more Russian intervention and further Novorossian military operations against Ukie forces. Is it not about time we begin asking who would benefit from such policies?

It has been an old trick of the US CIA to use the social media and the blogosphere to push for nationalist extremism in Russia. A well-known and respected Russian patriot and journalist—Maksim Shevchenko—had a group of people organized to track down the IP numbers of some of the most influential radical nationalist organizations, website, blogs and individual posters on the Russian Internet. Turns out that most were based in the USA, Canada and Israel. Surprise, surprise. Or, maybe, no surprise at all?

For the AngloZionists, supporting extremists and rabid nationalists in Russia makes perfectly good sense. Either they get to influence the public opinion or they at the very least can be used to bash the regime in power. I personally see no difference between an Udaltsov or a Navalnii on one hand, and a Limonov or a Dugin on the other. Their sole effect is to get people mad at the Kremlin. What the pretext for the anger is does not matter—for Navalny its "stolen elections," for Dugin it's "backstabbed Novorossiya." And it does not matter which of them are actually paid agents or just "useful idiots"—God be their judge—but what does matter is that the solutions they advocate are no solutions at all, just pious pretexts to bash the regime in power.

In the meantime, not only had Putin not sold out, backstabbed, traded away or otherwise abandoned Novorossiya, it's Poroshenko who is barely holding on to power and Banderastan which is going down the tubes. There are also plenty of people who see through this doom and gloom nonsense, both in Russia (Yuri Baranchik[195]) and abroad (M. K. Bhadrakumar[196]).

But what about the oligarchs?

I already addressed this issue in a recent post,[197] but I think that it is important to return to this topic here and the first thing which is crucial to understand in the Russian or Ukrainian context is that oligarchs are a fact of life. This is not to say that their presence is a good thing, only that Putin and Poroshenko and, for that matter, anybody trying to get anything done over there needs to take them into account. The big difference is that while in Kiev a regime controlled by the oligarchs has been replaced by a regime of oligarchs, in Russia the oligarchy can only influence, but not control, the Kremlin. The examples, of Khodorkovsky or Evtushenkov show that the Kremlin still can, and does, smack down an oligarch when needed.

Still, it is one thing to pick on one or two oligarchs and quite another to remove them from the Ukrainian equation: the latter is just not going to happen. So for Putin any Ukrainian strategy has to take into account the presence and, frankly, power of the Ukrainian oligarchs and their Russian counterparts.

Putin knows that oligarchs have their true loyalty only to themselves and that their only "country" is wherever their assets happen to be. As a former KGB foreign intelligence officer for Putin this is an obvious plus, because that mind-set potentially allows him to manipulate them. Any intelligence officer knows that people can be manipulated by a finite list of approaches: ideology, ego, resentment, sex, a skeleton in the closet

---

[195] Вот и конец байкам о войне «партии слива» и «партии войны» / Юрий Баранчик http://www.iarex.ru/articles/50896.html

[196] West beats retreat in Ukraine http://blogs.rediff.com/mkbhadrakumar/2014/09/24/west-beats-retreat-in-ukraine/

[197] Strelkov: from swimming with Piranhas to swimming with Great White sharks http://thesaker.is/strelkov-from-swimming-with-piranhas-to-swimming-with-great-white-sharks/

and, of course, money. From Putin's point of view, Rinat Akhmetov,[198] for example, is a guy who used to employ something like 200,000 people in the Donbass, who clearly can get things done, and whose official loyalty Kiev and the Ukraine is just a camouflage for his real loyalty: his money. Now, Putin does not have to like or respect Akhmetov, most intelligence officers will quietly despise that kind of person, but that also means that for Putin Akhmetov is an absolutely crucial person to talk to, explore options with and, possibly, use to achieve a Russian national strategic objective in the Donbass.

I have already written this many times here: Russians do talk to their enemies. With a friendly smile. This is even more true for a former intelligence officer who is trained to always communicate, smile, appear to be engaging and understanding. For Putin Akhmetov is not a friend or an ally, but he is a powerful figure which can be manipulated in Russia's advantage. What I am trying to explain here is the following:

There are numerous rumors of secret negotiations between Rinat Akhmetov and various Russian officials. Some say that Khodakovski is involved. Others mention Surkov. There is no doubt in my mind that such secret negotiations are taking place. In fact, I am sure that all the parties involved talk to all other parties involved; even with a disgusting, evil and vile creature like Kolomoiski. In fact, the sure signal that somebody has finally decided to take him out would be that nobody would be speaking with him anymore. That will probably happen, with time, but most definitely not until his power base is sufficiently eroded.

One Russian blogger believes[199] that Akhmetov has already been "persuaded" (read: bought off) by Putin and that he is willing to play by the new rules which now say "Putin is boss." Maybe. Maybe not yet, but soon. Maybe never. All I am suggesting is that negotiations between the

---

[198] Rinat Akhmetov https://en.wikipedia.org/wiki/Rinat_Akhmetov

[199] Вот и конец байкам о войне «партии слива» и «партии войны» / Юрий Баранчик http://www.iarex.ru/articles/50896.html

Kremlin and local Ukie oligarchs are as logical and inevitable as the US contacts with the Italian Mafia before the US armed forces entered Italy.

But is there a 5th column in Russia?

Yes, absolutely. First and foremost, it is found inside the Medvedev government itself and even inside the presidential administration. Always remember that Putin was put into power by two competing forces: the secret services and big money. And yes, while it is true that Putin has tremendously weakened the "big money" component (what I call the "Atlantic Integrationists") they are still very much there, though they are more subdued, more careful and less arrogant than during the time when Medvedev was formally in charge. The big change in the recent years is that the struggle between patriots (the "Eurasian Sovereignists") and the 5th column now is in the open, but it if far from over. And we should never underestimate these people: they have a lot of power, a lot of money and a fantastic capability to corrupt, threaten, discredit, sabotage, cover-up, smear, etc. They are also very smart, they can hire the best professionals in the field, and they are very, very **good** at ugly political campaigns. For example, the 5th columnists try hard to give a voice to the National-Bolshevik opposition (both Limonov and Dugin regularly get airtime on Russian TV) and rumor has it that they finance a lot of the National-Bolshevik media (just like the Koch brothers paid for the Tea Party in the USA).

Another problem is that while these guys are objectively doing the US CIA's bidding, there is no proof of it. As I was told many times by a wise friend: most conspiracies are really collusions and the latter are very hard to prove. But the community of interests between the US CIA and the Russian and Ukrainian oligarchy is so obvious as to be undeniable.

The real danger for Russia

So now we have the full picture. Again, Putin has to simultaneously contend with:

1) A strategic psyop campaign run by the US/UK & Co. which combines the corporate media's demonization of Putin **and** a campaign in the social media to discredit him for his passivity and lack of appropriate response to the West.

2) Aa small but very vociferous group of (mostly) National-Bolsheviks (Limonov, Dugin & Co.) who have found in the Novorossian cause a perfect opportunity to bash Putin for not sharing their ideology and their "clear, simple, and wrong" "solutions."

3) A network of powerful oligarchs who want to use the opportunity presented by the actions of first two groups to promote their own interests.

4) A 5th column for whom all of the above is a fantastic opportunity to weaken the Eurasian Sovereignists.

5) A sense of disappointment by many sincere people who feel that Russia is acting like a passive punching-ball.

6) An overwhelming majority of people in Novorossiya who want complete (de facto and *de jure*) independence from Kiev and who are sincerely convinced that any negotiations with Kiev are a prelude to a betrayal by Russia of Novorossian interest.

7) The objective reality that Russian and Novorossian interests are not the same.

8) The objective reality that the Anglo-Zionist Empire is still very powerful and even potentially dangerous.

It is very, very, hard for Putin to try to balance these forces in such a way that the resulting vector is one which is in the strategic interest of Russia. I would argue that there is simply no other solution to this conundrum other than to completely separate Russia's official (declaratory) police and Russia's real actions. The covert help to Novorossiya—the Voentorg—is an example of that, but only a limited one because what Russia must do now goes beyond covert actions: Russia must appear to be doing one thing while doing exactly the opposite.

It is in Russia's strategic interest at this point in time to appear to:

1) Support a negotiated solution along the lines of: a unitary non-aligned Ukraine, with large regional right for all regions while, at the same time, politically opposing the regime everywhere: UN, media, public opinion, etc. and supporting both Novorossiya and any Ukrainian opposition.

2) Give Russian and Ukrainian oligarchs a reason to if not support, then at least not oppose such a solution (for ex: by not nationalizing Akhmetov's assets in the Donbass), while at the same time making sure that there is literally enough "firepower" to keep the oligarch under control.

3) Negotiate with the EU on the actual implementation of Ukraine's Agreement with the EU while at the same time helping the Ukraine commit economic suicide by making sure that there is just the right amount of economic strangulation applied to prevent the regime from bouncing back.

4) Negotiate with the EU and the junta in Kiev over the delivery of gas while at the same time making sure that the regime pays enough for it to be broke.

5) Appear generally non-confrontational toward the USA while at the same time trying as hard as possible to create tensions between the US and the EU.

6) Appear to be generally available and willing to do business with the AngoZionist Empire while at the same time building an alternative international systems not centered on the USA or the Dollar.

As you see, this goes far beyond a regular covert action program. What we are dealing with is a very complex, multi-layered, program to achieve the Russian most important goal in the Ukraine (regime change and de-Nazification) while inhibiting as much as possible the AngloZionists attempts to re-created a severe and long lasting East-West crisis in which the EU would basically fuse with the USA.

Conclusion: a key to Russian policies?

Most of us are used to think in terms of superpower categories. After all, US presidents from Reagan on to Obama have all served us a diet of grand statements, almost constant military operations followed by Pentagon briefings, threats, sanctions, boycotts, etc. I would argue that this has always been the hallmark of Western "diplomacy" from the Crusades to the latest bombing campaign against ISIL. Russia and China have a diametrically opposed tradition. For example, in terms of methodology Lavrov always repeats the same principle: "*we want to turn our enemies into neutrals, we want to turn neutrals into partner and we want to turn partners into friends.*" The role of Russian diplomats is not to prepare for war, but to avoid it. Yes, Russia will fight, but only when diplomacy has failed. If for the US diplomacy is solely a means to deliver threats, for Russia it is a the primary tool to defuse them. It is therefore no wonder at all the US diplomacy is primitive to the point of bordering on the comical. After all, how much sophistication is needed to say "comply or else." Any petty street thug know how to do that. Russian diplomats are much more akin to explosives disposal specialist, or a mine clearance officer: they have to be extremely patient, very careful and fully focused. But most importantly, they cannot allow anybody to rush them lest the entire thing blows up.

Russia is fully aware that the Anglo-Zionist Empire is at war with her and that surrender is simply not an option any more (assuming it ever was). Russia also understands that she is not a real superpower or, even less so, an empire. Russia is only a very powerful country which is trying to de-fang the Empire without triggering a frontal confrontation with it. In the Ukraine, Russia sees no other solution than regime change in Kiev. To achieve this goal Russia will always prefer a negotiated solution to one obtained by force, even though if no other choice is left to her, she will use force. In other words:

Russia's long-term end goal is to bring down the Anglo-Zionist Empire. Russia's midterm goal is to create the conditions for regime change in Kiev. Russia's short-term goal is to prevent the junta from overrunning Novorossiya. Russia's preferred method to achieve these goals is negotiation with all parties involved. A prerequisite to achieve these goals by negotiations is to prevent the Empire from succeeding in creating an acute continental crisis (conversely, the imperial "deep state" fully understands all this, hence the double declaration of war by Obama and Poroshenko.)

As long as you keep these basic principles in mind, the apparent zigzags, contradictions and passivity of Russian policies will begin to make sense.

It is an open question whether Russia will succeed in her goals. In theory, a successful junta attack on Novorossiya could force Russia to intervene. Likewise, there is always the possibility of yet another "false flag," possibly a nuclear one. I think that the Russian policy is sound and the best realistically achievable under the current set of circumstances, but only time will tell.

I am sorry that it took me over 6400 words to explain all that, but in a society where most "thoughts" are expressed as "tweets" and analyses as Facebook posts, it was a daunting task to try to shed some light to what is turning to be a deluge of misunderstandings and misconceptions, all made worse by the manipulation of the social media. I feel that 60,000 words would be more adequate to this task as it is far easier to just throw out a short and simple slogan than to refute its assumptions and implications.

My hope that at least those of you who sincerely were confused by Russia's apparently illogical stance can now connect the dots and make better sense of it all.

September 27, 2014

YET ANOTHER HUGE DIPLOMATIC VICTORY FOR RUSSIA

Unless you read Russian or monitor the free blogosphere, you might not have noticed this, but something big just happened in Russia: Kerry, Nuland and a large State Department delegation have traveled to Sochi where they met with Foreign Minister Lavrov and then with President Putin. With the latter they spent over 4 hours. Not only that, but Kerry made a few rather interesting remarks, saying that the Minsk-2 Agreement (M2A) was the only way forward and that he would strongly caution Poroshenko against the idea of renewing military operations.

To say that this is a stunning development would be an understatement.

For one thing, this means that the so-called "isolation of Russia" is now officially over, even for the "Indispensable Empire." Second, this is, as far as I know, the first official US endorsement of M2A. This is rather humiliating for the US considering that M2A was negotiated without the Americans.

Third, for the very first time the US has actually warned the Ukronazi junta against a military attack. This, at a time when the Ukronazis are in a state of bellicose frenzy and Poroshenko just promised to re-conquer not only the Donetsk Airport, but all of the Donbass, and even Crimea, show that for the very first time the US and Kiev are not on the same page.

Fourth, the USA has, for the first time, declared that if M2A was implemented, EU and US sanctions would be lifted. Interestingly, the Russians were not even interested in discussing the topic of sanctions.

So what does that all mean?

At this point, nothing much.

Americans are terrible negotiators and in every single US-Russian negotiation over the conflict in the Ukraine the Russians completely outnegotiated their American "geostrategic partners" (the quasi-official ironic Russian term describing the West) every time. What typically happens, is that Kerry caves in, then comes back to Washington and changes his tune by 180 degree. The Russians know that and the Russian media stressed that in its analyses.

Still, the USA can zig and then zag as many times as they want, reality does not zag. If anything, the recent presence of Chinese and Indian troops on the Red Square showed that the notion of "isolating Russia" is a non-starter whether Kerry & Co. accept it or not.

Then, there was the rather interesting behavior of Nuland, who was with Kerry's delegation, she refused to speak to the press and left looking rather unhappy.

Finally, a quick check of the Imperial Mouthpieces reveals that the Imperial Propaganda Department does not really know what to make of it all.

So what is going on, really?

Honestly, this one is too early to call and, as I said, the chances for yet another US "zag" are very high.

Still, what "might" be happening is that the Americans have finally (!) figured out a few basic facts:

1. Russia will not back down
2. Russia is ready for war
3. The Nazi-occupied Ukraine is collapsing
4. Most of the world supports Russia
5. The entire US policy toward Russia has failed

All of the above is rather obvious to any halfway competent observer, but for an administration completely intoxicated with imperial hubris, crass ignorance and denial these are very, **very** painful realities to catch up with. However, denying them might, at the end of the day, get the USA nuked. As the expression goes, if you head is in the sand, your ass is in the air.

Thus it is possible that what just happens is the first sign of a US sobering up and that what Kerry came to explore with Lavrov and Putin is some kind of face-saving exit option. If that is so, then this is terminal news for Poroshenko, as this means that the US has basically thrown in the towel in utter disgust with the freaks in power in Kiev.

Furthermore, this might be a sign that US military analysts have taken a very negative view of the Ukronazi changes of success in their planned "Reconquista" of the Donbass. By going to Russia and officially endorsing M2A Kerry might be sending a message to Poroshenko: *forget it, it isn't happening*!

Still, I would strongly caution against any premature optimism. I consider a US "zag" to be a quasi-certitude. My hope is that the "zag" will be limited in magnitude and that when it happens, it will be more about face-saving exit for Obama than about a denial of reality.

What is certain though, is that Russia has won yet another battle is this long war, and that all the signs are pointing at the inevitable defeat of the Empire.

May 13, 2015

PART IV: ANGLO-ZIONISM

ANGLO-ZIONIST: SHORT PRIMER FOR THE NEWCOMERS

"To learn who rules over you, simply find out who you are not allowed to criticize"

Voltaire

Dear new-to-this blog friends,

Why do I speak of "AngloZionists"? I got that question many times in the past, so I will make a separate post about it to (hopefully) explain this once and for all.

1) Anglo

The USA is an Empire. With roughly 1000 overseas bases (depends on how you count), a undeniably messianic ideology, a bigger ~~defense~~ offense budget than the rest of the planet combined, 16+ spy agencies, the dollar as world currency there is no doubt that the US is a planetary Empire. Where did the US Empire come from? Again, that's a no-brainer—from the British Empire. Furthermore, the US Empire is really based on a select group of nations: the ECHELON[200] countries, Australia, Canada, New Zealand, the UK and, of course, the US. What do these countries have in common? They are the leftovers of the British Empire and they are all English speaking. Notice that France, Germany or Japan are not part of this elite even though they are arguably as important or more to the USA then, say, New Zealand and far more powerful. So the "Anglo" part is undeniable. And yet, even though "Anglo" is an ethnic/linguistic/cultural category, while "Zionist" is a political/ideological one, very rarely do I get an objection about speaking of "Anglos," or the "Anglosphere."

[200] ECHELON https://en.wikipedia.org/wiki/ECHELON

2) Zionist

Let's take the (hyper-politically correct) Wikipedia definition of what the word "Zionism"[201] means: it is *"a nationalist movement of Jews and Jewish culture that supports the creation of a Jewish homeland in the territory defined as the Land of Israel."* Apparently, no link to the US, the Ukraine or Timbuktu, right? But think again. Why would Jews—whether defined as a religion or an ethnicity—need a homeland anyway? Why can't they just live wherever they are born, just like Buddhist (a religion) or the African Bushmen (ethnicity) who live in many different countries? The canonical answer is that Jews have been persecuted everywhere and that therefore they need their own homeland to serve as a safe haven in case of persecutions. Without going into the issue of **why** Jews were persecuted everywhere and, apparently, in all times, this rationale clearly implies if not the inevitability of more persecutions or, at the very least, a high risk thereof. Let's accept that for demonstration sake and see what this, in turn, implies.

First, that implies that Jews are inherently threatened by non-Jews, who are all at least potential anti-Semites. The threat is so severe that a separate Gentile-free homeland must be created as the only, best and last way to protect Jews worldwide. This, in turn, implies that the continued existence of this homeland should become an vital and irreplaceable priority of all Jews worldwide lest a persecution suddenly breaks out and they have nowhere to go.

Furthermore, until all Jews finally "move up" to Israel, they had better be very, very careful as all the *goyim* around them could literally come down with a sudden case of genocidal anti-Semitism[202] at any moment. Hence all the anti-anti-Semitic organizations à la ADL or Union des Etudiants Juifs de France (UEJF), the Betar clubs, the network of sayanim,

---

[201] Zionism https://en.wikipedia.org/wiki/Zionism

[202] Michael Neumann: What Is Anti-Semitism? http://www.counterpunch.org/2002/06/04/what-is-antisemitism/

etc. In other words, far from being a local "dealing with Israel only" phenomenon, Zionism is a worldwide movement whose aim is to protect Jews from the apparently incurable anti-Semitism of the rest of the planet. As Israel Shahak[203] correctly identified it, Zionism postulates that Jews should "think locally and **act globally**" and when given a choice of policies always ask THE crucial question: "*But is it good for Jews?*"[204]

So far from being only focused on Israel, **Zionism is really a global, planetary, ideology** which unequivocally split up all of mankind into two groups (Jews and Gentiles), which assumes that the latter are all potential genocidal maniacs (which is racist) and believes that saving Jewish lives is qualitatively different and more important than saving Gentile lives (which is racist again). Anyone doubting the ferocity of this determination should either ask a Palestinian, or study the holiday of Purim, or both. Even better, read Gilad Atzmon[205] and look up his definition of what is brilliantly called "pre-traumatic stress disorder."

3) Anglo-Zionist

The British Empire and the early USA used to be pretty much wall-to-wall Anglo. Sure, Jews had a strong influence (in banking for example), but Zionism was a non-issue not only among non-Jews, but also among US Jews. Besides, religious Jews were often very hostile to the notion of a secular Israel while secular Jews did not really care about this quasi-Biblical notion. World War II definitely gave a massive boost to the Zionist movement while, as Norman Finkelstein[206] explained it, the topic of the "Holocaust" became central to Jewish discourse and identity only many years later. I won't go into the history of the rise to power of Jews

---

[203] Israel Shahak: *Jewish History, Jewish Religion: The Weight of Three Thousand Years* (Get Political)

[204] Lawrence Davidson: But Is It Good for the Jews? http://www.informationclearinghouse.info/article39558.htm

[205] Gilad Atzmon: *The Wandering Who*

[206] Norman Finkelstein: *The Holocaust Industry: Reflections on the Exploitation of Jewish Suffering*, New Edition, 2nd Edition.

in the USA, but from roughly Ford to G.W. Bush's neocons it has been steady. And even though Obama initially pushed them out, they came right back in through the back door. Right now, the only question is whether US Jews have more power than US Anglos, or the other way around. Before going any further, let me also immediately say that **I am not talking about Jews, or Anglos, as a group**, but I am referring to the top 1% within each of these groups. Furthermore, I don't believe that the top 1% of Jews cares any more about Israel or the 99% of Jews, than the top 1% of Anglos care about the USA or the Anglo people. So, here my thesis:

The US empire is run by a 1% (or less) elite which can be called the "deep state" which is composed of two main groups: Anglos and Jews. These two groups are in many ways hostile to each other (just like the SS and SA, or Trotskyists and Stalinists), but they share 1) a racist outlook on the rest of mankind 2) a messianic ideology 3) a phenomenal propensity for violence 4) an obsession with money and greed and its power to corrupt. So they work together almost all the time.

Now this might seem basic, but so many people miss it, that I will have to explicitly state it: **to say that most US elites are Anglos or Jews does not mean that most Anglos or Jews are part of the US elites**. That is a straw man argument which deliberately ignores the **non-commutative** property of my thesis to turn it into a racist statement which accuses most/all Anglos or Jews of some evil doing. So to be very clear:

When I speak of Anglo-Zionist Empire I am referring to the **predominant ideology** of the one-percenters elites which for this Empire's "deep state."

By the way, there are non-Jewish Zionists (Biden, in his own words) and there are (plenty of) anti-Zionist Jews. Likewise, there are non-Anglo imperialists and there are (plenty of) anti-imperialists Anglos. To speak of "Nazi Germany" or "Soviet Russia" does in no way imply that all Germans were Nazis, or all Russian s Communists. All this means it that the predominant ideology of these nations at that specific moment in time was National Socialism and Marxism, that's all.

My personal opinion now

First, I don't believe that Jews are a race or an ethnicity. I always doubted that, but reading Shlomo Sand[207] really convinced me. Jews are not defined by religion either (most/many are secular). Truly, Jews are a tribe. A group one can chose to join (Elizabeth Taylor)[208] or leave (Gilad Atzmon). In other words, I see "Jewishness" as a culture, or ideology, or education or any other number of things, but not something rooted in biology. I fully agree with Atzmon when he says that Jews are racist, but not a race. Second, I don't even believe that the concept of "race" has been properly defined and, hence, that it has any objective meaning. I therefore don't differentiate between human beings on the basis of an undefined criterion. Third, since being Jew (or not) is a choice, one to belong, adhere and endorse a tribe (secular Jews) or a religion (Judaics). Any choice implies a judgment call and it therefore a legitimate target for scrutiny and criticism. Fourth, I believe that Zionism, even when secular, instrumentalizes the values, ideas, myths and ethos of rabbinical Judaism (aka "Talmudism" or "Phariseeism") and both are racist in their core value and assumptions. Fifth, both Zionism and Nazism are twin brothers born from the same ugly womb: 19th century European nationalism (Brecht was right, ""The belly is still fertile from which the foul beast sprang"). Nazis and Zionists can hate each other to their hearts' content, but they are still twins. Sixth, I reject any and all form of racism as a denial of our common humanity, a denial of the freedom of choice of each human being and—being an Orthodox Christian—as a grievous heresy.

---

207 Shlomo Sand: *The Invention of the Jewish People*

208 Jessica Ravitz: Exploring Elizabeth Taylor's Jewish conversion http://religion.blogs.cnn.com/2011/03/24/making-sense-of-elizabeth-taylors-jewish-conversion/

To me people who chose to identify themselves with, and as, Jews are not inherently different from any other human and they deserve no more and no less rights and protections than any other human being.

I will note here that while the vast majority of my readers of Anglos, they almost never complain about the "Anglo" part of my "Anglo-Zionist" descriptor. The vast majority of objections focus on the "Zionist" part. You might want to think long and hard about why this is so and what it tells us about the kind of power Zionists have over the prevailing ideology. Could it be linked to the reason why the (openly racist and truly genocidal) Israeli prime minister gets more standing ovations in Congress (29)[209] than the US president (25)?

Some objections:

Q: It makes you sound like a Nazi/redneck/racist/idiot/etc.

A: I don't care. I don't write this blog for brainwashed zombies.

Q: You turn people off.

A: If by speaking the truth and using correct descriptors I turn them off, then this blog is not for them.

Q: You can offend Jews.

A: Only those who believe that their ideas cannot be challenged or criticized.

Q: But you will lose readers!!

A: This is not a popularity contest.

Q: Your intentions might be good, but they are easily misinterpreted.

A: This is why I define my words very carefully and strictly.

Q: But why are you so stubborn about this?

A: Because I am sick and tired of those in power hiding in the dark: let's expose them and freely challenge them. How can you challenge something which is hidden?

---

[209] Justin Elliott: Netanyahu gets more standing ovations than Obama http://www.salon.com/2011/05/24/netanyahu_standing_ovations/

Q: But I am a *hasbarachnik* and I need to get you to stop using that expression!!

A: Give it up and find an easier target for your efforts. You will still get paid.

A: I have a much better term.

Q: Good! Use it on your blog then.

That's it for now.

Actually no, there is one more thing, while I am at it:

Open message to those objecting to my use of the article 'the' in front of the word "Ukraine": before lecturing others, learn Russian and learn a little something about the history of the Ukraine.

In conclusion, a plea: can we pretty please stop this nonsense now? There are far more important things to analyze and worry about than my use of this or that expression, word or description. If you don't like it—great. Just consider that I am wrong (I often am, so I won't take offense). Can we please stop pretending like Jews and Jewish related issues are **T**he **M**ost **I**mportant **T**hing **I**n **T**he **U**niverse (TMITITU) and deal with the really important issues?

Thanks,

The Saker

PS: **IMPORTANT ADDENDUM**: you are more than welcome to comment discuss this topic all you want, but I have wasted enough of my time on this kind of nonsense. Not being a Jew myself, I don't have to share in any ethnocentric notion of exceptionalism and self-aggrandizement and this is why I said that the topic of Jews and Jewish issues is not TMITITU, at least not for me. So **I will not respond to comments to this post**, sorry. Careful though—I still loathe racism in all its forms, including anti-Jewish racism (even if Jews are not a race!), so don't bother posting long anti-Jewish rants as I will toss them all to /dev/null. Fact based, logical and otherwise substantive comments are, of course, not only welcome, but requested. Racist shit, pardon my French, is not.

September 3, 2014

DADDY—WHAT'S A 'NEOCON'?! ETHNIC MAFIA WARS IS THE USA

[Amy Goodman interviews Andrew Cockburn on *DemocracyNow]!*[210]

> Here is a most revealing exchange which occurred at the end of the interview:
>
> AMY GOODMAN: In 2006, you write that George W. Bush said to his father, "What's a neocon?"
>
> ANDREW COCKBURN: That's right. One of the rare moments of sort of communication between the two. Bush said to — they were out at Kennebunkport, and Bush Jr. says, "Can I ask you a question? What's a neocon?" And the father says, "Do you want names or a description?" The President says, "I'll take a description." He says, "I'll give it to you in one word: Israel," which is interesting on all sorts of levels, including the confirmation that our president doesn't really read the newspapers.
>
> AMY GOODMAN: Explain what you mean when you say that. And how do you know that this conversation took place at their vacation home?
>
> ANDREW COCKBURN: Well, I can't really say who told me, but it's someone who was — I have absolute confidence in both in their — that they're telling the truth and also in their position to be aware of this conversation.

I find this exchange most interesting. From my own observations of the power elites in Washington, DC (I was very close to them in the 1986-1991 years) I became aware of an highly significant albeit very covert struggle taking place: the old Anglos were being pushed out by Zionist

---

[210] Amy Goodman interviews Andrew Cockburn on DemocracyNow! http://www.democracynow.org/article.pl?sid=07/03/07/1436239)]

Jews. Here is what I was told, under strict secrecy, by one of the "old Anglos" in 1990:

"When Ronald Reagan was elected, Jews realized that the Democratic Party would not see power for one hell of a long time. So what they did is switch allegiance to the Republican Party. In various think tanks they began by contributing large amounts of money and, pretty soon, they were in the position to impose their own executive directors and research fellows. This is what happened at the Heritage Foundation and this is what is happening here (sorry—I cannot name this institution, VS)"

At that time I did not make too much of this, and I soon left the USA only to return only a decade later. Now I am observing how the Anglos are fighting back using the upcoming attack against Iran as their chance to discredit the "neocons." Hence the Mearsheimer, Walt, Scheuer (and pretty much most of the old CIA guard), Carter, Brzezinski, Buchanan, Kwiatkowski, Scott Ritter, & Co, overtly attacking the "neocons" and Israel (does anyone believe that all these guys suddenly and miraculously acquired an anti-imperial conscience?!)

The neocons are not blind to the real nature of the attack. Here is what Jonah Goldberg says about that:

"The term [neocon] does more damage than good because it allows people to hide their real intent. People who want to denounce the influence of Jews get to use the word "neocon' when they really mean "Jewish conservatives" without being held accountable."

My best guess is that is what happened with Baby Bush's election. Papa Bush was firmly in the "old Anglo" camp (Baker & co.) and he tended to despite the pro-Israeli "neocons" calling them the "crazies in the basement." He had to compose with them because of their power and money, but his real loyalties were always with the Anglo oil lobby. The climax of this takeover came with the presidential election in which Baby Bush decided to run and the Zionist Jews cleverly pushed the candidacy of Dubya which, on the face of it, appeared to be an Anglo, and being Papa's boy the Anglos backed him. But being the semi-literate failure that he is, Baby Bush became a perfect pawn in the hands of the Zionist lobby and the neocons. After 9/11 however, the neocons took him under total control, and the lame attempt of the Anglo camp (Baker & Hamilton) to get him "back on track" failed. The neocons easily overcame this challenge.

So who are these guys? According to the *Christian Science Monitor* (CSM),[211] these are the main neocon players:

Irving Kristol

Widely referred to as the "godfather" of neoconservatism, Mr. Kristol was part of the "New York Intellectuals," a group of critics mainly of Eastern European Jewish descent. In the late 1930s, he studied at City College of New York where he became a Trotskyist. From 1947 to 1952, he was the managing editor of *Commentary* magazine, later called the "neocon bible." By the late 1960s, Kristol had shifted from left to right on the political spectrum, due partly to what he considered excesses and anti-Americanism among liberals. Kristol built the intellectual framework of neoconservatism, founding and editing journals such as *The Public Interest* and *The National Interest..* Kristol is a fellow at the *American Enterprise Institute* and author of numerous books, including "*Neoconservatism: The Autobiography of an Idea.*" He is the father of a *Weekly Standard* editor and oft-quoted neoconservative William Kristol.

Norman Podhoretz

Considered one of neoconservatism's founding fathers, Mr. Podhoretz studies, writes, and speaks on social, cultural, and international matters. From 1990 to 1995, he worked as editor-in-chief of *Commentary* magazine, a neoconservative journal published by *the American Jewish Committee.* Podhoretz advocated liberal political views earlier in life, but broke ranks in the early 1970s. He became part of the *Coalition for a*

---

[211] This *Christian Science monitor article* has been taken down.

Democratic Majority founded in 1973 by Senator Henry "Scoop" Jackson and other intervention-oriented Democrats. Podhoretz has written nine books, including "Breaking Ranks" (1979), in which he argues that Israel's survival is crucial to US military strategy. He is married to like-minded social critic Midge Decter. They helped establish the *Committee on the Present Danger* in the late 1970s and the Committee for the Free World in the early 1980s. Podhoretz' son, John, is a New York Post columnist.

Paul Wolfowitz

After serving as deputy secretary of defense for three years, Mr. Wolfowitz, a key architect of the Iraq war, was chosen in March 2005 by President Bush to be president of the World Bank. From 1989 to 1993, Wolfowitz served as undersecretary of defense for policy in charge of a 700-person team that had major responsibilities for the reshaping of military strategy and policy at the end of the Cold War. In this capacity Wolfowitz co-wrote with Lewis "Scooter" Libby the 1992 draft *Defense Planning Guidance,* which called for US military dominance over Eurasia and pre-emptive strikes against countries suspected of developing weapons of mass destruction. After being leaked to the media, the draft proved so shocking that it had to be substantially rewritten. After 9/11, many of the principles in that draft became key points in the 2002 *National Security Strategy of the United States,* an annual report. During the 1991 Gulf War, Wolfowitz advocated extending the war's aim to include toppling Saddam Hussein's regime.

Richard Perle

Famously nicknamed the "Prince of Darkness" for his hardliner stance on national security issues, Mr. Perle is one of the most high-profile neoconservatives. He resigned in March 2003 as chairman of the Pentagon's Defense Policy Board after being criticized for conflicts of interest. From 1981 to 1987 he was Assistant Secretary of Defense for international security policy. Perle is a chief architect of the "creative destruction" agenda to reshape the Middle East, starting with the invasion of Iraq. He outlined parts of this agenda in a key 1996 report for Israel's right-wing Likud Party called "*A Clean Break: A New Strategy for Securing the Realm.*" Perle helped establish two think tanks: The Center for Security Policy and The Jewish Institute for National Security. He is also a fellow at the American Enterprise Institute, an advisor for the counter-terrorist think tank Foundation for the Defense of Democracies, and a director of the Jerusalem Post.

Douglas Feith

The defense department announced in January 2005 that Mr. Feith will resign this summer as undersecretary of defense for policy, the Pentagon's No. 3 civilian position, which he has held since being appointed by President Bush in July 2001. Feith also served in the Reagan administration as Deputy Assistant Secretary of Defense for negotiations policy. Prior to that, he served as special counsel to Richard Perle. Before his service at the Pentagon, Feith worked as a Middle East specialist for the National Security Council in 1981-82. Feith is well known for his support of Israel's right-wing Likud Party. In 1997, Feith was honored along with his father Dalck Feith, who was active in a Zionist youth movement in his native Poland, for their "service to Israel and the Jewish people" by pro-Likud Zionist Organization of America at its 100th anniversary banquet. In 1992, he was vice president of the advisory board of the *Jewish Institute for National Security Affairs.* Mr. Feith is a former chairman and currently a director of the *Center for Security Policy.*

Lewis "Scooter" Libby

Mr. Libby is currently chief of staff and national security advisor for Vice President Dick Cheney. He's served in a wide variety of posts. In the first Bush administration, Mr. Libby served in the Department of Principal Deputy Under Secretary (Strategy and Resources), and, later, as Deputy Under Secretary of Defense for Policy. Libby was a founding member of the Project for the New American Century. He joined Paul Wolfowitz, William Kristol, Robert Kagan, and others in writing its 2000 report entitled, *Rebuilding America's Defenses—Strategy, Forces, and Resources for a New Century*. Libby co-authored the once-shocking draft of the *Defense Planning Guidance* with Mr. Wolfowitz for then-Defense Secretary Dick Cheney in 1992. Libby serves on the advisory board of the Center for Russian and Eurasian Studies of the *RAND Corporation*.

John Bolton

In February 2005, Mr. Bolton was nominated US ambassador to the UN by President Bush. If confirmed, he would move to this position from the Department of State where he was Under Secretary for Arms Control, the top US non-proliferation official. Prior to this appointment, Bolton was senior vice president of the neoconservative think tank American Enterprise Institute. He also held a variety of positions in both the George H. W. Bush and Ronald Reagan administrations. Bolton has often made claims not fully supported by the intelligence community. In a controversial May 2002 speech entitled, "*Beyond the Axis of Evil*," Bolton fingered Libya, Syria, and Cuba as "other rogue states intent on acquiring weapons of mass destruction." In July 2003, the CIA and other agencies reportedly objected strongly to claims Bolton made in a draft assessment about the progress Syria has made in its weapons programs.

Elliott Abrams

In February of 2005 Elliott Abrams was appointed deputy assistant to the president and deputy national security advisor for global democracy strategy. From December 2002 to February 2005, Mr. Abrams served as special assistant to the president and senior director for Near East and North African affairs. Abrams began his political career by taking a job with the Democratic Senator Henry M. "Scoop" Jackson. He held a variety of State Department posts in the Reagan administration. He was a senior fellow at the Hudson Institute from 1990 to the 1996 before becoming president of the Ethics and Public Policy Center, which "affirms the political relevance of the great Western ethical imperatives." Abrams also served as chairman of the US Commission on International Religious Freedom. In 1991, Abrams pleaded guilty to withholding information from Congress about the Iran-Contra affair. President George H. W. Bush pardoned him in 1992. In 1980, he married Rachel Decter, daughter of neocon veterans Norman Podhoretz and Midge Decter.

Robert Kagan

Mr. Kagan writes extensively on US strategy and diplomacy. Kagan and fellow neoconservative William Kristol co-founded the Project for a New American Century (PNAC) in 1997. Kagan signed the famous 1998 PNAC letter sent to President Clinton urging regime change in Iraq. After working as principal speechwriter to Secretary of State George P. Shultz from 1984-1985, he was hired by Elliott Abrams to work as deputy for policy in the State Department's Bureau of Inter-American Affairs. He is a senior associate at the Carnegie Endowment for International Peace (CEIP). He is also an international affairs columnist for *The Washington Post*, and contributing editor at *The New Republic* and *The Weekly Standard*. He wrote the bestseller *Of Paradise and Power: America and Europe in the New World Order*. Kagan's wife, Victoria Nuland, was chosen by Vice President Dick Cheney as his deputy national security advisor.

Michael Ledeen

Seen by many as one of the most radical neoconservatives, Mr. Ledeen is said to frequently advise George W. Bush's top advisor Karl Rove on foreign policy matters. He is one of the strongest voices calling for regime change in Iran. In 2001, Ledeen co-founded the Coalition for Democracy in Iran. He served as Secretary of State Alexander Haig's advisor during the Reagan administration. Ledeen is resident scholar in the Freedom

Chair at the *American Enterprise Institute*, where he works closely with Richard Perle. He is also a member of the *Jewish Institute of National Security Affairs'* advisory board and one of its founding organizers. He was Rome correspondent for the New Republic magazine from 1975-1977, and founding editor of the Washington Quarterly. Ledeen also wrote *The War Against the Terror Masters*, which advocates regime change in Iraq, Syria, and Saudi Arabia.

William Kristol

Son of "godfather" of neoconservatism Irving Kristol, Bill Kristol is currently chairman of the Project for a New American Century, which he co-founded with leading neoconservative writer Robert Kagan. He is also editor of the influential *Weekly Standard.* Like other neoconservatives Frank Gaffney Jr. and Elliott Abrams, Kristol worked for hawkish Democratic Sen. Henry "Scoop" Jackson. But by 1976, he became a Republican. he served as chief of staff to Education Secretary William Bennett during the Reagan administration and chief of staff to former Vice President Dan Quayle during the George H. W. Bush presidency. Kristol continuously called for Saddam Hussein's ouster since the 1991 Gulf War. With the like-minded Lawrence Kaplan, Kristol co-wrote *The War Over Iraq: Saddam's Tyranny and America's Mission.* He is on the board of advisors of the *Foundation for the Defense of Democracies*, established as a counterterrorist think tank after 9/11.

Frank Gaffney Jr.

Mr. Gaffney is the founder, president, and CEO of the influential Washington think tank Center for Security Policy, whose mission is "to promote world peace through American strength." In 1987, President Reagan nominated Gaffney to be Assistant Secretary of Defense for international security policy. He earlier served as the Deputy Assistant Secretary of Defense for Nuclear Forces and Arms Control Policy under then-Assistant Secretary Richard Perle. In the late 1970s, Gaffney served as a defense and foreign policy advisor to Sen. Henry "Scoop" Jackson. He is columnist for the *Washington Times* and a contributor to *Defense News* and *Investor's Business Daily*. He is a contributing editor to *National Review Online, WolrdNetDaily.com* and *JewishWorldReview.com*. Gaffney is also one of 25 mostly neoconservative co-signers of the Project for a *New American Century's Statement of Principles*.

[BTW—one important name is missing from this list: Eliott Cohen.][212]

The mere fact that the CSM would make and publish such list with all-not-too-subtle references at Israel & Jewish institutions is telling of how desperate and determined the old Anglo guard is.

This list of neocons includes several non-Jews such as Bolton or, for that matter, Cheney himself who, while missing on this list, is certainly a major neocon player. This goes to show that equating Jews to neocons is as wrong as equating any Anglo person with what I call here the "old Anglo" camp. While ethnicity does play an important role here (principally by making any attack on neocons subject to accusations of anti-Semitism, and by making any criticism of Israel, and the unconditional support of it by the USA as total "crimethink") it is not the key element. The key thing is two mafia cliques fighting for power and these cliques are composed of people from the same ethnicity just as the Italian or Irish mafias were. Neocons do not speak for Jews any more than Joseph Stalin spoke for Georgians, or Putin for ethnic Russians. However, there can be little doubt that Stalin did try hard to promote supporters from non-Russian (and non-Jewish I would add) stock, while today Putin is promoting Russians over the Yeltsin era people (who were often Jews),

It is in fact a very sad but real danger that people disgusted with the neocons will blame "Jews" for what is happening in the USA today. This is why it is essential to separate these two concepts and keep reminding

---

[212] This reference has been taken down.

people of the many Americans Jews who are at the forefront of the struggle against the neocons today (Chomsky, Fingelstein, Neumann, Goodman, etc.) and who have to put up with constant accusations of being "self-hating Jews."

Dubya was clearly chosen by the neocons not in spite of, but "because" he is so utterly clueless about pretty much any issue, including the behind-the-scenes power politics in the USA. Speaking of which:

The CIA and the FBI seem to have been bastions of the old Anglo guard, which is why there was this truly huge purge at the CIA over the past years. This is also one of the main sources of leaks to the press about the planned war against Iran. As for the FBI the upcoming trial of the AIPAC officials for espionage goes to show that the FBI still is trying to hurt the Zionist power. Ditto for the Scooter Libby trial which is a non-so-subtle attempt to get at Cheney and his office.

As for the Pentagon, my best guess is that the top brass there is totally neocon co-opted, but that the middle-top layer is fighting back, again with leaks about Iran and all the stuff about the (now defunct) Office of Special Plans.

How to deal with Iran is the issue which brought these two camps in an overt confrontation. Simply put, the Anglos have "nothing" to gain form a war with Iran (and everything to lose), while the neocons clearly realize that Dubya's presidency is the last chance to get the USA to fight one more war on Israel's behalf (and deliver a final blow to the old Anglo guard in the process).

So who will prevail?

My guess is that the Anglos are "out" and have lost power for one heck of a long while. Even if the Republicans lose the presidency in 2008, the conference in Herzilia and the recent speeches of all the main Democratic presidential candidates at the AIPAC meeting clearly show that the Democratic Party is even more pro-neocon that the Republican one.

Only a "third party" (really a "true" second one) which would eject "both" the Anglo-oil and the neocon-Israeli lobbies from power would be an alternative and this, I sadly have to say, is not something I see happening anytime soon.

The USA is really, really in very bad shape and its foreseeable future looks very bleak.

May 2, 2007

HOW A MEDIEVAL CONCEPT OF ETHNICITY MAKES NATO COMMIT YET ANOTHER A DANGEROUS BLUNDER

Acting as one—which of course they are—President Bush[213] and the US House of Representatives announced[214] yesterday that they both favor the entry of the Ukraine and Georgia into NATO. That Dubya would take such an idiotic position is of no surprise of course, but that the House would pass such a resolution *unanimously* is quite shocking: not a single representative had the brains to understand what kind of message such a vote would send to Russia. Either that, or they did not care. I am not sure which is worse. Not even the fact that most Ukrainians want nothing to do with NATO could influence the crazed neocons who nowadays run the USA: as always, *knew they were right.*[215] So let's look at the bigger picture here and consider what exactly is going on.

NATO was founded with the unequivocal mandate to protect its member from any aggressor, i.e. the Soviet Union. Considering that Stalin had just absorbed all of Eastern Europe into his communist empire the establishment of NATO made sense. For all the bombastic statements about D-day, the RAF, Patton and Montgomery Western strategists knew full well that it was the Soviet Union which had defeated Hitler and that the Western Front was little more than a sideshow to the real thing.

The only thing which the West could oppose to the might of the Soviet Army was the power of the US nuclear arsenal. It was therefore absolutely essential to demonstrate to the Soviets that any attack on Western Europe would involve the vital interests of the USA. Thus "a nuclear tripwire called NATO was laid down along the Iron Curtain to draw a

---

[213] Bush backs Ukraine on Nato bid http://news.bbc.co.uk/2/hi/europe/7324035.stm

[214] U.S. House of Representatives backs Ukraine and Georgia NATO bids http://www.sputniknews.com/world/20080401/102732967.html

[215] Jacob Heilbrunn: They Knew They Were Right: The Rise of the Neocons

line in the sand" (at least this is how the media pundits and the talking heads would have phrased it). Soon, however, the Soviets detonated their own nuclear device and it became clear to all the parties involved that a war, any war, could potentially rapidly escalate into MADness, as in Mutually Assured Destruction. Later, MAD was revised to a more elegant "*flexible response*," but the underlying ideas always remained the same: making a war unwinnable.

The thing to remember here is that NATO was created as an organization of last resort, something like the sniper's hand grenade: something which could only be used in a truly desperate, hopeless, situation; something which only an existential threat could justify.

When in the late eighties the Soviet leaders agreed to withdraw from Europe and to dismantle the Soviet Union they were given all sorts of promises by the West about how the West would never take advantage of this situation; they were given solemn promises of Western support and they were told that new democratic Russia would forever be considered a friend and a partner.

Not a single one of these promises has been kept. Not one. Quite to the contrary, the West embarked on what can only be called a systematic campaign to encircle and threaten Russia.

The USA withdrew from the Anti-Ballistic Missile Treaty, the US Navy continued to aggressively patrol right off the Russian territorial waters. The West has not only absorbed all of Eastern Europe into NATO, but it has even admitted the Baltic countries (never mind that two of the latter endlessly violated the human rights of their not-so-small Russian minority). The West bombed Yugoslavia, a Russian ally, in a clear violation of the UN Charter. The West has even given full support to the crazed Chechen separatists even though the latter committed numerous atrocities reminiscent of the worst moments of the civil war in Sierra Leone. After 9/11, when the American public suddenly discovered Wahhabi terrorism, this pro-Chechen stance was rapidly abandoned in favor of the new priorities of the GWOT.

Now US neocons are pushing for the deployment of elements of an anti-ballistic missile system (clearly directed against Russia) in Eastern Europe. Frankly, short of declaring war on Russia on behalf of Yakut separatists I don't see how the West could have been more vindictive, provocative and hostile to Russia.

But why does the West hate Russia so much?

First, it's of course not "the West." What we are talking about here are the Western political establishment or, in other terms, the neocons which now are firmly in power in most key Western nations.

And what is a neocon, if not a former Trotskyite? (just need to google "neocon" and "Trotsky" and see for yourself). Of course, the neocons have adapted their ideology to new circumstances, but the core of this ideology and the psychological makeup of its proponents has not changed very much since the times of Trotsky. But then, what is a Trotskyite?

Following the Bolshevik Revolution of 1917, the term "Trotskyist" really only had one possible meaning in the Russian language: it simply meant a Jewish Bolshevik.

While most Russian Jews were not Bolsheviks at all (many were Mensheviks, Bundists, Anarchists, etc.) a majority of Bolsheviks was Jewish and a super-majority of members of the secret police, the infamous ChK, were Jewish Trotskyists. These were the folks who butchered the Russian peasantry, the Russian nobility, the Russian intelligentsia, the Russian Orthodox clergy in what can only be considered a systematic campaign to exterminate any expression of the Russian culture (which, at that time, very much included the Ukrainian culture and people too, hence the many years of terror in the Ukraine and the carefully orchestrated "Golodomor" or famine).

There are many theories for why these Jewish Trotskyists hated everything Russian or Orthodox with such a passion, some of them good, and many of them nonsense. Whether the Ukrainian pogroms are the cause of this hatred, or the Czarist discriminatory policies toward Jews, or whether there are far more fundamental religious reasons behind this hatred is beside the point. What matters is that Trotskyists indisputably suffered from a russophobia of a truly genocidal magnitude and that this hatred made them kill far, far more people than Hitler could have ever dreamed of exterminating.

The modern neocons, who are the descendants and intellectual heirs of the Trotskyists (primarily in an ideological sense, but sometimes even literally) still very much feel this hatred—hence all this talk about a "resurgent Russia" and the danger it presumably represents for the West.

The crucial thing to understand here is that far from seeing themselves as the butchers of Russia, the Trotskyite/neocons see themselves as greatly victimized by the Russians. Why is that? Because, as any history book will tell you, the original Trotskyists were eventually themselves persecuted (and often executed) by Stalin and his goons.

Stalin himself was a Georgian who could not even speak Russian properly, and his accomplices, whether ethnically Russian or not, can hardly been seen as a manifestation of Russian identity. Still, Stalin skillfully used the Russian national sentiment to promote his policies and, later, to get the Russian masses to fight the Nazis (who had originally been greeted as liberators from the Red Terror). Following the Soviet victory in 1945 Stalin never returned to the original Bolshevik "internationalism."

Stalin's purges did imprison and kill many Jews, but there were still plenty left in the Party apparatus. The point here is not to make ethnic distinctions, at least not at this stage, the point is to realize that when one Bolshevik group replaced another one of these groups had a very strong ethnic component. Here is how I would characterize the two groups:

a) **The Trotskyists**: they were primarily intellectuals who truly believed in the ideas of communism; their aim was to spread communism to the rest of the world; they viewed terror as something which accelerates the course of history toward the inevitable triumph of communism;

they believed in the Party as the collective vanguard of the people. Lastly, though Trotskyists had no interest in, or need for, Judaism (or any other religion) most of them definitely saw themselves as culturally Jewish, communist "internationalism" notwithstanding. While this might sound rather bizarre to the modern reader one needs to remember that the Russian Empire was in its nature and structure multi-ethnic (just as the Byzantine or the Ottoman Empires had been) and that at the turn of the 19th century 97% of all Jews of the Russian Empire spoke Yiddish and not Russian in their homes. There was no such thing as a "Russian Jew" in 1917. There were Jews, and there were Russians (a baptized Jew was, by the way, considered as Russian; even more interestingly, Karaites[216] were not considered Jews at all).

b) **the Stalinists**: they were basically criminal thugs who believed in nothing besides power, and while they were more than happy to use the communist ideals as a justification for their struggle for power they did not care in the least about "world communism" and any other ideological nonsense. What they wanted is power in the Soviet Union. Period. For them terror was both a means toward the goal of absolute power and an end in itself, a method of ruling over Russia. Stalin understood that as long as the Party could exist as an aggregation of factions and individuals (as it had been originally; see democratic centralism[217]) his power would not be absolute, he therefore aimed at transforming the Bolshevik into a party which he would absolutely control. Since many, if not most, top Party officials were Jews, Stalin's purges did, of course, affect many Jews, but it would be a mistake to think that these purges were aimed at Jews as such—they were aimed at the Party and its internal diversity. Ethnicity did not matter in the least to Stalin at least as long as he did not feel that some ethnic group might threaten his power.

---

[216] Karaite Judaism https://en.wikipedia.org/wiki/Karaite_Judaism

[217] Democratic centralism https://en.wikipedia.org/wiki/Democratic_centralism

We can observe exactly the same psycho-political divide among the Nazis, by the way. In this case, the ideologues, the "true believers" would be Goebbels, Himmler, SS and Hitler himself and the "petty thugs"—Röhm, Goering and the SA. I suppose that the same types can be found in any revolutionary movement which combines "intellectual terrorists" with petty criminals.

This digression is important because Stalin's purges and the gradual erosion of the influence of Jews in the CPSU between the 1930s to the end of the Soviet Union has left a very bitter sense of victimization in the Jewish circles which eventually spawned off the neocon movement. This sense of victimization culminated in the mass emigration of Soviet Jews to Israel and the USA which was only made possible by a major political confrontation between the West and the Soviet leaders. The fact that non-Jews had no right to emigrate at all was given no attention whatsoever by the Western political elites. Neither was the fact there were still plenty of Jews inside the Soviet elites. The order of the day was clear: "let my people go!!" said the US Congress led by neocon Senator "Scoop" Jackson and Representative Vanik[218] and let go they were indeed.

The historical facts are important here, but they are not crucial. What is crucial is the Jewish/Trotskyite/neocon **narrative about Russia**: pogroms, Stalin's purges, "anti-Semitism," the "dissident movement" and struggle over emigration, the Soviet assistance to Arab countries and the Soviet nukes aimed at the USA—this is what shapes the neocon worldview. The fact that no pogrom ever took place in Russia proper (they all occurred in the Ukraine), that Stalin's purges were not anti-Jewish at all, that Jews constituted high proportion of the Soviet nomenklatura right up to the fall of the Soviet Union, that non-Jews had even fewer rights to emigrate than Jews or that US nukes were also aimed at the Soviet Union (and that influential generals suggested that only ethni-

[218]Jackson–Vanik amendment https://en.wikipedia.org/wiki/Jackson%E2%80%93Vanik_amendment

cally Russian areas of the Soviet Union should be included in the Single Integrated Operational Plan) did not matter: this simplistic anti-Russian narrative fully permeated the worldview and cultural fabric of the neocons. Today, this narrative is still the prime factor defining neocon policies toward Russia.

Whether the neocons nowadays hate everything Russian or Orthodoxy Christian more than they hate everything Arabs or Muslim is debatable (it probably depends on the individual neocon anyway). What is sure is that these two hatreds are of a similar order of magnitude and that they are without equivalent. Once this is fully understood, the West's policies toward Russia since the end of the Soviet Union suddenly make perfectly good sense: *Russia, just like Iran, is considered as an "existential threat" by the neocons, although political expediency does not make it possible for them to openly say so.*

It is important to note here that for a typical modern person, "ethnic politics" just make no sense and any analysis based on ethnicity just sounds too bizarre to be true. The danger here is to assume that because one believes that ethnic policies are plain racists, everybody else must think likewise. Sadly, this is not the case. **There are plenty of people out there who very much think in ethnic or even racial categories, and Jews are among those most inclined toward this kind of thinking** (for an earlier article on this issue please check out *Daddy, what's a Neocon? Ethnic mafia wars in the USA*[219]).

The late Israel Shahak[220] used to say that Jewish extremists have reversed the old *Friends of the Earth*[221] slogan "think globally—act locally"[222] into a far more ominous **"think locally—act globally"**[223] (locally'

---

[219] Daddy – what's a 'neocon'?! Ethnic mafia wars is the USA http://thesaker.is/daddy-whats-a-neocon-ethnic-mafia-wars-is-the-usa/

[220] Israel Shahak https://en.wikipedia.org/wiki/Israel_Shahak

[221] Friends of the Earth https://en.wikipedia.org/wiki/Friends_of_the_Earth

[222] Think globally, act locally https://en.wikipedia.org/wiki/Think_globally,_act_locally

should not be understood in a strictly geographical sense here, but also as a parochial, 'single-issue priority setting' meaning). **The truly crazed idea of admitting the Ukraine and Georgia into NATO can only be understood in the context of such an neocon ideological mind-set.**

Could there be a pragmatic reason to admit the Ukraine and Georgia into NATO? Of course, not! Both of these countries are highly unstable politically, their ruling elites are corrupt to the bone, their military forces are not even close to meet NATO standards and their geographic location truly begs the question of what kind of threat an entry into NATO would protect them from. Of course, Dubya explained that NATO was not an anti-Russian alliance at all, but that is laughable. NATO can **only** be anti-Russian as nothing else can justify its existence.

By the way, American strategists fully realize that NATO is becoming meaningless in any other context besides a war ("cold" or "hot") against Russia. This is why they talk about "coalitions of the willing" or a "*league of democracies.*"[224] From the neocon point of view NATO has become useless (see the mess in Afghanistan) and only ad hoc coalitions can work jointly for the promotion of the interests of the neocon Empire. Thus NATO's "sole" role remains to isolate Russia politically and threaten it militarily and that can only be explained by the neocon's deep hatred and fear of Russia. **The fact is that a medieval concept of ethnicity shared by a very small group of people has been allowed to become the determining factor in the formulation US and Western policies toward the only major nuclear power besides the USA. This is both frightening and sad because, as with any policy based on threats and violence, this will result in even more blowback for the US and its European allies.**

April 1, 2008

---

[223] Original reference for this term has been removed.

[224] This reference points to John McCain's speech that has been removed.

Part V: Russia and China

TODAY'S VICTORY DAY CELEBRATIONS IN MOSCOW MARK A TURNING POINT IN RUSSIAN HISTORY

Today is truly a historical day. For the first time ever, the West has boycotted the Victory Day parade in Moscow and, also for the first time ever, I believe that this is a profoundly symbolic shift and one which makes perfectly good sense.

The past

For one thing, Russia and China suffered more from World War II than any other country (see for yourself).[225]

Now take a look at the casualties suffered by the "boycotting countries" and everything becomes clear (the only exception to this rule is Poland, which lost a huge proportion of its population). The fact is, that for all the Hollywood movies produced about World War II, the Anglo countries suffered very little, compared to the huge losses of Russia (25+ million) and China (15+ million). *For details, see here*[226] and *here.*[227] As for continental Europe, its resistance to the Nazis, while very real and heroic, was a feat of the few, not a true national resistance (like in the Soviet Union, Poland or Yugoslavia). But there is much more to this than just numbers.

The real reason why the US/NATO/EU countries have boycotted the celebrations in Moscow is, of course, not their very modest contribution to the defeat of Nazi Germany, but their unconditional support for Nazi Ukraine: the "country" which considers Stepan Bandera a national hero, the OUN-UPA death squads as a "heroic liberation movement" and the liberation of the Ukraine as a "Soviet occupation." It is also a fact that the

---

225 Today's Victory Day celebrations in Moscow mark a turning point in Russian history http://thesaker.is/todays-victory-day-celebrations-in-moscow-mark-a-turning-point-in-russian-history/

226 World War II casualties https://en.wikipedia.org/wiki/World_War_II_casualties

227 Second Sino-Japanese War https://en.wikipedia.org/wiki/Second_Sino-Japanese_War#Chinese_casualties

Anglos have always shared these feelings and that had developed several plans for total war against the USSR were considered right at the end of the war which I have already mentioned them in the past[228]:

Plan Totality[229] (1945): earmarked twenty Soviet cities for obliteration in a first strike: Moscow, Gorki, Kuybyshev, Sverdlovsk, Novosibirsk, Omsk, Saratov, Kazan, Leningrad, Baku, Tashkent, Chelyabinsk, Nizhny Tagil, Magnitogorsk, Molotov, Tbilisi, Stalinsk, Grozny, Irkutsk, and Yaroslavl.

Operation Unthinkable[230] (1945) assumed a surprise attack by up to 47 British and American divisions in the area of Dresden, in the middle of Soviet lines. This represented almost half of the roughly 100 divisions (ca. 2.5 million men) available to the British, American and Canadian headquarters at that time. (…) The majority of any offensive operation would have been undertaken by American and British forces, as well as Polish forces, and up to 100,000 German Wehrmacht soldiers.

Operation Dropshot[231] (1949): included mission profiles that would have used 300 nuclear bombs and 29,000 high-explosive bombs on 200 targets in 100 cities and towns to wipe out 85% of the Soviet Union's industrial potential at a single stroke. Between 75 and 100 of the 300 nuclear weapons, were targeted to destroy Soviet combat aircraft on the ground.

Ask yourself a simple question: why were these plans never actually implemented? The answer is both simple and obvious: because the West feared the Red Army. And since the West was terrified of the Red Army, what do you think the Western guests felt each time they watched the Victory Day parade in Moscow? Were they thinking about how the Sovi-

---

[228] Revanchism and russophobia: the dark undercurrents of the war in the Ukraine http://thesaker.is/revanchism-and-russophobia-the-dark-undercurrents-of-the-war-in-the-ukraine/

[229] Plan Totality https://en.wikipedia.org/wiki/Plan_Totality

[230] Operation Unthinkable https://en.wikipedia.org/wiki/Operation_Unthinkable

[231] Operation Dropshot https://en.wikipedia.org/wiki/Operation_Dropshot

et Army defeated the Nazis, or about how the Russian Army kept them in check? Again, the answer is obvious.

Beautiful Square for the Victory Day parade, the Western *leaders* do not: not only did the Anglos carefully nurture and promote Hitler, they always saw him as "their SOB" whom they hoped to unleash against the Soviet Union. Their plan failed, of course, but that only increased their russophobia ("phobia" in the double sense of "fear" and "hate"). To see the Western leaders "missing" today is, therefore, a very good thing and I personally hope that they never get invited again (I know, they will, but I wish they weren't).

The present

The Anglo-Zionist Empire and Russia are at war. Of course, the presence of nuclear weapons on both sides makes this a special kind of war. It is roughly 80% informational, 15% economic and 5% military. But *it is a very real war nonetheless*, if only because the outcome of this war will decide the future of the planet. The Donbass or the Ukraine are, of course, of exactly zero interest to the West. What is really at stake here is the survival of one of two different models.

Anglo-Zionist Unipolar Imperial Model	Russian Multipolar Model
One world hegemon	Collaborative development
Might makes right (national and international)	Rule of law (national and international)
Single societal model	Each country has its own societal model
Ad hoc "coalitions of the willing"	Respect for international law
Secularism and relativism	Central role for religions and traditions

Military violence as preferred solution	Military violence as option of last resort
Rule of the 1%	Rule of the 99%
Ideological monism	Ideological pluralism
White supremacism	Multi-culturalism

Both Russians and Americans are quite aware of what is at stake and neither side can back down. On one hand, if the US/NATO/EU prevail, they will have succeeded in breaking the Russian "back" and Russia will rapidly be submitted. Should that happen, all the BRICS countries will soon follow, including China. On the other hand, if Russia prevails in the Ukraine, then the US grip on the EU will soon be weakened and, possibly, lost altogether and the entire world will see that the Empire is crumbling. Should that happen, the entire international financial system will escape from the Anglo-Zionist control and liquidate the petrodollar. The consequences of such a collapse will be felt worldwide.

The presence of Xi Jinpin next to Putin on this historic day, the participation of the Chinese military in the parade and the presence of People's Liberation Army Navy ships alongside the Russian Black Sea Fleet, is a direct and powerful message to the world: in this titanic struggle, China is fully throwing her weight behind Russia.

[Sidebar: In the photo of Xi and Putin that there is one more absolutely crucial figure sitting next to the war veteran: Nursultan Nazarbaev, the president of Kazakhstan. The crucial role this man has played to shape today's world has not been recognized, but with time I am sure it will. Long before Putin, it was Nazarbaev who did everything in his power to prevent the breakup of the Soviet Union, the creation and strengthening of the Commonwealth of Independent States and the creation of the Eurasian Economic Union. I would note that Putin has, on several occasions, expressed his deep admiration for, and gratitude to, Nazarbaev whom he has explicitly described as the "father" of the new Eurasian Union.]

This is the "new Russia"—one literally flanked by her two allies, China and Kazakhstan. It is hard to over-estimate the importance of this event: for the first time in 400 years Russia has finally fully turned her face to her natural ecosphere—the East.

Many languages and culture have an expression which basically says that you recognize your true friends in times of hardship. I believe that this is true. This is even truer in international politics. And if you apply this criterion to the history of Russia, you come to a simple, but inevitable conclusion: the West has never been Russia's friend (of course, I am talking about the ruling class, not the common people!) By turning toward Asia, Russia is finally "coming home."

Chinese units have never marched on the Beautiful Square before, and to see them there today also sends a clear message to the West: we are standing with Russia!

The future

Today's Victory Day parade in Moscow marks a turning point in Russian history: now, for the first time ever, there is a consensus in Russia that instead of looking West, Russia must look north (Siberia, the Arctic), east (Asia) and south (Latin America, Africa). There will be no "big break" with the West, however, as Russia will continue to hope for the decolonization of Europe. In part, this process has already begun in Greece and Hungary, and it is simmering in Serbia, France, Italy and even Germany. The potential for a European decolonization is definitely there and Russia should not, and will not, give up on Europe.

Another major priority of Russia will be to try to facilitate a rapprochement between the two other BRICS "heavyweights": China and India. Tensions between these two giants are an inherent risk for all the BRICS members and cannot be allowed to remain.

Russia will also try to strengthen her informal but still very real alliance with Iran, Syria and Hezbollah. These three are natural allies for Russia and while it is too early to include Iran or Syria in the BRICS or the *Shanghai Cooperation Organization*,[232] where Iran already has an observer status, eventually this should happen. Iran could also become the first non-ex-Soviet country to join the *Collective Security Treaty Organization.*[233]

Still, the single most important development in the future will be the deepening of the symbiotic relationship between China and Russia, the one I call the "China-Russia Strategic Alliance" which Larchmonter445 has so brilliantly analyzed in his "*Vineyard of the Saker White Paper: the China-Russia Double Helix*":[234] while remaining externally two separate countries, Russia and China will form a single economic, political and military entity, fully integrated and fully dependent on each other (Xi and Putin have again signed a list of mega-contracts between the two countries).

Unless of course, a full-scale war breaks out between the Empire and Russia.

I personally have no hope for a peaceful solution for the Ukrainian civil war. There is nothing which could be meaningfully negotiated between Russia and the Nazi regime in Kiev. Besides, all the indicators and warnings seem to agree on the fact that an Ukro-Nazi attack on Novorossiya is all but inevitable. At that point, there are only two possible outcomes: either the Novorossians are defeated and Russia has to openly intervene, or the Ukro-Nazis are defeated and the Novorossians go on the offensive and liberate most, or even all, of Novorossiya and the Donetsk region. I am cautiously optimistic and my sense is that the Ukronazis will be defeated for a third time. When that happens, the regime in Kiev will most likely rapidly collapse.

---

[232] Shanghai Cooperation Organisation https://en.wikipedia.org/wiki/Shanghai_Cooperation_Organisation

[233] Collective Security Treaty Organization https://en.wikipedia.org/wiki/Collective_Security_Treaty_Organization

[234] Vineyard of the Saker White Paper: the China-Russia Double Helix http://thesaker.is/vineyard-of-the-saker-white-paper-the-china-russia-double-helix/

Conclusion

I am under no illusion that the end of World War II brought happiness and freedom to all of mankind, even less so in Eastern Europe. In reality, it brought an untold number of horrors and suffering to many nations, especially Germany. I don't see Victory Day as a celebration of communism or of the Soviet regime, but as a victory over one of the most abhorrent regimes in history. It was the victory of *all* the people who fought against the Nazis and not of one specific political ideology or order. But, by the same token, I don't think that it makes sense to deny that Stalin and the Communist Party of the Soviet Union played a key role in this victory. The notion that the Russian people prevailed "in spite of Stalin" really makes no sense as he, and his commanders, played a key role in every single major battle of this war, just as Hitler and his commanders did on the other side. As I said before, this victory belongs to all those who helped defeating the Nazis and that very much includes Stalin, his commanders and the CPSU. Hence the Red banners do belong to this parade.

Finally, this day is also a day of celebration for all those who, today, are still resisting the true "heir" of the Nazi regime—the Anglo-Zionist Empire, with its global hegemonic ambitions and never ending colonial wars. Thus today is a day of celebration for all of us in the Saker community, our brothers (and sisters!) in arms and all our friends and allies in this global resistance to global Empire.

I congratulate you and wish you a joy-filled and peaceful Victory Day!

The Saker

PS: We all probably have our own favorite iconic photo for World War II. Mine is one of Sergei Makarovich Korolkov minutes before his execution by the Germans. It shows a Russian soldier, Sergei Makarovich Korolkov, who has just been captured by a German unit and is about to be executed. I love his look of self-confident defiance, which, to me, symbolizes the real "ultimate weapon" of the Russian people: an unbreakable willpower, even in the face of defeat or death.

PPS: check out the excellent article "*To be Russian*"[235] by Andre Vltchek.

[235] Andre Vltchek:"To be Russian" by http://www.counterpunch.org/2015/05/08/to-be-russian/

A TALE OF TWO WORLD ORDERS (UNZ REVIEW COLUMN)

Dear friends,

I was recently contacted by Ron Unz,[236] who asked me if I would be willing to write a column for ***the Unz Review.***[237] I replied that I was, of course, interested but I wrote to him to warm him that I have a very strong propensity for "crimethink" and that I needed to know if there were any topics he would want me to stay away from. His reply was exactly what I wanted to hear: *"As you can probably tell from reading my Mission Statement or browsing the current articles and posts on the Home Page, I'm willing to publish articles containing "exceptionally" high levels of crimethink, both Left and Right. Among my regular columnists and bloggers, many of whom are "notoriously" controversial, I'm never hesitated to publish a single one of their pieces uncensored in almost two years, so including their republished archives, the current record is almost 40,000-to-zero."* To make things even better, Ron also added that I was free to repost my columns for *the Unz Review* on my blog. Finally, a quick look at the list of columnists[238] (which features names like Pat Buchanan, Patrick Cockburn, Tom Engelhardt, Philip Giraldi, Michael Hudson, Ron Paul, Paul Craig Roberts or Mike Whitney) convinced me that this was a great opportunity and I happily accepted.

Today I am posting the first column for the *Unz Review* and I hope that there will be many more.

Kind regards,
The Saker

---

[236] Ron Unz https://en.wikipedia.org/wiki/Ron_Unz

[237] The Unz Review: An Alternative Media Selection http://www.unz.com/

[238] The Unz Review Columnists http://www.unz.com/columnists/

A tale of two world orders

(originally written for the *Unz Review*)[239]

Two historical summits are taking place this week: the crisis talk in France and Germany about the Greek crisis and the simultaneous meeting of the BRICS and SCO countries in Ufa, Russia. These two meetings could hardly be more different.

The Eurobureaucrats are scrambling to prevent a domino effect in which Greece would leave the Eurozone and set a precedent for other Mediterranean countries such as Italy, Spain or even France. But there is really much more at stake here than the comparatively small Greek debts, the solvency of European banks or even the future of the Euro. What is really at stake is the credibility and future of the entire "Euro project" and thus the future of the oligarchy which created it.

The EU elites have put an immense amount of political and person capital into the creation of what one could call a "*Bilderberger Europe*," one run by the elites and on behalf of the USA-promoted New World Order. Just like the US elites have put their full credibility behind the official 9/11 narrative against all empirical evidence, so the European have put their full credibility behind a "grand EU" project even though it was obvious that this project was not viable. And now reality is coming back with a vengeance: simply put, the EU is way too big. Not only was the expansion of the EU to the East a huge mistake, but even the western EU is really the artificial assembly of a Mediterranean Europe and a Northern Europe as Nigel Farange so aptly put it here.[240] Finally, it is pretty obvious that the current EU was built against the will of many, if not

[239] A Tale of Two World Orders http://www.unz.com/tsaker/a-tale-of-two-world-orders/

[240] Your moment has come, Mr. Tsipras, take back control of your country - UKIP leader Nigel Farage https://www.youtube.com/watch?v=94UcyJnRcGU

most, of the people of Europe. As a result, the Eurobureaucrats are now fighting to keep their dying project alive as long as possible.

VII BRICS - and SCO - in Ufa

What we are witnessing these days in Ufa, Russia, could not be any more different. The simultaneous meeting of the BRICS (Brazil, Russia, India, China and South Africa) and the SCO countries (China, Kazakhstan, Kyrgyzstan, Russia, Tajikistan, and Uzbekistan) marks the gathering of a future world order, not one directed at the USA or the West, but one simply built without them, which is even more humiliating. In fact, the BRICS/SCO "combo" is a real nightmare for the Anglo-Zionist Empire (for the precise reasons for the use of this term, please see here.[241]

It has already been announced the India and Pakistan will become full members of the SCO. So the full list of BRICS/SCO members will now look like this: Brazil, China, India, Kazakhstan, Kyrgyzstan, Pakistan, Russia, South Africa, Tajikistan and Uzbekistan. The BRICS/SCO will thus include two Permanent UN Security Council and four countries with nuclear weapons (only three NATO countries have nukes!) Its members account for a full third of the world's land area, they produce 16 trillion dollars in GDP and have a population of 3 billion people or half of the global world population. The SCO population stands at 1.6 billion people, or one fourth of the Earth population which produces $11.6 trillion in GDP. Furthermore, the BRICS/SCO countries are already working on a new development bank whose aim is to create an alternative to the International Monetary Fund (IMF) and World Bank. But most importantly, the SCO is growing even further and might soon welcome Belarus and Iran as full members. And the door is wide open for more members, possibly even Greece (if the Grexit happens).

The core of this alternative New World Order are, of course, Russia and China. Without them, neither the BRICS nor the SCO would make

[241] Terminology http://thesaker.is/terminology/

any sense. The most amazing feature of this Russian-Chinese "core" is the way it was formed. Rather than creating a formal alliance, Putin and Xi did something which, as far as I know, has never been done in the past: they have turned their two super-countries (or ex-empires, pick your term) into **symbionts**, two **separate** organisms which **fully depend** on each other. China has agreed to become fully dependent on Russia for energy and high technology (especially defense and space) while Russia has agreed to become fully dependent on China economically. It is precisely because China and Russia are so different from each other that they form the perfect match, like two puzzle figures, who perfectly fit each other.

For centuries the Anglo-Saxons have feared the unification of the European landmass as a result of a Russian-German alliance, and they have been very successful at preventing it. For centuries the major sea powers have ruled the world. But what no Western geo-strategist had ever envisioned is the possibility that Russia would simply turn East and agree to a symbiotic relationship with China. The sheer size of what I call the Russian-Chinese Strategic Partnership (RCSP) makes not only German, but even all of Europe basically irrelevant. In fact, the Anglo-Zionist Empire simply does not have the means to influence this dynamic in any significant way. Had Russia and China signed some kind of formal alliance, there would always have been the possibility for either country to change course, but once a symbiosis is created, the two symbionts become inseparable, joined not only at the hip, but also at the heart and lungs (even if they each keep their own separate "brains," i.e. governments).

What is so attractive to the rest of the world in this BRICS/SCO alternative is that neither Russia nor China have any imperial ambitions. Both of these countries have been empires in the past, and both have paid a huge price for that imperial status. Furthermore, they both have carefully observed how the USA has arrogantly overstretched itself over the entire planet resulting in a dialectical anti-American reaction worldwide. While the White House and the corporate media keep scaring those still willing to listen to them with tales about the "resurgent Russia" and the "assertive China," the reality is that neither of these two countries has any desire at all to replace the USA as the world hegemon. You will never see China or Russia covering the globe with 700+ military bases, or fighting elective wars on a yearly basis or spend more on "defense" (i.e. aggression) than the rest of the planet combined. They will not built a 600-ship navy or even a fleet of twelve aircraft carriers to "project power" worldwide. And they will most definitely not point a "space gun" at the entire planet with megalomaniacal projects such a Prompt Global Strike.[242]

What Russia, China and the BRICS/SCO countries want is an international order in which security is truly collective, according to the principle that "if you feel threatened then I am not safe." They want a cooperative order in which countries are allowed (and even encouraged) to follow their own societal development model. Iran, for example, will not have to cease being an Islamic Republic after joining the SCO. They want to get rid of the *comprador* elites whose loyalty lies with foreign interests and encourage the "sovereignization "of each country. Finally, they want an international order ruled by the rule of law and not by the "might makes right" principle which has been the hallmark of the European civilization since the Crusades. And the key thing to understand is this: they don't want that because they are so kind and noble, but because **they sincerely perceive this to be in their pragmatic self-interest**.

So while the European ruling plutocracy is trying to find a new way to further dispossess the Greek people and keep southern Europe subjugated to the rule of international bankers and financiers, the participants of the double summit in Ufa are laying the basis of a new world order, but not at all the New World Order predicted by George H.W. Bush. One could say that they are building an anti-New World Order.

Predictably, the Western elites and their corporate media are in a "deep denial" mode. Not only do they not comment much about this tru-

---

[242] Prompt Global Strike https://en.wikipedia.org/wiki/Prompt_Global_Strike

ly historical event, but when they comment about it they assiduously avoid discussing the immense implications which these events will have for the entire planet. This borders on magical thinking: if I close my eyes hard enough and long enough this nightmare will eventually vanish.

It won't.

What will happen is that the US dollar will gradually be pushed out of the BRICS/SCO zone and that US military power will not be challenged, it will be made irrelevant by a completely changed international environment in which even 700+ military bases worldwide will make no difference and, thus, no sense.

The meeting in Ufa will be remembered as the moment in history when the so-called "West" began being irrelevant.

July 10, 2015

PART VI: JE NE SUIS PAS CHARLIE

JE NE SUIS PAS CHARLIE

I am NOT Charlie

Okay, let's be clear. I am not a Muslim. I oppose terrorism. I don't even support the death penalty. I loathe Takfirism. I oppose violence as a means to make a political or ethical point. I fully support freedom of speech, including critical speech and humor.

But this morning I am most definitely NOT Charlie.

In fact, I am disgusted and nauseated by the sick display of collective hypocrisy about the murders in France. Here is why:

Charlie Hebdo for the Darwin Awards

The folks at Charlie Hebdo had it coming. Here is what I wrote about them in September 2012 when they published their famous caricatures of the Prophet Mohammed: *Worthy of the Darwin Awards,*[243] *if you ask me. Excellent, the "gene pool" of the French "caviar-left" badly needs some cleaning.*" Today I fully stand by my words.

Just a stupid dare?

Let me ask you this: what would be the point of, say, taking a nap on train tracks? You don't have to "agree" with the train which will run you over, but it still will, won't it? What about taking a nap on train tracks specifically to make a point? To prove that the train is bad? To dare it? To make fun of it? Would that not be the height of stupidity? And yet, that is "exactly" what Charlie Hebdo did. I would even argue that that this is how Charlie Hebdo made its money, daring the "Muslim train" to run them over. You think I am exaggerating? Check out the caricature which one of the folks who got murdered yesterday had just posted. The text reads: "*Still no terrorist attacks in France—Wait, we have until the end of January to send you are best wishes.*" The crazy person shown in the

[243] Darwin Awards https://en.wikipedia.org/wiki/Darwin_Awards

drawing is packing a Kalashnikov and wearing an Afghan "Pakol"[244]—the typical "crazy Muslim" in Charlie Hebdo's world. Talk about a stupid dare...

"Spitting in people's souls"

There is an expression in Russian: spitting in somebody's soul. It fully applies here. Muslims worldwide have be unambiguously clear about that. They take blasphemy very, very seriously, as they do the name of the Prophet and the *Quran*. If you want to really offend a Muslim, ridicule his Prophet or his Holy Book. That is not a secret at all. And when *Charlie Hebdo* published their caricatures of the Prophet and when they ridiculed him the a deliberately rude and provocative manner, they knew what they were doing: they were very deliberately deeply offending **1.6 billion** Muslims worldwide. Oh, and did I mention that in Islam blasphemy is a crime punishable by death? Well, it turns out that of 1.6 billion Muslims **exactly three decided** to take justice in their own hands and kill the very deliberately blaspheming Frenchmen. You don't have to be Muslim or to approve of the death penalty for blasphemy to realize that this was inevitable and *that this has nothing to do with* Islam as a religion. Offend any group as large as 1.6 billion and sooner or later you will find one to five folks willing to use violence to make you pay for it. This is a statistical inevitability.

Are some victims more equal than others?

So twelve deliberately "soul-spitting blasphemers" were murdered and all of France is in deep mourning. The media worldwide does such a good job presenting it all as a planetary disaster that many thousands people worldwide say "*I am Charlie*," sob, light candles and take a "courageous" stance for freedom of speech.

Crocodile tears if you ask me.

---

[244] Pakol https://en.wikipedia.org/wiki/Pakol

The fact is that the AngloZionists have carefully and lovingly nurtured, organized, armed, financed, trained, equipped and even directed the Takfiri crazies for decades. From the war in Afghanistan to Syria today these murderous psychopaths have been the foot soldiers of the Anglo-Zionist Empire for decades. But, apparently, nobody cares about their victims in Afghanistan, in Bosnia, in Chechnya, in Kosovo, in Libya, in Kurdistan, in Iraq or elsewhere. There these liver-eating murderers are "freedom fighters" who get full support. Including from the very same media which today is in mourning over *Charlie Hebdo*. Apparently, in the Western ethos some victims are more equal than others.

And when is the last time somebody in Europe shed a single tear over the daily murders of innocent people in the Donbass whose murder is paid for and directly directed by the Western regimes?

How stupid do they think we are?

And then this. Even a drooling idiot knew that Charlie Hebdo was THE prime target for that kind of attack. And I promise you that French cops are not drooling idiots. Yet, for some reason, they were nowhere to be seen that day. Only a van with two (or one?) cop was parked nearby (hardly an anti-terrorist protection detail) and one poor cop was shot and then executed with an AK shot to the head while he was begging for mercy. Is this the best the French state can do?

Hardly.

So what is going on here? I will tell you what—the EU one-percenters are now capitalizing on these murders to crack down on their own population. Sarkozy already met Hollande and they both agreed that new levels of firmness and vigilance need to be implemented.[245] Does that not reek of a French 9/11?

---

[245] Sarkozy a demandé à Hollande d'augmenter "le niveau de fermeté et de vigilance" http://www.franceinfo.fr/actu/politique/article/sarkozy-demande-hollande-d-augmenter-le-niveau-de-fermete-et-de-vigilance-628421

So no, I am most definitely NOT Charlie this morning and I am disgusted beyond words with the obscene display of doubleplusgoodthinking "solidarity" for a group of "caviar-lefties" who made their money spitting in the souls of billions of people and then dared them to do something about it. And I am under no illusion whatsoever about the fact that cui bono clearly indicates that the French regime either organized it all, or let it happen or, at the very least, makes maximal political use of it all.

But most of all, I am disgusted with all those who play along and studiously avoid asking the right questions about all this. I guess they really are "Charlies" all of them.

I am not.

The Saker

January 8, 2015

IN THE CHARLIE HEBDO PSYOP DOUBLE STANDARDS, LOGICAL FALLACIES AND CRASS IGNORANCE ARE EVERYWHERE

Many of pointed out that apparently the French and most westerners seem to be much more upset when twelve people die in Paris then when hundreds, thousand and tens of thousands die elsewhere. It appears that the 1980s slogan "*don't touch my pal*"[246] which was originally supposed to denounce racism now has been "re-worked" into a, if not racist, then at least a chauvinistic mode: don't kill French leftists no matter how offensive their discourse is. I won't make that case again here, but because by now anybody still capable of critical thought "got it," but I will look at another, much less noticed case of double standards: the one about the issue of moral pain.

Here is what the official doxa tells us: Muslims have no right to whine about their Prophet being insulted, this is part of free speech. It is disingenuous for them to claim that they have been hurt by these caricatures, in reality they have not been hurt, they just had their feathers ruffled by a bit of disrespectful speech. How can you possibly compared such ruffled feathers with issues of life and death?

So is there such thing as moral pain and can it be compared to physical pain?

Let's look at the record as it stands in **the West**:

Any psychologist will explain to you that not only does moral pain exist, but it can be worse than physical pain. This is why some people confess to crimes (whether real or not) when they are told that their family members will be tortured next even though they themselves had found

246 SOS Racisme https://en.wikipedia.org/wiki/SOS_Racisme

the internal courage not to yield to torture inflicted upon them. An idea can hurt more than physical pain.

The Geneva conventions specifically forbid mock executions even though all they inflict is fear (a form of moral pain).

In France, it is currently illegal to even **question** the official version of the so-called "Holocaust" precisely because doing so would cause moral pain to the very few actual "Holocaust survivors" still alive. This protection from moral pain even extends to the relatives and descendants of "Holocaust survivors," who were born already after the war and how never suffered from any ill-treatment themselves.

At the famous Nuremberg trial Julius Streicher[247] was sentenced to death, even though he never committed any other crime than "*infecting the German mind with the virus of anti-Semitism.*" He was, by the way, also viciously tortured[248] before his execution. His crime? He was the founder and editor of a newspaper, *Der Stürmer,*[249] a nasty racist propaganda paper whose name can be roughly translated as "The attacker" or "The stormer." Apparently, hate speech can even get you the death penalty in the West.

The Eighth Amendment[250] of the US Constitution prohibits "cruel and unusual punishment" especially if it is "degrading to human dignity." Apparently, for the Founding Fathers human dignity was an extremely valuable and real thing which deserved to be protected.

Even in Guantanamo (hardly a bastion of civilization and human rights!) following the 2005 scandals about the desecration of the Quran,[251] it was decided that the rules about the manipulation of the

---

[247]Julius Streicher https://en.wikipedia.org/wiki/Julius_Streicher

[248]The Torture of Julius Streicher (in his own words) at Nuremberg- April '46 https://archive.org/details/TheTortureOfJuliusStreicherinHisOwnWordsAtNuremberg-April46

[249] Der Stürmer https://en.wikipedia.org/wiki/Der_St%C3%BCrmer

[250] Eighth Amendment to the United States Constitution https://en.wikipedia.org/wiki/Eighth_Amendment_to_the_United_States_Constitution

[251] 2005 Quran desecration controversy https://en.wikipedia.org/wiki/2005_Quran_desecration_controversy

Quran (which had already existed in the past[252]) would be strictly implemented. So even in waterboarding GITMO insulting the Prophet is considered beyond the norms of civilized behavior. Apparently not in Paris.

What about law defending against slander? Are they not here to protect people from the pain resulting from somebody else's speech? Do we not care if somebody dear to us is insulted or ridiculed?

So who are we kidding here? Do I need to bring further examples to make my point everybody in the West already knows that caricatures like the one published by *Charlie Hebdo* **really** bring on real pain to Muslims. We are not talking about ruffled feathers or irritation, we are talking about real moral and psychological distress here, the kind which normally Western civilizational and legal norms try to protect people form.

The truth which others dare not speak, but which I will spell out for you here is simple: Western elites have the same attitude toward Muslims as Victoria Nuland has for the EU: f**k them! That is the real message not only *Charlie Hebdo* but the entire teary circus around the Paris massacre sends to Muslims worldwide: **bleep you, your religion and your Prophet, bleep you and your victims—thousands and even millions of your dead Muslims (Iraq anybody?!) are not worth twelve of our guys, and we get to limit your speech, but don't you dare limit ours!**

And if a Muslim dares to object, he is instantly reminded about "his" stonings, burkas, terrorist attacks, etc. with the inevitable punch line: Islam is in no position to give lessons to the civilized West. Sadly, Islam is vulnerable to such attack because of its support for the death penalty and its use of various frankly inhuman execution methods, but that is far from being the full picture.

First, until recently the West ALSO had plenty of execution methods which are infinitely worse than those legal in Islam (anybody doubting

---

[252] U.S. Long Had Memo on Handling of Koran http://www.washingtonpost.com/wp-dyn/content/article/2005/05/16/AR2005051601320.html

this better read the Wikipedia entry under Robert-François Damiens[253] or remember that the French abolished the guillotine only in 1981 and against the popular will). Second, at least Islam is honest about its punishments. Compare that with the USA were people are officially sentenced to prison terms like in other civilized countries, but where it is well known, understood and **accepted** that your chances of being brutally assaulted or anally raped are very high, especially if you are weak, and where people are held in supermax isolation units which the UN correctly defines as torture.

Second, it is artificial to compare two (or more) civilizations by only comparing their penal codes. Why not compare other forms of violence such as warfare or genocides. Here, even the worst of the worst Muslims (the Ottomans) compare very favorably with the Europeans, I am sorry if I offend the latter, but that is a fact. Though, of course, there have been plenty of examples of Muslim atrocities (by the Ottomans and the Persians in particular), but compared to what the West did to entire continents (African, North and South America) these are truly minor incidents. Of course, folks in the West are not too knowledgeable about all this, and the comforting narrative is that Europe was civilized, a heir to the Greek and Roman civilizations (a lie—post Frankish Europe **re**-discovered antiquity thanks to Muslims and Jews!) whereas the Muslims are just goat herders from the deserts of the Arabian Peninsula. Comforting narrative for sure, but factually wrong. Muslims, however, are very much aware of this history and don't like to be looked down by the very westerners which they see as rather brutish and always bloodthirsty.

Third, there is a feature of modern Western civilization which does set it apart from pretty much all others. The quasi-total absence of the sacred. For a modern, secular and educated person in the West there is very little which is truly sacred. In the past, wives and mothers still used

[253] Robert-François Damiens https://en.wikipedia.org/wiki/Robert-Fran%C3%A7ois_Damiens

to be sacred, and telling an Italian or Spaniard "**cornuto**" or "**hijo de puta**" could get you knifed. Nowadays a French rap group proudly calls itself "Nique Ta Mère."[254] Some will say this is progress, I suppose. In the USA, the flag is sacred. At least to some. And, apparently, for millions of people in France—free speech, including deliberately offending free speech, is sacred. Except when it is directed at Jews, in which case it can land you in jail. For most Muslims, the prophets are so sacred that every time they mention their name they add "*sallallahu alayhi wasallam*" (peace be upon him). Now, you don't have to be a Muslim yourself or to approve of the Prophet to be capable of understanding that the Prophet Mohammed is truly dear and even sacred to Muslims. The fact that there is nothing sacred left in the West does not mean that the rest of the world has slouched down to a similar degree of degeneracy or that those who hold nothing for sacred have a license to impose their lack of anything sacred or their indifference on everybody else and offend them to their (sick) heart's content.

The most disgusting kind of westerner is the kind that actually **takes pride** in offending the feelings of those who still do have things which are sacred to them. This is what *Charlie Hebdo* was all about. Theirs was not a "discourse," it was an endless quest to become the most offensive, vulgar and crude newspaper in Europe. And, by the way, before the latest *Charlie Hebdo* psyop, this disgusting and stupid paper printed 60,000 copies for a country of 66,000,000 people. But then, apparently, some French matter more than others (what else is new?). Double standards again.

When considering any aspects of the *Charlie Hebdo* psyop you will inevitably find that double standards and logical fallacies are **everywhere**. That some speech is freer than other, that some victims matter more than others, that some atrocities are more atrocious than others and that some pain gets more respect than other. But the worst for me is this sickening

---

[254] Suprême NTM https://en.wikipedia.org/wiki/Supr%C3%AAme_NTM

solidarity with those who made insulting others into some kind of noble feat, these "heroes" are lionized for their "courage" to generate real moral pain in others. I see nothing noble in that at all and the fact that they were brutally and viciously murdered by, apparently, a gang of Takfiri freaks does not make then anyway more respectful.

One more thing: some of you have expressed outrage at the fact that Sheikh Imran Hosein said that the biggest evil the world has ever seen will rule from Jerusalem. Clearly, the good Sheikh is a vicious anti-Semite, right?

(Sigh)

I wish that those who speak about the "Christian West" actually knew a little something of Christianity, especially of Christian eschatology. What the Sheikh was saying is in no way different from what the Church Fathers said, including that the Antichrist would rule over the world from Jerusalem. A 5min search on the Internet gave me these pretty decent sources:

Early Church Fathers on the Timing of the Rise of Antichrist[255]

Prophesies of the Antichrist By Early Church Fathers[256]

Hippolytus of Rome Treatise on Christ and Antichrist[257]

Islamic eschatology is, by the way, remarkably similar to the traditional Christian one. A quick search under the term "Dajjal[258]" yielded these sources:

- Who is the evil Dajjaal (the "antichrist")?[259]
- Who is the Dajjaal and what are his attributes?[260]

---

[255] Early Church Fathers on the Timing of the Rise of Antichrist http://biblelight.net/fathers-on-antichrist.htm

[256] Prophesies of the Antichrist By Early Church Fathers http://www.unitypublishing.com/prophecy/AntichristbySaints.htm

[257] Hippolytus of Rome Treatise on Christ and Antichrist http://www.earlychristianwritings.com/text/hippolytus-christ.html

[258] Masih ad-Dajjal https://en.wikipedia.org/wiki/Masih_ad-Dajjal

[259] Who is the evil Dajjaal (the "anti-Christ")? http://www.islaam.org/al_mahdi/dajjaal.htm

- Lecture on Dajjal Antichrist by Imran N. Hosein[261]

As for Sheikh Imran Hosein's advice to the Muslims of France to leave while they can, it is fully in line with this admonition of Christ Himself who told his apostles "*And whosoever shall not receive you, nor hear your words, when ye depart out of that house or city, shake off the dust of your feet. Verily I say unto you, It shall be more tolerable for the land of Sodom and Gomorrha in the day of judgment, than for that city.*" (Matt 10:14-15). One does not have to agree with what the Sheikh says, but that is hardly a reason to call him crazy or anti-Semitic.

Frankly, what I see taking place is mostly a **lashing out against Islam and against Muslims which is first and foremost based on crass ignorance**. I personally am not a Muslim, and I vehemently disagree with some teachings and practices of Islam. And I am on record saying that I fully support what I call "Putin's ultimatum" to the Takfiri freaks: stop or we will exterminate you. And, when needed, Putin did exactly that: since 2000 Russia has literally executed every single leader of the Chechen insurgency, *every single one*. Some were killed in Russia, others in Chechnya, others even elsewhere, but they are all dead. And the Wahhabi "Icherkian" insurgency has been literally exterminated too. Not only that, but Putin has fully backed Assad, the other man who has not hesitated to physically exterminate as many Takfiri freaks as possible (and Assad did such a good job of it that they had to retreat to Iraq). And I am on record supporting Assad too. And, finally, I have always fully supported Hezbollah and Sheikh Hassan Nasrallah, not only in their war of national liberation against Israel, but also in their struggle against the so-called "Syrian opposition" (where the freaks who murdered the *Charlie Hebdo* people came from!) I don't think that anybody even minimally honest can ac-

---

[260] Who is the Dajjaal and what are his attributes? http://islamqa.info/en/8806

[261] Lecture on Dajjal Anti-Christ by Imran N. Hosein https://www.youtube.com/playlist?list=PL60F84B368D3270FF

cuse me of having any sympathies for the Takfiri/Wahhabi terrorists or for their actions in Paris.

But to those of you who take issue with my statement that the "West" cannot win against the Muslim world I say this: take the example of Russia and realize that the **Russians can kill Wahhabis, but they cannot kill Wahhabism. It took a Muslim man like Akhmad Kadyrov and his son to defeat the Wahhabi ideology in Chechnya**. The same goes for the West: no matter how many ISIS or al-Qaeda terrorist the Western security services kill (or, pretend to kill!), the ideology of Takfirism will only be defeated by other Muslims (who, by the way, are always the first and main victims of the Takfiri freaks!)

Just take one look at Hollande, Merkel or Obama and tell me that they have anything at all to say other than vapid platitudes and insipid lies? Do you really believe that they have anything to oppose to the ideas of Osama bin Laden, Abu Bakr al-Baghdadi or even Muhammad ibn Abd al-Wahhab or Taqi ad-Din Aḥmad ibn Taymiyyah?

Methinks that the Western leaders are both too arrogant and too ignorant to face this reality and that they think that they can outsmart the devil on their own—hence the unleash the Takfiri demon against Muslim world and the Nazi demon against the Donbass. I say that with leaders like that the West has exactly "zero" chance to prevail. And considering that with each passing year the Western leaders become even dumber, more arrogant, more pathetic and more clueless, I see no reason to believe that the West will win the "clash of civilizations," it itself created.

January 18, 2015

PART VII: SYRIA AND IRAN

WHAT COULD A SUSTAINED AIR CAMPAIGN BY THE US/ NATO/CENTCOM SUPPORTED BY NUMEROUS CRUISE MISSILE STRIKES REALLY ACHIEVE IN SYRIA?

For many months now I have been warning that what is happening in Syria is really what I call "*Bosnia v5, Chechnia v4, Kosovo, v3 Libya v2, Syria v1*" and, indeed, the basic Anglo strategy is exactly the same one: destabilize a country by using real popular grievances, trigger civil unrest, fan the violence, escalate the clashes into an insurgency, then carefully orchestrate some kind of "humanitarian" pretext to bypass the UNSC and intervene militarily. Remember how the Iraqis were allegedly tossing Kuwaiti babies out of their incubators? How the Serbs lobbed mortar rounds (in an physically impossible trajectory) into the Markale market in Sarajevo? Remember the Srebrenica genocide? The Racak massacre? How the Serbian "Chetniks" used "rape as a weapon of ethnic cleansing" (even though their enemy was of the same ethnicity)? Do you remember how Gaddafi gave Viagra and condoms to his soldiers? How Saddam could launch chemical warheads at the UK in 45 minutes? Ok, it appears that now Assad has used chemical weapons against the Free Syrian Army (FSA). Never mind that this narrative categorically contradicts even a superficial attempt at understanding what is going on in Syria by using common sense.[262] Hey—if Anglo politicians say it's true, then you can take it to the bank. After all, we all know that Anglo politicians never lie, don't we?

Anyway…

---

[262] Is there really no limit to how idiotic the anti-Assad propaganda can get?! http://thesaker.is/is-there-really-no-limit-to-how-idiotic-the-anti-assad-propaganda-can-get/

Well, it appears that the Anglo Empire is about to engage in some type of military intervention in the war on Syria and this intervention can be articulated around three basic options:

a) sending more weapons to the Takfiris

b) imposing a no-fly zone

c) embarking upon a cruise missile and air strikes campaign

Or, of course, a combination of the above.

I have addressed the first option in a previous post[263] and I will not repeat it all here. I will just say this: the insurgency has plenty of money and weapons and this entire "we needs weapons" thing is a complete canard. Even if the US floods the insurgency with the newest anti-tank weapons and MANPADS this will only marginally help them as their real problems are very different: poor training and even worse command, a poorly organized and primitive logistics and support structure, popular opposition to their ideology and a magnificent performance of the Syrian military which very skillfully adapted to a new set of tactics.

Today, I will look at the possible consequences of imposing a no-fly zone and a cruise missile and air strikes attack. Let's begin by something rather obvious and which is often overlooked by commentators: option b) and option c) are, in reality, one and the same. What I mean to say is that the **US/NATO cannot impose a no-fly zone over Syria without first embarking on a cruise missile and airstrikes campaign**. The notion that the Anglos will somehow "patrol the skies" from high above an only prevent the Syrian Air Force from flying combat missions is absolutely ridiculous. Even in Bosnia—and God knows the poor Bosnian-Serbs never had anything but a totally symbolic air force—the Anglos had to bomb to keep their no-fly zone halfway effective. Later, in Kosovo (which, in reality, meant in Kosovo, Serbia and Montenegro) the Anglos

---

[263] Rapid acceleration of events in the US/NATO war on Syria: comparing threats http://thesaker.is/rapid-acceleration-of-events-in-the-usnato-war-on-syria-comparing-threats/

embarked on a huge, strategic, bombing campaign. Ditto in Libya, although the latter was a much softer target requiring a much smaller intervention.

So the real question is this: what could a sustained air campaign by the US/NATO/CENTCOM supported by numerous cruise missile strikes really achieve in Syria?

To answer this question we need to look at the official and real purposes of such a campaign. Officially, of course, the primary goal of such a campaign would be to "protect the civilian population" and prevent the "regime" from using "weapons of mass destruction" against "innocent civilians." In reality, of course, the goals would be different:

1) Destroy the Syrian air-defense capabilities to be able to safely impose a no-fly zone.

2) Make the regime pay for its defiance of the Anglo Empire by destroying key government facilities.

3) Weaken the regime by substantially destroying the equipment and key installations of specific military units perceived as "elite" and "pro-regime."

4) Reduce the mobility and Syrian forces on the ground.

5) Disrupt the Syrian military's supply lines.

6) Weaken as much as possible the regime's ability to command and control its forces, to communicate with them, to obtain intelligence, etc.

7) Provide close air support to Anglo special forces embedded in the insurgency. And last, but not least:

8) Make the population pay for its support for Assad.

The last one is, of course, never mentioned, but it is an absolutely crucial goal in the bombing campaign against Serbia, the bombing campaign of Israel against Lebanon, and it will be a key objective in any future attack on Syria or Iran: **make the civilians pay for their support for the "wrong" regime.**

This goal-set need to be evaluated against the actual target list presented by the Syrian government, armed forces and society.

I have found some pretty decent descriptions of the Syrian military's order of battle[264] but, as is often the case, such "static" outlines do not give the real picture. I will therefore have to make a number of educated guesses. I will assume that the Syrian military is roughly organized along Soviet lines, that the bulk of the Syrian forces have not been put on full mobilization, that the government has been aware of the threat of a US/NATO attack since at least a year or more, and that the local civil defense and security organizations are already in high gear. Finally, I will assume that the Syrian military has very carefully studied the Israeli attack on Lebanon in 2006 and that the Syrian high command is in close contact with their Russian and Iranian counterparts.

At this point, I want to get one red herring out of the way: the issue of the Russian S-300 in Syria and their effect on US/NATO plans. Let us assume that there are already four batteries of S-300 in Syria and that each battery can engage 24 targets simultaneously with a probability of kill of.8 (these are all very optimistic assumptions, the real figures are probably closer to twelve targets at.7). In this case a saturation attack with 50 incoming missiles would be enough to defeat the S-300 (in reality such calculations do not work, the issue is much more complex, but we can use that as a tool just to think about these issues).

Now, I don't know what the cruise missiles stocks of NATO or CENTCOM are, but we can be sure that there are enough such missiles to saturate these 4 batteries. In fact, one Russian general estimated that Syria would need 10-12 S-300 batteries to protect itself.[265] And keep in mind that there are other options open to the US Central Command (CENTCOM) to destroy these batteries (such as special forces attacks). If needed, the USAF can bring in bomber from Diego Garcia, B-2 bombers from the USA, submarine based cruise missiles, etc. You can think of

---

[264] Syrian military's order of battle http://www.understandingwar.org/sites/default/files/SyrianArmy-DocOOB.pdf

[265] Syria needs a dozen S-300 batteries to protect itself – Russian general; Kerry Denounces Plan http://www.juancole.com/2013/06/batteries-general-denounces.html

CENTCOM as "NATO 2" because it was originally designed to stop a Soviet invasion of Iran (I know—stupid idea, but that was the fear in those days) and it only got more powerful over the past decades. The combined might of CENTCOM plus NATO is absolutely immense and the notion that just a few Russian air-defense systems—even very good ones—could defeat it is ludicrous. Yes, the S-300 is a superb system, yes it is better than the US Patriot, yes the Anglos do fear them, but no—it will never stop them.

I think that we should assume that NATO/CENTCOM will be able greatly degrade the Syrian air defenses and that they will also be to establish air superiority over the entire Syrian territory. How long this will take them will depend on many factors, not least the skills and determination of the Syrian military, but the inevitable outcome will not change. So let's assume that this phase is already over.

At this point nothing will prevent the Anglos to engage in a "shock and awe" kind of campaign similar to what they did in Baghdad in 2003. The results would also be similar: main ministry buildings will be destroyed, as will most TV stations (which the Anglos consider a legitimate target—see the case in Belgrade), most *Mukhabarat* (the various security and intelligence services) headquarters will be blown up, as will communication nodes, radar installations, bridges, etc. A number of military bases will be destroyed along with any equipment stored at that location. This is also the time when we could expect a GPS-guided missile to hit the Russian embassy in Damascus or a cruise missile to mistakenly explode in the harbor of Tartus.

This is when objectives 1 through 4 above will be practically achieved and CNN & co. will declare it yet another brilliant victory for the Anglo Empire, Obama will go on the air to congratulate the troops for a brilliant performance, and pundits will predict that Assad's regime will shortly collapse.

At this point the key issue is how much all this will affect the balance between the Syrian military and the Takfiri insurgency. Actually, I am inclined to think that, if anything, this type of campaign could further tilt the balance of power in favor of the Syrian government. Why?

Well, first and foremost, these types of air campaigns have a very poor record against deployed military forces. In Kosovo the entire air campaign had a negligible effect on the Serbian army corps deployed in Kosovo (the 2nd Army Corps if I recall correctly). Air operations in Bosnia were only marginally more effective while Israeli air operations in Lebanon practically failed to affect Hezbollah. In Iraq the results were more checkered, but that is primarily due to the fact that the inept Iraqi deployment presented an almost ideal target for this kind of assault.

Most combat in Syria happens on a company-battalion level meaning that mobility is not crucial (there are no deep envelopment operations or real "fronts" to breach with heavy concentrations of forces). Furthermore, most combat in Syria also happens in an urban setting which makes close air support difficult and "blue on blue" incidences of fratricide more likely. Even locating a target from the air can be very difficult in these circumstances and requires experienced and well trained forward air controllers.

Furthermore, the Syrian forces currently engaged in the battles against the insurgency do not require large amounts of ammunition, petroleum, oil or lubricants and their supply dumps are probably very well camouflaged. In fact, considering that the Syrian military has probably been seriously preparing for an Israeli invasion for many years, I suspect that such supply dumps are already prepositioned throughout the country and that the current counter-insurgency operations have not even come close to seriously depleting them. Also, if the Syrians have adopted Russian, Iranian and Hezbollah tactics, there are going to be a lot of fake targets scattered all over the country to complicate US planning and assessment efforts. Finally, an Anglo bombing campaign will probably even further antagonize and infuriate the local population against the US, if only because such air campaign do cause a lot of "collateral damage" in terms of killed and maimed innocent civilians.

And here we have now come to the crucial difference between, on one hand, Bosnia, Kosovo, or Libya and, on the other hand, Syria: leadership.

In the case of Bosnia and Kosovo it is almost never remembered that Slobodan Milosevic betrayed his Serbian brothers in both territories. During the war in Bosnia, "Slobo" even imposed sanctions upon the Bosnian-Serbs. In the case of Kosovo, Milosevic agreed to let NATO occupy Kosovo in exchange for a promise to leave him in power in Belgrade. The bottom line is this: the Serbs in Bosnia and in Kosovo were betrayed. Assad and the Alawite officer corps will not betray themselves and those Syrians who were willing to betray their country have already done so a long time ago (remember the series of defections early on in the war?) In the case of Libya, we had a mentally deranged leader who had built a rather decentralized political system which was used by tribal minorities to overthrow him. Again, this is not at all what we observe in Syria where the regime is a rather centralized and powerful one. The point I am trying to make here is really crucial: the Anglo "victories" over the Serbs and Libyan were never military victories, but *political* victories. What eventually gave the upper hand to the Anglos is not their military prowess, but their undeniable skills at subverting, deceiving, and manipulating. The Assad regime in Syria has already successfully overcome this stage of the typical Anglo offensive and it has come out of this phase even stronger than before. At this point in time all the signs are that both the political regime and the Syrian armed forces are determined to fight and resist and that the popular support for the regime is only growing with each passing day.

The point of "shock and awe" is, as its name clearly shows, to induce a state of, well, shock and awe. It is to startle, to impress, to induce panic, a sense of futility of any resistance, if you want. It is very, very hard to be at the receiving end of such a campaign, but Hezbollah has proven that this can be done. Even the usually clueless Hamas did, to a certain degree, show during the Israeli attacks on Gaza that it could overcome this initial moment of panic. And so once the "shock and awe" phase has failed to produce any signs of shock or of awe—what happens next?

Then the ugly and difficult business of warfare truly takes over and here the Anglo options are very limited: neither the US nor NATO are actually going to put "boots on the ground" as this would only serve to truly turn this civil war into a war of national liberation. Any such move will finish off an already completely disunited opposition. Then, US boots on the ground in Syria will trigger an immediate influx of Hezbollah fighters all too happy to realize their long held dream to make minced meat of as many Yankees as possible. Furthermore, can you actually imagine US Marines and al-Nusra combatants fighting side by side? Then, to even make things worse, an Anglo invasion of Syria might well trigger an influx of Shia volunteers from Iran, Iraq and Lebanon; that would also offer Iran the perfect opportunity to "send in volunteers" (remember that the students who took over the US embassy in Tehran were also "volunteer civilian students" and that the revolutionary government denied having any control over them). No matter how stupid, ill-informed or delusional US politicians are, I cannot imagine the Joint Chiefs ever agreeing to such a lunacy.

What about the option of not sending boots on the ground, but of a sustained campaign to support the Takfiri insurgency? It might appear as a viable option until you consider the following: the fact that the US or NATO cannot send troops in hardly means that the Iranians, the Iraqis or Hezbollah could not do that. In fact, what could the US do if, say, Moqtada al-Sadr decided to send some of his followers to fight the Takfiris in Syria? Protest and threaten, but there is really nothing much else they could do (short of re-invading Iraq?)

This is the huge weakness in the US/NATO posture: while the US/NATO/CENTCOM capabilities to engage in a massive bombing and cruise missile strikes are truly formidable, they have nothing else to follow up with. Everybody in the Middle East knows that the Americans do not have what it takes to go toe-to-toe against an insurgency. These are the folks who used B-2 stealth bombers over Afghanistan but who a full decade later failed to even control most of Kabul in daytime. This is why Khamid Karzai, even in his best days, was not called "president of Afghanistan" by his opponents but "mayor of Kabul."

The Americans and the Europeans are just like the Israelis: they are masters at remote, electronic warfare and but they simply do not have what it takes to get down into the dirty business of close contact warfare. Their tactics work against unprincipled traitors (Milosevic), arrogant imbeciles (Saddam and Gaddafi) but not against a smart and determined resistance (Taliban, Hezbollah). And all the signs are that the Syrians are both very smart and very determined. That they will not break down under a "shock and awe" campaign, and that just like Hezbollah or the Taliban, they are quite willing to fight for as long as it takes to resist the foreign occupation of their country. In other words, achieving objectives 5-7 will not be possible as long as the Syrians hold their ground. All the signs are that they will.

Which leaves only option 8: make the Syrian people pay for their support for the "wrong" regime. Unfortunately, this is an objective which the Anglos will be able to achieve, just as the Israelis did in Lebanon and Gaza. Of course, this will not win the hearts and minds of this population, but it will make the Anglos feel good about themselves—"we kicked the butts of these sand niggers"—and it will send a strong and clear message to the rest of the planet: submit and obey, or else "we will bomb you to the stone age" to use Secretary Baker's threat to Tarek Aziz. The Anglos have a long and distinguished history of making the civilians pay for the "wrong" political choices: from the bombings of Dresden and Hiroshima, to the crippling sanctions against Iran and Iraq, to the subversion of Cuba, Nicaragua, San Salvador and Venezuela, to the bombings of Serbia and Montenegro, to the comprehensive deconstruction of the Iraqi and Libyan polities, to the wrecking of the Afghan and Pakistani societies: the same "solution" has been used by the Anglo Empire over and over again. The beauty of this option, at least in the eyes of the Anglos, is that it can either lead to "victory" (Serbia, Libya) or the possibility to "declare victory and leave" (Vietnam, Iraq, Afghanistan), another old US military tradition.

So this is really what this is all about: not turning the tide of the civil war, but making the Syrians pay for their defiance of the New World Order. Is this goal really worth the many risks involved? I personally don't think so, but I don't get to vote.

The best we can hope for now is a totally symbolic "mini" cruise missile attack against some Syrian "chemical weapons factory." Not against a storage area, of course, since that would risk releasing the toxic gases. So maybe the US can strike an pharmaceutical plant, like they did in al-Shifa in Sudan,[266] and declare it a great achievement. I am personally encouraged by the fact that the Americans are speaking about a "limited use of chemical weapons" because if the fictional chemical weapons use was "limited" then so might therefore also be the "just retaliation," no?

One more thing: the notion that the Russians could somehow protect Syria or meaningfully oppose US/NATO plans is laughable. The Russian Navy presence in the Mediterranean is entirely symbolic and Russia has no other assets in the Middle East which it could use to engage the Anglos. To understand Russian policies in the Middle East and the conflict in Syria it is absolutely crucial to always remember that Russia is acting from a position of great weakness. It will take decades for Russia to be able to establish a more than symbolic Navy presence in the Mediterranean. The first step toward that goal would be to rebuilt the aging Black Sea Fleet which currently is only a shadow of its former self. Again, the Russian Navy's presence off the coast of Syria is an important factor, but only as a symbol of Russia's determination to stand up for the rule of law in international affairs and a sign of solidarity with the Syrian people. Symbols are important, and this is an important symbol, but symbols are

[266] Al-Shifa pharmaceutical factory https://en.wikipedia.org/wiki/Al-Shifa_pharmaceutical_factory

still only that—symbols. Those who fantasize about the Russian Navy "scaring away" the US Navy from Syria simply do not understand naval (or any other type of) warfare.

June 14, 2013

OBAMA MAKES A STRATEGIC MISTAKE IN SYRIA AND NOW ITS "GAME OVER" FOR THE US STRATEGY FOR THE MIDDLE EAST

In a recent post[267] I wrote the following:

> And so once the "shock and awe" phase has failed to produce any signs of shock or of awe—what happens next? (...) an Anglo invasion of Syria might well trigger an **influx of Shia volunteers from Iran, Iraq and Lebanon**; that would also offer Iran the perfect opportunity to "send in volunteers" (remember that the students who took over the US embassy in Tehran were also 'volunteer civilian students' and that the revolutionary government denied having any control over them) (...) consider the following: **the fact that the US or NATO cannot send troops hardly means that the Iranians, the Iraqis or Hezbollah could not do that.** In fact, what could the US do if, say, Moqtada al-Sadr decided to send some of his followers to fight the Takfiris in Syria? Protest and threaten, but there is really nothing much else they could do (...) This is the huge weakness in the US/NATO posture: while the US/NATO/CENTCOM capabilities to engage in a massive bombing and cruise missile strikes are truly formidable, they have nothing else to follow up with. **Everybody in the Middle East knows that the Americans do not have what it takes to go toe-to-toe against an insurgency.** These are the folks who used B-2 stealth bombers over Afghanistan but who a full decade later failed to even control most of Kabul in daytime.

[267] What could a sustained air campaign by the US/NATO/CENTCOM supported by numerous cruise missile strikes really achieve in Syria? http://thesaker.is/what-could-a-sustained-air-campaign-by-the-usnatocentcom-supported-by-numerous-cruise-missile-strikes-really-achieve-in-syria/

As is so often the case, the events on the ground actually developed even much faster than I thought.

I can confirm on the basis of information received from three different sources that the Iranians have begun moving a large military force into Syria. One of these sources I can quote: Robert Fisk who wrote the article "Iran to Send 4,000 Troops to Aid President Assad Forces in Syria[268]" for the *Independent.* There is also evidence of volunteers from Lebanon.

I think that we can safely make the assumption that the 4000 Iranians sent to Syria are just a beginning and that Tehran can send as many soldiers as needed.

I can also add here that we are not talking about well-meaning civilians here, but highly trained Pasdars[269]—**you can think of them as "the people who trained Hezbollah."** One of my best sources tells me that *this entire operations is closely coordinated with Russian specialists while another source even mentions Russians on the ground with the Iranians.*

It therefore appears that Tehran has decided to pre-empt a US/NATO attack on Syria by moving in forces even before the shooting start. I have to sincerely say that this is nothing short of a brilliant move as there is nothing at all the Anglo Empire can do to stop this at this point in time and once the full force is in place it will be impossible to target it separately.

I can add here that the idea of sending in "international brigades" has been discussed in specific Russian and Ukrainian military circles, but that it is likely that the Russian authorities want to keep the visible presence of ethnic Russian to a minimum. *What they can do is send it Russian ethnic groups which do not externally appear as Slavs.* I am thinking, believe it or

[268] Iran to send 4,000 troops to aid President Assad forces in Syria http://www.independent.co.uk/news/world/middle-east/iran-to-send-4000-troops-to-aid-president-assad-forces-in-syria-8660358.html

[269] Army of the Guardians of the Islamic Revolution https://en.wikipedia.org/wiki/Army_of_the_Guardians_of_the_Islamic_Revolution

not, of anti-Wahhabi Chechens who are fully integrated into the Russian military intelligence service GRU (the Russians already did something similar once in Lebanon).

Both Russian and Iranian sources confirm that the two government are very closely cooperating on this entire operation and that uninterrupted close consultations are taking place.

In the meantime, most Hezbollah units are withdrawn from Syria and repositioned to defend Lebanon from a possible Israeli attack.

Bottom line: it is already becoming clear that Barack Obama made a huge—strategic—mistake with his "crossing the red line" nonsense about a "limited use of chemical weapons" by the government forces. Obama probably wanted to give the insurgency a better bargaining position for the Geneva II negotiations, but all he succeeded in doing is fundamentally changing the strategic balance on the ground. It is one thing to fight the Syrian military, it is a qualitatively other one to fight the Iranian Revolutionary Guard Corps. By committing these forces already now, the Iranians are sending a chilling message to Washington: "we do not fear you, and our commitment to Syria is open ended."

As a military analyst specializing in strategic analysis I have to marvel at the superb elegance of the Iranian move because it essentially checkmates the USA's entire strategic plan for the Middle East. When I wrote that there is no way the US would put any boots on the ground, I assumed that they would not dare to do that against the Syrians. But, at least, some really naive Americans could have hoped that with enough bombing of Syrian civilians (a la Kosovo) the regime would eventually have to give in. With thousands of Iranian Pasdars on the ground this is categorically not an option.

This development, apparently only noticed by Robert Fisk, is really a game changer. **What this means for the USA/NATO/CENTCOM/-Israel/al-Qaeda is this: "GAME OVER!"**

The Russian-Iranian alliance has done what it does best: it has responded asymmetrically to the US moves. While the entire world was focusing on S-300s deliveries and Russian Navy moves, it essentially negated the entire US strategy by qualitatively changing the facts on the ground before the US could even react.

US options at this point are extremely limited. Yes, it can still engage in an orgy of civilian killings just to punish the Syrians and prevent elections. It can also denounce the Iranian intervention, but since the entire planet by now knows that the insurgency is largely foreign and supported by the USA's own admission (!), this would be rather hollow. It can also do the wise thing and strenuously look away from the Iranian presence on the ground and pretend like nothing happened. If it decided to do that, it could even try to get some kind of face-saving deal at Geneva II. Attacking Iran is not an option (even less so after the beautiful elections the Iranians just had). Blaming Russia is not an option either as there is exactly zero proof of Russian involvement.

The war itself is, of course, not quite over yet. This will all take time to play itself out. But yes, **this is most definitely the beginning of the end.** To the disgraceful defeats in Afghanistan and Iraq, the US can now add a no less disgraceful defeat in Syria. Good.

June 18, 2013

WHAT DOES THE CIVIL WAR IN SYRIA REALLY MEAN FOR IRAN, RUSSIA AND CHINA?

I was recently asked by a reader to update two of my past articles, *Iran's asymmetrical response options*[270] and For *Israel war is the continuation of national suicide by other means,*[271] and that is an excellent idea, considering that the first one was written in 2007 and the second one in 2010. I did touch upon these issues in a more recent article, *Iran in the crosshair again,*[272] which does to a certain degree update the former two, but this might be a good time to look at the big picture of what is taking place and try to get a feel for where it all might be headed. If the three above mentioned articles (which I recommend you read—if you have not already— before reading on further) looked at the possible outcomes of an attack on Iran primarily from a military point of view, it might be interesting to look at where the most changes have occurred: in the political field. After all, military conflicts never take place in a vacuum and, if anything, the war in Kosovo has shown that the side which militarily "wins" (the Serbs) can at the same time lose politically. So let's look at what the major political shifts are not from the point of view of some reporter sitting in Los Angeles or Rome, but from the point of view of Iran and Israel.

The creation of an anti-Shia front:

The outcome of the war in Iraq and the de facto takeover of Iraqi politics by Shia parties resulted in "push-back" reaction in many Sunni Arab

---

[270] Iran's asymmetrical response options http://thesaker.is/irans-asymmetrical-response-options/

[271] For Israel "war is the continuation of national suicide by other means" http://thesaker.is/for-israel-war-is-the-continuation-of-national-suicide-by-other-means/

[272] Iran in the crosshair again? http://thesaker.is/iran-in-the-crosshair-again/

states, in particular in Bahrain and Syria. The behind-the-scenes but direct involvement of Gulf states like Qatar in the war in Libya and the transformation of the Arab League into a "US/NATO invitation committee" clearly shows that the rich oil sheikdoms are becoming concerned and have decided to counter what they perceive as the "Shia crescent's"[273] threat.

But let's remind ourselves of what we are talking about here: the Shia crescent is nothing else but a list of countries where the Shia have been systematically and brutally repressed and excluded from the political process either by secularist (Shah in Iran, Saddam in Iraq), Wahhabi zealots (Bahrain, Saudi Arabia) or a mix of both (Lebanon).

It also happens that these are the parts of the Middle East in which most oil can be found.

In other words, the Shia crescent is nothing else, but the territories where the Western empires have used local Sunni **proxies to oppress and impoverish the majority population while stealing their natural wealth**. This is what all this nonsense about the "terrorist mullahs" and the "Shia threat" really is designed to conceal: that **the Shia, inspired by Iran and Hezbollah, are engaged in a national liberation struggle, which threatens all those billionaires who have been in bed with the British, the USA, and the Israelis since day one.**

Everywhere you look, Sunni leaders, and in particular of the Wahhabi type, have been working hand-in-hand with the Zionist-American interests, even at the clear detriment of the interests of the local Muslim population (Balkans, Caucasus, Afghanistan, Pakistan, Somalia, etc.) Oh sure, there are regular clashes between the US and various Wahhabi groups worldwide, but they are tactical, local, in nature. In the big picture the West and the Wahhabis have always walked in lockstep with each other (as seen recently in the case of Libya).

---

[273] Shia Crescent https://en.wikipedia.org/wiki/Shia_Crescent

And don't let the fact that the Shia mostly deny all this deceive you: that denial of the obvious reality is an old Shia survival technique destined to blame any Shia-Sunni tensions on any and all conceivable causes but the obvious one: the religious one. I think that this is a very misguided approach, but it has been historically the one most Shia have chosen: Shias would much rather believe themselves to be a part of the big Islamic "*Ummah*"[274] than to contemplate the outright distressing possibility that most of the Muslim world is hostile toward them (which is what the historical record shows).

The civil war in Syria really brought it all out in the open and if in the past one could debate the putative successes of Iranian diplomacy with its Gulf neighbors and the various smiles and hugs it resulted in, but the fact is that Iran's neighbors are now all joining forces against it. Even Turkey, which tends to be cautious in its policies toward Iran is now fully involved in the external intervention in Syria, which is another bad sign for Iran.

As for Hezbollah, it always knew that all the Arab and Sunni expressions of support for its causes were just that—empty words, lip service to the personal popularity of Hassan Nasrallah, but that in reality Hezbollah had no other friend or ally except Iran. In his famous 2006 "*Divine Victory speech*"[275] Hezbollah's leader Hassan Nasrallah said the following:

> The people of Lebanon gave strong proof to all the peoples of the world. The Lebanese resistance provided strong proof to all Arab and Islamic armies. Arab armies and peoples are not only able to liberate Gaza and the West Bank and East Jerusalem, they are simply capable of regaining Palestine from sea to river by one small decision and with some determination. The problem is that when one is torn between two choices and is asked to choose between his people and his throne, he chooses his throne. When he is asked to choose between Jerusalem and

---

[274] Ummah https://en.wikipedia.org/wiki/Ummah

[275] "Victory" Rally Speech Transcript: Hasan Nasrallah http://muslimobserver.com/victory-rally-speech-transcript-hasan-nasrallah/

> his throne, he chooses his throne. When he is asked to choose between the dignity of his homeland and his throne, he chooses his throne. What is distinct about the resistance movements in Lebanon and Palestine is that they chose the dignity of their people, holy places, and freedom and offer their leaders, sons, and dear ones as sacrifices to join the throne of God Almighty.

These words are a direct slap in the face of all the hapless Sunni and secular (Baathist) Arab leaders who literally for decades drowned the world in fiery speeches and yet have never achieved anything: from the Wahhabi fat cats of the Gulf, to the Masonic ~~Baath~~ (*corrected typo*) Phalangist leaders of Lebanon, to the "*progressive/ popular*" secular leftists leaders of the various Palestinian factions, none of them ever managed to score even a modest victory against Israel. Compare that to the Shia who defeated the USA in Iran, then defeated the USA again in Iraq, and then defeated Israel's four brigades, three reserve divisions and entire Air Force and Navy with roughly one thousand second rate Hezbollah soldiers (the best Hezbollah fighters were all kept north of the Litani river). What Hassan Nasrallah is saying is this: the reason why the Arab and Islamic world was always defeated is because it was led by unworthy leaders who care about their thrones more than anything else. Such talk is tantamount to a death threat to all these leaders and they are now "circling the wagons" under the protection of Uncle Sam and his Israeli overlords to stop the Shia liberation movement.

The USA has re-grouped and has Iran surrounded:

Juan Cole has recently published a map of US bases all around Iran which really says it all.[276]

What this map is not showing is how the spread of force levels has changed since, say, 2007. Nor does it show to what degree the US lines of supply have become shorter (in Afghanistan) or disappeared altogether

---

[276] Iran has US Surrounded, All Right http://www.juancole.com/2011/12/iran-has-us-surrounded-all-right.html

(Basra is no more a key transit area). While there still is an important US presence in Iraq, most of it via its huge mercenary forces, the bulk of the US Army combat units has been withdrawn to safer locations and is now available for deployment.

That still leaves plenty of US bases as potential targets of an Iranian retaliatory missile strike, but at least the Iraqi Shia allies of Iran have less of a chance to easily hit US military personal in Iraq.

Finally, should the USA decide to mount a sustained campaign of air and missiles strikes against Iran, it now has the regional resources to so. Iran is now as surrounded as Kosovo was.

The civil war in Syria as the litmus test of Western power:

I have said that many times already, and I will say it again: I despise the Baathist regime of Assad Jr. almost as much as I despised the regime of his father. To me, what is happening to Assad today is exactly what happened to Gaddafi, Saddam, Noriega and so many faithful servants of the US Empire who have been dumped by their American masters as soon as they became useless. Assad, specifically, was all too willing to torture "suspects" "rendered" to him by the US CIA, and there is no doubt in my mind that his regime let Israeli agents kill Imad Mughniyah. And, of course, Assad is yet another example of a leader, who only cares about his "throne" to use Hassan Nasrallah's expression, and who will do anything to hold on to it. So please don't mistake any of what I say below as a defense of Assad or his regime.

Just as was the case with the anti-Gaddafi forces in Libya, there is no doubt in my mind that the anti-Assad forces are nothing but US/NATO puppets, from the diplomatic prostitutes of the Arab League, to the Wahhabi snipers in Homs, to all the *doubleplusgoodthinking* "humanitarians" who flood the Internet with crocodile tears about the civilians victims in Syria, but who strenuously fail to say anything about the butchery of the Bahraini Shia.

Libya provided this bizarre hodgepodge of wannabe humanitarians with a grand rehearsal for their current operation; the big difference was that Gaddafi and his sons were clueless clowns whereas Assad seems to be a more sophisticated player. That, and the fact that the Alawi and Christian communities are probably terrified of what will happen to them if the Wahhabis take power in Syria, makes Assad a tougher opponent than Gaddafi.

What makes things worse in Syria is that it has the misfortune of being at a strategic crossroads of the entire Middle East and that it plays a crucial role not only for Iran, but even more so for Hezbollah. That, in turn, means that the "throne-loving" leaders of the Middle East, the US/NATO and the Israelis all see in the civil war in Syria the perfect opportunity to deal a severe blow to their Shia enemies. Hence the toxic "sacred alliance" against the Assad regime, all in the name of democracy and human rights, of course.

I can't call the outcome of this civil war yet. There are too many variables and too many possible developments. My personal feeling is that the fate of the Assad regime might well be decided in Moscow and Beijing as I don't see the Assad regime indefinitely resisting against the combined onslaught of all the forces arrayed against it. As for Iran, it also does not have the political weight necessary to save Assad from eventually losing power.

In contrast, Russia and China have enough weight, in particular in the form of money, to throw around to strongly influence the events on the ground, but will they do so? That, at least for me, is the big question.

So far Russia and China have a checkered record at best, which includes the betrayal of Iran and Libya at the UNSC, but which also includes the recent veto of the anti-Syrian resolution at the UNSC as well as numerous statements that no military action against Iran is acceptable to them.

I think that many people are making way too much over the recent visit of the Russian mini carrier group[277] (one aircraft carrier, one frigate, four tankers, one tug and two corvettes) to the Syrian port of Tartus. This was very much a political visit, scheduled a long time ago, and not at all the deployment of a real task force to "defend the Assad regime" against any US or NATO attack. In fact, the Russia flotilla was a mix of Northern Fleet and Baltic Fleet vessels whose area of responsibility does not include the Mediterranean. Yes, it is true that the Russian Navy would be interested in having a permanent base in Tartus, but this would be a re-supply and maintenance base, and not at all a military base designed to project Russian military power in the region, much less so intervene in internal Syrian political strife. So let's make something absolutely unequivocally clear: **neither Russia nor China will ever use military means to oppose a US/NATO intervention anywhere in the world unless it is against Russian or Chinese territory or forces.** Those who believe otherwise are dreaming.

This being said, it's not the Russian or Chinese military power which might influence the outcome of the civil war in Syria, but Russian and Chinese "soft-power." mainly in the form of money: in the form of official loans, of course, but also by means of behind the scenes pay-offs and bribes of various key actors, combined with technical assistance to the regime, and diplomatic pressure on the West (Russia and China do have excellent political "levers" which they could potentially use against the West). What is not so clear to me is whether Russia and China are willing to use much of their capital (financial and/or political) to save this week, corrupt and untrustworthy regime from collapsing.

Sure, for Iran and Hezbollah a collapse of the Assad regime would be a disaster, but for Russia or China?

---

[277] Syria hails visit of Russian warships to Tartus
http://www.sputniknews.com/russia/20120109/170675862.html

Looking at even the bigger picture, would even a US/Israeli war on Iran be a disaster for Russia and China?

The sad reality is that, at least so far, the *Shanghai Cooperation Organization*[278] and, even more so, the *Collective Security Organization* (CSO)[279] have failed to live up to the idea of being a counter-weight to NATO and the US. NATO has the huge advantage of being an organization totally controlled and operated by the USA, with the rest of the Alliance playing the role of a symbolic fig-leaf concealing the ugly fact that Europe is a US colony. In military terms, NATO is just another combined joint task force[280] operated by the US military. The SCO has two independent heavyweights, Russia and China, who remain in many ways suspicious of each other and who both want to retain their full independence. The CSO is much more Russian controlled, but that also means that it has a much smaller, strictly regional, role and importance.

The US therefore enjoys the immense advantage of having a fully integrated NATO as the cornerstone of its imperial project, supported by a list of local entities (Arab League) all capable of acting in full unison once the order is given by Uncle Sam (or his Zionist overlords). Add to this an immense and sophisticated propaganda machine, the Western corporate media, and you come to the inevitable conclusion that there is nobody out there who can really stand up to the US/Israeli Empire and make it back down. Oh sure, the Russians did make the US and NATO back down over Georgia in 2008, but the Russians were actually willing to have a full-scale war with NATO and the US over this issue, whereas most leaders in the West did not give a damn about Georgia or Saakashvili. Like in Chechnya, the West would have preferred to win, but a small loss was really no big deal for them.

---

[278] Shanghai Cooperation Organisation https://en.wikipedia.org/wiki/Shanghai_Cooperation_Organisation

[279] Collective Security Treaty Organization https://en.wikipedia.org/wiki/Collective_Security_Treaty_Organization

[280] Task force https://en.wikipedia.org/wiki/Task_force#Combined_Joint_Task_Force

I am afraid that the exact same logic, but in reverse, might be applied to Syria and Iran: whereas the West, fully controlled by Zionists interests, is hell-bent on a confrontation with Syria and Iran, the Russians and Chinese are show very little desire to really take a firm stand on this issue. Syria is not in the South China Sea or the Caucasus and its economy is too small to really matter to Moscow and Beijing. In contrast, Iran is awfully close to the Russian Caucasus and a war involving Iran might have a spillover effect on the Russian southern border. Not only that, but Iran's economy is far more important to Russia and China, so my guess is that there would be far more willingness in Russia and China to prevent the West from returning Iran into its sphere of influence than to do much about Syria.

And yet, consider this: if my 2007 analysis is still correct and the USA and Israel cannot 'win' in Iran, at least not in the sense of achieving regime change, and if Syria does not really matter enough to Moscow and Beijing, is there any rationale at all for direct Russian or Chinese intervention in either conflict (other than the usual loud protests and other expressions of outrage at the UN?).

Conclusion: an international anti-Shia coalition

First, it appears that an international anti-Shia coalition has been successfully formed by the USA in its efforts to support Israel. The primary aim of this coalition is to weaken Iran's influence in the Middle East by all possible means. Second, the USA is now in a much safer position than it was in 2007 to be able to respond to an Israeli strike on Iran or even to launch a missile and air campaign of its own. Third, there are as of now no signs that Russia or China are willing to directly intervene to save the Assad regime in Syria. In the case of Iran, since regime-change is probably not achievable in the first place, there is not clear rationale for a direct Russian or Chinese intervention in a possible war between Israel, the US and Iran.

If the above is correct, that leaves Iran and, even more so, Hezbollah, in a very difficult position. One could say that they are the victims of their own successes, Iran in Iraq and Hezbollah in Lebanon. In this context, I think that it is fair to say that the Assad regime has proven to be a fantastic liability for both Iran and Hezbollah, and that suggests a possible solution to this problem: the replacement of Assad and his band of highly secularized minions by some regime more committed to the Iran-Hezbollah alliance. The problem with that is that unlike the Shia of Bahrain or Iraq, the Shia in Syria are a minority[281] (13% split into three factions) and that the Alawis are tainted by the role in the Assad regime. So where would such a leader come from?

Syria always was the weak link of the Iran-Hezbollah alliance, and most definitely the weak link of the so-called "Shia crescent." By striking there the West has correctly identified this civil war as a low-cost operation (for itself, of course, not for the Syrian people) with very high potential rewards and it is now using all its power to win this battle.

Iran and Hezbollah might want to take heed of the US expression, "hope for the best, prepare for the worst, and settle for anything in the middle" and pray that the worst, whatever that may be, does not happen in Syria. Still, it remains highly likely that once the dust settles in Syria, both Iran and Hezbollah will find themselves in far weaker and vulnerable situation than before the conflict began.

And Israel in all that? The fact that I did not mention it at all in this analysis should not be taken as meaning that it is irrelevant to these processes. Israel is crucial to it all since it is on Israel's behalf that the entire US policy in the Middle East is conducted. Let me repeat this: the grand purpose of the entire Imperial operation against the Shia is to help Israel deal with Iran and Hezbollah. The question remains, of course, whether the Israeli leadership is willing to listen to reason and stay put while the

---

[281] Syria: International Religious Freedom Report 2006 http://www.state.gov/j/drl/rls/irf/2006/71432.htm

Americans are doing their bidding, or whether they will commit yet another folly and strike at Iran with no possible hope to achieve anything tangible (other than feeling good about themselves).

I would say that the past record clearly shows that the Israelis have never missed an opportunity to do something stupid, and that this time, pushed by, on one hand, their own rhetoric and, on the other, their belief that they can get Uncle Sam to rescue them from even a self-created disaster, they will end up attacking Iran probably sooner, than later.

February 23, 2012

IS A SYRIAN "DOMINO EFFECT" BEING USED IN A POWER STRUGGLE IN THE US DEEP STATE?

(written specially for ***the Asia Times***)

Following the ratification by all parties of the recent Joint Plan of Action between Iran and the P5+1 countries,[282] it is worth looking again at the official narrative explaining this "sudden breakthrough." It goes something like this:

"Iran was ruled by President Ahmadinejad, a notorious anti-Semite and Holocaust denier, who did everything in his power to deny the international community the monitoring rights it demanded and to keep the Iranian nuclear program unimpeded in its progress. Then the people of Iran elected Hassan Rouhani, a moderate, who accepted the terms of the P5+1 countries and a deal was finally signed."

That is pretty much the official version.

Of course, every sentence in the above paragraph is absolute nonsense.

The new President of Iran

Iran is not ruled by its president, but by its *Supreme Leader*,[283] Ayatollah Ali Khamenei,[284] who selects the six of the twelve members of the *Guardian Council*[285] which, in turn, vets all aspiring Presidential candidates before they can run for office and which also can veto any decision of the *Iranian Parliament*. The Supreme Leader also appoints all the members of the *Expediency Discernment Council*[286] which can resolve any

[282] P5+1 https://en.wikipedia.org/wiki/P5%2B1

[283] Supreme Leader of Iran https://en.wikipedia.org/wiki/Supreme_Leader_of_Iran

[284] Ali Khamenei https://en.wikipedia.org/wiki/Ali_Khamenei

[285] Guardian Council https://en.wikipedia.org/wiki/Guardian_Council

[286] Expediency Discernment Council https://en.wikipedia.org/wiki/Expediency_Discernment_Council

disagreements between the Parliament and the Guardian Council. Hassan Rouhani was appointed as a member of the Expediency Discernment Council by Ayatollah Ali Khamenei and his bid to run for president was also approved by the Guardian Council. In other words, not only did Mahmoud Ahmadinejad never have the political authority to independently take any crucial political decisions, but his successor has the 100% approval of the Supreme Leader. Thus, while there is a very clear difference in style between Ahmadinejad and Rouhani, it is ridiculous to suggest that the replacement of the former by the latter is the real cause of the "sudden" breakthrough in the negotiations between the P5+1 and Iran. The fact is that Rouhani has the full support of the Supreme Leader and that his election, while not trivial, cannot be considered as a real change in Iranian policies, including nuclear ones.

P5+1?

The media speaks of the P5+1[287] as if it was a body formed of more or less equal partners taking decisions together. This is also nonsense. Who are the P5+1? The five permanent members of the UNSC plus Germany: China, France, Russia, the United Kingdom, the United States (P5) and Germany[288] (+1; officially added for economic reasons). P5+1 is really a misnomer as it should be called "1+1(+4)": Those who matter—the USA and Russia—and those who don't China (which is happy to follow the Russian lead on this issue), France, the UK, and Germany (who will pretend to have an opinion but who will let the USA deal with the serious stuff). And since Russia under Putin is a strong ally of Iran, this really only leaves the "Big One" i.e., the USA as the negotiating counterpart to Iran.

---

[287] P5+1 https://en.wikipedia.org/wiki/P5%2B1

[288] Role of Germany in P5+1 https://en.wikipedia.org/wiki/P5%2B1#Role_of_Germany

So why this "sudden" breakthrough in negotiations between the USA and Iran. Could it be that the big change which made it possible did not occur in Iran but in the United States?

I have a different interpretation to offer.

It is my belief that it all began in September when, following a few dramatic days which almost saw a US attack on Syria, Barack Obama had to accept "*Putin's gambit*":[289] the US would not attack Syria in exchange for the full destruction of Syria's chemical weapons arsenal. I believe that this absolutely tectonic reversal US foreign policy has now triggered what I would call a "domino effect" which is still ongoing and which might result in further unexpected changes in US foreign policy.

Let's look at this domino sequence of events one by one:

Domino 1: Barack Obama accepts Putin's gambit

Whether it was really Barack Obama himself or his puppeteers is really irrelevant here. The president being the official Commander in Chief he is the person who had to announce that an agreement had been reached and that a US attack on Syria would be delayed/scrapped. Let's set aside for a moment the exact reason(s) why the US took this decision (we will come back to this crucial issue later) and just say that this was a major change for the following reasons.

a) This meant that the US would have to delay and, in all likelihood, *give up on its long-standing objective of "regime change" in Syria.*

b) This also meant that the US would *now have to negotiate with the Syrian government.*

c) Since chemical weapons were completely irrelevant to the military dynamic on the ground and since US had committed not to strike government forces, this meant that *the USA was essentially giving up on its plan to help the insurgency win the war.*

---

[289]Obama accepts the Russian gambit http://thesaker.is/obama-accepts-the-russian-gambit/

d) This removed the last pretext(s) possible for the US to continue to stall and avoid a Geneva II conference.[290] From now on, the US had to *get serious about Geneva II or lose it all.*

Before this development the USA had two possible ways to deal with a *Geneva II* conference: to try to sabotage it or to try to use this opportunity to achieve something. As soon as Obama accepted Putin's gambit only the second option remained. Indeed, since regime change in Syria is clearly not an option any more, and since the US foreign policy in the Middle East was predicated on regime change in Syria, the US now had to reconsider it all. This meant that the best possible option for the US was to try to use Geneva II to actually finally get something done. However, there is one truism which the US diplomats had to take into account: no solution in Syria will ever be achieved unless Iran approves of it. In other words, having accepted Putin's gambit, the US was not only committed to negotiations with the Syrians, but also with the Iranians. This the real causes of the "sudden" breakthrough between the "P5+1 and Iran": the defeat of the US in Syria literally forced the White House to negotiate with Iran, at which point to continue to stonewall at the negotiations over Iran's nuclear program became counter-productive and, frankly, absurd.

Domino 2: the USA and Iran finally agree on the nuclear issue.

As I have written it many times in the past, nobody in the US (or elsewhere), really believes that the Iranians are secretly building a nuclear weapon right under the nose of International Atomic Energy Agency (IAEA) inspectors (who are still working in Iran) while remaining a member in good standing of the NPT Treaty (no NTP member has ever developed nuclear weapons). The real US objective has always been to prevent Iran from becoming a regional economic superpower and, if possible, to find a pretext to isolate and destabilize the Iranian regime. By

[290] Geneva II Conference on Syria https://en.wikipedia.org/wiki/Geneva_II_Conference_on_Syria

accepting to negotiate with Iran, the USA is not "making the world safe from nuclear-armed Mullahs" but accepting the reality that Iran is, and will remain, a regional superpower. This is really what is at stake here, and all that talk about Iran nuking Israel in a "second Holocaust" is just a pious fig-leaf used to hide the real US policy objectives. Now that the US had given up on the notion of attacking Syria it made no sense to continue to act as if an attack on Iran was still possible. This left only two possible solutions: let the Iranians do whatever they want and appear to have failed to persuade Iran to take into consideration US objections, or actually find a mutually acceptable compromise which would be to the advantage of both sides. The US, wisely, chose the second option.

So far, Dominos 1 and 2 have fallen, but let us take a look at what might be happening next if nothing stops the momentum generated by these two dominos.

Domino 3: the two big losers—Saudi Arabia and Israel

It is rather obvious that the Saudis and the Israelis have done literally everything in their power to prevent the fall of Dominos 1 and 2 from happening and that they are now the big losers. Both countries hate and fear Iran, both countries were deeply involved in the Syrian war and both countries appear to be outraged by the actions of the White House. When all the signs indicated that a deal would be struck, the Saudis and the Israelis even sent their top decision-makers (Bandar and Netanyahu) not to Washington, but to Moscow in a (futile) attempt to prevent what they see as an absolute catastrophe from happening.

Now that a deal has been reached, both Israel and the KSA are now showing all the signs of "losing it" and are turning to crude forms of terrorism to lash out at their enemies: according to Hezbollah, the Saudis are behind the bombing of the Iranian Embassy in Beirut[291] while the Is-

---

[291] Saudi Arabia behind Iran embassy bombing: Nasrallah http://www.presstv.ir/detail/2013/12/03/338088/saudi-arabia-behind-iran-embassy-bombing/

raelis are behind the murder of a Hezbollah commander,[292] also in Beirut. One can dismiss these Hezbollah accusations as politically motivated, but I personally find them very credible simply because they "fit the picture" perfectly (and Hezbollah does have an excellent record of making only truthful statements). Whether one chooses to believe Hezbollah or not, nobody denies that there are now real and deep tensions between Israel and the KSA on one side and the USA on the other. That would also explain the rather amazing "rapprochement"[293] taking place between Israel and the KSA who now have a common problem (the USA) and lots of common enemies (first and foremost Iran, of course).

Considering the huge power of the Israel Lobby and, more discreet but also very powerful, the Saudi Lobby in the USA, it is by no means certain that the new KSA-Israeli alliance shall not eventually prevail over what I would call the "USA-firsters" (in contrast to "Israel-firsters"). I shall also come back to this topic later, but let us assume that the current US policies will not be reversed and that the US will sign a long-term agreement with Iran in six months or so. What could happen next?

Domino 4: goodbye US anti-missile "defense shield" in Europe?

Think about it: if the USA accepts the notion that Iran will not develop nuclear weapons, why insist on deploying an anti-nuclear missile defense shield over Europe? Russian Foreign Minister Lavrov has already clearly said that much and that is likely to remain a Russian policy position for the foreseeable future: now that the putative "threat" from Iran has been dealt with by means of negotiations—why should the US still deploy anti-missile systems in Europe?

---

[292] Hezbollah Official Assassinated in Hadath, Israel Held Responsible http://www.almanar.com.lb/english/adetails.php?eid=123792&cid=23&fromval=1&frid=23&seccatid=14&s1=1

[293] Officials: Israelis in secret trip to inspect Saudi bases. Could be used as staging ground for strikes against Iran http://kleinonline.wnd.com/2013/11/24/officals-israelis-in-secret-trip-to-inspect-saudi-bases-could-be-used-as-staging-ground-for-strikes-against-iran/

Of course, the US could plow ahead with this project as if nothing had changed, but would it not be logical to at least talk to the Russians to see if some modifications could be made to the US anti-missile system which would satisfy the Russian side? Having agreed to negotiate with Syria and Iran, would it not also make sense to seriously sit down with the Russians and find a mutually acceptable compromise?

After all, Russia (backed by China, of course) can easily prevent any deal between the US and Iran (by a UNSC veto for example) and that would leave the USA is a very vulnerable negotiating position: to be in a great need of a deal with Iran while Iran would not feel equally interested in negotiating. And, of course, a breakdown in negotiations between Iran and the USA on the nuclear issue would mean very bad news for the USA in Syria. The fact is that the USA will desperately need Russian collaboration to hammer out a long-term deal with Iran. And that, in turn, will have major consequences for a host of other issues, including European foreign policy.

Domino 5: an end to the European "Drang nach Osten"?[294]

Not since the days of Hitler has Europe been so hysterically anti-Russian as in the last decade. Of course, some of that russophobia has been fed by US propaganda needs, but one quick look at the European press and will show anyone that the worst of this Russia-bashing really comes from Europe, especially the UK. As for the EU and NATO, their offensive toward the East is really reminiscent of Hitler's, the only difference is that it is pursued with different means. Of course, West European revanchism is only part of the picture. There is definitely a desire by many East Europeans to become "true Europeans" combined with a hope that a EU+NATO combination would protect them from Russia. Never mind that Russia is not in the least interested in invading them—most East Europeans are generically afraid of what they perceive as a resurgent

[294] Drang nach Osten https://en.wikipedia.org/wiki/Drang_nach_Osten

superpower in the East. And if getting the "protection" of NATO and the EU means accepting a semi-colonial status in the US empire—so be it. Better to be a serf of the US empire than a serf in the Russian one. That is an ideological position which cannot be challenged by facts or logic. Most East Europeans probably understand that Russia has no interest in invading them, and most of them must be aware that joining the EU has been disastrous in economic terms for countries like Bulgaria, or the Baltic states. Frankly, most people don't care. They look at German highways, French stores or Dutch airports and want to get a share of that wealth even if that is only a pipe-dream.

As for the West Europeans, they shamelessly feed that illusion, promising much and delivering nothing. As for NATO, it continues to follow Hitler's example and attempts to push its influence into the Caucasus. As a result, the EU+NATO offensive now spans a "front" from Estonia in the Baltic to Georgia in the Caucasus—an exact copy of Hitler's strategy for his war on Russia.

Hitler and his promised "*1000 year Reich,*" of course, was defeated in only 12 years and the EU is not doing too well either. In fact, it is facing a systemic crisis that it has no idea of how to tackle.

I am not even referring to the so-called "PIGS"[295] (Portugal, Italy, Greece and Spain), but also to the supposedly "better off" nations of northern Europe. Did you know that only three of the seventeen nations of the Eurozone have a AAA credit rating[296] or that while no fewer than seven of the world's top rated nations are in Europe, most are either not in the Euro (Denmark, Sweden) or not in the EU at all (Norway, Switzerland)? Anyone doubting the full magnitude of the social and economic crisis which has hit the Eurozone should read the report recently published by the International Federation of Red Cross and Red Crescent

---

[295] PIGS (economics) https://en.wikipedia.org/wiki/PIGS_%28economics%29

[296] Dutch downgraded: EU shoots messenger http://www.rt.com/op-edge/dutch-credit-rating-downgraded-635/

Societies entitled "*Think differently: humanitarian impacts of the economic crisis in* Europe" (makes me wonder if anybody in the Ukraine has read this one!) Europe is in a deep crisis and this begs the obvious question: can Europe really afford a new Cold War with Russia? What about the US—does it need a new Cold War in Europe? Isn't it about time to set aside this crazy Drang nach Osten and accept that a non-imperial Europe would have much more to gain from a partnership with Russia than from another Cold War?

Time will show whether this last domino will also fall. What matters for our purposes here is not to accurately predict the future, but to look at the opportunities such a different future would offer. Let's ask a key question: if all the dominos above did fall, would the USA be better or worse off? My personal reply is that the USA would be far better off, as would be Europe. And if that is the case, one can wonder, did the US really stumble into a situation which triggered a domino effect or what this the plan all along? Could it be that some forces of the USA have decided to use the failure of the US policy in Syria to trigger a much larger change?

A project of the "USA-firsters"?

As I have written in a recent article,[297] I believe that the Presidency of Barak Obama has resulted in a shift of power in the US "deep state" which had the previously almighty neocons pushed aside from the Executive Branch and replaced with what I call "*old Anglo imperialists.*" They could also be called "USA-firsters" (as opposed to "Israel-firsters"[298]). As a rule, they are far more sophisticated actors than the neocons. Typically, the USA-firsters are better educated, more cautious in

---

[297] 1993-2013: is the twenty years long "pas de deux" of Russia and the USA coming to an end? http://thesaker.is/1993-2013-is-the-twenty-years-long-pas-de-deux-of-russia-and-the-usa-coming-to-an-end/

[298] Why I am using "Israel firster" again http://mondoweiss.net/2012/06/why-i-am-using-israel-firster-again

their discourse and methods and, unlike the neocons, they can count on the support of patriotically-inclined Americans in the armed forces, State Department, CIA, and elsewhere. Finally, they enjoy the big advantage over the neocons in the fact that they have no need to hide their real agenda: in their foreign policy they care first and foremost about US national interests (internally, of course, both the USA-firsters and the neocons are the prototypical "one percenters" whose real objective is to defend their class interests while keeping the remaining 99% in serf-like conditions).

So could it be that this "domino sequence" was deliberately initiated by Anglo USA-firsters who seized the opportunity to promote their agenda while pushing the neocon Israel-firsters aside?

Let's look at "Domino 1″ again.

I think that there is a preponderance of evidence that Obama accepted Putin's gambit against a background of absolute chaos both in Syria and in the USA. Iranian forces were covertly entering Syria to fight, a powerful Russian naval task force was positioned right off the coast of Syria, the British Parliament had refused to support an attack on Syria, demonstrations were taking place all over the USA—and elsewhere—against an attack, and all the signs were that Congress would not approve a military operation. It is hard to prove a negative, of course, but my sense is that the first domino fell pushed by all these factors and not a result of a deliberate change in US policies.

What about "domino 2″ then?

In contrast to domino 1, there is strong evidence that domino 2 clearly "fell" as a direct result of a political decision made in Washington. If we accept that the only change in the Presidency of Iran was mainly a cosmetic one, then we also have to agree that the USA *deliberately* decided to open negotiations with Iran. Could it be that somebody in the White House or in the US deep state realized that the fall of "domino 1″ presented real opportunities for the USA and the interests of the USA-firsters and decided to *deliberately add momentum* to "domino 1" and also push "domino 2"?

I believe that the sequence of events in Syria and Iran does offer a fantastic opportunity for the USA to finally rid itself from the disastrous legacy of many years of neocon rule (in my opinion from 1993-2009). I should immediately stress that I am **not** saying that the neocons are "out" as they still control the US corporate media and Congress with an iron hand. I am only saying that I am detecting the signs of a major change in US foreign policy which appears to be breaking free from the "Wahhabi-Zionist alliance" of the combined lobbies of Saudi Arabia and Israel. Again, the fact that both Netanyahu and Bandar felt the need to travel to Moscow **to stop Washington** is absolutely unprecedented and amazing, and I have to interpret that as a real sign of panic.

How far can the US really go?

A shift in the power equation inside the US does not mean regime change, far from it. In most circumstances US politicians will continue to mantrically repeat "there is no light between the U.S. and Israel,"[299] the constant verbal genuflection before everything Jewish, Israeli or Holocaust-related will continue, and it is quite possible that the next Israeli Prime Minister to address Congress will also get more standing ovations than the US president.[300] However, it is also quite possible that between closed doors the Israelis and the Saudis will be told to "tone it down or else" and that the US support for these two regimes will become contingent of them not doing anything crazy (such as attacking Iran).

Let's look again at Dominos 4 and 5 (basically, a stop in anti-Russian policies) from a non-Zionist and non-Wahhabi point of view: would the USA gain or lose from such a development? It could lose some money if

---

[299] "No Light Between the U.S. and Israel" http://www.thedailybeast.com/articles/2013/05/23/there-is-no-light-between-the-u-s-and-israel.html

[300] Netanyahu gets more standing ovations than Obama http://www.salon.com/2011/05/24/netanyahu_standing_ovations/

the European missile defense "shield" was scrapped, but the Russians are offering two alternative solutions: either let the Russian military become full partner in this system (thereby removing the threat to Russia) or move the entire system to Western Europe away from the Russian borders (thereby also removing the threat to Russia). Since the Russian asymmetrical response (special forces, relocation of launchers, special missiles) will defeat the proposed system anyway—why not accept either one of the Russian offers?

Politically, such an agreement would open the doors for far more important collaborative opportunities (in Central Asia and the Middle East) and it would remove the USA from the "collision course with the rest of the planet" it has been on since 9/11.

Clearly, a deal with Russia would be very beneficial for the USA.

What about Palestine?

Here, unfortunately, I have to remain as pessimistic as ever. As so many times in their history, the Palestinians have again committed something of a "strategic suicide" when they decided to support the anti-Assad forces in Syria. Just as with Saddam, the Palestinians are yet again with the losing side and, which is even worse, their only halfway decent resistance movement—Hamas—has now been taken over by Saudi interests which basically puts them under Israeli control no less than Fatah. The last "real" resistance movement in Palestine is now the Palestinian Islamic Jihad, but it is comparatively small and weak and cannot be a partner in any real negotiations with the USA and Israel. In this context, it is likely the Israelis will simply impose whatever "solution" they want on the ground without having to negotiate with any Palestinians at all. This is very sad and this did not have to be, but the Palestinians really did it to themselves and they only have themselves to blame now.

Bottom line: no domino effect in Palestine.

Conclusion: a real window of opportunity

The future is by no means certain and the Israel-firsters and their Saudi allies have many options to reverse this process (just imagine Hillary as president!!) And yet it is also possible that the USA might shift away from the disastrous course it has been following for the past two decades and return to a more traditional, pragmatic, foreign policy: it will remain an imperial power with global imperialist goals, but at least it will be driven by pragmatic—if cynical—considerations and not foreign ideological interests. In contrast to what the USA has been doing for the past two decades, it is possible that the developments in the Middle East will convince the USA that negotiations and compromise are more effective foreign policy tools than threat and military actions.

Historically, Republicans have had a comparatively better foreign policy record than the Democrats and senile psychopaths like McCain are not typical of Republican leaders. In contrast, US Democrats have often provided the most ideological and arrogant leaders and the very real possibility of Hillary running for the presidency is a frightening indicator that what appears to be the current phase of pragmatism might be short-lived. The good news is that both parties have an opportunity to seize the moment and nominate halfway sane candidates for the next presidential election. Of course, if what we end up with is a Sarah Palin—Hillary Clinton race all bets are off and the world will be in for some very, very bad times. But if the USA-firsters can give the boot to the Israel-firsters currently controlling the key positions inside both parties (folks in the model of Rahm Israel Emanuel) then there is a real possibility that the US could break free from its current subservience to Zionist and Wahhabi interests and resume a more pragmatic, reasonable, foreign policy.

Do these USA-firsters really exist? Honestly, I don't know. I hope that they do and I want to believe that the fact that the fall of the Syrian domino was followed so soon by the fall of the Iranian domino might be a sign that somebody inside the US deep state has decided to use this opportunity to try finally rid the USA from the foreign interests which have literally hijacked the country.

If after six month a permanent deal is agreed upon and signed by the P5+1 and Iran and if more or less at the same time the US begins serious negotiations with Russia such a scenario will become credible. At this point, it is too early to tell.

December 8, 2013

PART VIII: THE FRENCH RESISTANCE

ISRAEL LOBBY COMMITS MAJOR BLUNDER IN FRANCE: TRIES TO SILENCE A COMEDIAN

Amazing stuff is happening in France. It all began with a relatively well-known French-Cameroonian comedian, Dieudonné M'bala M'bala[301] was invited to participate on a TV show on the channel France 3. The show also featured a Maghrebian artist and Dieudonné decided to impersonate an extremist Israeli settled infuriated by the presence of an Arab on a French show (for those of you who understand French, you can see an excerpt of his appearance that day here).[302]

Dieudonné who, in the past, had always enjoyed ridiculing pretty much every segment of French society clearly had never expected the hysterical uproar that his humor would trigger that day: the huge constellation of French Zionists organizations lead by the notorious CRIF ("Representative Committee of Jewish organization in France"—the French version of AIPAC) immediately attacked Dieudonné, suing him for racists comments and suing him for "anti-Semitism" (a criminal offense in France). This was hardly the first time that the French Zionist mob had decided to crush an outspoken critic of its role in French politics or its unconditional support for the last racist state on the planet: Israel. But this time, the Ziomob miscalculated, badly.

Dieudonné began making the accusations of anti-Semitism made against him a central piece of his shows. Here is a sampling of the kind of the hilarious skits Dieudonné came up with:

---

[301] Israel lobby commits major blunder in France: tries to silence a comedian Dieudonné M'bala M'bala https://en.wikipedia.org/wiki/Dieudonn%C3%A9_M%27bala_M%27bala

[302] The video has been removed.

- *Les racistes anonymes*[303]
- *L'antisemitisme*[304]
- *Peuple Elue*[305]
- *Mes excuses premiere partie*[306]
- *Mes excuses deuxieme partie*[307]
- *J'ai fait le con*[308]
- *Dieudonné et Faurisson au Zenith de Paris*[309]
- *Dieudonné et Faurisson 1*[310]
- *Dieudonné et Faurisson 2*[311]

This was not at all what the Ziomobsters in France had hoped to achieve when they attacked Dieudonné for his appearance on France 3. In response to his defiant stance, they then used their total control over the French political class to shut down his shows under the pretext that they would "threaten the public order." Dieudonné immediately replied that France is capable of providing the security needed for an event like the G8 summit, but not to let one comedian make his show.

Still, while in the past he had filled the biggest concert halls in France, Dieudonné was forced to perform his skits in a rented bus (you can see a report about this here[312]). But Dieudo, has he is known, had one more thing up his sleeve.

---

[303] Dieudonné, association des racistes anonymes https://www.youtube.com/watch?v=jkA5FSVu4L0

[304] The video has been removed.

[305] The video has been removed.

[306] The video has been removed.

[307] The video has been removed.

[308] The video has been removed.

[309] The video has been removed.

[310] Dieudonné Faurisson le sketch (1ère partie) https://www.youtube.com/watch?v=nOORJHWW1Os

[311] Dieudonné Faurisson le sketch (2ème partie) https://www.youtube.com/watch?v=P9uUmffBDO0

[312] Dieudonné persiste et signe...dans un bus https://www.youtube.com/watch?v=9AmygPgytBg

His logic was simple: if I cannot use my freedom of speech as a comedian, why not use it as a politician?

Dieudo had already tried one to run for office a couple of times, but he never achieved any measure of success. This time, however, he came up with a stunning argument. Basically, Dieudo claims that the Left-Right chasm is an artificial and meaningless chasm in French politics and that the real issue which separates the parties in France is their attitude toward the Zionist ideology, the state of Israel, and the role of the Israel Lobby in France. Check out his press conference here:

Conference de presse de Dieudonné 1[313]

Conference de presse de Dieudonné 2[314]

Conference de presse de Dieudonné 3[315]

Conference de presse de Dieudonné 4[316]

Needless to say, the French political elites had a total hysterical breakdown at such impudence. *Doubleplusgoodthinking* reporters and commentators declared that his political party had to be banned[317] and that Dieudonné was probably mentally insane[318] (the latter reminds me of the old trick invented by Yuri Andropov's KGB who used to declared that Soviet dissidents were "obviously" insane because how could any mentally sane person oppose the Soviet rule: QED).

Still, Dieudo did not back down and he has recently presented some of the members of his political movement "the Anti-Zionist Movement" running as candidates for the European Parliament. Here is the press conference of this event:

---

[313] The video has been removed.

[314] The video has been removed.

[315] The video has been removed.

[316] The video has been removed.

[317] Dieudonné revu et tabassé 1/2 https://www.youtube.com/watch?v=2Pe0cphvwcs

[318] Dieudonné revu et tabassé 2/2 https://www.youtube.com/watch?v=qrKX4fVwVYc

- Conference de presse liste UE 1[319]
- Conference de presse liste UE 2[320]
- Conference de presse liste UE 3[321]
- Conference de presse liste UE 4[322]
- Candidats du Parti anti-sioniste: presentation[323]

What is most interesting in this list is that its candidates come from every political movement imaginable. Unionists, nationalist conservatives, Roman-Catholics, Muslims, ex-Communists, Socialists, etc. Ethnically, everybody is also present. It appears that the Zionist threat is truly uniting many of those who until recently were virulently opposed to each other.

What is the potential of this political movement?

On one hand, the entire weight of the French political establishment is now coming crashing down on Dieudonné. Every politician, every newspaper, every commentator either completely ignores Dieudonné and his movement or, when they speak of him at all, it is with a vitriolic loathing which cannot be imagined. The French newspaper even calls him a "comedian" in quotation marks, showing that such a hideous figure as Dieudonné cannot be called a comedian or somebody who makes people laugh. The fury of the establishment is such that I find it very likely that Dieudonné's political movement will be simply banned and declared a criminal organization (in France, the membership in an organization declared illegal is considered a crime in itself). If not, Dieudonné might do very, very well.

The fact is that there are literally millions of French citizens from all parts of the society who are sick and tired of being ruled by a small group

[319] This video has been removed.

[320] This video has been removed.

[321] This video has been removed.

[322] This video has been removed.

[323] This video has been removed.

of mutually interchangeable elite (all of which is 100% loyal to anything Zionist or Israeli). The fact is that in the French "banlieue" (suburbs) there are hundreds of thousands of Muslims who are outraged by the events in Gaza, the war in Iraq, the war in Afghanistan and the constant threats against Iran. The fact is that the economic crisis has hit France—and the rest of the Eurozone—very badly and that more and more people are making the link between the Israeli-American model of globalization and the economic collapse of the world markets. In fact, I would say that the potential of Dieudonné's movement is huge and that it represents a very real threat to the French and, beyond that, USraelien elites in the West.

The fact that Dieudonné himself is (half) Black, and that he succeeded in federating very different currents of the French society under his stance, will make it impossible to simply ignore him. Can the French political establishment engage Dieudonné and prevail over him in an open political debate? Not in a million years. Banning Dieudonné's political party will, at best, be a stop-gap solution as we can be certain that Dieudo will sue the French courts in Brussels and that, if needed, he will simply re-compose his movement under another name.

Under the influence of the recent immigrants to France, the French society is changing and it appears that while the "native" French did not have the wits and guts to take on the Ziomob in power, those who immigrated to France do have what it takes.

It is amazing to listen to these recent immigrants defending the secular and multi-ethnics nature of the French Republic and denouncing the ethnic and tribal nature of Jewish organizations in France. For example, Dieudo was once asked what he thought of the attempts made by such French Blacks to create an organization which would speak for them. Dieudo rejected this approach, saying that the organization which should speak for them should be the French Parliament. Amazing idea, no?

Thanks to Dieudonné, Zionism is now finally being denounced as a tribal and racist, ideology and support for Israel is now becoming as morally repugnant as support for apartheid. The entire intellectual edifice which was carefully built by the Zionists in France for many decades is not coming crashing down because once these issues are out in the open, the Ziomob has already lost the key battle. In fact, Dieudo has said that he has already won the next election.

What will happen next? Dieudonné does not take his participation in the upcoming elections too seriously. As a typical comedian, he can sit there and say "I will bring you all to the light" with a serious face. When asked if he is really serious, her replies that nobody in French politics is serious and that the difference between him the rest of the French politicians is that they are lousy comedians whereas he is a professional.

Humor as a weapon of liberation can be very powerful. The ridicule which Dieudonné is now heaping on the previously sacred cows of French Ziopropagnda, such as the "The Eternal Memory of the Shoah" (all in caps), and all the rest of the Zionist brainwashing toolkit might well prove to be a formidable weapon, for which the Ziomob does not have a standard answer.

It will be very interesting to see what happens between now and June 7th—the next election.

In the meantime, here are some links to Dieudonné's non-political skits. Enjoy!

- *L"equipe du 11*[324]
- *Avant le mariage*[325]
- *Apres le mariage*[326]
- *Le garagiste*[327]
- *La prison*[328]

---

[324] Dieudonné - la fine équipe du 11 https://www.youtube.com/watch?v=QucwSU_ArbA

[325] Dieudonné Avant le mariage https://www.youtube.com/watch?v=mrOcUe3bQBo

[326] Dieudonné après le mariage ttps://www.youtube.com/watch?v=aN1UMD6EotI

[327] Dieudonné - Le garagiste https://www.youtube.com/watch?v=hQe3lvVE2sk

[328] Dieudonné - La prison https://www.youtube.com/watch?v=pfH6zDWKFOU

- *Le journaliste premiere partie*[329]
- *Le journaliste deuxieme partie*[330]
- *L'institutrice*[331]
- *L'avocat*[332]

May 18, 2009

[329] Dieudonné - Le journaliste 1/2 https://www.youtube.com/watch?v=0Iw01Mh5xUM

[330] Dieudonné - Le journaliste 2/2 https://www.youtube.com/watch?v=n604t5GH0RI

[331] Dieudonné - L'institutrice https://www.youtube.com/watch?v=IcNezh2AOX4

[332] Dieudonné - L'avocat https://www.youtube.com/watch?v=75ZQNfRM2GQ

Dieudonné's anti-Zionist campaign in full swing in France

(For those of you who do not know who Dieudonné is, or what he does, please check my previous article on this topic here[333]).

First, the big news is that the French government has not succeeded in outlawing Dieudonné's Anti-Zionist Party or the list he has presented for the upcoming European elections. Official polls put the party's estimated support at 4% which, considering who is running such polls in France, probably means that Dieudo has at least 8-10% support. That is, of course, not enough to make a difference in the European political scene, but that is more than enough to keep openly challenging the Zionist lobby in France.

In fact, Dieudo's campaign is in full swing. Check out the new posters his list has released: Translation:

> "For a Europe free from censorship, communitarianism (ethnicity based politics—VS) and NATO speculators—The Antizionist List"

I would add that it is rather amazing that such a movement would be allowed to exist anywhere in the West, and even more so in France as the power of the Zionist lobby is far greater in France than it is in the USA or, should I maybe say, it is more brazen, more arrogant, more overt. The one factor which proved decisive in this case is the fact that France, like all European countries, has a multi-party political system whereas the USA has, in essence, only one party split into two vaguely competing factions. A "Dieudonné" in the USA is simply impossible as long as a third party is impossible.

---

[333] Israel lobby commits major blunder in France: tries to silence a comedian http://thesaker.is/israel-lobby-commits-major-blunder-in-france-tries-to-silence-a-comedian/

Another interesting feature in the Anti-Zionist Party's campaign is the support it is getting from French rap singers in videos.[334]

Amazing, no? Considering the explosive tensions between the French "banlieue" (suburban-ghettos) and the government, this double endorsement of Dieudonné and his anti-Zionist platform spells out major troubles for the Zionist lobby in France.

As is well known, French banlieues are heavily black and Maghrebian which potentially gives an ethnic character to any governmental policy toward them. It now appears that Dieudonné's movement is turning what used to be the alienation of the French youth against the establishment directly at the most powerful component of that establishment: the Zionist lobby. This could very easily repeated in the rest of Europe. I would even argue that this evolution is probably inevitable. This simple truth has now been re-discovered: Zionist is a form of racism (which *UN Resolution 3379*[335] clearly declared before being revoked[336]); it is also a form of neo-colonialism, imperialism and it is fundamentally anti-democratic.

The other interesting feature of this movement is that it clearly links the Zionist lobby, Israel and the USA into one power structure, what Dieudonné once called "The Axis of Goodness" (again using humor to ridicule and denounce). The Israeli bloodbath is perceived as much as an American or French policy as an Israeli one. This analysis is, of course, fundamentally correct.

Considering how immensely unpopular the USA has become during the Dubya years and his Global War on Terror the merging of the ideas

---

[334] These videos have been removed.

[335] The resolution of 1975: 3379 (XXX). Elimination of all forms of racial discrimination https://en.wikipedia.org/wiki/United_Nations_General_Assembly_Resolution_3379#The_resolution_of_1975

[336] United Nations General Assembly Resolution 46/86, adopted on 16 December 1991, revoked the determination in Resolution 3379, which had called Zionism a form of racism. https://en.wikipedia.org/wiki/United_Nations_General_Assembly_Resolution_3379#Revocation

of USA and Zionist in the minds of the French and, possibly, European youth is a very worrying development for the Zionist lobbies everywhere. It would not be incorrect to see all this as a case of "blowback" for what Israel did, and still does, in Gaza.

Dieudonné supporters see themselves as opponents of racism, of course, but also of imperialism, capitalism, globalization and neo-colonialism. They see countries like Russia, Iran, Venezuela or Bolivia as potential allies. In fact, the number 2 on Dieudonné's list, Alain Soral, spoke of Russia as "our future." It appears that a growing segment of the alienated French youth has evolved from the mindless rage stage (throwing stones at cops) to a much more conscious and informed opposition to the system in place and its immoral policies.

All this is rather fascinating and I encourage you all to keep a close eye on the situation in France.

For those who speak French, check out the latest press conference of Dieudonné's list.[337]

Further information:

Anti-Zionist Party[338] (in French)

Anti-Zionist List[339] (in French)

June 05, 2009

---

[337] These videos have been removed.

[338] Anti-Zionist Party http://www.partiantisioniste.com/

[339] Anti-Zionist List http://www.partiantisioniste.com/

IS A NEW REVOLUTION QUIETLY BREWING IN FRANCE?

Today I am beginning a series of articles about what I believe is the extremely deep crisis taking place in Europe and about the potential of this crisis to result in some cataclysmic events. I will begin by taking a look at what has been going on in France, probably the country in Europe I know best, and also one which I think has be biggest potential to generate an explosion with far reaching consequences.

One could look at France's economic and financial situation (catastrophic) or at the many social problems plaguing an already very frustrated population, but I want to focus on one specific aspect of the current French crisis: the complete alienation of the majority of the people from the ruling elites which I will illustrate by one very telling example: the growing hysteria of the French elites about a brilliant philosopher—Alain Soral—and one standup comedian—Dieudonné M'bala M'bala.

I have already written about these to remarkable people (*here,*[340] *here*[341] and *here*[342]) and I urge you to read these past articles to get a better picture of what is taking place now. For those who are really not willing to read a few background pages, I will begin by the following mini-introduction.

Dieudonné M'bala M'bala[343] is a French-Cameroonian comedian which was by far the most popular comic in France until he made one

[340] Israel lobby commits major blunder in France: tries to silence a comedian http://thesaker.is/israel-lobby-commits-major-blunder-in-france-tries-to-silence-a-comedian/

[341] Dieudonné anti-Zionist campaign in full swing in France http://thesaker.is/dieudonnes-anti-zionist-campaign-in-full-swing-in-france/

[342] Russia's prevailing ideological consensus: sovereignism and anti-capitalism http://thesaker.is/russias-prevailing-ideological-consensus-sovereignism-and-anti-capitalism/

[343] Dieudonné M'bala M'bala https://en.wikipedia.org/wiki/Dieudonn%C3%A9_M%27bala_M%27bala

short sketch about a religious Israeli Settler on French TV. The sketch was not particularly funny, but it really enraged the French equivalent of the US AIPAC—called CRIF in France—which began a systematic campaign to smear, ban and silence "Dieudo" as he is known in France. Dieudo refused to roll over and retaliated by making fun of those persecuting him which made him the darling of many of those who hated the financial elites running France since 1969. Now completely banned from any public media, Dieudo is still the most popular comic in France.

Alain Soral is a French author and philosopher whose political career included a membership in the French Communist Party and the National Front. He is credited with developing the concept of "*gauche du travail—droite des valeurs*" (literally "left of labor—right of values") which can be summarized as the simultaneous advocacy of socialist/social ideas and measures in economic and social issues combined with conservative moral, ethical and religious values in ideological, ethical and cultural issues. He is the founder of an extremely interesting movement called "*Egalité et Reconciliation*" which aims at reconciling native French people (called "*Français de souche*" or "root French") with those French people who recently immigrated to France (called "Français de branche" or "branch French") and to make them coexist in complete equality. Because of his numerous "politically incorrect" ideas and very overt statements, Soral is absolutely hated and feared by the French ruling class. Even though Soral has also been completely banned from any public media, he remains immensely popular with the general public and his books are all best sellers.

Soral and Dieudo are very different people, they have very different backgrounds and they have very different personalities. There even used to be a time when they were sharply critical of each other. But when the French elites decided to basically destroy them they became closer together and now they are good friends, and they openly support each other, as a result we have this truly bizarre phenomenon: a white philosopher, and a black comedian have jointly become a kind of "two-headed Emmanuel Goldstein[344]" of modern France: the elites absolutely hate them, and the media is gone into a completely Orwellian "*two minute of hate*"[345] frenzy mode trying to convince the French people that Soral and/or Dieudo are almost a reincarnation of Adolf Hitler. Needless to say, this thesis is so stupid that Dieudo makes fun of it in his shows while Soral ridicules it in his books and uses it to show that France is run by a tiny elite of vicious and arrogant SOBs.

In truth, one has to admit that the French elites are facing two formidable enemies. Dieudonné is truly one of the most talented French comedian ever while Soral is without any doubt the most original and brilliant philosopher France has seen since World War II. Furthermore, French law makes it rather difficult to completely ban a show or a book. God knows, the French elites have tried, and both Dieudo and Soral have been taken to court numerous times for "racism" and "anti-Semitism," both of them have been physically assaulted several times by the thugs of the "LDJ" (Jewish Defense League) and both of them are constantly harassed by the authorities (the French version of the IRS and the FBI). Yet, this systematic campaign of persecutions has clearly backfired against its authors and given Dieudo and Soral a (well-deserved) martyr status. Finally, Dieudo and Soral have shown that they are extremely sophisticated users of the Internet where their shows, special events, interviews, books, monthly news roundups have been extremely popular and are seen by many millions of people in France and abroad.

Gradually, Soral and Dieudo have built a real political movement which is active both on the internal front and on international issues.

As I mentioned, "*Egalité et Reconciliation*"[346] or "E&R" stands for a full acceptance and integration of Muslim immigrants into the French society. This is crucial because unlike the French National Front, E&R

---

[344] Emmanuel Goldstein https://en.wikipedia.org/wiki/Emmanuel_Goldstein

[345] Two Minutes Hate https://en.wikipedia.org/wiki/Two_Minutes_Hate

[346] Egalité et Reconciliation http://www.egaliteetreconciliation.fr/

does not advocate the expulsion of immigrants out of France. Not only that, but E&R even denies that immigrants are the real problem. Of course, E&R does not deny that unemployment is huge in France, nor does it deny that a large percentage of crime and violence in France are committed by immigrants, but they see that as an *effect* of previous political mistakes and not as a cause of the problems of France.

Likewise, E&R is very openly pro-Muslim. Not in a truly religious sense, most members of E&R are not deeply religious people, but rather in the cultural sense. E&R primarily see Islam and French Roman-Catholicism as two sources of ethnics, morality and civilization as for whether one is religious or not and accepts the theology of these religions is left to the individual member. This is quite different from the utterly sterile "ecumenical dialog" which seeks to find common teachings to Jesus Christ and the Prophet Mohammad while desperately trying to overlook the very real and deep theological disagreements between these two religions. Instead, E&R advocates a common stance on most, if not all, issues faced by French Muslims and Christians. And that makes sense.

Think about it: both Islam and Christianity are clearly opposed to the values of capitalism, profit maximization, speculation, usury, sexual immorality, the destruction of the traditional family, imperialism, etc. While the theological roots of Islam and Christianity are different, most of their ethical philosophical teachings are very similar. Frankly, I can think of only one big difference and that is the fundamentally different views Muslims and Christians have on the death penalty, but since the death penalty has been abolished in France in 1981 this hardly matters today.

Of course, both Christianity and Islam have their crazy perverted deviations such as the plutocratic and genocidal policies of the Papacy in the past or the liver-eating Wahhabis the world is facing today, but E&R has no problems rejecting and condemning them. On the Christian side, E&R advocates a type of popular Roman-Catholicism seen in the pre-1789 France which has little to do with some of the worst excesses of the

Papacy. On the Muslim side, E&R is especially close to the teachings of Sheikh Imran Hosein[347] and Sayyed Hassan Nasrallah. They are also close to the Iranian supported Center Zahra[348] in Paris. I would say that the type of Muslims attracted to E&R are exactly the same as the type Christians attracted to it: politically progressive, religiously strict, observant, but tolerant. Needless to say, the potential of this radically new movement is absolutely huge because it unites Left and Right, Christian and Muslim, religious and secular (as long as they are not anti-religious), native and immigrant, white and black, rich and poor. But what seems to really trigger the panic of the French elites is the deep penetration of this movement into the notorious French banlieues, the destitute suburbs which over the past decades were filled with immigrants from Africa and which have turned into no-go zones of lawlessness and crime.

To understand this phenomenon, it's crucial to understand the following: crime in France is not, repeat "not," the product of recent immigrants or religious Muslims. Recent immigrants and religious Muslims have strong roots in their culture, families and lifestyles which categorically prevent them from being criminal. And poverty has nothing to do with this either. I personally have lived for twenty years right next to a big mosque attended by huge crowds of dirt-poor Muslims from sub-Saharan Africa, the Maghreb, the Balkans and the Middle East. I can attest that **never**, I mean that literally, **never**, was any crime committed in my neighborhood by the folks who came to this mosque. Quite to the contrary, these mosque attending Muslims were far better behaved, and more courteous, than the locals. In fact, it was clear that these people were going out of their way to show the (initially rather frightened locals) that they had no cause to fear them. The worst "crime" these Muslims regularly committed was to park their cars on the curb and that was because there were not enough parking places available. Finally, at the end

347 Sheikh Imran Hosein http://www.imranhosein.org/

348 Centre Zahra http://www.centre-zahra.com/

of each Holy Month of Ramadan, the Muslims invited the entire neighborhood to join in the celebrations, to sample the many delicious dishes offered, and to visit the mosque. To say that these Muslims were perfect citizens would be an understatement.

The so-called "Muslim crime" in France is always linked to **second** generation youth gangs who have lost their cultural and religious roots and who know little or nothing about them but who are also rejected by the local, native, population. As Soral likes to say "*nobody goes from the mosque straight into a gang-raping spree.*" It's really either/or—but not both. Soral calls these thugs "*Islamo-racaille*" which can be loosely translated as "Islamo-thugs"—a very nasty and dangerous type with no sense of right and wrong who exteriorizes his alienation by abusing the natives whom he hates. These are exactly the types who feel a deep attraction for the crude brutality of Wahhabism and who end up killing cops in France or joining the liver-eaters in Syria. Their "Islam" is really only a pretext, a pious justification, for their psychopathic thuggery. I suspect most Crusaders were exactly of the same psychological makeup.

Most young immigrants are, of course, somewhere in between the family-educated and observant type and the out of control lawless thugs. And for the very first time a relevant political movement offers them a very attractive option: E&R.

In essence E&R tells them "instead of being neither, be both—be Muslim and be French, don't hate the natives who have the same oppressors as you do and who are your best friends and allies, our enemies are trying to turn us against each other to better rule over all of us, let us therefore unite and stand together." This is an absolutely new and original message.

In the past, only two movements openly dealt with the immigration issue. On one hand you had the National Front who advocated policies such as the "national preference" (better social and labor laws from the natives), the crackdown on crime (more police, stricter laws, more and bigger jails) and the expulsion of all immigrants (except, possibly, those with a French passport—and even that was debated). On the other hand, you had an organization created by the Socialist Party called "SOS Racisme" which openly advocated the rejection of the native French culture by the immigrants who, under the nice-sounding slogan of "right to be different," were encouraged to hate the natives and demand a full acceptance of their cultures of origin by the French society. Over the past twenty years the "tag team" of the National Front and SOS Racisme has only served to make the issue of immigration in France infinitely worse. The latest, and particularly ugly, development on this front has been the new political line promoted by the French elites.

The very same elites who 20 years ago created and covertly financed SOS Racisme and its moronic slogan "*Touche pas a mon pote*" (don't touch my buddy) have now declared that Muslims are, after all, a serious problem. While in the past these elites were systematically ridiculing Christianity, they are now saying that "Islam is not compatible with the Republic." As for the youth in the *banlieues* they are now presented as potential terrorist or al-Qaeda sleepers. As a result, when the French elites are not legalizing homosexual marriages they are busy banning the hijab in schools and complaining about too much halal meats in the stores. And while only a tiny percentage of Muslim woman in France cover their faces, the French elites have now officially banned the burqa and the niqab in public places. Clearly, Muslim immigrants in France have now been downgraded from "buddies" to enemies.

It is against this background that more and more young immigrants are flocking to Soral, Dieudonné and E&R whose popularity is rapidly growing. Recently, an absolutely incredible event took place, something unthinkable just a few years ago.

In one of his sketches Dieudo sang a song called "Shoananas" a rather basic play on the words "Shoah" (from the Hebrew "HaShoah" or "disaster"—name by which the French Jews often refer to the "Holocaust") and "ananas" (pineapple). Sure enough, the CRIF, SOS Racisme and other organization sued Dieudo for "incitement to hatred." Dieudo was sentenced to a 20,000 Euros fine and he appealed the decision. On the day Dieudo's appeal was heard by the court, something absolutely extraordinary happened. I found two YouTube videos which show the event and which I will provide links to both because of the high probability that one, or both, of these videos will be banned (guys—download them now while you can!). Here they are[349]: and longer version[350]:

For those of you who do not understand French, let me summarize what we see.

Members of the Jewish Defense League (LDJ) show up to scream insults at Dieudo and his supporters who, in turn, shout all types of abuse at the LDJ members and wave pineapples at them while singing "Shoananas." The cops keep the two sides apart as best they can. Then the supporters of Dieudo begin to chant "*liberté d'expression*" (freedom of speech) to which the LDJ members reply "*am Israel hai*" ("Israel is alive" in Hebrew) and begin to sing the Israeli national anthem. At this point the supporters being to sing the French "La Marseillaise" from the top of their lungs totally drowning out the completely overwhelmed LDJ activists. Now take a close look at the faces singing "La Marseillaise"—do you see that a lot of the people singing it are clearly brown and black? These are precisely the type young people taken mostly, but not only, from the notorious *banlieues*. These could be the same people who in 2001 and 2002 booed the French national anthem during soccer matches (a big scandal at the time).

The Marseillaise is first and foremost a revolutionary song, and when it is not so much sung as it is shouted by a large crowd waving fists, this is a very, very serious development. Needless to say, none of that was ever shown on the French media. But you can bet that the elites saw it all and one can only imagine the fear they felt as these images.

---

[349] Face à la LDJ, les fans de Dieudonné chantent la marseillaise! https://www.youtube.com/watch?v=HDnAzoO1AJo

[350] Procès Dieudonné : Quenelles, LDJ, ananas et compagnie! https://www.youtube.com/watch?v=TWRVXIAzvMA

Coincidence or not, but the fact is that when the cops heard the crowd behind them singing the Marseillaise, they began pushing the LDJ activists out of the court-building. This is not very surprising considering the immense popularity Dieudo and Soral enjoy in the various uniformed services (more about that below).

Something very important and very new is happening in France. The traditional political paradigm of Right versus Left is falling apart if only because the official "Right" and the official "Left" have become indistinguishable from each other. And in the meantime, the E&R phenomenon is becoming not only bigger, but **deeper**. More and more young Frenchmen are looking back at the history of France since 1945 and they are gradually coming to the realization that the country has been ruled by an arrogant cabal of plutocrats, who overthrew de Gaulle in 1968, and who replaced this remarkable national leader with a protégé of the Rothschild family, Georges Pompidou, who began his career as a director of the Banque Rothschild and who was later picked by the French elites to replace de Gaulle. The French plutocracy which, together with the CIA, had covertly orchestrated the "May 68" riots to achieve "regime change" in France, now had free rein to radically change the "sovereignist" political course chartered by de Gaulle. Can you guess when the policy of mindless import of cheap foreign labor into France began? Under Pompidou, of course! Now, thanks for E&R both native and immigrant French people are re-discovering their **common** history and are beginning to understand that they both were victims of the same politicians.

In the meantime, the regime in power commits one blunder after the other. The latest one is both very funny and very serious. This is the huge scandal surrounding the "*quenelle.*"

Originally, the *quenelle*[351] was a French dish which, if well prepared, could be quite delicious.

---

[351] Quenelle https://en.wikipedia.org/wiki/Quenelle

The elongated shape of the *quenelle* has also given a 2nd, slang, meaning to this word. Let's just say that the French expression to "put you a *quenelle*" would have a very similar meaning to the English "up yours!"

Dieudonné did probably not realize the far reaching consequences of his words when he began referring to each of his jokes mocking of the regime in power as a quenelle. To add some emphasis, Dieudo than began to show, with his arms, the various sizes of quenelles which he, or his supporters, were "putting" to the elites. The small ones were shown has having the length of about a hand, while the big ones, the really successful ones, where shown as having the full length of an outstretched arm. Imagine a typical image of Dieudo showing a "big quenelle." This gesture rapidly went viral and became an Internet meme and more and more people began making this gesture as sign of something like "f"ck the system," "screw the government" or "here is for you, Mr. President!"

To make things worse, it became something of a sport to approach well-known personalities and to have a photo taken next to them while flashing the quenelle. People were making quenelles everywhere, especially when photographed next to regime officials.

Check this photo of the French Minister of the Interior, Manuel Valls, a rabid Zionist who has openly called for the repression of Dieudonné and Soral in a major speech in from the a congress of the Socialist Party:

Valls is the clueless grinning idiot in the middle, surrounded by a group of young Frenchmen flashing the quenelle. Needless to say, when this photo was published the entire country exploded in laughter, making the quenelle even more famous.

In the meantime, the League against Racism and anti-Semitism (the equivalent of the US Anti-Defamation League in France) declared that the quenelle was an "*inverted Nazi salute and a symbol of the sodomization of the victims of the Shoah.*"[352] I kid you not! Predictably, the French Internet exploded in laughter. The regime did not find that funny at all

[352] Page non trouvée

and it reacted with the kind of paranoia which one would expect from dictators like Stalin or Saddam Hussein: it literally launched a witch-hunt to try to detect more or less overt quenelles and when such a gesture was detected, it attempted to punish those responsible if they were civil servants, especially in the police and military. And, sure enough, the Internet was flooded with all types of folks flashing the quenelle in defiance of the regime's wrath.

Dieudo, of course, invited uniformed officials to come to his theater in Paris to perform a quenelle onstage, with him. He also created a website solely dedicated to photos of uniformed people defiantly flashing the sign.[353]

Now the regime is completely lost and confused. On one hand, it is simply impossible to sanction all the people who flash such signs, even disciplining only those in uniform is impossible. Initially, the French Chief of Staff had demanded "exemplary sanctions" against the first two soldiers who flashed a quenelle (in front of a synagogue they were ordered to guard), but now he have to punished entire crowds of defiant soldiers, most of whom hate the regime anyway. On the other hand, how can the regime ignore the fact that it is being openly defied, mocked and ridiculed?

Here we are reaching a topic whose importance cannot be overstated: how **can one achieve regime change in a democracy who has been completely bought and paid for by a plutocracy**? This is question which is as absolutely crucial for France, as it is for the USA, the UK or any other EU country and the reply to this crucial seems to have eluded most of the millions of people in the West who are completely disgusted with the regime in power but who see absolutely no realistic way to change it.

Violence is clearly not an option. The regime has been very clever to label any form of "direct action" as "terrorism" while creating a monstrous spy-state which would dwarf Ceausescu's Securitate. If you try as

353 http://www.dieudosphere.com/les-"quenelle"s.html

much as throwing a brick at a politician, they will call you a terrorist and lock you up for many decades.

Playing the electoral game is futile. The plutocrats own the media which, standing on the shoulders of folks like Edward Bernays has learned how to brainwash a population far more effectively that Hitler or Kim Il-Sung ever could. Basically, as shown by yesterday's vote in the US state of Washington,[354] elections are bought. Period. "One man one vote" has long been replaced by "one dollar one vote."

Trying to convince people by regular information campaigns has proven useless too. If anything the double facts that the 9/11 Truth movement has proven far beyond reasonable doubt that the Twin Towers and WTC7 have been brought down by controlled demolition AND the fact that his has had exactly **zero** impact on the political process in the USA proves that most people have been either zombified beyond rescue or have given up hope in complete disgust and despair.

And yet we, the common folk, do have one formidable weapon left: we can demonstratively show our total lack of respect for this regime and its values. Like Dieudo, we can do that through humor and laughter. God knows we all need a reason to laugh nowadays! And we can do it by showing our complete contempt for all the institutions the regime tries so hard to make us respect. First and foremost, we need to "diss" the voice of the regime—the corporate media—and we need to "diss" the holy liturgy of the regime—the elections. But we cannot do just that as this is only a first step. Next, we need to follow the example of Dieudo and Soral and use each opportunity to openly express our absolute contempt for every shill showing respect of this regime and its values. Not only that, but we need to denounce these propagandists as "paid regime stooges" (which, of course, they are). Lastly, we need to force the regime to show its true face by forcing it to take action against us.

---

[354] Washington votes against GMO labeling – preliminary results http://www.rt.com/usa/washington-no-gmo-labeling-282/

Humor plays a crucial role here because—at least for the time being—it has not been declared illegal. Humor is also a formidable weapon to attack a regime's legitimacy. Here I think of the many sketches which the late George Carlin[355] made about the regime in the USA.

Carlin was brilliant, but he did not have the immense opportunity which Dieudo and Soral are now using with devastating effectiveness: a large percentage of the population which is already not only deeply alienated by the regime in power, but which has the cultural, religious and historical roots to dare look at another model: I am talking about the Muslim immigrants in France.

Sure, the USA has the Nation of Islam (NOI) led by a pretty interesting leader, Louis Farrakhan, but the problem with the NOI is that its teachings are not truly Islamic and that cuts them off from the rest of the much larger Islamic world. Besides, ever since the murder of Malcolm X by two NOI activists I suspect that the NOI has been thoroughly infiltrated by FBI plants.

In France, however, the Islamic community has a much more organic link to the Islamic world, including to countries like Iran which fosters a far more refined and sophisticated look at the flaws of modern society than either the pro-regime mosques in France and abroad or the Wahhabis.

It is, of course, ironical that the French who for many years have seen the Muslim immigration to their country as a curse are now coming to slowly realize that this might well have been a blessing. I do not mean to paint a rosy picture of Islam in France: there are plenty of unsolved problems to tackle both for the natives and the immigrants, and certain forms of Islam are probably really not compatible with the original French traditions and culture. And yes, there are many signs that the current social brew might explode sooner or later. But the phenomenon of Dieudo,

[355] George Carlin: The Illusion Of Choice https://www.youtube.com/watch?v=SC_wjQtfhZQ

Soral and E&R gives me the hope that this explosion does not have to be a destructive one, that it could also be a liberating one.

What I am sure of is that some form of explosion will happen. Not only is France ruined economically, but the regime in power is losing its legitimacy literally day by day. Should it come to a confrontation, and that is a very real possibility in France, it is by no means certain that the police and security forces will continue to remain loyal to the plutocracy in power which, after all, has only made the life of the regular cop much worse. I can easily imagine a "bank holiday" turning into a violent uprising and after that, anything could happen. One of the most knowledgeable observers of the French political scene—economist and author Pierre Jovanovic[356]—believes that President François Hollande will not even be able to finish his current term in office.

Of course, I do not expect Dieudo or Soral to become president or prime minister, neither will E&R become a big political party anytime soon (not to mention that its creators did not register it as a party). That is not the point. What I do hope for is that this movement will trigger a re-definition of the French political scene and create a force bold enough to take on the current power establishment head-on, something which has not happened since May of 1968 (the National Front, whose rise was secretly aided by the French Socialists in order to split the French right, has long been fully co-opted into the system). Considering the many deep systemic and structural crises currently plaguing Europe, France could lead by example, if only because France's problems are not much different from those facing the rest of Western Europe.

November 7, 2013

---

[356] Pierre Jovanovic http://www.jovanovic.com/

"QUENELLE WARFARE" IN FRANCE—A "REPORT FROM THE TRENCHES"

The warfare around the quenelle gesture[357] is reaching new heights in France where representatives of the plutocratic elites are now seriously considering the following options:

a) banning the latest show of Dieudonné;

b) closing down his theater in Paris;

c) jailing Dieudonné;

d) making the quenelle gesture a criminal offense; and, I kid you not,

e) creating a special cell with representatives of the Ministry of Justice, Ministry of Internal Affairs and the Ministry of Economy to bankrupt Dieudonné (this is not the official reason, but that is clearly the aim).

In the meantime, more and more people are breaking free from their zombified state and joining the many thousands of people who are openly defying the state by going on record making the quenelle gesture. What is particularly distressing for the *doubleplusgoodthinking* French elites is that the "quenelle movement" achieved something which the elites claimed as an objective and which now turn into a true nightmare for them: it unites whites, blacks, Arabs, immigrants, natives, Papists, Muslims, agnostics, young, old, male, female—you name it, they have it. This is truly a mass grass-roots phenomenon which knows, quite literally, no barriers. Can I just give you one example? Alain Soral made is latest Internet video in a t-shirt sent to him by the French Prime Minister's personal protection service! Yes, even there.

Anyway, I refer here to a video "from the trenches," which really does not need translation, featuring Bertrand Delanoé, lapsed Freemason,

---

[357] Is a new revolution quietly brewing in France? http://thesaker.is/is-a-new-revolution-quietly-brewing-in-france/

lapsed Papist, current homosexual, high-raking apparatchik of the French Socialist Party and current Mayor of the City of Paris (make sure to listen to the part where Bertrand goes hysterical).[358]

No doubt, there is much more to come, much, much more, in the near future.

I will keep you posted.

Reporting from the frontlines of the "quenelle wars."

January 06, 2014

[358] Dieudonné est-il antisémite? - Reportage du 04/01/2014 https://www.youtube.com/watch?v=-NZ_18RmElI#t=13

STATE REPRESSION IN FRANCE ONLY MAKES THE RESISTANCE GROW STRONGER

Last November I wrote a piece entitled "*Is a new revolution quietly brewing in France?*"[359] in which I described struggle which was taking place between the French people and the Zionist plutocracy which has ruled France over the past decades (roughly since 1969) and today I am returning to this topic as events have rapidly accelerated and taken a sharp turn for the worse. A number of most interesting things have happened and the French "Resistance" (I will use this collective designator when speaking of the entire Dieudonné/Soral movement) is now being attacked on three levels.

Intellectual level:

This is, by far, the most interesting "counter-attack." A well-known French commentator, Eric Naulleau, agreed to a "written debate" with Alain Soral in which both sides would discuss their differences and the transcript would be published in a book entitled "*Dialogues Désaccordés*"[360] (which can roughly be translated as "detuned dialogs" or "dialogs out of tune" or even "disagreeing dialogs"). To explain the importance of this publication I have to say a few words about Naulleau himself.

Everybody in France knows Eric Naulleau as one of the two partners of a "journalistic tag team" called "*Naulleau and Zemmour*" in which one of the partners—Eric Naulleau—is a left-leaning progressive and the other—Eric Zemmour[361]—is a right-leaning conservative. Together they form a formidable and, sometimes, feared team of very sharp and outspoken critics and commentators which has been featured on various

[359] Is a new revolution quietly brewing in France? http://thesaker.is/is-a-new-revolution-quietly-brewing-in-france/

[360] Alain Soral, Eric Naulleau: Dialogues Désaccordés (French) Paperback – 2013

[361] Éric Zemmour https://en.wikipedia.org/wiki/%C3%89ric_Zemmour

shows on French TV. Zemmour, in particular, is an extremely intelligent and very charming person whose wonderful sense of humor combined with an outspoken attitude often got him in trouble. He is one of the few French Jews who actually got sued by the notorious LICRA[362] (rabid Zionist organization formed by Trotskyists to attack those opposing them) for daring to say "French people with an immigrant background were profiled, because most traffickers are blacks and Arabs... it's a fact" on TV. Together, Naulleau and Zemmour are known for being formidable debaters and very tough and even blunt critics who can take on pretty much anybody.

Naulleau explained that, according to him, it made no sense at all to ban Soral from the mass media because that still gave the option for Soral to record his shown on the Internet where they would be viewed by millions of people (that is not an exaggeration, by the way, Soral's videos do score more views than some national TV channels!). Naulleau explained that in his videos Soral was always alone, free to say whatever he wanted, without anybody contradicting or challenging him and that his goal was precisely that—to unmask, challenge and defeat Soral in an open debate in which he would show all the fallacies and mistakes of Soral's theses. To say that Naulleau failed in his goal would be an understatement. Soral absolutely crushed every single one of Naulleau's arguments to the point, where I personally felt sorry for Naulleau (whom I like a lot as a person). Worse, not only did Soral absolutely obliterate Naulleau, he also made a prediction and said: "you will see the shit-storm, which will hit you for agreeing to make this book with me!" And that is the crux of the disagreement between Soral and Naulleau: do the Zionists control the French media yes or not? Can they blacklist somebody or not? Is there a shadow "Zionist censorship" in France or is public speech still free? Soral's thesis is that France is in the iron grip of a "behind the scenes" Zionist mafia

[362] International League against Racism and Anti-Semitism https://en.wikipedia.org/wiki/International_League_against_Racism_and_Anti-Semitism

which is exactly Naulleau vehemently denies. The problem for Naulleau is that he proved Soral to be right.

The French media immediately attacked Naulleau for "providing Soral with a platform to spew his hateful theories" to which Naulleau logically replied that Soral was already doing so on the Internet and that, besides, he—Naulleau—did not believe in censorship, but in a strong and free debate. Naulleau also got attacked for not saying this or not saying that—in reality for getting so totally defeated by Soral in the debate. The book, by the way, became an instant bestseller with, indeed, made it possible for even more French people to think through Soral's arguments, and make up their own mind. So, ironically, and even though Naulleau clearly wanted to challenge Soral, he did him a huge favor by allowing him to break the media blockade around his name—Soral is never ever invited on talk shows—and by allowing the ideas of Soral to come right back into the public debate via this book, Naulleau de facto helped Soral. Some have even speculated that Naulleau might be a secret sympathizer of Soral and that he did all of this deliberately. I don't believe that at all—Naulleau is sincere, and Naulleau is also naive: he is now only slowly coming to grips with the fact that Soral's core thesis—that the Zionists completely control the French media—is a fact, and that Soral's prediction about Naulleau getting in trouble for this book was spot on. Right now, Naulleau and his friend Zemmour still have a show on a small local TV station, but clearly Naulleau has now deeply alienated the French plutocracy. As far as I know, nobody has dared to speak in Naulleau's defense. The funniest thing of all is that even though both Soral and Naulleau are officially coauthors of this book and even though Naulleau attempts to deny that Soral is blacklisted, only Naulleau got interviewed on the French talk shows, never Soral. Not once. What better way could there be to prove Soral right?

"Personalities lynch-mob" level:

While Naulleau was trying to defend himself against attacks from all sides for daring to coauthor a book with Soral, something absolutely unprecedented took place: day after day after day, media personalities were shown on TV trashing Dieudonné and his quenelle gesture. This really looked like a "virtual lynching," or a Stalinist trial—politicians, journalists, comedians, commentators, actors—you name it—all took turns to ridicule, insult, denounce, and otherwise express their hatred for Dieudonné. This truly became an Orwellian "two minutes of hate" in which Dieudonné was designated as the target of an absolutely vicious hate campaign.

A mediocre comedian named Nicolas Bedos was even given twelve minutes of uninterrupted air time to compare Dieudonné to both Hitler **and** Osama Bin Laden and his shows to a Gestapo interrogation room. It was surreal, really. If an extraterrestrial had just tuned in and watch this display of vicious hatred he would have imagined that Dieudonné was a second Hitler about to invade France with a huge army of bloodthirsty Nazis. For me, it was clear that the reason why all these different personalities were standing in line for the chance to outdo each other in taking a shot at Dieudonné was to prove their loyalty to the Zionist "deep state." This was as transparent as it was sickening. And again, it proved that Soral was right and that, if anything, he was understanding the degree of control of the Zionist plutocracy over France.

State level:

Finally, from more or less covert, the persecution of Dieudonné and Soral by the French state became completely overt. I already mentioned how in early January the French Minister of the Interior, Manuel Valls, used his powers to ban the latest show of Dieudonné (see here[363] and

---

[363] "Quenelle warfare" in France – a "report from the trenches" http://thesaker.is/quenelle-warfare-in-france-a-report-from-the-trenches/

here).[364] Over the last weeks, this repression has reached a new level with even more lawsuits against Soral **(12 simultaneous lawsuits**, see Google-translated list here) and administrative harassments (evening "visits" by bailiffs, abusive arrests, threats, police search of his small theater in Paris) against Dieudonné. All these events taken together—and it is really not hard at all to connect the dots—for a very clear picture: the power of the state is used to persecute, harass and repress Dieudonné and Soral. And that, of course, just goes even further in proving that Soral is right in his central thesis about France being run by a shadow occupation "deep government" whose loyalties are not to the French people, but to the Zionist plutocracy and Israel.

The reaction against this state of affairs is also becoming stronger and the amount of people supporting Dieudonné and Soral has literally skyrocketed. The reason for that is not only that a lot of French people share the same views as Soral and Dieudonné, but also a deep running French cultural tradition of admiring rebels and disliking the state. Add to this that Hollande is the most hated president in French history and that the French economy is doing down the tubes triggering untold suffering and rage in the people suffering from the crisis, and you get a very explosive mix: the so-called "*Day of Rage.*"[365]

The videos discussed below were available on YouTube (like this one[366] and this one[367]).

Anybody who knows France well will tell you that this is very serious stuff because unlike other demonstrations which typically oppose a law, or a policy or a specific event, **these demonstrators clearly are rejecting**

---

[364] A few news updates from the virtual trenches of the "Quenelle war" http://thesaker.is/a-few-news-updates-from-the-virtual-trenches-of-the-quenelle-war/

[365] La manifestation JOUR DE COLERE du 26 janvier 2014 (Clip de Morgan Priest) https://www.youtube.com/watch?v=AWeB9jevQ8M

[366] Jour de colère : interview de manifestants https://www.youtube.com/watch?v=TX57O-l7T_g

[367] La manifestation "Jour de colère" dégénère https://www.youtube.com/watch?v=y71qWzu3xKs

the legitimacy of the entire political system: *they want regime change.* So far, the French media has tried to minimize the coverage of this event and the French elites are trying hard to pretend like this is some small, fringe, extremist group, which is utter nonsense. France is bubbling with rage.

Zionist panic:

The Zionists are actually aware of that, and they are now in the panic mode. Just take a look at the headlines of this Israeli-French website:[368]

On the top right, you can see the Israeli founder of this website—Jonathan-Simon Sellem and on the top left you see Arno Klarsfeld, a well-known "French" (Israeli/German/French) lawyer and rabid Zionist. Here is what they are quoted saying:

Jonathan-Simon Sellem: "Dieudonné, you will never be a martyr. You will not a hero. Your name will be cursed in history, by history."

Arno Klarsfeld: "They is a crucial moment in history: Jews are already beginning to leave France."

Clearly, these two gentlemen see Dieudonné as some modern mix of Agag, Hamman, Titus, Hitler and Bin Laden—a terrifying, bloodthirsty and infinitely dangerous and evil man who threatens the survival of the Jewish race (never mind that Jews are not a race).

Could that be a little bit of an over-reaction?

What are these folks so terrified of?

I think that the answer is obvious: what they are so terrified of is not that Dieudonné and Soral will reopen Auschwitz somewhere near Paris, or that French Jews will be expelled from France. They know that this is paranoia (which Gilad Atzmon calls "Pre-Traumatic Stress Disorder") is absolute crap: French Jews are safe, happy and welcome in France and nobody is seriously out there to do them any harm. No, what this small

---

[368] Vidéo: « Jour de colère » dégueule sa haine: « Juif, la France n'est pas à toi! » http://jssnews.com/2014/01/26/video-jour-de-colere-degueule-sa-haine-juif-la-france-nest-pas-a-toi/

clique of Zionist Jews (representing a tiny fraction of the much more diverse French Jewry) really fears is that the truth about them and their power over the French deep state will come out. And this is not only about Jews. There is a non-Jewish plutocracy formed around the Jewish core of French bankers and financiers which is also completely in bed with the Zionists and whose future depends on maintaining the Zionist control over France: politicians, of course, but also actors, journalists, academics, etc.—a full constellation of *Shabbos Goyim*[369] willing to do Israel's Sayanim's[370] dirty job for them. It is this entire elite and the system which it built, which is threatened by Soral and Dieudonné and by what the movement "*Equality and Reconciliation*" stands for: a union of all the French people (native or immigrants) which together are determined to resist the Zionist oppression of France and who, just as in World War II, will resist the occupier until the Liberation.

When and how could such a "Liberation" occur?

I don't know. These events are very complex and multi-dimensional and it is, I believe, impossible to predict what could happen. What I am sure of, is that this movement, this Resistance, will not be crushed, nor will it somehow magically disappear. To paraphrase the Communist Manifesto, the French people "have nothing to lose but their chains": their country is ruined and they are ruled by an evil foreign occupier. In terms of dynamics, every move which is made against Soral and Dieudonné only makes things worse for the occupation regime—the harder the strike, the harder the blowback. The legitimacy of the regime, in particular, is greatly affected by such absolutely ridiculous actions like the "overkill" of a Minister of Internal Affairs using the highest court in the country (the State Council) in an emergency session to ban a single comedian's stand-up show.

---

[369] Shabbos Goyim https://en.wikipedia.org/wiki/Shabbos_goy

[370] Victor Ostrovsky https://en.wikipedia.org/wiki/Victor_Ostrovsky

Sure, for the time being most people in France comply, obey, or look the other way. But everybody know, everybody understands and very few believe in the official lies, especially in the younger generation.

This all reminds me of the Soviet Union of the 1980s where externally nothing much was happening and where the system itself looked ugly but safe. Russians were making anti-Brezhnev jokes at private parties while the KGB from time to time attested dissidents. But nobody—not even the KGB officers—had any respect for the system, the regime, the official ideology and its propaganda. Everybody did what they were told, but nobody believed in what they were doing. That is the exact situation not only for the French cops who are constantly used to ban, harass and arrest Dieudo and his supporters, but also of an increasing percentage of the general public.

Right now the pressure on the dam is getting stronger and stronger, and the cracks more and more visible. So far, the elites have had enough fingers to stick into the cracks, but this is clearly a futile attempt to delay the inevitable. And when the French dam will burst, it will impact on only France, but also a good segment of Western Europe. So while the pro-US Ukrainian nationalists want to subordinate their country to the EU, the EU is threatened with an inevitable and violent explosion. But, like on the sinking *Titanic*, the media's "orchestra" will be playing its music until the last second.

January 29, 2014

Solzhenitsyn and Sakharov in the USSR—Soral and Dieudonné in France

A minor but oh-so-telling example of the power of the Zionist regime in France:

French comedian Dieudonné was sentenced to a two months suspended sentence for "condoning terrorism" because he posted on FB: "*I feel like Charlie Coulibaly.*"[371]

French comedian Nicolas Bedos[372] was cleared from any wrongdoings even though he had called Marine LePen a "*Fascist bitch.*"

In the case of Bedos, the court declared that it was "perfectly clear to any reader that the column in question was being deliberately provocative."

This begs the question of whether Dieudonné was not provocative enough, or if he was too provocative. Either way, it is pretty darn clear that some in France are more equal than others.

Not that I feel particularly sorry for Marine LePen who, unlike her father, has been doing all she can to be accepted as "one of our own" by the regime. She engaged in the obligatory Islam-bashing which is now "*de rigueur*" after the Charlie Hebdo false flag, and she also cozied up to the all-powerful French Zionist lobby. This apparently, is not enough groveling as shown by the fact that neither she or her party were invited to the "*Je suis Charlie*" mega-demonstration.

In the meantime, Alain Soral is threatened with a 250,000 Euros (1/4 million!) fine for having taken a photo of himself making the now famous *quenelle*[373] at the Holocaust Memorial in Berlin.

---

[371] French comedian sentenced for 'condoning terrorism' in FB post http://www.rt.com/news/242045-french-condoning-terrorism-facebook/

[372] French court defends comedian for calling Le Pen 'fascist b*tch' http://www.rt.com/news/242665-lepen-court-fascist-comedian/

What is so amazing in this case is that this gesture was never banned by any court. In fact, it was not even **defined**. All it took is a few statements of the heads of the main French Jewish organization in France who declared that, I kid you not, it was an "inverted Nazi salute" and the "sodomization of the victims of the Shoah" (this term meaning "catastrophe" in Hebrew and is used interchangeably with "Holocaust" in France). The crime had been defined, the heresy denounced!

France, of course, has no such thing as a First Amendment, but at least in theory, speech is supposed to be free unless it is illegal. In this case, Soral should logically win, but considering how tightly the French courts have been controlled by the Zionist lobby, anything could happy.

The irony is that while Jewish organizations claim that the quenelle symbolizes the "sodomization of the victims of the Shoah" there are, indeed, plenty of sodomizations going on every day at the Holocaust Memorial in Berlin: it is a well-known meeting place for the homosexual community. Anybody doubting this is welcome to click here[374] to see the short video made by E&R about what takes place in this location (no translation needed!) Apparently, a sodomy-related gesture is far more offensive that an actual act of sodomy. Go figure…

If all this was not so scary and dead serious, it would be hilarious. But funny it is not—what this shows is that the regime in France will stop at nothing to crack down on the modern French Resistance. In fact, since neither Soral nor Dieudonné are showing any signs of backing down it is likely that non-suspended prison sentences will be meted out to them or their supporters in a not too distant future.

Already several absolutely unprecedented events have taken place recently. The highest court in France banned a show by Dieudonné[375] (on

---

[373] Is a new revolution quietly brewing in France? http://thesaker.is/is-a-new-revolution-quietly-brewing-in-france/

[374] Coming out! http://www.dailymotion.com/video/x2jr7p2_coming-out_news

[375] A few news updates from the virtual trenches of the "Quenelle war" http://thesaker.is/a-few-news-updates-from-the-virtual-trenches-of-the-quenelle-war/

grounds of risk to the public safety!) and now the sale of the DVD of the show is also banned (it is unclear on what ground). This is the first time in French (European) history that a "show" is banned (even though there has never been a single instance of a show by Dieudonné resulting in any clashes or, much less so, threats to the public safety!). Needless to say, this gave such a visibility to this (excellent!) show that if can be found all over YouTube (see here[376] or here[377]). The website of the movement *Equality and Reconciliation* is probably the next target of the French regime's censorship efforts.

But that is not the scariest thing of all.

What is "really" frightening is that in a country which strongly believes that Voltaire once said "*I don't agree with what you say but I will defend to the death your right to say it*" (he never said that!) **nobody** seems to care that was is at stake is not "good" versus "bad" humor, but freedom of speech itself, the very concept of freedom. Millions of "Charlies" are sniveling at an obvious false flag, but when two men are viciously and **illegally** persecuted by the entire state apparatus—everybody looks away. Here, I want to quote the beautiful words of Yehuda Bauer who said:

> Thou shalt not be a victim.
> Thou shalt not be a perpetrator.
> And above all,
> Thou shalt not be a bystander

And yet, most French intellectuals, authors, journalists, party leaders, social leaders and everybody else are remaining silent, trying very hard to look away or, at least, to find some reason to blame Soral and Dieudo for what is being done to them. As for the media—it rambles on about the "right to blasphemy" but, apparently, this right is only to be used when

---

[376] "Dieudonné Spectacle Dieudo..." This video is no longer available due to a copyright claim by Les productions de la Plume.

[377] This video is unavailable.

targeting religions. And yet, in a paradoxical way, Dieudo and Soral are winning just as Solzhenitsyn and Sakharov were winning against the Soviet regime: they forced the Kremlin to expel one of them (Solzhenitsyn) and exile the other one (Sakharov). And by doing so, it showed by its true, ruthless, face but also its weakness and paranoia. This is exactly what the French regime is doing now.

By persecuting two men for clearly illegal and ridiculous reasons, the Zionist regime in France is showing its true, ruthless, face and its paranoia. When the Prime Minister of a nuclear-armed member of the UN Security Council openly declares "war" on a comedian all pretense of "democracy" is clearly gone. When an entire power structure is terrified of a simple gesture you know for sure that its legitimacy is based on deceit and that its ability to con people is melting.

When the Soviet regime persecuted Solzhenitsyn and Sakharov. they have very little support in the USSR. Just as in France today, most people preferred to look away, or blame them for their plight. This is a sadly human way to cope with the cognitive dissonance of letting somebody innocent being mistreated without defending that person. And yet, within a decade or so, the Soviet regime collapsed, mainly because nobody had any respect for it. I am absolutely convinced that this will also happen in France.

PS: before some *doubleplusgoodthinking* folks accuse me of saying something I never did—let me clarify that I am not comparing the personalities, values or actions of Solzhenitsyn, Sakharov, Soral or Dieudonné. All I am saying is that as somebody who lived through the Cold War and remembers these events very well, I recognize the same pattern taking place. That's all.

March 21, 2015

FRANCE'S CRIF-RUN REGIME HAS UNLEASHED A VICIOUS PERSECUTIONS CAMPAIGN AGAINST DISSIDENTS

Thou shalt not be a victim.
Thou shalt not be a perpetrator.
And above all,
Thou shalt not be a bystander.

Yehuda Bauer

For many months already the political situation in France[378] has been largely overlooked by events in Greece or the Ukraine and even on this blog I have mostly been mentioning France in relation to the debacle with the sale of the French Mistral class ships to Russia. But that hardly means that the political situation France did not change over the past year or so. In fact, it did change, dramatically, and for the worse. Here is a short summary of what has happened since last year:

1. The French economy is in free fall. Reading the French corporate media, however, you would never find out about it. One of the very few specialists who regularly reports about this is Pierre Jovanovic, an independent economy/finance reporter (if you speak French, check out his YouTube channel where he makes a monthly and very interesting press

---

[378] Note: for those who are not familiar with the real political situation in France, please read the following background material:

http://thesaker.is/israel-lobby-commits-major-blunder-in-france-tries-to-silence-a-comedian/

http://thesaker.is/dieudonnes-anti-zionist-campaign-in-full-swing-in-france/

http://thesaker.is/is-a-new-revolution-quietly-brewing-in-france/

http://thesaker.is/state-repression-in-france-only-makes-the-resistance-grow-stronger/

http://thesaker.is/quenelle-warfare-in-france-a-report-from-the-trenches/

review).[379] There are a few others, but they have no access to the mass media.

2. The French Zionist lobby has now completely broken cover and is now engaged in a campaign of persecutions against those few who dare openly challenge its influence in France. All parties have been given an ultimatum: submit or be destroyed. The level and nastiness of the propaganda on French TV is now worse than anything I have seen in the USA or Soviet Russia.

3. As I had predicted a long time ago, Marine Le Pen has caved in to the pressure of the Zionist lobby and has turned against her father, Jean-Marie Le Pen, the founder of the National Front, who has now been basically booted out of his own party (for his allegedly anti-Jewish views). The Zionist lobby appears to be unimpressed and continues to ostracize even this emasculated National Front.

4. Alain Soral and Dieudonné are now the object of an open and systematic persecution by the French authorities, especially the Prime Minister Manuel Valls. The kind of persecutions methods used very much remind me of what the Soviet regime did under Leonid Brezhnev: constant bureaucratic harassment, police searches, lawsuits, smear campaigns, threats, etc. I don't even know how many lawsuits both Dieudonné and Soral are facing right now, but the total sum for which Soral is being sued right now is 264,523 Euros. Since Soral cannot and will not pay (on principle) it looks like he will have to go to jail, though before that he promised to appeal as high up as the *European Court of Human Rights*.

5. The political scene in France is dead. With the sole exception of the tiny *Égalité et Réconciliation* there is no more resistance against the Zionist regime in power. Like in the rest of Europe, the Left and the Right have more or less merged into an "extreme center," which caters to the

---

[379] Pierre Jovanovic - La Revue de Presse https://www.youtube.com/channel/UCG6Zpr_CnDxASjeHyBHtQMw

need of the comprador elites in power, and which is totally subservient to the USA.

It is important to keep in mind that the French Zionist lobby is even more powerful and more arrogant, in a uniquely "in our face" kind of attitude, than, say, AIPAC in the USA. The French CRIF[380]—a Likud controlled outfit—is basically in full control of the three branches of government, and the French media. To even mention that fact is a death sentence for the career of any politician, author, or journalist. Even the National Front has now caved in and made a pretty clear, if futile, attempt at showing a total subservience to this Zionist Lobby (Marine Le Pen's betrayal of her father).

[Sidebar: Of course, formally, the CRIF has no power whatsoever and it would be incorrect to assume that the CRIF leaders have a direct organizational control of all the numerous agents of the Zionist lobby in the French state or media. The CRIF is the ultimate **symbol** of the Zionist control of France, but those who are actually in control of that lobby are in Israel, not in France.]

There are now rumors that some new "real" opposition party or movement might be created by Jean-Marie Le Pen. Soral has already indicated that *Égalité et Réconciliation* might support such efforts. Under the current circumstances, I personally expect the repression to only get harsher and overt—the goal being not only to crush those who dare oppose the CRIF, but also to terrify everybody else. And since everybody else is, indeed, scared shitless of being labeled as, or even associated with, anything "anti-Semitic" this terror tactic works very well. All the other parties and movement make truly heroic efforts **not** to notice what is being done to Soral and Dieudonné. It is as disgusting as it is amazing.

---

[380] Conseil Représentatif des Institutions juives de France https://en.wikipedia.org/wiki/Conseil_Repr%C3%A9sentatif_des_Institutions_juives_de_France

To illustrate all of the above, I want to share with you a recent press conference of **Soral and Dieudonné**[381] which Paul Matthews has translated and Marta Begemot subtitled (my most heartfelt thanks to both of them!).

I love France and I have an immense affection and respect for the French people whom I do not blame for what has been done to them. The story of how de Gaulle was "regime changed" by the US CIA in 1968 and replaced by what can only be called an *occupation regime spearheaded by a cabal of international bankers* has happened to many other countries before and after that date. And I am sure that France will, eventually, come to see the day of her liberation. But before it gets better, it will get worse, much worse. Once the crackdown on dissent becomes as vicious and ruthless, as it has now become in France (just think of the "Charlie" false flag), there is no turning back, things will only get worse. But I am confident that the values of social justice, national tradition, equality and reconciliation will inspire enough young French patriots to eventually overthrow the regime in power and create a new, multi-confessional and multi-ethnic France.

August 2, 2015

[381] Alain and Dieudonné on "I'm not Charlie" / Summer 2015 [Eng Subs] https://www.youtube.com/watch?v=WuKntWdR_Po

THE RESISTANCE IN FRANCE—SUPPRESSED, BUT NOT BROKEN

It has been a very long while since I have written about the popular resistance movement in France embodied by the philosopher Alain Soral and the humorist Dieudonné.

For those who have missed these articles, they can be found here.[382]

My purpose today is to update you on what has been happening to the only meaningful anti-system Resistance movement in France

The first thing to say is that the state repression against Dieudonné got much more vicious: both of them are now being sued for huge amounts of money.[383] The list of lawsuits filed against Alain Soral now takes a full page on his website and the total sum for which he is being used is a stunning 489,292 Euros. I don't know the exact figures for Dieudonné, but I do know that attempts are being made at seizing both his home and his theater in Paris.

Next to that financial repression, the "minutes of hate" against Dieudonné and Soral have now become a quasi-permanent fixture in the French media and the doubleplusgoodthing blogosphere: they are ac-

---

[382] [Sidebar: for those who have missed these articles, they can be found here: •Israel lobby commits major blunder in France: tries to silence a comedian

- Dieudonné anti-Zionist campaign in full swing in France
- Is a new revolution quietly brewing in France?
- "Quenelle warfare" in France – a "report from the trenches"
- A few news updates from the virtual trenches of the "Quenelle war"
- State repression in France only makes the Resistance grow stronger
- Dieudonné music video and an appeal to French speakers (updated)
- La "quenelle" now in music!! (in French with English subs)

These are just a few examples, use the search option for more]

[383] Liste des procès en cours impliquant Alain Soral et Égalité & Réconciliation http://www.egaliteetreconciliation.fr/Liste-des-proces-en-cours-impliquant-Alain-Soral-et-Egalite-Reconciliation-22084.html

cused of Nazis, anti-Semites, homophobes and, of course, the inspiration of various terrorist movements. Dieudo is also accused of being a crook. Some individuals do not shy away from overtly racist slurs like the Rabbi Rav Dymovisz who said that Dieudonné proves that Darwin was right and he is the living proof that some humans are descendants from monkeys "*most probably a gorilla.*"[384]

There have been even numerous attempts to censor both Soral's books and Dieudo's shows, including efforts in the French State Court, but these have run into that pesky problem that French law does not foresee political censorship. Hence the two tricks most used have been the standard accusation of anti-Semitism and "risk of trouble to the public order." In reality, of course, both Soral and Dieudo are completely non-violent and their ideology is one of reconciliation and equality, not hatred. They, however, have been attacked physically many times, but the police has always denied them any protection and their aggressors have walked away with, at most, a gentle little slap on the wrist. Since Soral and Dieudo are, of course, losing most of their lawsuits, it appears inevitable that prison sentences will inevitably replace fines because they will be tried as "repeat offenders."

And yet, for all these efforts by the French one-percenters to crush them, the popularity of both men has continued to steadily grow, but mostly in the disenfranchised classes and the immigrant communities. Dieudo only plays to full theaters, while Soral's books are best sellers. As for their websites, they have more viewers than the national TV channels. The French elites, however, including the putatively freedom-loving intelligentsia, prefer to look away as if not noticing what is taking place or, worse, then join into the chorus of the "official" ideological lynch mob.

Still, Dieudo and Soral are not giving up the struggle. They have even decided to form a *Equality and Reconciliation* (**E&R**) party. These men are smart and they know that they cannot win, but what they can do is

[384] This video is unavailable.

get two things, which the state desperately tires to deny them: a platform and money. Becoming a party can get them both.

In the past Soral and Dieudo have supported the short-lived Anti-Zionist Party which did remarkably well considering the political reality in France, but make no mistake, in this case "remarkably well" means single digit figures or less. There is absolutely no reason to believe that their new party will do any better, at least visibly. This is why:

There are really two "Frances" today: one, the official, visible one, appears to be one of consensus, of democracy, of relative well-being. The other, the "invisible one," is one of deep alienation, of rage, of despair and of revolt. And these two Frances are not always where one would expect them to be found. For example, in the very same French police that is used by the state to persecute Dieudonné and Soral the popularity of both men is very high. The same goes for the military, the fire departments, and a host of other government agencies. Likewise, even though neither Dieudo or Soral are Muslim (both are Christian Latins, though in the case of Soral this is more of a cultural affinity), they get a great deal of support from the Muslim immigrés in France who understand and respect their message.

As for the French "Far Right," it mostly dislikes them, often with no less intensity then the rest of the Establishment. The problem here is a generational one. If Dieudo and Soral both respect Jean-Marie LePen and if both of them are still close to him both ideologically, they both have accused the National Front of having basically joined the Establishment, of having been co-opted and corrupted, and they have strongly criticized the anti-Muslim stance of Marine LePen.

The second ideological struggle which is taking place is that Dieudo and Soral are also on the offensive against a French author named Eric Zemmour, whom they accuse of being a fake dissident. Zemmour recently wrote a book entitled *The French Suicide* in which he strongly criticizes almost all French policies and politicians since 1968 and in which he, a French Jew, openly criticizes the use for petty political purpose of the

Nazi persecutions of Jews. He even went as far as to declare on national prime time TV that Pétain had saved French Jewry. Among his many theories, Zemmour is also known for declaring that Islam is not compatible with the French republic, and that immigrants should be assimilated. This is where he enters into a direct conflict with Dieudo and Soral.

They accuse him of being the new "Bernard-Henri Levi," the new "*official ideologue*" who is now in charge of Islam-bashing in the name of French patriotism. Their proof? That Zemmour is constantly invited to all the major talk shows on French radio and TV whereas they are quasi-officially blacklisted.

Frankly, I think that in this case they are simply wrong. First, I do not agree with Zemmour's view of Islam at all, but to say that he is simply wrong or mistaken does not imply that he is being used. There is a very simple explanation of why he is being invited everywhere: he is not Soral, or Dieudo. Really, his views are very similar to the ones of Soral on many topics, you can think of him as a "Soral light," and that is precisely why to invite him to the official media makes sense for the Establishment: it is a safe(r) way to "prove" that there still is freedom of speech in France, and that even a "quasi-Soral" gets airtime.

Zemmour is a brilliant man and speaker, and he is also a formidable debater who, unless he is shouted down, usually makes minced meat of his opponents while keeping a smile all along. Zemmour is also very direct and, in my opinion, intellectually honest man, and I don't see him at all as the next "BHL" or somebody who is corrupted by the system. However, I also think that Zemmour is completely wrong about Islam and, even more importantly, wrong about France. The France which he would like to see is one, which is gone forever, and though he does not really deny that, he also does not want to accept it. In a way, he reminds me of Strelkov, many of whose views I share, but who appears to me to lack the realism needed to get things done in the modern world and the reality of today's Russia. Whatever may be the case, Zemmour, who is usually associated with the French far right, is also a target of Dieudo and Soral.

Thus it is completely wrong to classify them with the "Right." In fact, both of them admire Jean Marine LePen and Georges Marchais, the charismatic leader of the French Communist Party until 1994. The issue for them is not one of "Right vs. Left" but one of real opposition versus selling out to the system.

Neither Soral or Dieudo have ever endorsed the political program of the National Front or the Communist Party. What they did do is praise these two forces for being truly revolutionary (in the literal meaning of the word—wanting change) and not a fake opposition. But if under Marchais and Jean-Marie LePen the Communist Party and the National Front were truly speaking "for the masses," then after their retirement both parties turned into tools for the elites. I fully agree with that analysis. This is why I say that today the only real opposition in France is E&R.

As for Zemmour, he is a nostalgic of the past and therefore neither a revolutionary nor a supporter of the current system which his views can only mildly annoy, but not threaten.

Can Dieudo and Soral, unlike Zemmour, threaten the system?

I strongly believe so. But in the long run only.

For one thing, they are appealing to the disenfranchised masses which are, by definition, the majority. The rest of the political scene in France only appeals to the elites. Second, while the Establishment tries as hard as it can to create fake non-issues (homosexual marriages) while obfuscating the vital ones (poverty and exploitation), E&R brings the real problems to the forefront of its discourse. Furthermore, while the official (Masonic) French ideology is both anti-Christian and anti-Muslim E&R is pro-Islam and pro-Christian. This is why the key slogan of E&R is "*la gauche du travail la droite des valeurs*" (the Left of Labor and the Right of Values) meaning that its economics are very similar to those of traditional Socialist parties whereas its ethics and morals are more typical of the ones of religious conservatives (Zemmour, by the way, would disagree with both, even though he likes to quote Marx and defends Christian ethics). In fact, **I would argue that the ideas of Soral, Dieudo and E&R ap-**

peal to moral categories taken straight out of Christian, Islamic and Marxist traditions and that they recombine and adapt them to modern realities. This is, I think, very, very interesting stuff, especially for me since this is also what I see happening in Russia.

Resistance to Empire can take many forms. Sometimes, this resistance is armed, as in the case of Hezbollah. Sometimes this resistance is purely ideological, as was the case with Gandhi. But sometimes, it begins on the purely ideological level and eventually becomes incarnate in a very material way. For example, I would argue that today's continuator of Alexander Solzhenitsyn's ideas is Vladimir Putin. And yet, Solzhenitsyn will be remembered as possibly the biggest foe of the KGB whereas Putin was an officer in that organization. These are the amazing paradoxes of history which show over and over again that the power of ideas is far stronger than the power of the state and its institutions.

Today, Soral and Dieudo are in a position very similar to the one of opponents in the former Soviet Union. Sure, the methods have changed, and there is no GULag in France (for the time being), but the French courts are now clearly used to silence dissent. How long until they begin being used to send thought-criminals to jail?

Soral and Dieudo are typically French phenomena and so is their resistance. But they are also part of a much larger planetary Resistance to Empire. They are part of the same struggle as Evo Morales, Ali Khamenei, Vladimir Putin, or Xi Jinping. Just like these men, they are not always right, and we don't have to endorse all of their views. But I think that it is vital to recognize them as fellow resistants and, therefore, comrades.

November 18, 2014

PART IX : THE WEST AND SEX

MOSCOW BANS HOMOSEXUAL "PRIDE" PARADES FOR THE NEXT 100 YEARS

First, when I saw the RT news item announcing that "*Moscow bans gay pride for century ahead*"[385] I went "no way!" and had the giggles thinking of how the doubleplusgoodthinking Lefties in the West would cry in outrage if such a decision had really been taken. Then I saw an outraged statement by Human Rights First[386] confirming that the folks on Moscow had really taken such a decision. Now some of you might wonder what a self-proclaimed "Left Libertarian" like myself might think of all that. Let me tell you:

I am totally DELIGHTED by this decision!

Now before the inevitable verbal stoning beings, let me explains my reasons, okay? Then you can hate me for being the bigot that I am…

Before I begin making my case, I would like address two issues: one semantic and one dialectical one. First, I refuse to use the word "gay" *on principle*, as it should not be applied to homosexuals because it is a "value-loaded" use of an otherwise perfectly legitimate word designed to shape any discussion of the topic. Furthermore, there is nothing gay about gays, any psychologist or addiction specialists will confirm that to you (if only in a private conversation). Frankly, I always thought that "gays" should really be called "sads," but that would be loaded too. So I will thus use "homosexual"—an accurate and value-neutral descriptor. Second, I will not use any religious arguments in discussing this topic for a very simple reason: most religions already have a clear stance on homosexuality which should be normative for the followers of these religions

---

[385] Moscow bans gay pride for century ahead http://www.rt.com/politics/moscow-city-court-gay-247/

[386] Page not found http://www.humanrightsfirst.org/2012/06/07/gay-pride-parade-banned-for-100-years-in-russia

but which are also irrelevant for everybody else. Simply put—to discuss the topic of homosexuality to religious folks is preaching to the choir. So there shall be no mention of "sin" or "fallen human nature" in my argument below. Now let us turn to the issue itself.

What is homosexuality, really? Here is what Wikipedia[387] reports about it:

> In 1973, the American Psychiatric Association declassified homosexuality as a mental disorder. The American Psychological Association Council of Representatives followed in 1975. Thereafter other major mental health organizations followed and it was finally declassified by the World Health Organization in 1990.

It is interesting to get some background on how this decision was taken. I have found the following details in the article of Philip Hickey *Behaviorism and Mental Health.*[388] Here is what the author writes (stress added):

> Then in 1970 gay activists protested against the APA convention in San Francisco. These scenes were repeated in 1971, and as people came out of the "closet" and felt empowered politically and socially, the APA directorate became increasingly uncomfortable with their stance. In 1973 the APA's nomenclature task force recommended that homosexuality be declared normal. The trustees were not prepared to go that far, but they did vote to remove homosexuality from the list of mental illnesses by a vote of 13 to 0, with two abstentions. This decision was confirmed by a vote of the APA membership, and homosexuality was no longer listed in the seventh edition of DSM-II, which was issued in 1974. What's noteworthy about this is that the removal of homosexuality from the list of mental ill-

---

[387] Homosexuality and psychology https://en.wikipedia.org/wiki/Homosexuality_and_psychology

[388] Phil Hickey: Homosexuality: The Mental Illness That Went Away http://www.behaviorismandmentalhealth.com/2011/10/08/homosexuality-the-mental-illness-that-went-away/

> nesses was not triggered by some scientific breakthrough. There was no new fact or set of facts that stimulated this major change. Rather, it was the simple reality that gay people started to kick up a fuss. They gained a voice and began to make themselves heard.

Got that? Yup, this was a 100% political decision which had no scientific basis whatsoever. From a scientific point of view, it was as nonsensical as declaring—simply by vote—that cancer or schizophrenia are not more diseases, but are "normal." Wikipedia deals with this problem in a single, and yet very telling, sentence:

> While some still believe homosexuality is a mental disorder, the current research and clinical literature demonstrate that same-sex sexual and romantic attractions, feelings, and behaviors are normal and positive variations of human sexuality, reflecting the official positions of the American Psychiatric Association and the American Psychological Association.

Right. Brilliant. So "same-sex sexual and romantic attractions, feelings and behavior are normal and positive variations of human sexuality." And yet pedophilia is still considered a psychiatric disorder. What about incest?[389] Well, guess what? Psychiatry puts incest next to paraphilia, i.e. pathologic sexual activities which is a group name for every sexual activity that is considered unnatural in psychology and sexology. Apart from incest, paraphilia also includes pedophilia, sadism, masochism, sexual fetishism, exhibitionism, voyeurism, necrophilia, and nymphomania.

And how does one distinguish between "normal and positive variations of human sexuality" and paraphilia? Since up until 1974 homosexuality was considered a paraphilia,[390] why were no arguments presented to remove it from this category?

This is all utter nonsense, of course. There are only three possible solutions to this conundrum:

---

[389] Pedophilia https://en.wikipedia.org/wiki/Pedophilia

[390] Paraphilia https://en.wikipedia.org/wiki/Paraphilia

a) Declare that only one specific form of sexuality is "normal."

b) Declare that any form of sexuality is "normal."

c) Arbitrarily discriminate between various forms of sexuality with no logical basis for it.

Most developed countries have opted for the third option, making a completely arbitrary, illogical and absurd list of "normal" and "not pathological" sexual behaviors. By the way, the same dumb approach was used in dealing with sexual practices between consenting adults (the so-called "sodomy laws") or the codification of a legal age of sexual consent. Even a cursory look at these laws clearly shows that they are based on nothing except political expediency.

And what does "normal" really mean? It can mean one of two things: a) consistent with some average or minimum or b) within expected norms, for example, of society.

In the first case, I would gladly admit that homosexuality is "normal" simply because of its prevalence. But I would immediately add that so are many, if not all, of the forms of paraphilia. And I would also agree that homosexuality has become "normal" in the second meaning of the word simply because it is socially acceptable to most developed societies, in particular in the post-Christian "West." So to speak of the normalcy of homosexuality is absolutely nonsensical.

Furthermore, is there anything in the above which suggest that the decision of the City of Moscow to ban so-called "gay pride" parades is morally, ethically or even logically wrong?! Is it not the right of any society to establish its own social norms?

Furthermore, compare the situation of Russian homosexuals with the situation of Western pedophiles who are the victims of a systematic campaign of vicious persecutions. Oh, I am not saying that it is wrong to persecute pedophiles, I am only saying that I don't see any logical reason to viciously prosecute the adepts of one form of paraphilia while allowing the adepts of another form of paraphilia to engage in "pride parades." And if Moscow has no right to ban "gay pride parades" then the West has an obligation to allow "pedophile pride parades" in its Berlin, New York or Rome. But no, the West gets away with its massive anti-pedophilia campaign while, in July of 2011, the European Court of Humans Rights condemned Russia to pay 30,000 Euros in compensation to gay activists over its decision to ban so-called pride marches. Talk about absolute hypocrisy!

I would like to add one more thing here. I find militant homosexuals particularly offensive and irritating. Frankly, to each his own. There are plenty of sexual psychopathologies out there and plenty of people engaging in them. I don't force everybody to give a standing ovation to my own sexual preferences, and I don't see any reason why somebody would demand from me that I approve and cheer on his/her sexual preferences. Keep your bedroom in your bedroom and leave the rest of us alone. But no, that is not good enough for what I call the "Homo lobby."

Homosexuals are the only ones who, not content to be left alone, are demanding not only equal rights, but special protections. They have the nerve to demand that society treat them as some kind of oppressed minority, they want their "marriages" to be considered as equivalent to heterosexual ones, and they even want the right to form "single sex couples" and adopt children. Amazingly, the very same society which considers it to be a felony to possess photos of naked children on your computer finds its perfectly acceptable to give away its children to homosexual "couples"!

I am delighted that Moscow is pushing back against the "Homo lobby" and its cultural fascism which considers that "live and let live" only applies to individuals and not to nations. I say let the Western homosexuals do whatever the hell they want in their own countries—that is the West's problem—but don't let them engage in cultural imperialism and demand that the rest of the planet submit to their completely subjective and illogical system of double standards.

I have said above that I will not make use of any religious arguments to make my case in defense of the Moscow City Council. Since I have made my case on this topic, I will now add a few general comment about homosexuality, religion and society.

First, this entire topic is yet another illustration of Dostoevsky's truism that "if there is no God everything is permitted." The very concepts of "right" and "wrong" must, by logical necessity, either be anchored on some absolute (such as God) or become absolutely arbitrary and subjective. Secularists can bawl in impotent rage and frustration but there is no logical argument which can be made against this fundamental truth. In other words, no secular society will ever be able to logically distinguish between right or wrong (other than by convention), much less so in the case of sexuality.

Second, traditional Christianity affirms that since the Fall man has lost his original, true, nature and that his current fallen nature is the cause of his suffering. The fact that some percentage of any given population is affected by any one type of psychopathology is therefore something Christians fully expect from all humans. To the homosexual argument "I was born that way" a Christian simply replies "brother, we were all born dysfunctional in some way" and "what we now must do is reclaim our real nature and our full potential" (conversely, the word "sin" really means "missing the target" or "failing to act according to one's true potential).

Thus while Christianity never condemns a condition as such, neither does it consider any putatively "natural" condition as good or in any way "legitimate." In fact, the very purpose of life is, according to traditional Christianity, to reclaim our "true" human nature by a process of theosis (which I shall not describe here; those interested can read this).[391]

Third, the one and only reason why homosexuality is the only paraphilia which gets an official stamp of approval is that there is a strident,

---

[391] THEOSIS: The true purpose of human life http://orthodoxinfo.com/general/theosis-english.pdf

wealthy and well-organized "Homo lobby" (well, a LGBT[392] lobby, really). This lobby was very effective in presenting the issue as one of "homophobia" and "hate" against one of tolerance and diversity. Of course, there will always be some insecure idiots out there who think that their manhood will be somehow enhanced if they beat up a homosexual, preferably in a group. But to present any rejection of the Homo lobby's dogmas (because that is what they are!) as an expression of homophobia is, of course, a total misrepresentation of what is really happening. As far as I can tell, most people do not care at all about what adult and consenting homosexuals do in the privacy of their bedrooms. What bothers people is the extremely rude and strident "in your face" attitude adopted by what I call the "militant homosexuals." Frankly, if they did not dress like clowns (or birds! see photos) and if they refrained from organizing "gay pride" parades they would gain far more acceptance from most heterosexuals. My two cents.

June 8, 2012

[392] LGBT https://en.wikipedia.org/wiki/LGBT

WILL PEDOPHILIA BE THE NEXT PARAPHILIA TO BE DECLARED A "NORMAL AND POSITIVE VARIATION" OF HUMAN SEXUALITY?

A month ago I posted a commentary[393] in support for the decision of the city of Moscow to ban so-called "gay pride" parades. Just as I expected, the post resulted in somewhat of a firestorm of outraged reactions from those who believe that homosexuality is, to quote Wikipedia, a "normal and positive variation" of human sexuality. They were particularly outraged at the fact that I stated that homosexuality was just one form among many other of what is known is *paraphilia* which also includes such "orientations" as pedophilia, sadism, masochism, sexual fetishism, exhibitionism, voyeurism, necrophilia, nymphomania, etc. In fact, there is even an increasing body of scientific evidence[394] that pedophilia is not a choice, but a condition, that pedophiles where "born that way" to use one of the favorite slogans of the Homo lobby. But unlike homosexuals, pedophiles are still offered cognitive, behavioral and pharmacological therapies no, not to cure them—they are considered "incurable"—but to help them with their "symptoms"...

When I pointed out that while homosexuals were asking to be treated like a persecuted minority deserving of some special protections, pedophiles were severely persecuted and prosecuted (just think of the public "sexual predators" databases[395] which list the home address, photo and contact information of any person condemned for, among other crimes, possessing photos of nude children or having sex with an underage part-

---

[393] Moscow bans homosexual "pride" parades for the next 100 years http://thesaker.is/moscow-bans-homosexual-pride-parades-for-the-next-100-years/

[394] Pedophilia https://en.wikipedia.org/wiki/Pedophilia#Causes_and_biological_associations

[395] Family watchdog http://www.familywatchdog.us/

ner) the defenders of homosexuality pointed out that homosexuality is different from pedophilia because it involves two consenting adults whereas sex with underage children implies violence, whether direct or statutory.

What the homo-fanboys missed is that they were comparing apples and oranges.

From a legal point of view homosexuality and pedophilia are, indeed, totally different for the above mentioned reasons. However, from a psychological point of view, they are not. Let me clarify: nobody will ever send a person to jail for having pedophile inclinations, only for acting on them. Somebody who is sexually attracted to children is considered as having a sexual disorder (i.e. sick) and only considered a criminal if he/she acts on this psychopathology. But if we take this legal/psychopathological distinction to the issue of homosexuality we can just as easily accept the possibility that homosexuality is a psychopathology, a sexual disorder just like pedophilia, and that the only difference between homosexuality and pedophilia is that the latter is considered criminal by society if acted upon.

But are there any experts making the case that pedophilia is, to use this wonderful expression of Wikipedia, just a "normal and positive variation" of human sexuality? Turns out that yes, there are.

I just came across this rather amazing article,[396] which I want to share with you. I have bolded out the parts which appear most interesting to me.

Check out this article:

> Pedophilia a 'sexual orientation' experts tell Parliament (Canada)
>
> OTTAWA, Ontario, February 28, 2011 (LifeSiteNews.com)—In a recent parliamentary session on a bill relating to sexual offenses against children, psychology ex-

[396] Rebecca Millette: Pedophilia a 'sexual orientation' experts tell Parliament(Canada) http://www.freerepublic.com/focus/f-news/2682310/posts

> perts claimed that pedophilia is a "sexual orientation" comparable to homosexuality or heterosexuality, a definition that was questioned by one Member of Parliament who was present....
>
> "Pedophiles are not simply people who commit a small offence from time to time but rather are grappling with what is equivalent to a sexual orientation just like another individual may be grappling with heterosexuality or even homosexuality," emphasized Van Gijseghem
>
> "True pedophiles have an exclusive preference for children, which is the same as having a sexual orientation. You cannot change this person's sexual orientation." He added, however: "He may however remain abstinent."
>
> MP Serge Ménard later praised the witnesses. "Mr. Van Gijseghem and Mr. Quinsey," said Ménard, "corrected some of our impressions."
>
> However, MP Marc Lemay of the Bloc Quebecois challenged Van Gijseghem's definition. "I have to admit that I was not expecting, on this Valentine's Day, to be talking about this inappropriate type of love. It is not really love. It has more to do with violence and control. I am concerned, Professor Van Gijseghem ... because you say, if I am not mistaken, that pedophilia is a sexual orientation."
>
> "That is what I said," continued Van Gijseghem.
>
> Lemay pursued the point, asking if it therefore should "be compared to homosexuality."
>
> "Yes, or heterosexuality," responded Van Gijseghem ... "pedophiles do not change their sexual orientation."
>
> During his witness, Quinsey, professor emeritus of psychology at Queen's University, said that pedophiles' "sexual interests" "prefer prepubescent children." "There is no evidence," he said, "that this sort of preference can be changed through treatment or through anything else."

One columnist in the *Toronto Sun*, Brian Lilley, expressed shock at Van Gijseghem's testimony: "what really shocked me was the Université de Montreal professor, Dr. Hubert Van Gijseghem, who showed up to tell MPs pedophilia was a sexual orientation just like heterosexuality or homosexuality." He argued that "it's time to take our country back by ignoring the 'experts.'"

Speaking of pedophilia and its acceptance, did you know that Frédéric Mitterrand, former French Minister of Culture and Communication and nephew of the late President of France François Mitterrand, wrote a book called The Bad Life in which he openly admitted using boys in Thai brothels? Here is the relevant Wikipedia section on this book[397]:

Mitterrand's autobiographical novel **The Bad Life** (French: **La mauvaise vie**) was a best seller in 2005. In the book he details his "delight" while visiting the male brothels of Bangkok, and writes, "I got into the habit of paying for boys ... The profusion of young, very attractive and immediately available boys put me in a state of desire I no longer needed to restrain or hide." At the time of its release Mitterrand was applauded for his honesty, but he has had to defend his writings after he publicly defended Roman Polanski when Polanski was detained in Switzerland on an American request for extradition for having sex with a thirteen year old girl. On 5 October 2009, Marine Le Pen of the French National Front Party quoted sections of the book on French television, accusing him of having sex with underage boys and engaging in "sex tourism," demanding that Mitterrand resign his position as Culture Minister. Among others he was also criticized by the Socialist Party spokesman Benoît Hamon, who stated: "As a minister of culture he has drawn attention to himself by defending a film maker and he has written a book where he said he took advantage of sexual tourism. To say the least, I find it shocking." On the other hand, some conservatives supported Mitterrand, and a close aide to Nicolas Sarkozy said the French president backed his Culture Minister, describing the controversy around him as "pathetic." Mitterrand also insists the book isn't an autobiography, the publisher describes it as a "novel inspired by autobiography" and the BBC refers to

---

397 Frédéric Mitterrand: The Bad Life https://en.wikipedia.org/wiki/Fr%C3%A9d%C3%A9ric_Mitterrand#The_Bad_Life

it as "autobiographical novel." In his own defense Mitterrand stated, "Each time I was with people who were my age, or who were five years younger—there wasn't the slightest ambiguity—and who were consenting," and that he uses the term "boys" loosely, both in his life and in the book. He also declared, "I condemn sexual tourism, which is a disgrace. I condemn pedophilia, which I have never in any way participated in."

Now, notice something very interesting here. France has had many homosexual politicians and members of government, but Mitterrand was the first one to openly display his homosexuality. And what happens to him? Soon his "homo only" image gets marred by allegations of pedophilia, and then made even worse by Mitterrand's defense of another pervert, rapist cum pedophile Roman Polanski. Needless to say, nobody took Mitterrand's denials seriously, even if only a few dared to openly challenge it openly.

For decades now, homosexuals have vehemently denied any link between homosexuality and pedophilia/hebephilia, and yet before the Homo lobby got its way and found an army of experts to agree with such nonsense, a short look into the concept of pederasty[398] clearly showed that there is a strong link between the two. Heck, there is even an organization[399] openly advocating, quote, "for the end of the extreme oppression of men and boys in mutually consensual relationships." How do they propose to do that? By:

1. Building understanding and support for such relationships.

2. Educating the general public on the benevolent nature of man/boy love.

3. Cooperating with lesbian, gay, feminist, and other liberation movements.

4. Supporting the liberation of persons of all ages from sexual prejudice and oppression.

---

[398] Pederasty https://en.wikipedia.org/wiki/Pederasty

[399] NAMBLA http://nambla.org/

Also, make sure to check out their latest bulletin[400]: not only will it tell you everything you need to know about this "persecuted sexual minority," but it will even show you how they too compare their "persecutors" with Nazis. Priceless...

I am quite sure that Frédéric Mitterrand would feel right at home in this crowd...

I could go on for hours and hours giving examples not only illustrating the fact that there is no real inherent difference between the homosexual and pedophile psychopathologies, but also showing that these two are closely linked by the "pederasty" category.

And yet, Western society actively promotes one form of paraphilia (homosexuality) and harshly persecutes another one (pedophilia). This makes absolutely no logical sense at all, and just goes to show how confused and, frankly, degenerate this society has become. It reminds me of the Biblical city of Nineveh, "*in which dwell more than twelve myriads of human beings, who do not know their right hand or their left hand*" (Jonah 4:11). It is ironic that this society seems to suffer from what I would call a spiritual form of AIDS, an acquired deficiency of its "spiritual immune system" to differentiate between right and wrong, healthy and sick, fertile and sterile. This is a phase which many degenerating societies seemed to have reached before their inevitable collapse.

This is all rather pathetic, in particular coming of a society which fancies itself as some kind of leader of the rest of humanity and which has the arrogance of delivering yearly "human rights" reports to the rest of the planet while killings its unborn children by the millions or giving up its kids to "same-sex couples."[401]

Although all that is only a logical outcome of declaring any form of psychopathology a "normal and positive variation," is it not? And here,

---

[400] NAMBLA bulletin http://www.nambla.org/B25-3.pdf

[401] The little boy who started a sex change aged eight because he (and his lesbian parents) knew he always wanted to be a girl http://www.dailymail.co.uk/news/article-2043345/The-California-boy-11-undergoing-hormone-blocking-treatment.html

the blame cannot be put solely upon those who suffer from these pathologies. The main culprits of this pathetic state of affairs are all those who fully know, feel and understand that homosexuality is no more "positive" or "normal" than any other form of paraphilia but who lack the basic courage and decency to speak up. Why are they afraid? Because the Homo Lobby is very aggressive, very well organized and even violent. This lobby has learned all the tricks of the Zionist lobby, but it is using them in a much more brazen and arrogant manner.

For example, in France the French comic humorist Dieudonné has declared that poking fun at homosexuals might be even a bigger "crime" than making fun of Jewish organizations. In Russia the famous Russian sexologist Dilia Enikeeva became the object of a massive campaign of death threats against her and her family after she wrote her *book Gays and Lesbians* which enraged the "gay community." Again, the examples are all out there, but the corporate media is simply ignoring all the evidence proving that the so-called "gays" are, in reality, a nasty and powerful lobby who will not hesitate to hunt down anybody who dares to object to its propaganda and myths.

One last example? Sure. Recently, a Russian "feminist punk group" delicately called "Pussy Riot" has organized a "punk-prayer" asking the Virgin Mary to get rid of Putin. So far so good, except for these ladies organized their "punk-prayer" in front of the altar doors of the biggest Orthodox Church in Moscow, the Cathedral of the Christ Savior. The "performance" of these ladies can be found on video.

Predictably, they were eventually kicked out of the church building and eventually had to leave. What is more interesting, however, is that the authorities decided to prosecute them for "*hooliganism committed for motives of politics, ideology, race, national or religious hatred or religious hatred or hostility toward anybody for motives of hatred or hostility for any social group.*" It seems that the Russian authorities did detect a hate motive in this action and decided to treat this as a hate crime. Well, guess what? Amnesty International decided to declare that Pussy Riot were, I am not kidding you, "prisoners of conscience." They particularly objected to the fact that these ladies were held in preventive custody and that they risked a jail term. It seems that the "artists" of Pussy Riot did not anticipate that the Russian state would actually dare to defend the rights and freedoms of the simple Orthodox people whose beliefs and holy shrines they wanted to mock with impunity. They clearly miscalculated.

How is all this linked to the topic of homosexuality? Simple: not only are Pussy Riot at the forefront of the "struggle for gay rights" in Russia, but the Homo lobby has immediately used all its power in Russia and abroad to lionize "Pussy Riot" as the most heroic defender of sexual rights and persecuted "prisoners of conscience." Something tells me that if some neo-Nazi punk rock group (of which there are, alas, plenty in Russia) organized a spontaneous "prayer-concert" in, say, the Grand Choral Synagogue,[402] which is the largest synagogue in Russia, Amnesty International and its Homo lobby allies will not protest nearly as loudly, but that kind of double standards and hypocrisy is not anything new, not for Amnesty International nor for the Homo lobby.

Nikolai Alekseev, the main organizer of the Russian "grey-pride" parade has recently declared on a Russian TV talk show "I don't give a shit about the opinion of 99% of Muscovites." Pussy Riot and the rest of these "gay rights" "activists" are simply putting in action this wholly intolerant and overly aggressive mind-set: better support us or else …

So let's sum it up. "Gay rights" are neither about gaiety, nor about rights. This is the organized political expression of a group of psychologically sick people who are seeking to impose their sexual dysfunctions and pathology as a norm on the rest of society and which do so with the utmost regression and intolerance. History shows than these groups only prevailed in degenerating societies and that when they did achieve their objectives, the society which they submitted to their agenda rapidly collapsed.

---

[402] Grand Choral Synagogue https://en.wikipedia.org/wiki/Grand_Choral_Synagogue

A personal note in conclusion: this blog is mostly about ethics, politics and the quest for truth in all matters. I have no personal axe to grind with those whom I call the "sads." I am blissfully married for 18 years now, have three kids, and I am not really interested in dwelling in topics of sexual psychopathology. But I am observing how the issue of "gay rights" is becoming instrumentalized by the West in its current campaign to destabilize or, at least, discredit Russia and, I would add here, Iran. By turning "gays" some kind of kind of persecuted prisoners of conscience, the West is simply using another tool among many others to try to eliminate any regime which would dare to oppose its rule over the rest of the planet. The fact that they will fail, both Russia and Iran have a strong social consensus on this topic, is no reason not to denounce the substance and form of this type of campaigns. This is why I will conclude by repeating what I said in my first piece:

"Let the Western homosexuals do whatever the hell they want in their own countries—that is the West's problem—but don't let them engage in cultural imperialism and demand that the rest of the planet submit to their completely subjective and illogical system of double standards."

July 14, 2012

A SOCIETY OF SEXUALLY FRUSTRATED PINOCCHIOS

We live in a strange world. Check out just the recent news: putative European "democrats" support Nazis and don't seem to notice that the latter are using weapons of war, including chemical munitions, multiple-rocket launchers and ballistic missiles, against cities. We live in a world where it is apparently quite normal for the IMF/ECB/etc. to continue to send money to a bankrupt country in the midst of the civil war in total violation of their own statutes, but where an EU/NATO member like Greece cannot even get a few days' worth of credit extension. In the USA homosexuals will now be "playing marriage" and will continue to adopt children to pretend to be viable couples. In the Middle East the Israelis are happily continuing to commit acts of piracy on the high seas while Canada wants to pass a law making criticizing Israel a punishable form of "hate speech." Besides being revolting, is all this not just plain crazy?!

"Democratic" countries are ruled by the 1%, but "authoritarian regimes" like Russia, Iran or Syria all undeniably have the support of the masses (and the eternal hatred of the local wannabe one-percenters!).

And it is not just politics—this insanity reaches much deeper into our society. Man are not supposed to be manly any more, while women are now told that femininity is being stupid and submissive. Honor is now passé, as is obedience, kindness, faithfulness and humility.

We are supposed to be sexually free, yet there is a huge multi-billion dollar industry fully dedicated to cater to sexually dysfunctional people (sexually happy people need neither porn nor Viagra!). We are supposed to be politically free, but somehow the policies of our rulers seem to never change. We are supposed to be intellectually free (freedom of speech!!) and yet with each new generation the already disgraceful level of crass ignorance of the average citizen is getting worse and worse.

But that's no big deal as long as we maintain the illusion that the fake substitute is, in reality, the real thing. From top to bottom our entire society is based on a charade, a fraud, a pretense of reality, but none of it is real.

But when did this all start?

I know that many will disagree with me, but I see a direct cause and effect relationship between the denial of moral reality and the denial of physical reality. I can't prove that, of course, but here is my thesis:

Almost from day one, the early Western civilization began by, shall we say, take liberties with the truth, which it could bend, adapt, massage and repackage to serve the ideological agenda of the day. It was not quite the full-blown and unapologetic relativism of the 19th century yet, but it was an important first step. With "principles" such as the end justifies the means and the wholesale violation of the Ten Commandants all "for the greater glory of God" the Western civilization got cozy with the idea that there was no real, objective truth, only the subjective perception or even representation each person might have thereof. Fast forward another ten centuries or so and we end up with the modern "Gayropa" (as Europe is now often referred to in Russia): not only has God been declared 'dead' and all notions of right and wrong dismissed as "cultural," but even objective reality has now been rendered contingent upon political expediency and ideological imperatives.

Here is how Orwell defined *doublethink* in his book *1984:*

> "To know and not to know, to be conscious of complete truthfulness while telling carefully constructed lies, to hold simultaneously two opinions which canceled out, knowing them to be contradictory and believing in both of them, to use logic against logic, to repudiate morality while laying claim to it (...) To tell deliberate lies while genuinely believing in them, to forget any fact that has become inconvenient, and then, when it becomes necessary again, to draw it back from oblivion for just as long as it is needed, to deny the existence of objective reality"

The necessary corollary from this state of mind is that **only appearances matter, not reality**. This is how you end up with a society of sexually frustrated Pinocchios desperately trying to look respectable and relevant.

I had to pick the perfect symbol for our modern Western society it would be Michael Jackson: neither white nor black, neither young, nor old, neither a man nor a woman, at the same time both asexual and pedophile. And, most importantly, Jackson was the artificial creation of hundreds of hours of surgery and marketing.

In the political real the nearest equivalent to Jackson would be Obama. Obama has all the qualities of a car salesman: superficially charming, not too bright, but clever enough to learn sales techniques. And a world-class liar, of course. In many ways, both Clinton and Reagan had the same skills set. These are the man that sold the world ideas like the liberation of Grenada as a great triumph for the US military, the bombing of Serbia as a great triumph for human rights or the destruction of Libya as a great triumph for democracy. Characteristically, these statements are both **factually** and **morally** wrong. Thus we see the wonderful "marriage" of immorality and delusion—they always go hand in hand.

And as long as Europe was led by "*great supine protoplasmic invertebrate jellies*" (to use the wonderful words of Boris Johnson[403]) and the sub-pathetic Yeltsin was drinking himself to death in the Kremlin, this system could more or less function. But when Putin came onto the scene this house of card came tumbling down. When faced with a real man and an officer with an iron will and an excellent understanding of how the Western political system works, the likes of Obama, Cameron and Merkel found themselves completely outmaneuvered.

---

[403] Boris Calls London Assembly 'Great supine protoplasmic invertebrate jellies' https://www.youtube.com/watch?v=LI5oRTL-6rA

And now they are stuck. They would like to lie their way out of this predicament, but it is already too late for that. So they are doing what the French called "*la fuite en avant*": the situation in which you run forward even faster in the hope that this will mitigate the consequences of having chosen the wrong course of action.

But immorality and delusion only "work" as long as there is nobody willing to denounce them for the fraud they are. But, as the expression goes "*when you head is in the sand, your ass is in the air,*" and reality inevitably comes back, with a vengeance, making these sexually frustrated Pinocchios completely unable to resort to one of their habitual tricks. Not that any of that will stop them—they will continue, of course, it's all they can do, but at least their lies will have less and less effect.

July 1, 2015

HOMO LOGIC APPLIED TO THE OLYMPICS AND SPORTS IN GENERAL

This morning I was watching the pairs figure skating when it suddenly hit me: the couples were always one man and one woman. How reactionary! After all, the Homo lobby wants to be called the LGBT or Lesbian, Gay, Bisexual and Transgender community. Okay. But then, there is also an "asexual"[404] or "non-sexual" community out there. According to Wikipedia, that community can be subdivided in the following subcategories:

- **aromantic**: lack of romantic attraction toward anyone
- **biromantic** (also **ambiromantic**): romantic attraction toward men and women (but not necessarily at the same time), or romantic attraction toward two or more genders—the romantic aspect of bisexuality
- **heteroromantic**: romantic attraction toward person(s) of a different gender—the romantic aspect of heterosexuality
- **homoromantic**: romantic attraction toward person(s) of the same gender—the romantic aspect of homosexuality
- **panromantic**: romantic attraction toward person(s) of every gender—the romantic aspect of pansexuality
- **polyromantic**: romantic attraction toward multiple, but not all, genders. The romantic aspect of polysexuality
- **andromantic**, **gyneromantic**, and **ambiromantic**: romantic attraction toward person(s) expressing masculinity or femininity or intersex/third gender-mixing (respectively) without implying the gender of the individual experiencing the attraction; often used by asexuals with a non-binary gender identity. The romantic aspect of androphilia, gynephilia, and ambiphilia

[404] Asexuality https://en.wikipedia.org/wiki/Asexuality

- **demiromantic** or **demisexual**: a person who may identify as "grey romantic" or a "grey asexual," respectively, because they may feel romantic attraction or sexual attraction once a reasonably stable or large emotional connec- connection has been created

But to keep things simple, let's just add an "A" to the LGBT designation and make it into LGBTA. What does that mean for sports?

I think that, logically, the old-fashioned and thoroughly "passé" paradigm of men, woman and man + woman couple should be replaced by a much for natural and forward looking:

1. Man (hetero)
2. Man (homo)
3. Man (bi)
4. Man (asex)
5. Woman (hetero)
6. Woman (homo)
7. Woman (bi)
8. Woman (asex)
9. Trans

I think that this covers all the basics. And then, for pairs, would could either also use these basic categories or, which is much more fun and "diverse," we could make a matrix of all the possible combinations. That would initially complicate things, but it would also generate some memorable and refreshingly new events like, "man (asex) + trans" or a "man (bi) + woman (asex)" pairs skating.

A big problem with that system is that it discriminates against gender-identities which society reproves of, like pedophiles or hebephiles which, for the time being, is okay, but which, considering the speed at which yesterday's "bad" is declared today's "good," might be a problem tomorrow. So I suggest leaving a few empty spots for tomorrow's paraphilia.[405]

[405] Paraphilia https://en.wikipedia.org/wiki/Paraphilia

It is high time for us to break free from the confining categories of the old man-dominated system of patriarchal oppression and that we finally give the right to all the beautiful diversity of mankind—peoplekind—to freely blossom!

[**PS**: for my (serious) posts on this topic, see here,[406] here[407] and here.][408]

February 10, 2014

---

406 Moscow bans homosexual "pride" parades for the next 100 years http://thesaker.is/moscow-bans-homosexual-pride-parades-for-the-next-100-years/

407 Will pedophilia be the next paraphilia to be declared a "normal and positive variation" of human sexuality? http://thesaker.is/will-pedophilia-be-the-next-paraphilia-to-be-declared-a-normal-and-positive-variation-of-human-sexuality/

408 Why I say that the "homo rights in Russia" lobby is full of crap http://thesaker.is/why-i-say-that-the-homo-rights-in-russia-lobby-is-full-of-crap/

ONE LAST MENTION OF AN INCREDIBLY BORING TOPIC (OR HOW TO DEAL WITH OBNOXIOUS SINGLE-ISSUE INSECURE NARCISSISTIC MINORITIES)

I have finally found the time to sit down and reply to a question asked by Carrie under my recent post[409] about Obama's choices. Carrie asked:

> Could we have another less "sexist", less "macho" term than "sissy," do you think? For the female readers that contribute to your page view stats, the term smacks of "boys with toys (sigh)." For me, term detracts from the mostly excellent content.

As soon as I read that question I had a flashback to my student years when I was working toward my Master's Degree in Strategic Studies in Washington DC. One evening, we were sitting with a group of students and discussing various Russian study programs when I mentioned that one of the very best one I had ever seen was the Russian studies program[410] at Bryn Mawr College. I then mentioned that it was too bad that it was a "ladies-only college" (that was in 1990 or 1991—not sure if they are now coed or not). One American woman (you will see why I use this term in a few seconds) got very upset and told me the following: "*To use the word 'lady' is sexist and offensive because under a thin semblance of respect it really implies that woman are weak and need male protection.*" I asked her what the appropriate term would be and she said "women" (she left it unclear whether she would spell that "women" or "womyn"). At this point she and I reached a full agreement and I promised her that I

---

[409] Two quick pointers – Asia times and Obama's "sissy on steroids" option http://thesaker.is/two-quick-pointers-asia-times-and-obamas-sissy-on-steroids-option/

[410] The Bryn Mawr College Department of Russian http://www.brynmawr.edu/russian/

would never speak of her again as a "lady" but only as a "woman." Needless to say, I continued to refer to other adult females as "ladies." Still do.

That was the first time in my life that I was told that the word "lady" was offensive, but that sure was not the last time as I came to realize that the "feminist vocabulary police" was busy shaping many languages in the West. Jumping ahead of myself I would add that this "feminist vocabulary police" has now been joined by a no less aggressive "homosexual vocabulary police" so from now on I will be referring to this as "sexual vovocabulary police" (the "West's finest"?)

Now turning to my use of the word "sissy." Let's begin by a definition, this time taken from *Wikipedia*[411]:

> Sissy (derived from sister; also sissy baby, sissy boy, sissy man, etc.) is a pejorative term for a boy or man who violates or does not meet the standard male gender role. Generally, sissy implies a lack of courage, strength, coordination, testosterone, male libido, and stoicism, which have traditionally been important to the male role. A man might also be considered a sissy for being interested in traditionally feminine hobbies or employment (e.g., being fond of fashion), displaying effeminate behavior (e.g. using hair products or displaying limp wrists), being unathletic, or being homosexual. Sissy is, approximately, the male converse of tomboy (a girl with masculine traits or interests), but has none of the latter's positive connotations. Even among gay men, behavior thought of as sissy or camp produces mixed reactions. Some men reclaim the term for themselves. The term sissyphobia denotes a negative cultural reaction against "sissy boys" thought prevalent in 1974. Sissyphobia has more recently been used in some queer studies; other authors in this latter area have proposed effeminiphobia as an alternative term.

Awesome, no?!

First, this very accurately expresses my beef with Obama, Kerry, Hagel and all the other mediocrities sitting in the White House and Congress.

---

[411]Sissy https://en.wikipedia.org/wiki/Sissy

So my short reply to Carrie would be: **if the word "sissy' exactly conveys the meaning I was trying to get across, why should I not use it?**

The rest of the definition is the typical cocktail of idiotic issues which seem to preoccupy the insecure and narcissistic segment of our society which I call the "sexual vocabulary police." Think about it: however wrote the second part of this definition is clearly a "me, myself and I" kind of person who strongly feels that his or her sensitivities must be important to the rest of the population (hence the absolutely serious discussion about comparative merits of the terms "sissyphobia" versus "effeminiphobia" in the context of, I kid you not, "queer studies"!)

Fair enough—to each his own—but why would I care?!

Well, it gets better. Check out the rest of this Wikipedia entry:

> Term of affection toward women:
>
> Sissy (or sis) can also be a relationship nickname formed from sister, given to girls to indicate their role in the family, especially the oldest female sibling. It can also be applied to girls as a term of affection from friends who are not family members. (See Sissy Spacek.)
>
> In gender and queer studies:
>
> Gregory M. Herek wrote that **sissyphobia arises as combination of misogyny and homophobia.** Communication scholar Shinsuke Eguchi (2011) stated:
>
> The discourse of straight-acting produces and reproduces **anti-femininity and homophobia** (Clarkson. 2006). For example, feminine gay men are often labeled "fem," "bitchy," "pissy," "sissy," or "queen" (e.g., Christian, 2005; Clarkson, 2006; Payne,2007). They are perceived as if they perform like "women," **spurring straight-acting gay men to have negative attitudes toward gay feminine men** (Clarkson, 2006; Payne, 2007;Ward, 2000). This is called sissyphobia (Bergling, 2001). Kimmel (1996) supports that "**masculinity has been (historically) defined as the flight from women and the repudiation of femininity**" (p. 123). Thus, sissyphobia plays as the communication strategy for straight-acting gay men to justify and empower their masculinity. (p. 38).

> Eguchi added, "I wonder how 'sissyphobia' particularly plays into the dynamic of domestic violence processes in the straight-acting and effeminate-acting male same-sex coupling pattern." (p. 53).
>
> In sexual subcultures:
>
> In the **BDSM practice of forced feminization**, the male bottom undergoing cross-dressing may be called a sissy as a form of erotic humiliation, which may **elicit guilt or sexual arousal**, or possibly both, depending on the individual. In (paraphilic) infantilism, **a sissy baby is a man who likes to play the role of a baby girl.**

What in God's name are they talking about?! What is this cornucopia of sexual pathologies supposed to tell us? That the only proper way to use the word sissy is when trying to elicit sexual arousal in a man playing the role of a baby?!

Let's try to limit this discussion within the assumption that all the parties involved are basically balanced, mature and sane.

I notice that Carrie find my use of the word "sissy" objectionable even though she is a woman. Maybe, but I was not referring to a woman, I was referring to Obama or, even more accurately, to his "attack options" (which is a logical category, not even something alive or material). Besides, Wikipedia clearly says that when applied to women the terms "sissy" is a term of endearment. So what is the problem here?

I will wholeheartedly admit that women are treated terribly in the western world. From the appalling rape statistics, to poverty, to the misery of single mother homes, to widespread domestic violence, to the denial of any social recognition of the hard work of the "stay at home mom"—there is much to be offended by in our society. So why this obsession with **words**? Is it simply because it is easier to obtain a change in the use of a word then to change the reality we live in?

My personal conclusion is the following one: we are living in a society where **any** forms of sexual differentiation are being ostracized. God forbid you use a word which might be "female-specific" or "too feminine" because the simple use of that word reaffirms and reinforces the differences between genders and that, in turn, is offensive to those who find the very notion of differences in genders offensive. What this "sexual vocabulary police" really wants is to turn our daily use of words into a "linguistic Michael Jackson" who was neither white nor black, not really male or female, not quite an adult or a kid. Jackson was the ultimate non-identity acceptable to all because of the inherent (and, in reality, carefully constructed) vapidity of his stage persona.

Do you still remember what happened to Obama when he said about California Attorney General Kamala Harris: "She's brilliant and she's dedicated, she's tough, she also happens to be, by far, the best-looking attorney general in the country." He got attacked for being sexist! Never mind that Mrs. Harris goes out of her way to look good (check her photos for makeup, lipstick, jewelry, expensive dresses, etc.)—a president cannot acknowledge that because that is a gender-specific comment which, in turn, implies that women should or could be judged by their looks, which is, by logical implication, not something which would happen to a man.

And here the feminists and the homo lobbyists meet each other: both dead set to train us not to discriminate between genders or sexual behaviors. Thus even the word "discriminate" which really means being able to identify differences has now become associated with racism and injustice. How totally stupid can a society become?!

Speaking for myself, not only do I discriminate, I go out of my way to teach that skill to my kids. In fact, the more people get brainwashed into not discriminating, the more effort I put into teaching my kids how crucial discrimination is not only for biological life (that is what our immune system does 24/7—it discriminates), but also for our psychological and spiritual lives (which both feature the psychological and spiritual equivalents of our physiological immune systems). In fact, I am so sick and tired of the insecure narcissistic types and their constant demand that we all comply with their latest demands that I make it a point to not let this kind of wholly illegitimate behavior go unchallenged. Any my reply to the sexual vocabulary police" is this:

Live and let live. You like the infinite greyness of non-gender differentiated people—please, be my guest and enjoy. But let me enjoy and cherish masculinity in men and femininity in women. To me, every single difference between the character of man and woman is beautiful and deeply enjoyable—for both parties—and they are the basis of the wonderful complementarity of genders. I have been privileged to meet many truly intelligent, courageous, strong and otherwise "tough" women in my life, and yet all of them also remained truly feminine which only added to their other qualities. I find it very sad when a woman turns away from her femininity and tries to look like a man, because most of the time they succeed. This is just as sad as an Asian or African person trying to look white.

Socially, I come from a culture and a religion which energetically fosters and promotes gender differentiation and I like to think of our families as "gender differentiated families." When I see the modern kids who are left with two "Michael Jacksons" as "parents" I feel heartbroken for them because I know for a fact that it is impossible to raise a healthy child and balanced without a real father and real mother at home (I was raised by my mother with no father, so I speak of personal experience). Thanks to the "sexual vocabulary police" and the rest of the "sexual lobbies" out there our society is turning into a society of orphans, who have neither father nor mother and who are now even denied their gender. If that is what you like—fine. But you have no right to impose your preferences on the rest of us. You don't like discrimination? Please, poke out your own eyes and enjoy the discrimination-free darkness, but don't start coming after my eyes as I cherish them very much.

In conclusion I will say that I am really getting sick and tired of constantly discussing sexual issues. When Putin was in Holland he was amazed that this was the only topic of interest to the press corps. Well, he is a political figure and so he has to deal with this nonsense. I don't. I have made my views on homosexuality quite clear (here[412] and here[413]) and I have made my point of view about the "sexual vocabulary police" quite clear today. I think that anybody who has read these posts will be able to easily guess my opinion on feminism. As Michael Parenti recently put it, it is waste of time to discuss sexual orientation issues when most people come home from work too exhausted to have sex.

So now let's return to the truly important issues of our times and stop paying attention to the narrow agenda for a small part of our society which is insecure, narcissistic and yet very obnoxious. Let the corporate press deal with that topic. As for me, I am done with this incredibly boring topic.

PS: just when I wrote the last sentence above a friend of mine drew my attention to the following article in Salon:[414] *Richard Dawkins defends "mild pedophilia," says it does not cause "lasting harm."*

Yeah! There we go. Another "luminary" of the modern world has the courage to take it to the next level!!

Amazing...

September 12, 2013

---

[412] Moscow bans homosexual "pride" parades for the next 100 years ttp://thesaker.is/moscow-bans-homosexual-pride-parades-for-the-next-100-years/

[413] Will pedophilia be the next paraphilia to be declared a "normal and positive variation" of human sexuality? http://thesaker.is/will-pedophilia-be-the-next-paraphilia-to-be-declared-a-normal-and-positive-variation-of-human-sexuality/

[414] Richard Dawkins defends "mild pedophilia," says it does not cause "lasting harm" http://www.salon.com/2013/09/10/richard_dawkins_defends_mild_pedophilia_says_it_does_not_cause_lasting_harm/

PART X: RUSSIAN MILITARY

THE RUSSIA-U.S. CONVENTIONAL MILITARY BALANCE

(This column was written for the ***Unz Review***)[415]

In a recent column for ***the Unz Review*** [416]I wrote that "under any conceivable scenario Russia does have the means to basically completely destroy the USA as a country in about 30 minutes (the USA, of course, can do the same to Russia). Any US war planner would have to consider the escalatory potential of **any** military action against Russia."

This still begs the question of whether Russia could challenge the USA militarily if we assume, for demonstration's sake, that neither side would be prepared to use nuclear weapons, including tactical ones. If, by some mysterious magic, all nuclear weapons were to disappear, what would the balance of power between Russian and the US look like?

Why bean counting makes absolutely no sense

The typical reply to this kind of question resorts to what US force planners call "bean counting." Typically, journalists use the yearly *IISS Military Balance*[417] or a source like *Global Firepower*[418] and tallies of the number of men, main battle tanks, armored personnel carriers, infantry combat vehicles, combat aircraft, artillery pieces, bombers, missiles, surface ships, submarines, etc. each side haUs and presents them in a chart. The reality is that such bean counting *means absolutely and strictly nothing*. Let's take a simple example: if a war happens between, say, China and Russia then the fact that China has, say, 1000 tanks in its Yunnan

---

[415] The Saker: The Russia-U.S. Conventional Military Balance http://www.unz.com/tsaker/the-russia-u-s-conventional-balance/

[416] The Meaning of the US Saber-Rattling at the Borders of Russia http://www.unz.com/tsaker/the-meaning-of-the-us-saber-rattling-at-the-borders-of-russia/

[417] The Military Balance. The annual assessment of global military capabilities and defense economics https://www.iiss.org/en/publications/military-s-balance

[418] Global Firepower (GFP) http://www.globalfirepower.com/

province, will make no difference to the war at all, simply because they are too far. When we apply this caveat to the Russian-US conventional military balance we immediately ought to ask ourselves the following two basic questions:

a) What part of the US military worldwide would be immediately available to the US commanders in case of a war with Russia?

b) On how *many reinforcements* could this force count and how *soon* could they get there?

Keep in mind that tanks, bombers, soldiers and artillery do not fight separately—they fight together in what is logically called "combined arms" battles. So even the USA could get X number of soldiers to location A, if they don't have all the other combined arms components to support them in combat they are just an easy target.

Furthermore, any fighting force will require a major logistics/supplies effort. It is all very well to get aircraft X to location A, but if it's missiles, maintenance equipment and specialists are not here to help, they are useless. Armored forces are notorious for expending a huge amount of petroleum, oil and lubricants. According to one estimate, in 1991 a US armored division could sustain itself for only five days,[419] and after that it needed a major support effort.

Finally, any force that the US would move from point A to point B would become unavailable to execute its normally assigned role at point A. Now consider that "point A" could mean the Middle East, or Far East Asia and you will see that this might be a difficult decision for US commanders.

---

[419] Logistic support of an armored division in a deep attack http://www.dtic.mil/dtic/tr/fulltext/u2/a241430.pdf

"Heavy" warfare

We have one very good example of how the US operates: operation *Desert Shield.*[420] During this huge operation it took the US six months and an unprecedented logistical effort to gather the forces needed to attack Iraq. Furthermore, Saudi Arabia had been prepared for decades to receive such a massive force (in compliance with the so-called *Carter Doctrine*[421]) and the US efforts was completely unopposed by Saddam Hussein. Now ask yourself the following questions:

a) In case of war with Russia, which country neighboring Russia would have an infrastructure similar to the one of the KSA, prepositioned equipment, huge bases, runways, deep ports, etc.? (reply: none)

b) How likely is it that the Russians would give the USA six months to prepare for war without taking any action? (reply: impossible)

One might object that not all wars run according to the "heavy" scenario of *Desert Storm*[422]. What if the US was preparing a very 'light' military intervention using only US and NATO immediate or rapid reaction forces?

Light (or rapid reaction) warfare

I will repeat here something I wrote in December of last year:[423] "the Russians have no fear of the military threat posed by NATO. Their reaction to the latest NATO moves (new bases and personnel in Central Europe, more spending, etc.) is to denounce it as provocative, but Russian officials all insist that Russia can handle the military threat. As one Russian deputy said "five rapid reaction diversionary groups is a problem we can solve with one missile." A simplistic but basically correct formula. As

---

[420] Operation Desert Shield (Iraq) https://en.wikipedia.org/wiki/Operation_Desert_Shield_%28Iraq%29

[421] Carter Doctrine https://en.wikipedia.org/wiki/Carter_Doctrine

[422] Gulf War https://en.wikipedia.org/wiki/Gulf_War

[423] 2014 "End of Year" report and a look into what 2015 might bring http://thesaker.is/2014-end-of-year-report-and-a-look-into-what-2015-might-bring/

I mentioned before, the decision to double the size of the Russian Airborne Forces and to upgrade the elite 45th Special Designation Airborne Regiment to full brigade-size has already been taken anyway. You could say that Russia preempted the creation of the 10,000 strong NATO force by bringing her own mobile (airborne) forces from 36,000 to 72,000. This is typical Putin. While NATO announces with fanfare and fireworks that NATO will create a special rapid reaction "spearhead" force of 10,000, Putin quietly doubles the size of the Russian Airborne Forces to 72,000. And, believe me, the battle hardened Russian Airborne Forces are a vastly more capable fighting force then the hedonistic and demotivated multinational (28 countries) Euroforce of 5,000 NATO is struggling hard to put together.[424] The US commanders fully understand that.

In other words, "light" or "rapid reaction" warfare is where the Russians excel and not the kind of conflict the US or NATO could ever hope to prevail in. Besides, if the "light warfare" was to last longer than planned and had to be escalated to the "heavy" kind, who of the USA or Russia would have its heavy forces nearer?

Shock and awe

There is, of course, another model available to the US commanders: the "shock and awe" model: massive cruise missile attacks backed by bomber strikes. Here I could easily object that bombing Russia is not comparable to bombing Iraq and that the Russian air defenses are the most formidable on the planet. Or I could say that while the USA has an excellent record of success when bombing civilians, its record against a military force like the Serbian Army Corps in Kosovo is an abject failure.

[Sidebar: 78 days of non-stop US/NATO airstrikes, 1000+ aircraft and 38,000+ air sorties and all that to achieve what? Ten or so Serbian aircraft destroyed (most on the ground), 20+ APC and tanks destroyed and

---

[424] NATO Struggles to Muster 'Spearhead Force' to Counter Russia http://www.wsj.com/articles/nato-struggles-to-muster-spearhead-force-to-counter-russia-1417459067

1000+ Serbian soldiers dead or wounded. That is out of a force of 130,000+ Serbian soldiers, 80+ aircraft, 1,400 artillery pieces, 1,270 tanks and 825 APCs (all figures according to Wikipedia).[425] The 3rd Serbian Army Corps basically came out unharmed from this massive bombing campaign which will go down in history as arguably the worst defeat of airpower in history!]

But even if we assume that somehow the US succeeded in its favorite "remote" warfare, does anybody believe that this would seriously affect the Russian military or break the will of the Russian people? The people of Leningrad survived not 78, but 900 (nine hundred!) days of an infinitely worse siege and bombing[426] and never even considered surrendering!

The reality is that being on the defense gives Russia a huge advantage against the USA even if we only consider conventional weapons. Even if the conflict happened in the Ukraine or the Baltic states, geographic proximity would give Russia a decisive advantage over any conceivable US/NATO attack. American commanders all understand that very well even if they pretend otherwise.

Conversely, a Russian attack on the USA or NATO is just as unlikely, and for the same reasons. Russia cannot project her power very far from her borders. In fact, if you look at the way the Russian military is organized, structured and trained, you will immediately see that it is a force designed primarily to defeat an enemy on the Russian border or within less than 1000 km from it. Yes, sure, you will see Russian bombers, surface ships and submarines reaching much further, but these are also typical "showing the flag" missions, not combat training for actual military scenarios.

---

[425] NATO bombing of Yugoslavia https://en.wikipedia.org/wiki/NATO_bombing_of_Yugoslavia

[426] Siege of Leningrad https://en.wikipedia.org/wiki/Siege_of_Leningrad

The sole and real purpose of the US military is to regularly beat up on some small, more or less undefended, country, either to rob it from its resources, overthrow a government daring to defy the World Hegemon or just make an example. *The US military was never designed to fight a major war against a sophisticated enemy.* Only the US strategic nuclear forces are tasked to defend the USA against another nuclear power (Russia or China) or actually fight in a major war. As for *the Russian military, it was designed to be purely defensive and it has no capability to threaten anybody in Europe, much less so the United States.*

Of course, the Western corporate media will continue to "bean count" US and Russian forces, but that is pure propaganda designed to create a sense of urgency and fear in the general public. The reality for the foreseeable future will remain that neither the USA nor Russia have the means to successfully attack each other, even with only conventional forces.

The only real danger left is an unprepared and unforeseen sudden escalation which will lead to a confrontation neither side wants nor is prepared for. The Israeli attack on Lebanon in 2006[427] or the Georgian attack on Russian peacekeepers in 2008[428] are two scary reminders that sometimes dumb politicians take fantastically dumb decisions. I am confident that Putin and his team would never take such a dumb decision, but when I look at the current pool of US presidential candidates I will tell you that I get very, very frightened.

Do you?

July 24, 2015

---

[427] 2006 Lebanon War https://en.wikipedia.org/wiki/2006_Lebanon_War

[428] Russo-Georgian War https://en.wikipedia.org/wiki/Russo-Georgian_War

THE MEANING OF THE US SABER-RATTLING AT THE BORDERS OF RUSSIA

(This article was written for ***The Unz Review)***

Hardly a day ever passes without the Western corporate media reporting that USN warships have entered the Black Sea, the US Army is sending instructors to train the Ukrainian military, US joint task forces are organizing maneuvers in the Baltic or US Army units are making highly publicized movements from the Baltic states to Poland. And every time this happens, Russian diplomats and officials make protests and declare that such actions are only making matters worse and contributing to the destabilization of an already very tense situation. Russian officials also like to remind everybody that NATO is roughly four times bigger than the Russian military and that the US has bases all around Russia. So are we to conclude that the Pentagon is preparing to attack Russia or to intervene militarily in the Ukraine?

I believe that such a conclusion would be premature. Here is why:

The first thing to keep in mind is there is absolutely no need for the USA to forward deploy anything to attack Russia. I would even argue that forward deploying units or systems close to Russia put them at risk and make them a much easier target for Russia to strike. This is especially true of any USN ship entering the Black Sea which is completely "covered" by Russian coastal defense missiles. One Russian expert declared that Russia could destroy any ship anywhere in the Black Sea in 20 min or less. This is probably an accurate figure. If the Pentagon was preparing to attack Russia it would pull US units and systems "away" from the Russian border, not closer. The US has plenty of very effective long range strike capabilities including ballistic and cruise missiles.

The second undeniable fact is that under any conceivable scenario Russia does have the means to basically completely destroy the USA as a country in about 30 min (the USA, of course, can do the same to Russia). Any US war planner would have to consider the escalatory potential of any military action against Russia. It is theoretically possible that in the future the USA might have a means to protect itself from such a retaliatory attack by using a combination of its future **Prompt Global Strike**[429] **system**, the forward deployed **Active Layered Theater Ballistic Missile Defense system**[430] and the **US National Missile Defense programs.**[431] Personally, I don't believe that such a system would ever protect anybody against a Russian counter-attack, but even if it does, this will be far away in the future. Currently these systems are not operational and will not be so for the foreseeable future.

The entire notion of sending lethal aid to the Ukraine or instructors to train the Ukrainian military is utter nonsense. The Ukraine used to be in the Soviet second strategic echelon and it is absolutely full of weapons of all kind, and there are plenty of experts capable of using them. The problem of the Ukrainian military is neither a lack of weapons nor a lack of experts, but a lack of motivation by the vast majority of Ukrainian soldiers to go and fight in the Donbass against highly-motivated and very skilled Novorossian forces. Furthermore, it is abundantly clear for everybody (including the Ukrainians, of course) that should the Novorossian defenses crumble then Russia would have to intervene militarily to protect the Donbass. The Ukrainians can claim that they are already fighting hordes of Russian soldier and tanks (up to 200,000 according to a recent interview of Poroshenko[432]), but everybody in the Ukraine fully under-

[429] Prompt Global Strike https://en.wikipedia.org/wiki/Prompt_Global_Strike

[430] Active Layered Theater Ballistic Missile Defense https://en.wikipedia.org/wiki/NATO_missile_defence_system#Active_Layered_Theater_Ballistic_Missile_Defence

[431] United States national missile defense https://en.wikipedia.org/wiki/United_States_national_missile_defense

[432] Poroshenko claims there are 200,000 Russian troops in Ukraine without a shred of evidence https://www.youtube.com/watch?v=ft8jVIx3SLo

stands that it would take the Russians no more than 24 hours to completely wipe out the entire Ukrainian military.

Some would argue that what the US is doing is setting up a "tripwire force," just small enough to be attacked, but one whose destruction would warrant a full-scale US counter-attack. There are two problems with that theory. First, these deployments are happening in NATO member states whose areas are already protected by the "political tripwire" of **Article 5 of the Washington Treaty.**[433] There is simply no need for any kind of tripwire force in a NATO member state. Furthermore, nobody in his right mind would seriously believe that Russia might attack any European country. Sure, the EU and US politicians will try to terrify the Europeans with images of Russian hordes invading the Baltics, Poland or even Germany, but they all know that this is utter nonsense. For one thing, the Russian military is simply not configured to execute such a mission as it does not have the required power projection capability. And there is no political force in Russia even suggesting such a move. And why would Russia do that anyway? I cannot think of a single reason for such a crazy move.

In reality, what the US military is doing is called "showing the flag." This is purely a political statement and not, in itself, a preparation for an attack. In fact, I would argue that deploying US units in the Baltic states would be just about the worst possible way to prepare for an attack.

That does not mean that a war cannot happen. It very much can. First, there is the obvious risk of mistake and miscalculation. Then, it is really dangerous to see the kind of completely irresponsible statements regularly made by top US officials ranging from **Obama's idiotic claim that Russia is somewhere between ISIS and the Ebola virus in the list of major threats to the world**[434] or the more recent declaration of a **JCS**

---

[433] Article 5 of the Washington Treaty http://www.nato.int/terrorism/five.htm

[434] Full text of President Obama's 2014 address to the United Nations General Assembly http://www.washingtonpost.com/politics/full-text-of-president-obamas-2014-

Nominee General Joseph Dunford who seriously declared that "*Russia presents the greatest threat to our national security.*"[435] This kind of reckless fear-mongering can become a self-fulfilling prophecy and result in an actual war, if only because of the confrontational atmosphere it creates.

So why are the Russians so upset about this saber-rattling if it really presents no real risk for Russia?

The main reason is that these highly inflammatory actions and statements create a sense of crisis which contribute to isolate Russia from the rest of Europe—a key US foreign policy objective. This was also the main goal for all the US attempts at drawing Russian into the conflict in the Ukraine: to create a huge crisis and re-ignite a Cold War II in all of Europe. After all, the Europeans who are now busy with the Greek crisis, the tanking economy, social issues such as immigration and crime would rapidly turn to other issues if the main topic on all news shows became the "Russian threat to Europe." The politics of fear are well known: obedience, passive acceptance of the dismemberment of social, human, political and civil rights, the creation of a scapegoat on which any crisis could be blamed, etc. Having failed to re-ignite a Cold War II by means of a Russian "invasion" of the Donbass, the US now has fallen back on the option of acting as if such a military move did happen and that the rest of the Ukraine, the Baltics and Poland "are next." Hence the need to "protect" them by such public display of the US military presence.

Russia is walking a tight line here: she needs to avoid looking weak or frightened while also avoiding contributing to the further degradation of the situation. Hence the apparent Russian policy of "one step forward, one step backward" toward the US/NATO/EU.

The US will probably only achieve a moderate degree of success in its desperate campaign to present Russia as a threat to the world. After all,

---

address-to-the-united-nations-general-assembly/2014/09/24/88889e46-43f4-11e4-b437-1a7368204804_story.html

[435] Joint Chiefs nominee: Russia greatest threat to U.S. http://www.cnn.com/2015/07/09/politics/joseph-dunford-russia-greatest-threat/

there are only so many gullible doubleplusgoodthinkers out there willing to buy this silly notion. The problem is that regardless of the real feelings of most Europeans, the EU's comprador ruling class will continue to act as if the threat was real. The same goes for the Empire's propaganda machine (aka "corporate media").

The current saber-rattling is therefore likely to continue as long as the EU is run by US puppets.

July 18, 2015

RUSSIA PLANS TO INVITE INDIA, PAKISTAN AND IRAN INTO THE SHANGHAI COOPERATION ORGANIZATION (SCO)

This has been discussed for a very long time already, but this time it is official: Sergei Lavrov has just declared that at the next summit of the Shanghai Cooperation Organization (SCO) countries Russia will propose to the initiate the process of accepting Iran as a full member alongside India and Pakistan.

Quick reminder: the following countries are currently member of the SCO: China, Kazakhstan, Kyrgyzstan, Russia, Tadjikistan and Uzbekistan; the following countries are currently "observers" and, therefore, possible candidates: Afghanistan, India, Iran, Mongolia and Pakistan while Belarus, Sri Lanka and Turkey are "dialog partners". The near-future SCO would thus include all of the following full members: China, India, Iran, Kazakhstan, Kyrgyzstan, Pakistan, Russia, Tadjikistan and Uzbekistan.

[Sidebar: It is also important to remember that the SCO is a security organization with a strong military component to it. While its main goal is the coordination of members states in their struggle against terrorism, separatism and extremism, the SCO has conducted a number of military exercises. The SCO is not a formal military alliance but it has at its core countries which are members of the Collective Security Treaty Organization (CSTO) i.e., Russia, Armenia, Kazakhstan, Kyrgyzstan, Tajikistan, and Uzbekistan. We could very roughly say that the SCO has a function similar to NATO while the CSTO has a function comparable to the one of the Supreme Headquarters Allied Powers Europe (SHAPE). This comparison is not to be taken literally, but just as in Europe we can observe an economic alliance (the EU), a political security alliance (NATO) and a single purely military military command (SHAPE), so in Asia we see the Eurasian Economic Union (or EEU) being the economic alliance,

SCO as a political security organization and the CSTO as a purely military organization].

Needless to say, the White House is absolutely horrified by all this: not only did the US oppose the creation of the SCO, CSTO and EEU at every step of the way, but the consolidation of these organization is a vivid illustration of the loss of influence and power of the USA. The USA tried to stop it, lobbied hard to prevent anybody from joining it, and even tried to ignore it – and they failed: the SCO is growing in membership and influence.

To make things worse, the BRICS states have now become an open and direct challenge to the USA's economic hegemony over our planet. The folks in Washington are now very slowly becoming aware of the magnitude of the threat now faced by the Empire.

These developments also illustrate the dramatic contrast between US and Russian diplomatics methods and goals. While the US favors the classical "divide and conquer" method, Russia favors a "unite and lead" method which is designed to bring former enemies together (like India and Pakistan or China and India) and build large coalitions.

The prospect of Iran joining the SCO is seen by Washington as an overt provocation, as slap in the face of the Emperor, especially at a time when the US and the KSA are at war in Yemen precisely to isolate and "contain" Iran (of course, "containing" Russia, China and Iran all at the same time was not a very smart plan to begin with!). The US response is predictable: punish everybody involved with chaos. This time, it is tiny Macedonia which the object of US aggression (via the CIA-run UCK terrorists from Kosovo) with the deliberate desire to send everybody else the following message: side with Russia and you will pay, dearly. There have also been warnings by Russian analysts about the risks of ISIS/IS training in Georgia or a resumption of the Chechen insurgency, but this time around, with direct Ukronazi support. Uncle Sam is apparently trying to hit Russia in her "soft underbelly," but this plan has no chance of success because no such soft underbelly exists any more.

The myth of the soft underbelly of Russia

Amongst the many myths of old style geopolitics was the famous "soft underbelly of Russia." To be fair, there was some truth to that, but not much. Nowadays, however, this is absolutely false.

In reality, the combined results of the two wars in Chechnia, the war against Georgia, the civil war in the Ukraine, the terrorist threat in Dagestan, the Wahabi insurgency in Tadjikistan and the US-created chaos created in Iraq have all contributed to the definition and implementation of a long-term Russian policy to "armor her belly".

The earliest manifestation of this policy was the decision to deploy the elite 201 Motor-Rifle division in Tajikistan in direct support of the combined Russian-Tadjik border guard forces. Later, this division was renamed the 201st Base to reflect the unique capabilities of this unit. At the present time, subunits of this base are located in threeTadjik cities and "cover" all the critical areas. The 201 is, by any standard, a formidable force, far superior to anything Tajikistan or Afghanistan could deploy. But the Russians went one step further: they recently tested the ability of Russian airborne forces to deploy within hours to Tajikistan: without any warning, elements of the 98th Airborne Division were put on alert and transported with all their equipment and weapons to southern Tajikistan.

This exercise was specifically conducted under the aegis of the rapid reaction forces of the CSTO and was designed to test the Russian ability to project her military power right to the Tajik-Afghan border.

Currently, the Russian security posture towards Afghanistan relies on the following layers: first, maintaining a good working relationship with the Tajik population of northern Afghanistan; next—strengthening the Tadjik border guards and regular military forces by providing them with instructors and equipment; next deploying Russian border guard troops alongside their Tadjik colleagues; then, to maintain a powerful combat "fist" in the form of the 201 Base and, finally, to be ready to reinforce the 201st with Airborne Forces and aviation elements. As a result, Russia is now capable of deploying an extremely powerful combat group within 48 hours anywhere in, or near, Tadjikistan.

Another example of the "armored underbelly of Russia" is the no-less formidable 58th Army which is located in and around Chechnya whose recent combat record includes defeating the Chechen Wahhabis in 2000 and the Georgian military in 2008. The 58th Army is one of the best trained and best equipped army in the Russian armed forces. Now it can also count on the full support of the Chechen forces loyal to Ramzan Kadyrov which are beyond any doubt the most best trained and experienced forces in the Caucasus. Should the ISIS/IS crazies ever try to penetrate into the Caucasus (say, via Georgia) they would be met by an extremely powerful military force which would be superior to anything Syria or Iraq could deploy.

Finally, there is the Black Sea fleet which in the Soviet days was considered the least capable and, frankly, least important of the four Soviet Fleets (Northern, Pacific, Baltic and, last, Black Sea - in order of importance). Now, with the civil war in the Ukraine and after the war in Georgia, the Black Sea has re-acquired a new found importance, especially as "Crimea's Fleet." Russian officials have announced that they will greatly strengthen not only the group of forces in Crimea, but also the Black Sea Fleet.

The solution chosen by Russia was the creation in Crimea a separate "military grouping" comprising 96 formations and units and whose tasks will include not only the protection of Russian interests in the Black Sea and on the Crimean Federal District, but also to "meet the challenges in the long-range maritime zone." In other words—power projection.

The Crimean "fortress", the Black Sea Fleet, the 58th Army and the 201st Base are all part of a new, armored, Russian hard underbelly which is quite ready to deal with any threat coming from the south.

Conclusion

Over the past decades Russia has invested tremendous resources into the development of multi-dimensional policy towards the South and the East. On a political level, organizations such as the SCO, the CSTO and the BRICS are all forming a network of alliances which Russian can count on for support. On a military level, Russia has placed "military locks" her southern flank in the Black Sea, Caucasus and Central Asia and has developed the capabilities to send powerful reinforcements to these "locks". In effect, Russia has created a "cordon sanitaire" to protect herself from the instability on her southern border. This combination of political and military measure have given Russia a great degree of flexibility in responding to any crisis or challenge.

May 19, 2015

PART XI: RELIGION

Off-Topic but Apparently Needed: Judaism and Christianity—Back to Basics

I have received a lot of outraged comments for my statement that Orthodox Judaism is at its core just a type of "anti-Christianity." My critiques informed me of the fact that since Judaism was older than Christianity, it could hardly have been an anti-Christianity. Here are some samples of these comments:

> Well, the first cannot possibly be true as Judaism existed well over thousand years prior, and ever since was an introverted worldview. (If you don't know much about it, no need to put such sort of labels. Everybody has a right to preach his own religion, not just the Orthodox Christians).
>
> Surely you're aware that Judaism is MUCH older than Christianity, Saker? However some of them may feel toward the goyim, I think there's a good bit more to their religion than mere anti-Christian animosity.
>
> WTF!? and with that the fools and naive can point and chant "anti-semite"—and could you blame them? Well yes you could, but still. That one sentence pollutes any nuance, any thoughtful analysis, any factual argument Saker makes. Shame Saker is turning out to be a religious zealot—or at least an anti-Jewish one.

Sigh…

As is so often the case, modern propaganda works by a mix of ignorance and learned assumptions. You could say that this is a case of "unknown unknowns" to paraphrase Rumsfeld. This is case, all the self-righteous outrage above is based on a very simple fallacy: the assumption that what we call "Judaism" today is the religion of the Jews before, or until, the times of Christ. This assumption is **completely wrong**.

What we call "Judaism" today is basically the continuation of one of the many Jewish sects which existed at the time of Christ: the famous sect of the Pharisees. Specifically, it is the continuation of that part of the sect of the Pharisees which did not accept Christ (others did, Saint Paul was a Pharisee and so was the immensely famous teacher, Saint Gamaliel the Elder).[436] Besides being intellectually very sophisticated, one of the unique features of the Pharisees was that they met in "assemblies" to read the Scripture and worship. The word "assembly" in Greek (which was the *lingua franca* of the time) is συναγωγή "sinagoge"—or "synagogue" in modern English. When the Temple in Jerusalem was destroyed by the Legions of the Roman Emperor Titus in 70 AD the Pharisees were the only ones that had a ready structure which could be used in the absence of the Temple, the synagogue.

Please keep in mind that as such there were no "rabbis," at least not as an institution, before 70 AD. There were priests and teachers and some teachers were addressed as "rabbi," but "rabbinical Judaism" (which what modern "Judaism" really is) did not exist at that time.

The other crucial feature of the Pharisees was that they (correctly) believed that not all of the teachings of God had been written down and that oral tradition was as important as the written one. Other Jewish sects, just like modern day Protestant denominations, insisted that *sola scriptura.*

There is no overstating the catastrophic importance of destruction of the Temple in 70 AD. Not only did it take away the place of worship around which the lives of all the Jews of the entire Middle East centered at the time, but it also destroyed the building in which the Messiah had been predicted to come to preach and it happened at the time predicted by the Prophet Daniel. For those Jews who did not accept Christ, this was very, very bad news indeed. Something needed to be done urgently, and indeed it was. Here are the main axes this "response" took:

1) Under the pretext of correction and standardization the various Holy Books which we today think of as the "Old Testament" were ex-

[436] Gamaliel http://orthodoxwiki.org/Gamaliel

punged of the most evident passages that were referring to Christ. The Book of Psalms was especially butchered. A "new Old Testament" of sorts was created by a group of scholars called the Masoretes who produced a fraud, a re-worked collection of texts we nowadays call the *Masoretic Text*[437] of the Bible purged from all the key references to Christ. The "real" original text of the books of what we call today the Old Testament has not been preserved in Hebrew, but it exists in translations made from Hebrew into the Greek in the late 2nd century BC by 72 scholars working for Ptolemy Philadelphius, hence the translation is called the Septuaginta or simply LXX.

2) A new class of teachers tasked with the "correct" interpretation of the written and oral traditions emerged, the rabbis. Their main task was to "explain" what had happened in 70 AD and what that mean for the Jewish people.

3) A "new old oral tradition" was created and this time it was put in paper. This is what eventually became known as the Talmud (of which there are two, but never mind that), the anti-Christian book par excellence.

4) Exactly in accordance with the words of Christ and the apostles Paul and John the Evangelist, Devil worship and black magic also soon were integrated into the "new old" corpus of traditions and this is the basis of what today is called the Kabbalah.

5) Finally, and logically, the focus of worship turned from a worship of God to self-worship. In this recent addition, it is the entire Jewish people who are the innocent and suffering Messiah and the so-called "Holocaust" is that mystical sacrifice from which the salvation of the world will come. In this latest school of thought, the Jews are collectively called to "fix/repair" the world, to do the work of the Messiah.

Okay, now before there is the usual tsunami of outraged comments spiced up with the usual accusations of anti-Semitism and the rest of the

---

437 Masoretic Text https://en.wikipedia.org/wiki/Masoretic_Text

inevitable nonsense, let me tell you immediately that I have no intention at all to prove any of the above. I simply have no time for that. If you are interested, you can easily find all this information online, from books written by anti-Judaic scholars like Michael Hoffman to books written by authoritative Jewish scholars like Jacob Neusner. The latter will, of course, not at all put the same interpretation to these events as I do, but he will not disagree with the basic facts and chronology.

The point for me is this: you can take any good book or course on the history of what is called "Judaism" today and check for yourself that all the facts above are true. I particularly recommend "*The Way of Torah: An Introduction to Judaism*" by Jacob Neusner which, if I am not mistaken, exists in the form of audio lectures from the Teaching Company's "Great Courses" series. From an non-Judaic perspective I recommend the books *Judaism's Strange God* and, especially, the huge *Judaism Discovered* (over 1000 pages!) by Michael Hoffman. You can get them from an online bookstore or even in the form of a (possibly unauthorized and therefore free) PDF download. But even a short trip to your local library should give you enough confirmation that I am not making things up.

If you take the time to study the roots and evolution of what we called "Judaism," and which could be called something like "rabbinical/ Pharisaic Talmudism," you will come to the inevitable conclusion that modern "Judaism" is not the religion of Abraham, Isaac and Jacob but the religion of Maimonides, Karo and Luria. This religion has "nothing" in common with the religion of the Jewish people before Christ, just as modern Jews, especially the Ashkenazim, have no genetic connection to the Jewish people of 2000 years ago. We are dealing with a fraud whose main effort is to prove that it is the real thing, just as the Papacy is trying to prove that it is "the" original Church of Christ while in reality neither one of them have their roots in the times of Christ.

Depending on your personal beliefs there are only two religions today which can claim to be the real, true, continuation of the faith of Abraham, Isaac and Jacob: Orthodox Christianity (simply because it is the original form of Christianity which itself is the accomplishment of the ancient faith of the Jewish people) or Karaism (simply because it the closest non-Christian denomination to trace its roots to pre-Talmudic "Judaism" at least in the version of the Sect of the Sadducees).

I'd rather not have a long discussion about this fascinating, but complex, topic. I just wanted to explain why I wrote the modern Judaism is basically a form of anti-Christianity and try to calm down those who suffered a heart-attack or stroke from the indignation at hearing such a self-evidently ignorant and bigoted thought.

Now let's get back to the modern world and its numerous problems.

December 1, 2014

Non-political interlude: reply to two posts (religions haters please skip this one!!)

Today is a beautiful day in Florida. Yesterday we "survived" not one, but two tornadoes (they mostly hit a national wildlife refuge south of us, there never was any real danger, but this sounds better) and today we get one of those perfect Florida days: blue skies with a few white clouds, beautiful warm sunshine (26C/79F), a cool breeze from the northeast and which brings in the always refreshing smell of the Atlantic ocean (where my lucky son spend six hours surfing the waves this morning). I know that I have to work on my promised report on world opinion and media coverage of the Ukrainian crisis, but I want to "seize the day" and go for some nature photography this afternoon (shall I post some pics of sunny Florida here?). The report will have to wait a little. However, I got two questions recently which I find worth answering in a separate post.

[WARNING: these two questions deal with religion so those of you who hate religion—please just ignore this post.]

Here are the two issues I want to discuss today: James wants to know what the Church is while Mohamed wrote in a comment that the Scripture was corrupted. I will take them one by one (though there is a link between the two)

@James: What is the Church?

To reply to this question adequately one could write a PhD thesis. I will try to make a much shorter reply and point you to a few texts, fair enough?

Since you are a former Latin Christian let me begin by saying what the Church is not. It is not an organization nor a formal institution. You probably remember that in the Symbol of Faith (aka the Credo) it says "In one Holy, Catholic, and Apostolic Church." Most people do not seem to be aware that the words at the very beginning "I believe in" also apply to the section "In one Holy, Catholic, and Apostolic Church." In other words, not only do Orthodox Christians believe "**in one God**, the Father Almighty, Maker of Heaven and Earth and of all things visible and invisible (…) "**in one Lord Jesus Christ**, the Son of God, the Only-begotten, begotten of the Father before all ages. Light of light; true God of true God; begotten, not made; of one essence with the Father, by Whom all things were made" (…) in the Holy Spirit, the Lord, the Giver of Life, Who proceeds from the Father" but also "**In one Holy, Catholic, and Apostolic Church.**" *The Church itself requires an act of faith similar to the confession of the belief in God.* Orthodox Christians literally "believe in the Church" and this is why the Church is most definitely not an organization.

In theological language the Church is called the *Theandric Body of Christ.* Theandric derives from *Theanthropos* or "God-man" the central dogma of all Christianity. In other words, the Church is literally the Body of Christ no less than the Eucharist. This is also why the only valid Mysteries (called "Sacraments" in Western theology) can *only* be found inside that Church. Just like the Body of Christ, the Church cannot break into parts, have sub-groups, contradict itself, etc. This is why the Symbol of

Faith speaks of ONE Church, no more divisible that God Himself. Again, to accept that requires an act of faith.

The Church is called "Holy" because it is the Body of Christ and that it is filled with the Holy Spirit. This is why at the First Apostolic Council in Jerusalem (50 AD) those present wrote "For it seemed good to the Holy Ghost, and to us.." (Acts 15: 28). However, its individual members—laity and clergy—are not necessarily holy at all. The Church is also a **hospital for sinners** and not an elite club of perfect holy people.

The Church is called "Catholic" because of the Greek word καθολικός which means "universal," especially in the following two meanings: a) which includes and is not limited to one region, country, continent or part of the world and b) acts in a way which includes everybody. The first one is obvious, but the second one is not. In this sense, "Catholic" means "Conciliar" in reference to a "council of all" or, in Greek, a "Ecumenical" (including the whole world) council. The Russian term Соборный/соборность is very accurate here as it clearly points to a council ("sobor" in Russian). So being "Catholic / Conciliar" means that there is no "teaching Church" versus a "taught Church," no one instance or clerical rank which is the source of "authority" (to use a Latin concept) or unity. It is the **whole** Body of the Church, down to the last layperson, which acting as one has the "authority" of the Church. Not even a council of, say, 99% of all the Orthodox Bishops—never mind one bishop or one Patriarch—on the planet can claim to speak for the Church if the rest of the "Body" does not agree with it.

There have been plenty of instances in history were the vast majority of bishops who formally appeared to have remained Orthodox had, in fact, lapsed from the Church. These are the so-called "robber councils" which, at that time, looked legit and had all the external signs of legitimacy, but which the Body of the Church—the people, really—ended up denouncing and condemning later. Again, there is no external legitimacy, no authority from which legitimacy can be derived, no person or group of people who can deliver some "certificate of authenticity" to this or that local Church or bishop. So how do we know which is the one true Church as opposed to those who only **appear to be** so externally. Here are the criteria of truth:

1) Apostolic succession. Simple enough, does not need to be explained.

2) True confession of faith. The local Church has to confess the exact same faith which, in the words of Saint Athanasios "the *Lord gave, was preached by the Apostles, and was preserved by the Fathers. On this was the Church founded; and if anyone departs from this, he neither is nor any longer ought to be called a Christian.*" It has to be what I call "backward compatible" **meaning absolutely no innovation**. In the words of Saint Vincent of Lerins, it has to be exactly and fully the same as that ""which has been believed everywhere, always and by all." If they did not all believe and confess X in, say, the 5th century or the 8th century, then it is not Orthodox. Simple.

3) Unity of the Eucharist: simply put—if you are not in Eucharistic communion with the rest of the Body of Christ, you are not part of the Church.

I would note here that the unity of faith is a prerequisite for the Eucharistic communion: if you do not have the same beliefs as I do, we cannot share the same Eucharist. Nowadays some people have it exactly backward. They say "let us commune from the same cup, and then iron out our secondary differences later." This is modern nonsense. The Church has never **taught** that.

In the world the visible part of the Church is, for cultural and practical reasons, organized along several independent religious organizations: local Churches, independent ("autocephalous") Patriarchates which can be Russian, Greek, Paraguayan or Japanese. The pray in their own language, organize themselves in any way they want, have their own customs and traditions. Just like there were 12 and 70 apostles there can be plenty of local and autonomous Churches as long as they maintain the unity of faith and communion. In fact, if the One Church did not allow that it would not be truly "Catholic" either. And just like the apostles did not have some "Big Boss" over them, the Church has no Head other than Christ Himself. Sure, for administrative and pastoral issues each Church has a senior bishop (put in charge by a council of local bishops) but even that local boss has no more authority in matters of faith, of confession, that any layperson.

There have been plenty instances in the history of the Church when Patriarchs and entire councils strayed from the truth, and they were often reproved and even condemned by simple lay people. Speaking of which, there are only four clerical ranks in the Church: layperson (yes, that is a rank, a layperson can, in case of emergency, baptize in the name of the entire Church), deacon, priest and bishop. All the other fancy categories are only administrative or honorary. So folks with roaring titles like "His Beatitude the Archbishop of X" is no more than a simple bishop. A Protopresbyter is just a priest and an Archdeacon is just a deacon. Clergymen, by the way, are formally addressed with honorary titles "Most Reverend," "Your Grace," etc. but that really applies to the clerical rank, not the person carrying that rank. Same for kissing the hand of a priest—it's not because he is so worthy, but because of the high rank (charisma[438]) bestowed on him. He himself might be a dumb jerk (many are) or even a lying hypocritical ignoramus with a bad temper. Remember, the Church is a hospital for sinners, not a club of holy men. There is only one thing that really matters: the confession of faith of this clergyman needs to be 100% Orthodox and his personal sins must not be serious enough to ban him from serving and / or himself receiving the Eucharist (so no pedophilia, no sexual immorality, no killing, no apostasy, etc.).

Okay, I have to stop here even though we barely scratched the surface here. Let me give you a few good readings I recommend:

---

[438] Divinely conferred charisma https://en.wikipedia.org/wiki/Charisma#Divinely_conferred_charisma

Online texts on ecclesiology (what is the Church?):

Christianity or the Church? by Archbishop Hilarion (Troitsky)[439]

Essay on the Unity of the Church: the Church is one by Alexei Khomiakov[440]

General Information: The Church (any text on that page)[441]

General books on Orthodox Christianity:

The Faith: Understanding Orthodox Christianity by Clark Carlton[442]

The Orthodox Church by Timothy Ware[443]

Truth: What Every Roman Catholic Should Know About the Orthodox Church (Faith Catechism) by Clark Carlton[444]

Orthodox Dogmatic Theology: A Concise Exposition by Michael Pomazansky, translation of Seraphim Rose[445]

Theosis: The True Purpose of Human Life by Archimandrite George of Mount Athos[446]

I hope that this was useful. If not, I am sorry.

@Mohamed: was the Scripture corrupted?

---

[439] Christianity or the Church? by Archbishop Hilarion (Troitsky) http://www.pravoslavie.ru/english/christchurchilarion.htm

[440] Essay on the Unity of the Church: the Church is one by Alexei Khomiakov http://www.myriobiblos.gr/texts/english/komiakov_essay.htm

[441] General Information: The Church http://orthodoxinfo.com/general/gen_church.aspx

[442] The Faith: Understanding Orthodox Christianity by Clark Carlton http://www.amazon.com/The-Faith-Understanding-Orthodox-Christianity/dp/0964914115/ http://www.amazon.com/The-Orthodox-Church-New-Edition/dp/0140146563/

[443] *The Orthodox Church* by Timothy Ware http://www.amazon.com/The-Orthodox-Church-New-Edition/dp/0140146563/

[444] Truth: *What Every Roman Catholic Should Know About the Orthodox Church (Faith Catechism)* by Clark Carlton http://www.amazon.com/Truth-Catholic-Should-Orthodox-Catechism/dp/0964914182/

[445] *Orthodox Dogmatic Theology: A Concise Exposition* http://www.amazon.com/Orthodox-Dogmatic-Theology-Concise-Exposition/dp/0938635697

[446] *Theosis: The True Purpose of Human Life* by Archimandrite George of Mount Athos http://www.amazon.com/Theosis-True-Purpose-Human-Life/dp/B001UR1SI0/

Yes and no. Yes it was, but never successfully. Let me explain why.

First, if you accept that God did communicate with mankind by means of prophecy and that the prophets did put down the prophecies which they received, you would wonder why then God would let men distort or otherwise corrupt the message He sent us. Of course, all man can err, we are all sinful, and either by mistake or deliberately man have corrupted the Scripture, no question here, the pertinent question is rather could these men have gotten away with that?

In the *Third book of Esdras* [Ezra] we have an interesting episode. Esdras tells God that the Scripture has been burned and asks *"If then I have found favor before thee, send the **Holy Spirit** into me, and I will write everything that has happened in the world from the beginning, the things which were written in thy law, that men may be able to find the path, and that those who wish to live in the last days may live."* To which God replies *"Go and gather the people, and tell them not to seek you for forty days. But prepare for yourself many writing tablets, and take with you Sarea, Dabria, Selemia, Ethanus, and As'iel—these five, because they are trained to write rapidly; and you shall come here, and I will light in your heart the lamp of understanding, which shall not be put out until what you are about to write is finished."* And, sure enough, Esdras tells us *"So I took the five men, as he commanded me, and we proceeded to the field, and remained there. And on the next day, behold, a voice called me, saying, "Ezra, **open your mouth and drink what I give you to drink.**" Then I opened my mouth, and behold, a full cup was offered to me; it was full of something like water, but its color was like fire. And I took it and drank; and when I had drunk it, my heart poured forth understanding, and wisdom increased in my breast, for my spirit retained its memory; and my mouth was opened, and was no longer closed. And the Most High gave understanding to the five men, and by turns they wrote what was dictated, in characters which they did not know. They sat forty days, and wrote during the daytime, and ate their bread at night. As for me, I spoke in the daytime* *and was not silent at night. So during the forty days ninety-four books were written. And when the forty days were ended, the Most High spoke to me, saying, 'Make public the twenty-four books that you wrote first and let the worthy and the unworthy read them; but keep the seventy that were written last, in order to give them to the wise among your people. For in them is the spring of understanding, the fountain of wisdom, and the river of knowledge.' And I did so."*

Sorry for the long quote, but I want to illustrate a point: when needed God can command his faithful to restore even the full Scripture provided a) that they are worthy to receive the guidance of the Holy Spirit and b) that they receive the "drink like fire" which God gives them (note that this book was written long before the times of Christ!). What is certain is that the notion that God would grant a revelation through His prophets and then allow that revelation to remain corrupted for centuries is rather ludicrous.

There was, indeed, one grievous attempt at falsifying the Scripture. It occurred after the fall of Jerusalem in 70 AD. At that time the Jewish people were separated into two sects: those who believed that Christ was the Messiah and those who did not. The former become known as Christians, while the latter—mostly Pharisees—created their own group which developed a new spirituality which switched focus from the Old Testament to the Talmud, from the Temple to assemblies (synagogues), from priests to rabbis and from the original Scripture to a new "corrected" text. This texts had the official imprimatur of the rabbis who declared that it has been corrected by their sages, the scribes and scholars. Needless to say, what they really did is cut out or alter those parts of the Scripture that were inconvenient to them. At the time there was a great deal of hostility between the two groups and disputations centered around the Scripture, of course. The issue at hand was simple: did the prophesies about the Messiah in the Scripture match what actually happened in the life of Christ or not? Could the followers of Christ prove their case by using the Scripture? Well, the "guardians of the tradition," or "*Maso-*

retes"[447] as they became known, "corrected" the Scripture as much as possible to produce a forgery known today as the "*Masoretic text*"[448] (abbreviated MT).

Christians immediately saw through that and denounced the text as a fake. One of the earliest documents we have showing that Christians at the time were fully aware that the Jews produced a forgery is the "*Dialog with Trypho*"[449] in which Saint Justin Martyr[450] (2nd century) explicitly makes that accusation. The latter Fathers have also confirmed that.

You might wonder which text is the original and what happened to it. We only have parts of the original Hebrew "Old Testament" (which is, of course, not what they called it). Following the conquests of Alexander the Great much of what is today the Middle East was "Hellenized" and the language of the elites and the international language of the time was Greek. About two centuries before the birth of Christ, at the request of the local (Greek) ruler, *Ptolemy II Philadelphius*,[451] a translation into Greek of the Hebrew text was made for the famous Library of Alexandria[452] by 70 translators from the twelve tribes of Israel. This text is called the Septuagint[453] (abbreviated LXX) in memory of these 70 translators. This is the only text ever considered authoritative by the Church. Following the Latin schism, the LXX was almost forgotten in Western Europe where the Latin Church used a translation made by Saint Jerome called the Vulgate.[454] Because the Latin believed that only the "learned" clergy should read the Scripture and then teach and explain it to the "simple" folks, this text was not very widely circulated. In contrast, Luther wanted

---

447 Masoretes https://en.wikipedia.org/wiki/Masoretes

448 Masoretic Text https://en.wikipedia.org/wiki/Masoretic_Text

449 ST. Justin Martyr: Dialogue with Trypho http://www.earlychristianwritings.com/text/justinmartyr-dialoguetrypho.html

450 Justin Martyr http://orthodoxwiki.org/Justin_Martyr

451 Ptolemy II Philadelphus https://en.wikipedia.org/wiki/Ptolemy_II_Philadelphus

452 Library of Alexandria https://en.wikipedia.org/wiki/Library_of_Alexandria

453 Septuagint https://en.wikipedia.org/wiki/Septuagint

454 Vulgate https://en.wikipedia.org/wiki/Vulgate

each Christian to have access to the Scripture. Luther, who was opposed to the Latin clericalism and who suspected that the Latins might have corrupted the text, decided to base his teaching on what he apparently sincerely believed was the "original" Hebrew text, the Masoretic forgery. As a result, the vast majority of Bibles available in the western world are based on a text deliberately forged by Christ-hating rabbis, including the (otherwise beautifully written) King James Version. More recently, newer "corrected" versions of the MT have been made, but there is still only one, rather bad, translation of the LXX in English, the so-called "Brenton translation" (I hear that a new one is being worked on). But until very recently the West was simply too proud and too ignorant of Patristic thought to remember that only the LXX was the true text of the Old Testament.

I am going into all these details to illustrate a point: yes, Holy Writ can, and has been, corrupted both deliberately (Masoretes) or by ignorance (western Bibles). But **God never allows the original true text to simply vanish.**

I would also note that what the rabbis attempted is first and foremost a substitution: LXX by MT. They never claimed that the MT was the LXX. In fact, some Jewish holidays (such as Hanukkah[455]) have no scriptural basis in the MT but only in the LXX (in the book of Maccabees in this case). Unlike the West, the Jews never forgot about the LXX—they simply did not want to grant it authoritative status, for quite obvious reasons.

There are some sources which claim that an attempt to corrupt the LXX was also made by Jews, but I have seen no good evidence of that. For one thing, the LXX was simply too widely circulated (not as one text, but as a collection of books) to suddenly substitute another text. Really, the creation of the MT was for "internal consumption" and to beat back Christian polemicists.

---

[455] Hanukkah https://en.wikipedia.org/wiki/Hanukkah

So here is my main point: there is zero historical evidence to attest to the corruption of the original Holy Scripture. The only known case is the one I outlined above. We also know from the Scripture itself that God would never deprive his faithful from His Word, the example of Esdras (aka Ezra) above also shows that. Furthermore, simple logic suggests to us that it is impossible to corrupt a text which is both 1) widely circulated and 2) very closely analyzed and held for sacred.

Let me conclude here by saying that I personally believe that the Prophet Muhammad did hear about the Masoretic forgery and that this inspired him to look at the Christian Scripture with a strong suspicion that the text had been forged. Obviously, like Luther, he was not aware of the LXX. It is also possible that Muhammad might have had another reason to declare that the Christian Scripture was corrupted: the so-called Old Testament has absolutely no prophecy speaking of any figure like Muhammad, this is why some Muslim scholars have had to declare that the "Comforter" mentioned by Christ to His disciples was a reference to Muhammad and not to the Holy Spirit, an interpretation which even a superficial reading of the New Testament immediately invalidates and which not a single Church Father or theologian between the first and seventh century endorsed.

Whatever may be the case, the Muslim theory that the Scripture has been successfully corrupted is both illogical and ahistorical. One can, of course, chose to believe it, especially if one accepts that everything, including the historical record, has been forged, corrupted or lost, but at least to me faith and common sense should not contradict each other.

I think that it is undeniable that Christianity grew out of the religion of the Jewish people before the birth of Christ. Christ Himself constantly makes references to the books the Church has united into one volume called the "Old Testament." If the topic is of interest to you, see all the texts on this page,[456] especially this one[457] and this one.[458] In contrast, Is-

---

[456] On Holy Scriptures http://fatheralexander.org/page8.htm

lam has no other scriptural basis that itself or, rather, the book it produced: the Quran.

In conclusion I want to say that a closer look at history shows that the notion of "Judeo-Christian" is simply at least as nonsensical as speaking of a white-black or a dry-wet. As for the so-called "Abrahamic religions" they truly have nothing in common. Modern Judaism is really nothing else but an "anti-Christianity" while Islam is a faith which appeared *ex nihilo* and has no basis in either Jewish or Christian Scripture or oral tradition.

I hope that I have not offended anybody here, especially not my Muslim friends and readers, but I felt that it was important to lay out here the **original** Christian understanding of these issues. As any other Orthodox Christian I strongly feel that it is my personal obligation to preserve that which has been passed on to me (the "corporate memory and awareness" of the Church, if you want) and to share it with others if and when it is appropriate. As (hopefully) intelligent and considerate people, we can "agree to disagree," but to do that, you need to be made aware of the nature of what we might disagree on, right? By the way, I would welcome any offer to present a Muslim view of this—or any other—topic here and if somebody submits it (in the comment section for example) I will be glad to post it.

That's it for today. I will return to worldly topics tomorrow.

I wish you all an excellent week-end, kind regards.

May 17, 2014

[457] Concordance of Messianic Prophesies http://fatheralexander.org/booklets/english/prophecies_christ.htm

[458] The Old Testament Regarding the Messiah http://fatheralexander.org/booklets/english/old_testament_messiah.htm

PART XII: VARIA

HOW I BECAME A 9/11 "TRUTHER"

Eight years have now passed since the attacks of 911, and for these eight years I have steered clear from the debate about what exactly happened on 911. Mostly, I defined myself as a "911 agnostic" meaning literally that I had no knowledge of what took place that day. However, being an agnostic does not mean not thinking about a topic. I watched every single "truther" movie out there, read quite a few books on this topic, compared and contrasted the "truther" and "debunker" arguments and stances. Now, eight years later, a number of aspects of this debate have become clear in my mind.

From the very beginning one thing did strike me: the systematic vilification of those who doubted the official version of the events on 911 by not only the corporate media and their talking heads, but even a lot of people in the blogosphere. "911 kooks" was the most frequently used term to refer to the "truthers." From the outset I was shocked by that. Why should those who ask questions be vilified in such a manner? Does the US government not have a well-known history of false flag operations (think of the US "Operation Northwoods" or the joint US-Israeli "Operation Cyanide" - on the latter an excellent source of info is the BBC report "Dead in the Water"). Was the CIA not involved at every single step of the creation and growth of what became later known as al-Qaeda? If there any doubt at all that the folks who were in power on 9/11 are evil to the very core and more than capable of killing not thousands, but millions of innocent people to achieve their goals? Last, but not least, who benefited most from 9/11 if not the US Empire and the Israel Lobby?

The answers are rather obvious, aren't they?

But then why were "truthers" vilified? I suppose that the fact that there are real crackpots and kooks among the 9/11 Truth movement did not help. Some of these guys are, indeed, raving lunatics and plainly idiots.

And having the likes of Alex Jones screaming all sorts of things on the streets of NY with his megaphone did little to help the image of the 911 Truth movement (Alex Jones is the kind of guy I just love to hate. Everything about him offends me, his tone, his behavior and, worst of all, his voice). This is all true, but none of this is in any way a logical reply to the issues which were raised by the "truthers." I mean - if a person says "how could WTC7 collapse at free fall accelerations?" it is just not enough to answer "Alex Jones is a lunatic!!!!'" Even though the latter might be true, this is hardly an adequate reply. Yet this kind of "argument" is mostly what I saw from the alternative blogosphere.

The other thing which amazed me is that from day 1, the Dubya administration did pretty much everything it could to prevent a real investigation of 9/11. First, the opposed it, then they wanted Henry Kissinger (!) to head it, then they refused to let Bush testify without Cheney in the same room, etc. Why would they? The logical thing to do for them would have been to make a huge and open investigation looking into every single aspect of the 9/11 attacks with maniacal care. After all, if a bunch of Saudis armed with cutters lead by a small group of people sitting in a cave in Afghanistan really did commit these acts, as the government says they did, why not maximize the outrage of the public opinion by keeping an endless flows of details about this operation coming in day after day after day into the public domain? Why not expose it all step by step, event by event?

But no—every single step taken to investigate these events was at best a farce and at worst a pathetic attempt to bury the truth forever. Let's just take one simple example: there was enough debris left on 9/11 to send samples to every single laboratory on the planet. Yet, all of it was removed at warp speed and, of all things, sent to China! (keep in mind that legally speaking the debris from WTC1, WTC2 and WTC7 represented evidence on a crime scene). Now how can the politicos in Washington complain when the "truthers" allege that traces of thermite were found in the 911 dust? NIST, to this day, also adamantly refuses to test the dust for explosives even though such an investigation is required by law.

Not only that, but the government's story changed time after time after time. This is as true for the list of alleged hijackers as it is in the case of the mechanisms which brought down the buildings (see below). With that type of constantly changing stories, it is no wonder that people start asking questions, I would say.

Yet another kind of response to the Truth movement was what the Papist call the "argument of authority." It goes something like this "if Ron Paul does not question 911, neither will I."

Frankly, this is kind of dumb, in particular in the case of a politician who, no matter how courageous and honest, simply cannot afford to say anything and everything he thinks. Yet, a lot of people did exactly that, and not only Ron Paul supporters—exactly the same argument was made with Noam Chomsky's name. I personally have a great deal of respect for both Ron Paul and Noam Chomsky, but that respect does not translate into an automatic and unconditional support for everything they say or, in this case, do *not* say.

Another thing which got me thinking is the amazingly dishonest arguments used by "debunkers." Only yesterday evening I read the following thing on a debunker website: "the truthers say that a cruise missile hit the Pentagon, yet they also say that the way the light poles were cut down is suspicious - but how could a cruise missile cut down these poles? Obviously, an aircraft did this!"

This kind of "argument" is fundamentally un-scientific. The scientific method consists of making an observation, asking a question, form a hypothesis, conduct an experiment and then either accept or reject the hypothesis; in the latter case a new hypothesis has to be made taking into account the outcome of the experiment. In the case of 9/11, it is the government who presented us with a hypothesis (the official version) and this hypothesis did not fit the observed facts at all. What the truthers primarily did is to challenge this hypothesis. But the "debunkers" instead of re-working their initial hypothesis immediately challenged the "truthers" to present a more solid explanation. This is not logical or scientific at all.

Consider this: the "debunkers" love to call the truthers "conspiracy theorists." Yet these very same 'debunkers' fully buy into the official government version(s) which, as it happens, is nothing but a big conspiracy theory (and a utterly incredible one, I would add).

I realize that all of the above is little more than my personal, subjective, impressions and musings. True. And I don't claim to have all the answers. But one thing I do know is that 911 was never properly investigated or, even much less so, adequately explained. Therefore, ***the 9/11 Truth Movement demand for a new, independent, and fully transparent investigation is absolutely legitimate*** and to reject it is fundamentally undemocratic. If millions of dollars can be spend by the US taxpayer to investigate Clinton's sexual activities with Monica Lewinsky, then the death of 3000 Americans surely deserves a real and independent investigation, no?!

In reality, of course, the "truthers" did force many revisions of the official version (see below). It's just that the government and the debunkers will never admit to it. Who are the real "kooks" here - they folks who question the official theory or those who fully buy into it, even when *it changes over and over again*?!

For example, did you know that:

1. That in 2006 (already four years ago!) NIST dropped the famous "pancake theory" about how the WTC buildings fell on 9/11? Here is a quote from their final report:
2. **NIST's findings do not support the "pancake theory" of collapse,** which is premised on a progressive failure of the floor systems in the WTC towers (the composite floor system—that connected the core columns and the perimeter columns—consisted of a grid of steel "trusses" integrated with a concrete

slab; see diagram below). Instead, the NIST investigation showed conclusively that the failure of the inwardly bowed perimeter columns initiated collapse and that the occurrence of this inward bowing required the sagging floors to remain connected to the columns and pull the columns inwards. Thus, **the floors did not fail progressively to cause a pancaking phenomenon.** (source: NIST report FAQ) .[459]

3. Never mind the part about "the NIST investigation showed conclusively ...". My point is not to challenge their newest theory, but to **point out that the initial** "official" **theory was quietly dropped and that nobody seems to be aware of that**. Ask your friends and colleagues why and how the WTC buildings fell - and I betcha that you will get the "pancake theory".
4. **That NIST also admitted that WTC7 fell in free-fall**? Check out this video[460] showing how NIST had to cave in to "truthers" and reluctantly admit that free fall did occur. Check out this three part video:

So, no "pancaking" and an officially free falling WTC7...

So what is the "official version" of 9/11? Does anybody even ask this question?

Still, having myself spent eight years being a "9/11 agnostic" I certainly can relate to the incredulity of those who believe that while the US government has plenty of ugly deeds on its conscience, the idea that 9/11 was some kind of "inside job" is really "too much."

I would like to spell out here what exactly brought me around and made me into a committed "truther". The second thing I would like to

[459] NIST report FAQ http://www.nist.gov/el/disasterstudies/wtc/

[460] http://www.youtube.com/watch?v=eDvNS9iMjzA

do, is to give some "shortcuts" to those who are "on the fence" or confused about this entire topic.

Let's begin by the one thing which really opened my eyes. For this, I need to first identify the reasons for my previous 9/11 agnosticism. Basically - I believed that the US government could not have pulled off such a major operation as the covert installation of many tons of explosives inside WTC1, WTC2 and WTC7 without this somehow becoming public. Likewise, I did not believe that having used at least three planes (2 in NY and the one which crashed in Shanksville) the putative "conspirators" would have chosen a rather convoluted "no plane" option to strike the Pentagon. Finally, I did believe very strongly that the USA "had it coming" for decades already and that an organization like al-Qaeda had clearly warned the USA that it would retaliate for the perceived occupation of Saudi Arabia by "infidels" and for the US support Israel. So I applied Occam's Razor and decided that there is no need to seek some really complex and convoluted solution when the simple and straightforward explanation made sense and seemed to be supported by all the facts: 9/11 was a case of "blowback" for US imperial policies.

This reasoning looked all fine and dandy to me until I came to a truly momentous realization: the "official theory" did not explain one major fact: there is absolutely no way that 2 planes could have brought down the 3 buildings in New York. Not only that, but the way the buildings fell simply cannot be explained by a gravitational collapse induced by fire.

Let me stress something crucial here: one need not have an explanation for HOW something happened if this something is observed and irrefutably established. Or, put in another way—the fact that somebody cannot explain a phenomenon is not a logical basis to dismiss or deny the phenomenon itself.

Bottom line: the US government - through NIST - officially recognized the fact that the WTC7 building fell at a free-fall acceleration for 2,25 seconds. Do those 2,25 seconds really matter? Hell yes!! What this means is that the US government admits that for 2,25 seconds WTC7 fell without any kind of resistance to slow it down and this, therefore, means that there was nothing under the collapsing section. So this begs an obvious question: since we now know that there was nothing under the collapsing section and since we also know that there was a steel frame building there seconds before the collapse - what happened in between those two events? There is only one possible answer to this question: the steel-framed section of the building which would have normally slowed down the collapsing section of the building was removed a) extremely rapidly b) symmetrically. There is only one phenomenon which can explain that: explosives.

The above is simply not a matter of opinion. This is a fact. Likewise, it is a fact that fires could not have removed a section of WTC7 the way it was observed. At this point, we are faced with two basic and mutually exclusive options:

- to deny the reality of indisputably established facts
- to accept the compelling logic of Conan Doyle's Sherlock Holmes who said: "When you have eliminated the impossible (*in this case - fires causing the observed collapse*), whatever remains, however improbable, must be the truth."

Furthermore, we also know that WTC1 and WTC2 could not have collapsed as a result of the combined effects of the impact of the planes and the subsequent fires (anyone doubting that should watch 9/11 Blueprint for Truth—a presentation by Richard Gage of Architects and Engineers for 9/11 Truth,[461] an organization which now counts over 1000 members).[462]

Unlike the case of WTC7 for which we do have a de-facto government admission that only explosives could have cause the observed collapse, the case of WTC1 and WTC2 has not yet elicited any kind of oblique ad-

---

[461] http://www.ae911truth.org/

[462] http://vineyardsaker.blogspot.com/2010/01/milestone-reached-for-architects.html

mission by the US government. What Uncle Sam did was even more basic: its latest report officially analyzes the events leading up to the collapse, but does not look at anything which happened once the collapse was initiated.

The extent of NIST's explanation for the totality of the collapses and their many demolition-like features[463] is simply that the total collapse was "inevitable" once a collapse event was "initiated". A footnote in the Executive Summary reads:

> The focus of the Investigation was on the sequence of events from the instant of aircraft impact to the initiation of collapse for each tower. For brevity in this report, this sequence is referred to as the "probable collapse sequence," although it includes little analysis of the structural behavior of the tower after the conditions for collapse initiation were reached and collapse became inevitable.

The footnote is a re-worded version of a paragraph in the text of the Report's Draft, which read:

> ... although it does not actually include the structural behavior of the tower after the conditions for collapse initiation were reached and collapse became inevitable.

In other words - the government does not even have an explanation, theory or even hypothesis of what could have triggered the type of collapse which was actually observed by millions, if not billions, of people.

So let's now put it the simple and direct way: the ONLY explanation for the collapse of WTC1, WTC2 and WTC7 is a controlled demolition by pre-planted explosives. This is not "one of the" theories - it is the ONLY theory (a theory is an explanation which makes it possible to explain that which is observed). I need to repeat this again:

The US government has already admitted that WTC7 did collapse at free fall speed for 2,25 seconds and the US government has simply no ex-

---

[463] http://911research.wtc7.net/wtc/analysis/collapses/index.html

planation at all for the any of the building collapses which happened on 9/11.

Since all the WTC center building were highly secure (especially WTC7 which had all the following organizations as tenants: DoD, CIA, FBI, IRS, USSS and many others)[464] is unthinkable that any entity not affiliated with the US government could have covertly introduced hundreds of tons of high-explosives in these buildings, and most definitely not "al-Qaeda". Again, we need to turn to the compelling logic of Sherlock Holmes: "When you have eliminated the impossible (*in this case - a non-US government entity bringing in tons of explosives into WTC1/ WTC2/WTC7 without being caught*), whatever remains, however improbable, must be the truth."

That's it.

That is all it takes to establish beyond reasonable doubt that 9/11 was an "inside job."

There is no need to explain all the seemingly unexplainable events which happened on that day, nor is there any need to explain HOW what we know happened was actually organized and executed. When a crime is committed, the forensic experts can establish that, say a murder was committed with a knife before the police investigators establish who did it, why or how. Put it differently, the fact that the police cannot establish motive, means and opportunity or charge a suspect beyond reasonable doubt does not mean that no murder happened.

This is why the all the numerous members of the 9/11 Truth movement all agree on one key demand: a new, independent and free, investigation into the events of 9/11 (conversely, those who oppose such an investigation are accessories to a clear case of obstruction of justice!).

---

[464] http://www.wtc7.net/articles/FEMA/WTC_ch5.htm

What about the Pentagon?!

Here I need to caution any newcomers to the 9/11 Truth movement: the fact is that the 9/11 Truth movement is deeply divided on this issue. Many "truthers" are absolutely convinced that no plane ever hit the Pentagon, while many others are equally sure that only a plane could have caused the damage which was observed. The debate on this topic is so heated that both sides sometimes resort to exactly the same tactics as the other: dismissing eyewitnesses are "notorious unreliable" and accusing each other of being government plants, disinformation agents.

Let me candidly share my own view on this with you: I have seen many pictures of the damage on the Pentagon and I cannot imagine that an aircraft would simply vanish the way this one seemed to have vaporized itself. Not only that, but I think that a plane hitting a building at full speed would cause much more structural damage then what is actually seen on the photos. However, and this is a big however, I am not an expert on air crashes. Not only that, but the idea that whoever would have used three planes in New York would suddenly decide not to use one at the Pentagon makes no sense to me whatsoever. Nor do the "alternative" theories such as a cruise missile strike or a "bombing flyover" of the Pentagon by a mysteriously disappearing aircraft. On this issue I personally still remain a total "agnostic" and I am quite willing to be convinced either way.

I am aware of the fact that some 9/11 truthers are constantly warning the rest of us that there is a real risk that the US government is deliberately muddying up the waters around the Pentagon attack to commit as many truthers as possible to a "no-plane" theory only to better ridicule us all by eventually releasing an indisputable video showing a plane hitting the Pentagon (and we know that they have many such unreleased videos). I think that this warning should be taken very seriously by all.

But let's come back here to Occam's Razor. Here is how Wikipedia sums it up: "*When competing hypotheses are equal in other respects, the principle recommends selection of the hypothesis that introduces the fewest assumptions and postulates the fewest entities while still sufficiently answering the question.*"[465] In practical terms for the 9/11 Truth movement this translates into a fundamental principle: **we do not need to refer to whatever happened at the Pentagon to prove that 9/11 was in inside job**.

The official narrative (it does not even deserve to be called a "theory") so full of holes that even a fully empowered independent investigation would have a very hard time making sense of it all. There are literally dozens of issues which should be investigated: the damage to the Pentagon, of course, but also the real fate of United 93 (was it shot down?), the impossible phone calls made from the aircraft, the lack of debris in Shanksville, the close connections of the supposed hijackers to the CIA and FBI, the role of "high-fiving" Israelis and the so-called "Israeli students" spy network, the financing of the alleged hijackers by the Pakistani ISI (whose head was in DC on 9/11), etc.

These are all valid topics worthy of careful analysis, but they are not needed to establish that 9/11 was in inside job. The big news of 2009 was the publication by a group of prestigious scientists in the Open Chemical Physics Journal[466] of a peer-reviewed article entitled "Active Thermitic Material Discovered in Dust from the 9/11 World Trade Center Catastrophe"467 which established that the dust from the WTC buildings which was collected in NY is full of not only of residue of explosives, but even from unexploded materials (see also Jim Hoffman's paper "Explosives Found in World Trade Center Dust").[468] Not only had a "smoking gun" been found, a "loaded gun" had been found too. This was, of course, terrific news for the 9/11 Truth movement, a monumental

[465] https://en.wikipedia.org/wiki/Occam%27s_razor

[466] http://benthamopen.com/tocpj/home

[467] http://benthamopen.com/contents/pdf/TOCPJ/TOCPJ-2-7.pdf

[468] http://911research.wtc7.net/essays/thermite/explosive_residues.html

achievement for the scientists involved in the research and publication of this seminal paper. But establishing that explosives have now been found is not needed to make the case that 9/11 was in inside job.

Why is this so important? Because any discussion about HOW 9/11 was done can turn into a refutation of WHAT was done that day. For example, the explosives expert Ron Craig has regularly attacked Richard Gage with the following logical fallacy: since he—Ron Craig—would not have been able to bring down the WTC buildings with regular explosives without a number of phenomena which were not observed on 9/11 and since he—Ron Craig—knows of no other explosives which could have brought these buildings down the way they were seen to collapse, it follow therefore that explosives could not have been used and the cause of the collapse itself and all the phenomena seen and heard that day could only have been a gravity induced collapse. Ron Craig is basically saying this: "since I cannot explain it—it did not happen."

So here is what is so crucial: the 9/11 Truth movement should never accept to be placed in the position of having to explain what kind of explosives were used, how they were placed, how they were detonated, how they were brought into the buildings, or how they were manufactured. Our position should be crystal clear: we *know* that the buildings were brought down with explosives, we think that we have some solid evidence about at least some of explosives which were used, we even have a very good idea of how they might have been brought in, but none of that is central to our thesis that 9/11 was in inside job. What the 9/11 Truth movement needs to reply to the Ron Craigs out there is: we have proven that the buildings were brought down with explosives and since you claim to be an explosives expert we don't you find out how exactly this was done instead of denying the facts?!

The main point is this: the way those who are still 9/11 "agnostics" must focus their internal debate about what happened on 9/11 is exactly the same as those who have joined the ranks of the "truthers" must focus the debate when talking to sceptics: First, only stick to those few but crucial facts which are sufficient to prove that the WTC buildings were brought down by explosives as demonstrating this is enough to prove the fundamental thesis of the entire 9/11 Truth movement that 9/11 was an "inside job." Second—refer all other outstanding issues to a future independent 9/11 investigation. This way, we can transform each challenging question thrown at us into yet another reason for a new investigation.

This pretty much sums up the conclusions to which I have come. I am open to other opinions and to criticisms, and I am not in any way claiming that what I wrote above is THE truth about 9/11. It is simply an outline of where I am at this moment in time. My goal in writing all this is to "compare notes" with others in a similar situation and to encourage the doubting agnostics to take a second, hard, look at the facts. Lastly, my hope is that some newcomers (such as myself) might steer clear of some of the logical traps and pitfalls which are placed ahead of them by the proponents of the official narrative.

WHY AM I NOT HEARING THE ENDLESS RUMBLE OF JAWS DROPPING TO THE FLOOR?! (UPDATED!)

For those of you who have been regular readers of my blog it is no secret that after eight years of doubts and confusion I have finally come to the conclusion that 9/11 was an "inside job." I would refer those who are not aware of my fairly recent "conversion" to the "truther" camp and of the motives which caused it to my paper "*How I became a dedicated 9-11 Truther,*" which is actually a letter I wrote to a friend and it lays out why I strongly believe that there can be no doubt whatsoever about the fact that 9/11 was an "inside job." **Please do read it as I will write the rest of this post under the assumption that you have read my paper** [preceding chapter] where I substantiate and reference the following facts:

1) The US government and corporate media do not have any explanations about how the WTC1 and WTC2 fell. NIST simply did not investigate the events which followed the "initiation of collapse." In case you wonder what happened to the previously official version of the "pancaking" theory—NIST quietly dropped it. Let me repeat this once again. **THERE IS NO "OFFICIAL VERSION" FOR THE COLLAPSE OF WTC1 and WTC2.** None. Zilch. Nihil. Nuttin'. Niente. As in "absolutely no nothing." Got it?

You never heard about this?! I am not surprised. But it gets even better, watch this:

2) The US government admitted that WTC7 fell in free fall acceleration for 2.25 seconds. Why is that important? Simply because that means that a number of floors of WTC7 simply disappeared instantaneously and symmetrically from under the roof of WTC7. There is only one possible way to remove a section of a building instantaneously: by explosive power. Yes, the admission by Uncle Sam that the WTC7 feel for at least 2.25 seconds is an implicit admission that explosives were used. Let me

repeat this one too: **UNCLE SAM HAS DE FACTO ADMITTED THAT EXPLOSIVES WERE USED IN WTC7.**

Amazing, jaw-dropping stuff I would say, no? So why do I not hear the endless rumble of jaws hitting the floor all over the USA and the rest of the world? Maybe I should drive home the point even more forcefully? Ok, let me try this:

Since Uncle Sam has admitted that only explosives can explain what was observed on September 11th, Uncle Sam has also admitted that he is guilty of that crime. No outside agency, never mind some semi-mythical "al-Qaeda" could have had access to a super-secret building like WTC7. **Only Uncle Sam could have rigged that building to bring it down in a few seconds.**

I still do not hear the endless rumble of jaws hitting the floor all over the USA and the rest of the world ...

The "official narrative" (it's not even a theory) about 9/11 is so full of holes that one could easily write a 100 page-long paper analyzing all the impossibilities populating literally every aspect of it: from the exploded and non-exploded residue of thermitic material found in huge amounts in the WTC dust, to the impossible telephone calls allegedly made from the hijacked aircraft, to the non-existing plane wrecks in DC and Shanksville, to the absolutely amazing biographies of the putative hijackers all of whom seem to have been US government agents, to the role of Pakistan and Israel, to the ridiculous claims about recovered flight manuals, passports, letters, to the impossible flight profiles of the aircraft in DC and NY, etc.—none of it makes any sense at all. Every single one of these absolutely nonsensical parts of the official narrative deserves its own investigation and the good news is that it has already been done, very effectively, by the 9/11 Truth movement (my personal "9/11 electronic library" is currently at 22.6GB [!] of data, most of it high-quality research by very smart folks which have literally eviscerated all the absolute crap of the official narrative). Yet nobody seems to care.

Why?

In my training years I was taught that the process of intelligence revolves around three distinct phases, called the "three As": acquisition, analysis, acceptance.

The first one—acquisition—is all about collecting the data and that has been comprehensively done by thousands of folks since 9/11. The second one—analysis—centers on the careful analysis of the collected data, and I would say that the 9/11 Truth movement has also done a superb job in that respect too. Which leaves the last one—acceptance—which is the process by which the intelligence community brings its conclusions to the attention of the decision makers. It is in this final aspect that the 9/11 Truth movement has largely failed, at least so far: amazingly, even though the truth about 9/11 is out there, only a couple of computer mouse clicks away—*most people simply do not give a damn.*

Worse, those who do not consider themselves as "truthers" often reflect an amazing degree of bigotry and hostility. These are the folks who refer to "truthers" and their theories as "cooks," "garbage" and, my all-time favorite "conspiracy theories" (as if the official narrative is not one hell of an absurd conspiracy theory!). Why do these "skeptics" so naively accept an absolutely ridiculous official narrative and show such a vitriolic hostility toward those who dare question it?

David Ray Griffin wrote a brilliant open letter to the left-leaning wing of such "skeptics" entitled *Left-Leaning Despisers of the 9/11 Truth Movement: Do You Really Believe in Miracles?* Please do take the time to read it, it clearly shows that it is not the "truthers" who believe in miracles, but the so-called "skeptics." Griffin addressed his letter to left-leaning despisers, but he could have addressed it to the right-leaning despisers too—they are equally unwilling (or unable) to cope with the mind-boggling implications of the fact that 9/11 was beyond any doubt an inside job. Yes, the implications of this are truly appalling and, frankly, quite frightening and the aggressive reaction of the "despisers" is not so much a reflection of their careful analysis and subsequent rejection of the evidence as it is a reflection of their fear to take a hard look at reality. It is hard, if not impossible, to achieve "acceptance" when your audience is absolutely terrified by the implications of your analysis and conclusions.

The 9/11 Truth movement is composed of people who have all dared to think the unthinkable. Some from day one, some, like myself, from roughly day 3000, but who all eventually dared to plunge in the cold waters of facts and logic no matter where this might lead them.

In contrast, I find that most skeptics, in particular of the aggressive "despisers" variety are really what I call "*existential cowards*"—folks who choose delusion over the painful facts of reality.

There have been attempts by some in the 9/11 Truth movement to appeal to the common sense of the "despisers." One of my favorite ones is this video.[469]

Yet, one would have to admit that these efforts have not yielded the results one could have reasonably expected. If anything, the more evidence the 9/11 Truth movement produces, the most vociferous hostility it gets from the "despisers." So where do we go from here?

Social psychology has shown the many ways in which people can be led to believe the exact opposite of what their own eyes are showing them (check out, for example, the research known has the "Asch conformity experiments"[470]) or how figures of authority can elicit an amazing degree of obedience to "authority" (check out Milgram's work on obedience to authority[471]). Here I think of those who reject the evidence about 9/11 basically because Noam Chomsky or Ron Paul dismiss it.

We can, of course, find some solace in the words of Gandhi about how "*first they ignore you, then they laugh at you, then they fight you, then you win,*" but I would not hold my breath for a final "victory" any time

---

[469] WTC7 -- This is an Orange https://www.youtube.com/watch?v=Zv7BImVvEyk

[470] Asch conformity experiments https://en.wikipedia.org/wiki/Asch_conformity_experiments

[471] Milgram experiment https://en.wikipedia.org/wiki/Milgram_experiment

soon. Yes, there are some absolutely amazing people in the 9/11 Truth movement (the names of Richard Gage, Steven Jones and David Ray Griffin immediately come to my mind), but these are all specialists, our movement still lacks a unifying Gandhi who would have the authority to speak for all and loudly cry out "But he isn't wearing anything at all!"[472] when presented with the official myths and fairy tales about September 11th. Sooner or later such a person will appear, I believe, but in the meantime I say that we should just keep working on the already huge corpus of 9/11 research without expecting to ever hear the endless rumble of jaws dropping to the floor. Folks—it ain't coming and we might as well get used to this unpalatable fact.

Looking at how long it took my own jaw to drop (eight years!) I find some solace in the idea that we will be able to convince people, although not en masse, but one by one, one jaw at a time. That should be the objective—small steps in the right direction while remaining steadfastly unaffected by the never ending stream vitriol and scorn from the existential cowards who are freaked out by reality.

September 7, 2010

[472] The Emperor's New Clothes https://en.wikipedia.org/wiki/The_Emperor's_New_Clothes

SAKER'S "MAN OF THE YEAR 2013": THE SYRIAN SOLDIER

Yes, I know, this "man of the year" business is silly. But then, when I see the pathetic choices made for man of the year by the corporate media, I feel that if they can't even do a halfway decent job in that rather easy task, why should I not indulge myself and choose my own man, or woman, of the year. So anyway, here is my choice.

Runner up: Vladimir Putin

First, I thought of nominating Vladimir Putin. Pretty obvious, I would say. Not only did he stop the US in its planned attack on Syria, he thereby also prevented an almost inevitable domino effect of having Iran drawn in and then even possibly Russia. Throughout the Syrian war, Putin showed an ironclad consistency in upholding the rule of international law and demanding that a negotiated solution be found. If we consider that the US attack on Yugoslavia on behalf of the Kosovar guerrillas marked the official death of international law, the Russian move to stop the US attack just days before it occurred was, quite literally, the resurrection of international law. Just for that Putin deserves the Nobel Peace Prize while Obama should be stripped of his.

Putin also firmly resisted the Saudi offer of money in exchange for caving in on the Syrian problem, and even when Bandar threatened terrorist attacks on Sochi, Putin held firm. When Netanyahu showed up in Moscow with, basically, the same demands, Putin also warmly welcomed him, smiled a lot, and then sent him home empty handed.

Putin also did an absolutely stellar job of beating back the Anglo-Zionist propaganda machine: he did not yield on the homo lobby's campaign to organize a "pride parade" in Moscow, instead he actually got a law passed making the propaganda of homosexuality among minors a criminal offense. He did not yield in the infamous "Pussy Riot" case either—Amnesty International called these creatures "prisoners of conscience," but that did not prevent him from sticking them exactly where they belong: in the company of other petty criminals in a work camp. Nor did Putin yield even a millimeter to the liberal crowds who attempted to organize a color-coded coup similar to the one they later attempted on the Maidan square in Kiev. When Western oil interests dispatched Greenpeace's activist to try to stop Russia from exploring and exploiting its Arctic shelf, Putin showed that he did not intend to yield to that sort of pressure either, instead he made sure that Russia would develop the means and capabilities to defend its national interests on the North Pole. Last, but not least, he got two of his most formidable opponents (Berezovsky and Khodorkovsky) to plead for his mercy (the former was killed for doing so, the latter left Russia).

All of the above proved to the AngloZionists that Russia was no longer their colony and that Russia had recovered most, though not all, of its sovereignty. That is a huge achievement as for the first time since February 1917 a sovereign Russia reappeared on the world map.

And yet, I think that there is somebody which deserves even more praise and whom I will nominate my "man of the year 2013":

Saker's Man of the Year 2013: the Syrian soldier

Simply put—if it had not been for the amazing courage of the Syrian soldier Putin would not have had the opportunity to maintain his principled stance over Syria simply because Syria would have been run over by the Wahhabi liver-eaters and there would have been no more Syria to defend. Worse, the political and military "line of defense" would have been moved by to the Iranian border and across the Persian Gulf. As for Hezbollah, it would have been facing a much more dangerous environment stuck as it would have been between the Zionists on one hand and the medieval apes from the Gulf monarchies and their paid agents in Lebanon.

True, the Syrian military did get help from Iran and Hezbollah, and probably from Russia too, but that one remained mostly covert. Still, the Syrian soldier was literally the cornerstone of the entire Resistance in the

Middle East and if that Syrian soldier had been overcome or discouraged, the entire Resistance would have greatly suffered.

Of course, the Syrian soldier had to show courage to fight against the international coalition which brought together Western special forces officers and murderous Wahhabi thugs from all over the planet. But he also had to show a different kind of courage not to get discouraged with the so-called "friends of Syria" got together for that international meeting on how to crush Syria. It took a very special courage for the Syrian soldier not to get disgusted and bitter when he saw the wave of betrayals coming from all over the Muslim and Arab world, especially from the political prostitutes of Hamas and the rest of the Palestinian "intellectuals" who sided with Uncle Sam and his Empire. I can only imagine the anguish felt by the Syrian soldiers when they were told that Russia, Iran and Hezbollah would offer nothing more than words, while the West would offer money, guns and training to the insurgency. And yet the fighting spirit of the Syrian soldier did not break, even when some Syrian generals betrayed their fellow officers and defected to their Western handlers.

And yet, somehow, even those who truly want the Syrian people to be free seem to take for granted that the Syrian military would fight with no hesitation or doubts. Why? They are not robots. And I am quite sure that most of them are quite aware that the current Syrian regime is, shall we say, less than perfect and that the Syrian security services are not exactly beloved by the vast majority of the population. In the age of the Internet, I am quite confident that the vast majority of Syrian are fully aware of all the ugly aspects of the regime Bashar al-Assad inherited from his father. I guess they realize that he was simply not given the time to implement reforms he had been pondering as early as his years in the UK and they have forgiven him his clumsy handling of the earlier stages of the insurrection. Whatever may be the case, the Syrian soldiers have plenty of reasons to doubt and fear that they would be swiped away like Gaddafi's regime. And yet they stood firm, for two and a half long years and they held on long enough to finally see at least the general outline of a possible end to the conflict.

At the end of 2013 things definitely look better for Syria than in 2012 or 2011 and even though the Saudis are now clearly threatening a terrorist campaign, it is now possible to hope that 2014 will be a comparatively better year for the Syrian people.

Special distinction: Hassan Nasrallah

I have to mention another person who acted heroically in 2013: Hassan Nasrallah. At a time when the vast majority of the Muslim and Arab world had betrayed the Syrian people and basically sold out to the Anglos, Zionists and Wahhabis, Hassan Nasrallah took the very delicate decision to stand by the Syrian regime even though I am quite sure that he had little love for Assad or his brand of Baathism. Nasrallah also must have known how corrupt the Syrian regime was, that it was chock-full of CIA/MI6/Mossad/DGSE/etc. agents and simply corrupt officials, and yet he made the correct call, very early on, to stand by Syria and its less-than-perfect President. And when things got really tough, Hassan Nasrallah did send Hezbollah fighters to stand by the Syrian military even though that put him in a delicate political situation inside Lebanon. As for Hezbollah fighters, they performed as always—in an absolutely stellar way—and they play the crucial role of turning the tide of the entire war during the battle for al-Qusayr.

The main reason why I did not give the title of man of the year to Hassan Nasrallah is that he would be more deserving of the title of "man of the decade." Besides, think of it this way: in early 2011 who could have expected Hassan Nasrallah to act wisely and heroically? Everybody, of course. But who would have expected **the Syrian soldier** to show so much courage and fortitude? Not very many people, I think. What is sure is that Hassan Nasrallah remains one of the most popular leaders in the Middle East while very few people render homage to the Syrian soldier and this is why I decided to single him out as my (collective) "Man of the Year 2013."

What are your candidates?

December 25, 2013

THE 2014 "SAKER'S MAN OF THE YEAR": THE RUSSIAN SOLDIER

It's this time of the year again when the corporate media engages in the silly "man of the year" exercise and when I offer my own nominations just as a small sign of defiance toward the Imperial propaganda. Last year, I decided that the title of "Saker man of the year" should go to the Syrian solider[473] without whom neither Russia, nor Iran, nor Hezbollah would have been able to save Syria from the NATO-Wahhabi aggression. I also listed Vladimir Putin as a "runner up" and Sayyed Hassan Nasrallah as honored by a "special distinction." Looking back, I would say that these were very good nominations and I hope that this year I will get it right again. So here we go.

The 2014 Saker man of the year nomination goes to the masked Russian solider: the "Polite Men in Green" and the Novorossian Volunteer.

I decided that, if anybody, the Polite Man in Green deserved this honor because of the absolutely brilliant way he liberated Crimea and protected the Crimean people during the referendum while the Novorossian Volunteer deserved the distinction because of the no less brilliant way he defeated a much larger Ukrainian force.

The Polite Man in Green:

It is often forgotten that the Ukrainians had a very large force on the Crimean Peninsula composed of their best trained and equipped units. The operation to disarm them all with a minimum of violence was far from being risk free. Of course, the Ukrainians had no chance to prevail

[473] Saker's "man of the year 2013": the Syrian soldier http://thesaker.is/sakers-man-of-the-year-2013-the-syrian-soldier/

against the Russian Special Forces, but they sure had the manpower and resources to give them a very good fight. What prevented them from doing so what the lightning speed of the Russian operation as well as the overwhelming force clearly represented by a large number of fully equipped Spetsnaz operators. Simply put—the Ukrainians understood that they had no chance, none at all, against such a formidable enemy. The calm but very self-confident behavior of these Polite Man in Green psychologically crushed the Ukrainian will to resist.

But that is not why I wanted to honor these men. There are, after all, plenty of skilled soldiers worldwide. No, the main reason why I felt that these men deserved to be recognized is because they were truly liberators in the most noble sense of the world. The Anglo-Zionist Empire and the Nazi junta leader in Kiev had already decided that Crimea was theirs, the USN even had plans to build special facilities on the peninsula and they were all sure that there was nothing the locals could do about it, that they were irrelevant. The Polite Man in Green proved them wrong: they liberated them and gave them a chance to freely decide their future themselves, they gave them back a dignity which had been taken away from them by Nikita Khrushchev.

The Novorossian Volunteer

Here again I am honoring a collective "man," all those who did not wait for an order from above or for somebody else to do the right thing and who decided that I will not stand by and I will fight against the Nazi regime which is trying to oppress my people.

Unlike the Polite Man in Green, the Novorossian Volunteer had all the odds staked against him and even his hope that the Russian Federation would do for Novorossiya what she had done for Crimea was soon proven wrong: no Polite Man in Green were sent to Novorossiya (or **very few**). The Nazis had an overwhelming advantage in firepower, in armor, in artillery, in heavy weapons and they had a total control of the skies, yet—unlike the Ukrainian soldiers in Crimea—the Novorossian Volunteer did not let his will to resist be crushed, he fought on, very skillfully, and not only defeated his enemy but even launched a highly successful counter-offensive which was stopped on political grounds but which could have been sustained much further (though probably not as far as some believe it could have).

Together, the Polite Man in Green and the Novorossian Volunteer stand against the Empire and its Nazi allies just as the Syrian soldier stood against the Empire and his Wahhabi allies. All of them have proven, yet again, that the most powerful weapon in any conflict still remains the fighting spirit and the individual courage of the fighting man.

The runner up(s): Vladimir Putin and Xi Jinpin

For a second time I am going to choose Vladimir Putin as the runner up for "2014 Saker Man of the Year," but this time with Xi Jinpin. Together these two man have taken the unprecedented step for creating something much more complex than just a strategic alliance: they have decided to integrate their two nations in a symbiotic relationship which will truly turn them into a type of "Siamese twins" except that they will share most of their "vital organs" while keeping to separate "heads." Through a series of huge multi-billion contracts in such key areas as energy and defense (along many more comparatively smaller ones), the Russian and the Chinese leaders have basically decided to "marry" their two nations for a common future. Not only that, but by not following the US model of hegemonic and planetary full-spectrum dominance Russia and China are now offering a new model of international relations one in which multipolarity is actively sought, in which security is viewed as collective and in which the sovereignization, not subjugation, of the rest of the world promoted. Thanks to Vladimir Putin and Xi Jinpin, we will probably end up with a new world order, but most definitely not the one envisioned by Anglo-Zionist imperialists and for that I think that they most definitely deserved to be recognized.

Special distinction: Ramzan Kadyrov

For many years already Ramzan Kadyrov has been the driving force behind the Chechen miracle. Let's remember what Chechnya looked like in 2000: Grozny was in such ruins that many seriously advocated completely abandoning the city and relocating the capital of Chechnya elsewhere. All the Western "experts" predicted that the Chechen insurgency would never be defeated. Most importantly, it sure looked like Russians and Chechens hated each other with a dark and burning passion. Fifteen years later, Grozny has turned into a superb city, with the lowest crime rate in Russia, the Wahhabi insurgency has been comprehensively defeated, and traditional Sunni Islam is triumphant over Wahhabism which has been completely eradicated. As for the terrorist threat, it has become so low that when in the recent incident a group of Wahhabi terrorists penetrated deep inside Grozny the world found out that the city did not even have checkpoints or roadblocks because they had been removed by the authorities a long time ago.

Furthermore, Ramzan Kadyrov fully took on the role of "protector of the Russian people" not only politically, but by getting personally involved in the conflict in Novorossiya: many know that Chechen volunteers are fighting against the Nazi forces, but most people ignore that Chechnya is also accepting many Ukrainian refugees who are finding a safe heaven and, for many, a new home in the small republic.

And through this Ramzan Kadyrov arguably achieved his most amazing miracle: whereas by 2000 the Russian people hated and despised the Chechens whom they saw as vicious and evil enemies, nowadays Russian see Chechen as their most courageous and faithful allies. It is not an exaggeration to say that Ramzan Kadyrov has restored the honor of the Chechen people in a dramatically short period of time.

Needless to say, it is precisely for all these reasons that Kadyrov is absolutely hated by the Empire and its propaganda machine and Kadyrov is presented as a bloodthirsty thug. Truth be told, Kadyrov certainly did display some very thug-like behavior, especially in the past, but there is a lot more to the man than his natural swagger: he is a deeply principled, religious and patriotic leader who has shown in many difficult circumstances that he as fully inherited his father' wisdom and personal courage.

Now it is your turn. Who are **your** men/women of the year 2014?

December 23, 2014

THE EMPIRE'S WAR AGAINST THE SERBIAN NATION: LESSONS FOR THE RESISTANCE

Fifteen years ago the Anglo-Zionist Empire began the third phase of its war against the Serbian nation. It is important to take a few minutes to remember this war because the main purpose of this war was to show to the Russian people what could be done to them if they dared resist. Just as the US had bombed Nagasaki and Hiroshima primarily with the purpose of showing the Soviet Union what it could suffer, so did the AngloZionists bomb the Serbian people living in Croatia, Bosnia, Kosovo, Macedonia and Serbia primarily to send a "message" to the Russian people: if you resist—you are next. Besides a massive bombing and cruise missile strikes campaign, the Empire also unleashed the biggest propaganda campaign in history, presenting the Serbs as vicious, crazed, nationalist and sadistic mass murderers and all of their enemies as progressive, freedom-loving, democratic and heroic civilians who only had light weapons to resist the massive onslaught of Serbian heavy weapons. The narrative then further hyped the vilification by speaking of Serbian "concentration camps" and massive "ethnic cleansing" campaigns which included "rape as a weapon of war." Finally, and logically, the AngloZionists concluded that Milosevic was the "new Hitler" and that the Serbs were actually engaging in genocide.

At the time, practically everybody bought that narrative. There were a few exceptions here and there—the independent journalist Michel Collon[474] in Belgium deserves a special mention here with his book *Me-*

[474] Michel Collon https://en.wikipedia.org/wiki/Michel_Collon

diaMensonges[475] written as early as 1994—but by and large the Empire's campaign of "strategic psyops" was a stunning success.

I will return to the topic of this war on a regular basis because a lot of things still must be re-visited and re-explained, especially now that the Muslim world has found itself on the receiving end of exactly the same forces doing exactly the same thing in Libya and Syria. But for the time being, I just want to share an email exchange I had with one upset reader to whom my reply could serve as a useful starting point to begin to set the record straight.

Here is the email which I got last week:

> Dear Saker,
>
> Let me first congratulate you on excellent articles and commentaries on your site. I enjoy reading them, and agree with them.
>
> But, of course, there is one thing that bothers me in your writings, your obsession with "suffering" of Serbia and Serbs. Even in today's article you mentioned 78 days of "suffering" of Serbia. If you really needed good example of suffering from Balkans couldn't you use Siege of Sarajevo which lasted from 5 April 1992 to 29 February 1996, longer then Siege of Stalingrad, and guess who kept Sarajevo under the siege, yes your dear Serbian fascists.
>
> Few pictures[476] ...
>
> Enemy of my enemy does not have to be my friend, and a lot of progressive writers lose some of their credibility by portraying Serbs under Milosevic as another victim of US imperialism, they are the same shitty Nazis like those who are ruling Ukraine these days. They came in power by coup, they pushed

---

[475] Attention medias! Les mediamensonges du golfe-manuel anti-manipulation de Michel Collon http://www.amazon.fr/Attention-medias-mediamensonges-golfe-manuel-anti-manipulation/dp/2872620877/

[476] Google images https://www.google.ca/search?q=siege+of+sarajevo&client=ubuntu&hs=kzk&channel=fs&tbm=isch&tbo=u&source=univ&sa=X&ei=zIEsU-aLKYOsyAGOmoGAAg&ved=0CEUQ7Ak&biw=1458&bih=774&dpr=1

> other nations from Yugoslavia, they committed worst crimes during wars in ex-YU mostly in Bosnia, but also in Croatia and Kosovo!
>
> Best,
>
> Anonymous
>
> P.S. I was born and lived for 31 years in Sarajevo until Serbs forced me to leave in 1991.

Here is the text of my reply: (slightly corrected)

Dear Anonymous,

Thanks for your email. I have to honestly tell you that while I sympathize with your plight as I would do for the plight of any person suffering the consequences of civil war, I find your arguments wholly unconvincing. First and foremost, you have to ask yourself basic questions:

1) Who of the Croats, Bosnian Muslims or Serbs unleashed the devil of nationalism and who stood for a multi-ethnic and multi-cultural society? (Answer: Croats and Bosnian Muslims)

3) Which was the party which decided to use a symbol clearly associated with a Bandera-like regime? (Answer: the Croats with their checkerboard)

3) Whose side got the support of the so-called international community and even the USAF to bomb on their behalf? (Answer: Croats and Bosnian Muslims)

4) Which side did exactly what the Ukies do today and said: "we can secede from you, but you cannot secede from us"? (Answer: Croats and Bosnian Muslims)

5) Which side even got the al-Qaeda types to support them with money, guns and Wahhabi crazies? (Answer: Bosnian Muslims)

6) Which side used to hide inside United Nations Protected Areas (UNPAs) or UN safe havens and conduct attacks from there? (Answer: Croats and Bosnian Muslims)

7) Which side was backstabbed by its own people? (Answer: Bosnian Serbs whom Milosevic slapped with an embargo)

8) Which side had the most displaced persons/refugees? (Serbs from Croatia, Bosnia and Kosovo)

9) Which side organized false flag massacres (Markale I and II, Racak) to trigger intervention? (Answer: Bosnian Muslims)

10) Which side had to give up its so-called "heavy weapons" before the US and Croat forces attacked them? (Answer: Krajina-Serbs)

11) Which side turned a formerly progressive and liberal society into an obscurantist and intolerant one as portrayed in the Bosnian movie "Luna's choice"? (Answer: Bosnian Muslims)

12) Which side had the full 100% support of the US propaganda machine and the NWO media? (Answer: Croats and Bosnian Muslims)

13)Which side produced the worst collaborators with Hitler? (Answer: Croats and Bosnian Muslims)

14) Which side produced the strongest resistance against the Nazis? (Answer: Serbs with Tito and Mikhailovich)

15) Which side managed to get the support of BOTH the various Jewish lobbies AND of the Vatican? (answer: the Croats)

16) Which side benefited from nightly delivery of weapons from NATO and Turkey? (Answer: the Bosnian Muslims)

17) Which side first signed a peace agreement and then reneged on it? (Answer: the Bosnian Muslims)

18) Which side had crimes committed against it never punished by the Hague Tribunal? (Answer: the Serbs)

Also—let me tell you a little something about myself. I used to do military analysis for, among other assignments, the United Nations and I followed the wars in Croatia and Bosnia on a day-to-day basis, and not the public stuff, but classified UN Protection Force (UNPROFOR) reports. I also personally interviewed **many** UNPROFOR officers including UNPROFOR Force commanders. So, believe me, I know what did or did not happen in Bosnia, Croatia and, Kosovo. Yes, there were crazy Serbian nationalists and murderers who committed atrocities, no doubt here at all, but no more and no less then what the Croats or the Bosnian Muslims did. Second, I make a HUGE difference between Milosevic (both an ex-banker AND an ex-communist) and the Bosnian Serb people, including Karadzic and his aides. Milosevic was the scum of the earth, a fake nationalist, fake communist, and real capitalist SOB who betrayed his people at least twice (when he slapped sanctions against the Bosnian Serbs and when he betrayed the Kosovo Serbs), but Federal Forces in Bosnia committed the least atrocities and massacres and some Serbian paramilitary units—like the one of Capitan Dragan—had an excellent record on human rights. So to portray the Serbs as Nazis the way you do is simply not honest and, in the case of a person like me, futile—because I know what was going on behind the propaganda veil.

As for the leaders of the so-called "good guys" a lot of them were scum and professional liars (Tudjman, Silajdzic) or maniacs (Itzebegovich). Yes, Milosevic was a piece of shit too, but no worse than these guys.

Your vision is simple: bad Serbs, good Croats and/or good Bosnian Muslims. That is utter nonsense. Like in any other country, in all the ethnic/religious groups of the former Yugoslavia you had a majority of decent but passive people, a certain percentage of sick and evil folks who like to do evil, and a small group of heroes who kept their decency in the middle of the horror around them. And 90% of people did NOT want a way, much less so a civil one. And today, most people in Bosnia understand that they have been used by the US Empire and regret the civilized society and country which they lost. I think that if somebody did a public opinion survey in Bosnia and asked the people: "When you see the outcome today do you think that it worth triggering a civil war at the time?" the vast majority would answer "no." Well, that civil war was not started by the Serbs.

So, please, don't come tell me how bad the other guy is. Look at what "your" people did to "themselves" and try to learn something from it.

Kind regards,
The Saker

I did not get a reply, nor was I expecting one (though I do expect today's post to trigger an avalanche of outraged comments). The crisis in the Ukraine is far from over and there are other events to which I would like to turn to—like the absolutely barbaric condemnation to death of 528 members of the Muslim Brotherhood in Egypt.[477] The situation in Syria also deserves much more coverage then the zero-coverage I have been giving it since the crisis began in the Ukraine. Alas, I simply do not have to time to reply to all the comments and emails I get every day, never mind providing a focused coverage on several "fronts" so I always pick the one which appears to most important to me. All this is to explain that I will not be able to reply, especially in detail, to what I expect to be quite a few irate comments to this post. I sincerely apologize for that, but I promise to come back to this topic as soon as things cool down elsewhere.

For one thing, I consider it my moral obligation to address my many Muslim readers with a plea to "connect the dots" and realize that they have been lied to not only about Chechnya, but also about Croatia, Bosnia and Kosovo. I know that some of them have been reading this blogs for years and they know my views on nationalism, religion and Islam and that I really do try to live by Malcolm X's motto "I am for truth, no matter who tells it." The Empire's propaganda machine tried hard in presenting the wars in Chechnya and in the former Yugoslavia as a war of Orthodox Christians against Islam. Sadly, this propaganda campaign was nothing short of a total triumph, especially among Muslims. So today I want to submit to you all, but especially to my Muslim readers, the following exchange with a first-rate Muslim scholar and academic to whom I had written to express my enthusiasm for his book and my issue with

[477] Egypt court sentences 528 Morsi supporters to death http://www.bbc.com/news/world-middle-east-26712124

only once sentence in it. (I am not going to reveal the name of this person out of respect for him, especially since he is going through a great deal of suffering right now). Here is what I wrote:

Dear Sir,

My name is xxxxxx xxxxxxx and I am writing to you for two reasons. First, to express my gratitude for your most interesting essay on Wahhabism which was recommended to me by a Muslim friend as "the best book on Wahhabism." I can only agree wholeheartedly. At the end of the book though, one sentence immensely disappointed me and made me decide to write directly to you.

On page 68 you wrote that the US global war on terror was "waged in concert with allies such as Russia, its hands bloodied with the Muslims of Chechnya." I take issue with literally every letter of that sentence.

1) First, we now know from the testimony of Sibel Edmonds that not only did the USA not help Russia but, quite to the contrary, the USA fully supported the Chechen insurgency.

2) You make it sound like the wars in Chechnya were wars opposing Russians and Chechens. This is also patently false. There never was a united "Chechen side," not in 1995 and, even less so, in 1999. In fact, I would credit the Chechens of Akhmad and Ramzan Kadyrov with killing at least as many insurgents as the Federal Forces did.

3) You also make it sound like the wars in Chechnya were wars opposing Muslims and, by implication, non-Muslims. This is also patently false. Not only was there always a Chechen opposition to the insurgency, but there were plenty of non-Chechen Muslims in the Federal Forces, especially so during the 2nd Chechen War which, after all, began with a Chechen attempt to invade Dagestan where Muslim Dagestanis fought to their death to stop this invasion.

4) Now let's take the issue of whose hands were bloodied with Muslim blood. Do you really not know of the constant violence which was meted out by the government of the independent "Ichkeria" against its own citizens? Of all people, you should know best how Wahhabis treat non-

Wahhabi Muslims! Do you really believe that when the Wahhabis got to power in Chechnya they treated the local Muslims any better than what they have always done everywhere in the past and which your book so well explains? Why is it that when (putatively) non-Muslim Federal Forces kill Muslims this deserves a special mention whereas when (putatively) "Muslims" such as the Wahhabis kill (real) Muslims this gets no mention.

Now, you wrote the book in 2002 and you can be excused for not having guessed at that time what Chechnya would look like a decade later. I will honestly admit that I also could not have imagined that. Still, I think that now that we see the kind of butchery the Wahhabis are yet again engaged in in Syria, and following the disgraceful events which happened in Syria, you might want to ask yourself who the "good guys" and who the "bad guys" really were in Chechnya. I submit to you that what Putin and Kadyrov did is save the Chechen people from the horrors of Wahhabism and that this is exactly the situation Assad in now facing in Syria. The only difference is that Putin was always represented by the (US-funded) Muslim propaganda as some kind of bloodthirsty monster and Kadyrov as his "puppet."

In conclusion I want to express to you my deep disappointment that a person with your phenomenal culture and knowledge would fall for the "wrong or right—my Ummah" reflex. According to you, the Muslims in Bosnia, in Kosovo and in Chechnya were each time the "good guys" and the victims. As a specialist of the war in Bosnia I can assure you that this is false. The sad and admittedly embarrassing reality is that in all three of these wars the Muslims were used by the US as a tool for its imperial designs, just like the "Mujahedeen" had been in Afghanistan a few decades earlier. In Kosovo, the native Serbian population was ethnically cleansed, replaced by a regime of gangsters and mafia dons, the USA opened its huge "Camp Bondsteel" at the cost of a barbaric bombing of the entire civilian population of Serbia and Montenegro and now Kosovo is a criminal black hole. Is it not a disgrace for the Muslim world that it blindly sided with the Kosovar drug lords?

Sir, I see Wahhabism as a huge danger for the entire planet. As long as it was a small crazy sect in the sands of Arabia it was ugly and bloodthirsty, but it was limited. But as soon as the (always "brilliant") US CIA cooked up the plan to federate various neo-Wahhabi movement into one worldwide movement, which later became known as al-Qaeda, Wahhabism became a danger to us all, but first and foremost to Muslims and, among Muslims, first and foremost for the two forms of Islam the Wahhabis hate the most: the Shia and the Sufi. Now this is my key point here: non-Wahhabi Muslims need all the allies they can get to deal with this nightmare (just look at the situation in Syria as a proof of this). This, however means, that as long as even the most educated Muslims will instinctively stick to a "wrong or right—my Ummah" reflex you will deny yourself these allies.

Critics of the US and EU policies point at the logical absurdity of using military forces to destroy Wahhabis in Mali while at the same time arming the same forces in Syria. I agree, this makes no sense. But what of the mainstream Muslim stance of supporting Wahhabis in Chechnya or Bosnia while opposing them in Syria or Egypt? How is that less absurd?

In which country today do we see truly large numbers of Sunni Muslims live with the state protecting them from the Wahhabis? In which country does the state have as its declared and official policy to support and defend traditional Sunni Islam against Wahhabism? Which country has for the past two years played a key role in not letting the Wahhabis over-run Syria? Finally, which is the ONLY major country to have ALWAYS opposed Wahhabism, everywhere and at all times, regardless of the pretexts for war?

Russia, of course. The very same Russia you accuse of having Muslim blood on its hands.

This is factually wrong and this is morally wrong too. Finally, it is self-defeating and country-productive as it offends Russians like myself who refuse the Western canard that "all Muslims" are a threat to "our" civilization and that there is a clash of civilization happening.

I, Sir, believe that what Russia did in Chechnya was not "killing Muslims," at least **not** deliberately or because of their Islam, but killing many truly evil Wahhabi thugs and this is why so many Chechen commanders changed sides and are now deeply grateful to Putin. Putin did not try to shed Muslim blood any more than Assad tries nowadays in Syria. When faced with a violent, vicious, bloodthirsty and aggressive insurgency fully paid for by the Gulf states and supported politically by the USA Putin and Assad simply did the only thing which could save their country, including its Muslim population: they ruthlessly pursued and physically destroyed the Wahhabi-run insurgency. I submit to you that all non-Wahhabi Muslims owe them a great debt of gratitude.

Thank you for taking the time to read this letter and thank you again for an outstanding book.

Kind regards,

xxxxxx xxxxxxx

(Florida)

This is the reply I got:

> Dear Mr. xxxxxxx,
>
> There is much that I could say in response to your comments, but I have decided not to expend the effort. After all, you describe yourself as "a specialist of the war in Bosnia." I don't know what your credentials are in this respect. Having visited Bosnia both before and after the genocidal war waged against the Muslims, talked with the survivors and bereaved of Srebrenica, seen the soccer fields of Sarajevo turned into cemeteries, prayed in the ruins of mosques destroyed by your fellow Slavs, seen the remnants of the burnt manuscripts of the Orientalni Institut, talked to some of the women raped by the Serbs ... I find your assurance that it is false to regard the Muslims as the "good guys" and the victims quite simply repulsive. As for Kosova, yes there are gangsters there (as there are in your much cherished Serbia), and I can appreciate the

> fact that Russian mobsters will not welcome the competition. In Chechnya, yes, much of the opposition is Wahhabi-oriented, and the North Caucasus has not produced anyone even remotely comparable to Imam Shamyl of blessed memory, but does this justify the destruction of Grozny, the staged bombings used by Putin to justify the Second Chechen War, or the numerous crimes reported by journalists such as Politkovskaya whom the Kremlin found it necessary to assassinate?
>
> Your notion of a diabolical US-Wahhabi alliance against Muslims is at the very best curious. As for Russia being the protector of Muslims to whom a debt of gratitude is owed, are you try to make me laugh?
>
> You are disappointed that I have fallen prey to the "wrong or right—my Ummah" reflex. Plainly what you are suffering from is an advanced case of Pan-Slavism.
>
> I have already written more than I intended. This correspondence is now at an end.

At this point on, I knew that it was futile to try continue a discussion with my correspondent did not want to have, so my reply was short:

Dear Sir,

Though I am disappointed by the lack of substance in it, I thank you for your reply.

And, Sir, "all" the inhabitants of Bosnia are Slavs, including Muslims. As for Pan-Slavism, that silly idea died roughly 200 years ago.

Kind regards and all the best,

xxxxxx xxxxxxx

My hope in publishing these exchanges today is to at least set the stage for future discussions, especially with my Muslim readers, about these wars. Why? Because as long as the AngloZionists can divide us they will also rule over us. In France, for example, the Zionist lobby is making truly immense efforts to set the French Muslims against the French Latin Christians because they know that as long as these two groups fight against each other, they themselves will be safe and in control. The

French author Alain Soral says that what is taking place is a war between the "Old Testament" world (Judaism and Protestantism) against the "New Testament" world (Latin and Orthodox Christianity) and that the key strategy used by the Empire is to set Christians against Muslims. As you probably know, I have a big problem with the notion that Latin and Orthodox Christianity are on the same side, today's events in the Ukraine only prove the opposite, but this is irrelevant here: Soral's religious education is, frankly, sub-minimal (he considers himself a non-believing "cultural Catholic"), but his political acumen is world-class and what he says about France is absolutely true: the plutocratic elites are now in a complete panic because they see that the "stem French" (local, Latin Christian French) against the "branch French" (first or second generation Muslim immigrant) are joining forces against the Zionist domination of France and that this alliance has a huge potential.

Likewise, in Russia, we now see that the strongest and most determined defenders of Russia are the Chechen people (speaking of which: Chechen President Ramzan Kadyrov has declared that just as his special forces have killed Doku Umarov, they will hunt down and catch Dmitri Iarosh, "dead or alive—either way is fine by me" said Kadyrov). As for the Resistance on a global scale, we see today that it is led by Russia (Orthodox, Muslim) then China (Confucianist, Taoist, Buddhist), Iran (Muslim), Syria (Muslim, Christian) and Hezbollah (Muslim). The Empire, of course, tried hard to set Russia against Islam (Chechnya: failed), China against Russia (failed), Islam against Orthodox Christianity (Bosnia, Kosovo: success), Islam against China (in progress), Sunni against Shia (Syria: in progress), Christian against Shia (Lebanon: in progress), Islam against Latin Christianity (France: failed), Sunni against Shia (Iraq: success), Sunni against Shia (Iran: failed), Sunni against Shia (Bahrain: success), Muslim against Christian (Indonesia: in progress), Muslim against Christian (Mali, Sudan: success), etc.

This list is incomplete—but I think the point I want to make is clear: **the Empire has had a stunning success in using Muslims literally as**

cannon fodder to fight against its enemies. It is, I submit, therefore absolutely vital for Muslims worldwide to realize this and to refuse to be further lied to. The real enemy of Islam is exactly the same as the real enemy of Christianity: the Anglo-Zionist Empire. Sayyid Qutb[478] did see the real nature of the Empire, as did Malcom X. The real heir of their thought today are not al-Qardawi[479] and degenerate rulers of Saudi Arabia, but people like Sheikh Imran Hussein, Ramzan Kadyrov and Hassan Nasrallah (whose Hezbollah **party** includes only Muslims, but whose **military resistance** includes Christians).

What happened to the Serbian people is a grotesque injustice and nothing short of an abomination. It was also the precursor of what happened to the people of Libya and Syria and the Serbian people, now more than ever, have a moral right to have the truth finally be said about their plight. Furthermore, those of us who are determined to resist the Empire need to learn from our mistakes, if only to avoid repeating them in the future. This is the purpose of this post today and I hope that it will be understood by those who will read it.

March 24, 2014

---

[478] Sayyid Qutb https://en.wikipedia.org/wiki/Sayyid_Qutb

[479] Yusuf al-Qaradawi https://en.wikipedia.org/wiki/Yusuf_al-Qaradawi

US FABRICATED EXCUSES FOR MILITARY INTERVENTION FROM MARKALE TO GHOUTA?

One of the labels which I have been using more and more recently is the *"Bosnia v5 Chechnya v4 Kosovo v3 Libya v2 Syria v1"* which refers to the fact that the Empire uses exactly the same trick over and over again to justify its military aggressions.

Though history is replete with false flag attacks, the end of the Cold War saw a systematization of a specific **complex of measures** designed to give a sophisticated illusion of an undeniable fact. Here is how this works: I will present a theoretical model and one example.

First, a high-visibility target is identified. During the war in Bosnia, the most "visible" location was the city of Sarajevo, and the most "visible" location inside Sarajevo was the Markale market. By "visible" I, of course, mean "visible to the media."

Second, a specific moment is chosen for the attack. It can be right before or after a crucial negotiation, it can be made to coincide with an election, it can be matched to a religious or secular holiday or whatever other optimal moment in time is preferred. In Bosnia the first "Markale market massacre" was intended to justify the use of NATO airpower against Bosnian-Serb artillery position while the second Markale market massacre was intended to justify a second wave of airstrikes against Bosnian-Serb forces.

Third, the actual false flag attack is conducted with the triple aim of having a maximum amount of killed civilians, to secure the maximal amount of media coverage and to coincide with the exact moment when the forces needed for the military intervention are ready. The need for this maximization of casualties and coverage is explained by the fact that enough military specialists on the ground will inevitably have the expertise to see through the false flag and try to challenge the official version.

In Bosnia, the official narrative about the Bosnian-Serb responsibility was almost immediately challenged by no less than the UNPROFOR Commander Sir Michael Rose (for the first massacre) and by the UNPORFOR Sarajevo Intelligence Chief Colonel Andrei Demurenko (for the second massacre). And, just in case anybody has doubts about this, I would note here that the International Criminal Tribunal for the former Yugoslavia has had to acquit the Bosnian-Serbs initially charged with the crime.

Finally, even if the accusation is absolutely ridiculous (like Gaddafi giving Viagra to his soldiers to rape Libyan woman), the vast majority of Western politicians will go along with it just to avoid appearing not "strong" enough "on" whatever entity dares to resist the Empire.

As for those who actually conducted the attack, all they need is "plausible deniability" (a CIA-coined expression meaning that it is possible that the US was not behind the attack). I would even say that all the Empire needs is "short-term plausible deniability" just because even if with time the false flag nature of the attack is proven beyond reasonable doubt, nobody cares.

Think of 9/11. By now the fact that the destruction of WTC1, WTC2 and WTC7 was caused by controlled demolition has been proven beyond any reasonable doubt.[480] I would even argue that the US government has implicitly admitted to this through its NIST report on WTC1 and WTC2 and almost explicitly admitted that through its report on WTC7. So what? Does anybody even care by now? Of course not.

Most of the imperial false flag operations have been debunked, in most cases rather rapidly. But in a world ruled by political expediency and, let's be honest, an almost total indifference to the very concept of "truth," that kind of debunking, while historically important, is operationally easy to ignore. "We lied? So what? Whatcha gonna do about it."

---

[480] Why am I not hearing the endless rumble of jaws dropping to the floor?! (UPDATED!) http://thesaker.is/why-am-i-not-hearing-the-endless-rumble-of-jaws-dropping-to-the-floor-updated/

After Saddam's non-existing WMD the very notion that being caught lying is a problem has vanished. Now the imperial politicians can lie all they want, with no consequences for that at all.

Which brings me to so-called "Ghouta" chemical attacks.

Key imperial politicians, Fabius in France, but also UK and Sweden and others, have already stated that this was an attack by Syrian forces. They were in such a hurry to apportion blame that they could not even wait for any investigation. They just "knew"! Fabius even said that the guilty party should be punished by "force," but something tells me that he did not mean bombing the insurgents should the UN report blame them. Besides, France is "already" bombing al-Qaeda in Mali, how could it possibly do the same thing in Syria were al-Qaeda are the "good guys"?

According to the Anglo media, the US is preparing for cruise missile strikes.

Now, to understand what that really means, one has to understand what cruise missiles stand for in the collective psyche of the US Democrats: Democrats use cruise missiles not only to destroy a target, but also to simply "appear strong" and get the Republicans off their backs. I am thus quite sure that even if the White House fully understands that the Syrian military did not use chemicals two days after the arrival of the UN investigation team (if only because the attack might have been organized by the CIA), this will not at all prevent Obama from launching a series of cruise missile strikes just to appear strong, macho, with hair on his chest. It will be easy to tell, by the way:

If the White House launches a sustained cruise missile strike campaign of at least 5 days, with each round of damage assessment followed by repeat attacks—then they are trying to intervene militarily on the side of the insurgency and tip the balance on the ground.

If the White House launches a one-time series of cruise missile strikes lasting 24 or less, and then declares victory and stops, then it's just a way to deal with the crazy Republicans and neocons who always want blood, blood and more blood.

Finally, if the White House orders no strikes at all, then this means that this false flag operation was not a US or NATO one, but an "independent" effort of Wahhabi crazies, probably with Saudi or Qatari complicity.

We shall know very soon.

August 24, 2013

A FEW BASIC REMINDERS ABOUT WARS, CIVIL WARS AND HUMAN RIGHTS

Robert recently posted the following comment on this blog:

> Manicheanism tends to take over with civil wars. Both sides tend to believe all that is good is with them and all that is evil with the other and this usually leads to fiendish atrocities on both sides. The media often then gives selective reporting of atrocities by the side they favor. In a war with a foreign enemy you can respect the other guy because he's fighting for his country but in a civil war you are fighting an enemy within and it becomes bitter and cruel because each side regards the other as traitors who are destroying the country.

I think that he is absolutely right and I feel that I want to add a few observations of my own to this words. But first, let me remind everybody of a little-known fact: according to the fundamental positions of the Nuremberg Tribunal the worst crime possible is not genocide or any other crime against humanity. The worst possible crime is the crime of "aggression" because, according to the experts who set up the Nuremberg Tribunal, the crime of aggression "contains" all the other crimes (by the way, the International Criminal Court takes the same position). In the words of the chief American prosecutor at Nuremberg,[481] Robert H. Jackson,

> To initiate a war of aggression, therefore, is not only an international crime; it is the supreme international crime differing only from other war crimes in that it contains within itself the accumulated evil of the whole.

[481] Opening Statement before the International Military Tribunal https://www.roberthjackson.org/collection/speeches/

I think that this is an absolutely crucial insight and it is a bittersweet irony that it came from a scholar from the USA which is, beyond any possible doubt, the nation which waged the most wars of aggression of any nation in mankind's history.

I submit that this argument is also very much applicable to civil wars because civil wars are, by their very nature and inherently, far more vicious and prone to result in atrocities than conventional international conflicts. I can only repeat Robert's words:

> In a war with a foreign enemy you can respect the other guy because he's fighting for his country but in a civil war you are fighting an enemy within and it becomes bitter and cruel because each side regards the other as traitors who are destroying the country.

The Western propaganda machine has done its best to bolt out this idea for the public consciousness and discourse. Why? Because of all this "humanitarian intervention" nonsense. The Western recipe for war is really extremely simple:

Find out whatever issue is upsetting a sizable minority of the public, then support that agenda and foster demonstrations. When these demonstrations happen, make sure that a few cops and demonstrators get killed. The more violence the better. Then encourage an armed insurrection by the opposition and as soon as the government forces use force to crack down on the (now armed) opposition, scream to high heavens about "human rights violations," atrocities, etc. Then, all you have left to do is intervene, either indirectly or even directly.

Simple, no?

And the best part of this tactic is that while a few atrocities might be false flags, or exaggerations, or even complete fabrications, the real atrocities will "INEVITABLY" begin to happen. All you need to do is to grossly inflate the atrocities of the government forces and minimize or even better, totally ignore, the atrocities of the opposition. Now, how hard is that when the entire corporate press is completely under your control? Very easy, really!

This is what happened in Iraq, in Romania, in Bosnia, in Kosovo, in Chechnya, in Libya and now in Syria. This is also what is possibly going to take place very soon in Iran.

Indeed, according to Russian sources, the MEK are preparing for a series of terrorist attacks in Tehran and other major cities during the upcoming elections. While the "Gucci Revolution" of Mr. Mousavi and his patron and boss Rafsanjani lacked the needed level of violence (this is why the Basij and cops were plenty enough to contain it), the upcoming terrorist attacks will have as a goal to force the government to use the Pasdaran to impose law and order. At that point, it will be easy to whine and yell about all sorts of atrocities and horrors (whether real or imaginary).

There is another idea which the Western propaganda machine is trying to remove from the public consciousness and discourse. Simply put, this is my thesis: **in a pre-civil war or civil war situation the government side has NO interest in committing atrocities whereas the opposition/insurgency has a HUGE interest in generating atrocities**.

No, I am not saying that Ceausescu, Saddam Hussein, Milosevic, Gaddafi or Assad are tender-hearted doves who would weep over every innocent killed or that they are highly principled men of honor whose ethics and morals which would never allow them to commit an evil act. Nope. In fact, all these were ruthless individuals, with a sense of compassion and mercy as developed as the one of a blue-green algae. The point is that they all perfectly understood that any atrocities committed their watch would be disastrous for them.

You want an example?

Take Ratko Mladic. The so-called "butcher Srebrenica" and "genocidal war criminal." What did he do the day his forces entered Srebrenica? He drove to Srebrenica and addressed the surviving civilians and prisoners of war while on camera and surrounded by the press crops, and then *he personally guaranteed their safety.* Now, ask yourself a basic question: no matter how evil you think Mladic was, do you really believe that he would show up in person and deliver such a message right in front of numerous cameras if he had any intention of massacring anybody? Of course not! He would have made darn sure to be as far away as possible to generate what the CIA calls "plausible deniability." And then, let's look just one step further: at the time of the so-called "Srebrenica genocide" who was winning the war and who was losing it? The fact is that by 1995 the Bosnian-Serbs had comprehensively won the civil war. In this context, does anybody seriously believe that killed a large number of Bosnian Muslims was in their interest?

Of course not. So this is why the corporate press inevitably describes these people as "beasts" "monsters" "bloodthirsty Chetniks"[482] or equally "bloodthirsty Shabiha."[483] The idea here is not only to demonize, but to explain away seemingly illogical acts by suggesting that these people are such bloodthirsty monsters that they are unable to rationally assess their situation and that they are compelled to torture and murder just because of their bestial and maniacal nature. This, of course, is utter nonsense. Why?

Because while it is true that in any country, ethnic group or religion you will find a percentage X of people who will gladly indulge in horrors, massacres and other unspeakable atrocities, these people are very rarely in command positions and, when they are, then they still do not lose sight of their own self-interests. There is a reason why Lenin, Hitler, Churchill and all the American Presidents liked to kiss small children: it is to appear kind and decent. Even when they are genocidal maniacs, they engage in this kind of behavior only when they feel that it will give them a tangible advantage, not just because they like to torture or kill.

---

[482] Chetniks https://en.wikipedia.org/wiki/Chetniks

[483] Shabiha https://en.wikipedia.org/wiki/Shabiha

Notice that in Syria, Assad has just re-subordinated the Shabiha to the regular armed forces precisely to try to stop them from committing atrocities. This, by the way, exactly what Karadzic and Mladic were trying to do with Serbian irregulars in Bosnia, but now all this is down the memory hole ...

Bottom line: civil wars truly bring out the worst in people, and they provide an ideal environment for the small number of real bloodthirsty maniacs to indulge in atrocities. And this is why I submit that **the crime of initiating a civil war is even a worse crime than the crime of international aggression**.

This still leaves an important question: can there be norms of behavior in civil wars or do we simply have to accept that any civil war will inevitably result in a completely uninhibited orgy of unspeakable horrors for which nobody should be answerable?

Here I can only offer my subjective opinion, and I freely admit that I cannot prove my point. I want to share it with you only as a basis for discussion:

I believe that the killing of civilians in modern wars, both civil and international is simply inevitable. In an attempt to minimize so-called "collateral damage" specialists of international humanitarian law and the laws of war have come up with the concept of "proportionality." The basic idea here is that you not bomb a hospital just because there is a sniper hiding on its roof (well, hospitals should be protected anyway, and no armed combatants should have access to them, but never mind, you get the idea). It is a good idea, but not a practical one.

Any good military commander feels a profound sense of responsibility for the men under his command. In many cultures, the commanding officer is considered morally responsible before the parents of his soldiers for their well-being and survival. And many officers, in particularly good ones, take this responsibility very seriously. It is often the case that generals sometimes address their soldiers (though not officers) by such words as "my son." For such a commander the life of only one of his soldiers is far more important that the lives of even many enemies, in particular during a civil war where the hatred for the other side is particularly strong.

Ask yourself this simple question: if you are the commander of, say, and armored company, and while you pass a village your soldiers get shot from the rooftops, while you send your men in to do a house-to-house search (and inevitably suffer even more casualties) or will you call in an artillery strike?

Or this: you are the commander of a special operations unit deep inside the enemy territory and while you are moving at night you stumble upon young girl watching over a herd of goats. She sees you and your men. What do you do? If you let her go, she will report you to her village. If you take her with you, she won't be able to follow you and by her very presence she will compromise your security. Or do you quietly slit her throat and hide her body?

These are all real situations, which were shared with me by officers who had to take these decisions and who still suffer internally from what they had to do, but they did that to protect that which was the most precious thing for them: the lives of **their own men** whom they felt responsible for first and foremost.

And then there is this: in the good old days, wars used to have fronts and even battlefields. Armies had the good taste of fighting in the fields near little-known villages like Austerlitz or Borodino. Now, the very nature of war has completely changed.

To explain this, I will use an metaphor: traditionally wars looked very much like a American football game: a line of scrimmage, two lines of deployed adversaries, a clearly identifiable "front" and "rear." Modern warfare is much more like European soccer: both teams are deployed all over the field, and each player "covers" one other player, while the game is constantly in motion. What does that mean for civilians? That there is no more FEBA (forward edge of battle area) and no "front." As soon as hostilities begin the full strategic depth of each side becomes as much part of the area of operations, of the battlefield, as any other. In other words, from now on combat operations will always and inevitably happen right next to and in the middle of civilian areas. This is why the argument of "hiding behind civilians" is so stupid: civilians will be everywhere, you simply cannot fight at all unless you accept the fact that you will fight in civilians areas.

All this is inevitable for any modern war, civil or international.

Civil wars, however, do have their own unique horrors.

It is not politically correct to say so, but in most civil wars you do not take prisoners. At all. Zero. Why?

Well, for one thing the parties to the civil war rarely have the infrastructure to process and hold large groups of prisoners. Then, remember what Robert said, in civil wars your enemy is not a patriot of his country, he is a traitor to your country. And what do traitors deserve? Yup. Death. That is a universally accepted idea. Finally, in a highly mobile combat environment there is simply not enough time to deal with the issues of prisoners. So what normally happens is this: you try not to make prisoners in the first place. If you still end up taking some prisoners, you quickly interrogate them (we are talking for ten to fifteen minutes per prisoner unless the guy caught is really important), and then you shoot them and leave.

This is how it is done. I am not saying that this is right or that I approve of it. But this is how it is done by all sides in every conflict. This, sadly, is the norm. Again, if you don't like that, if these facts make you uncomfortable, don't start civil wars because this is how civil wars are fought. All of them.

So, are there things which are truly beyond the pale even in civil wars?

Yes.

Things like torture, rape, deliberate and useless execution of civilians. Not only are these simply unjustifiable—there can be no military rationale for such acts—but they are also extremely corrupting for the units engaged in them. Units who engage in these kind of practices always end up losing their cohesion and discipline and the necessary military hierarchy rapidly deteriorates and commanders and commanded all become **accomplices**.

By the way, the worst offenders in this kind of crimes are typically poorly trained and poorly commanded units. While a special operations commander might not hesitate to slit a girls throat to protect his men, he will never allow his men to engage in such behavior or, even less so, engage in it himself.

What about torture to extract information?

Well, as I just said, poorly trained and poorly commanded units might think that torturing an enemy prisoner might yield some important information. But the reality is that 99% of the prisoners have very little information worth sharing and that 99% of these prisoners will be so terrified and depressed anyway that they will talk hoping that this might save their life (it won't) and it makes no sense to spend more than ten to fifteen minutes to interrogate them. Sure, those are unlikely to be a pleasant ten to fifteen, you can expect threats, screams, punches, slaps, kicks and rifle-butts in your face, but nothing too gory or medieval. As for the high value prisoners, they will be sent away to be interrogated by specialists and, unlike what these morons in Guantanamo thought, the best way to "break them open" is not at all to torture them, but to outsmart and out-think them.

Again, none of the above applies to irregular units formed of self-proclaimed "patriots" who really are only poorly trained criminal thugs who love to torture and kill out of viciousness. Yes, they will also be out there during a civil war, but they will not be acting under orders of the regular military command who typically will feel an intense dislike and distrust for them (and rightly so, I would add).

I thought that it was important to write to these basic reminders of what wars and civil wars are really like. We are all too conditioned by a "CNN view" of wars which has no resemblance with reality at all. And I hope that the next time you hear some pious outrage about some horrible dictator and "new Hitler" engaging in all kinds of atrocities you will keep these few considerations in your mind to try to make sense of what has really happened or not.

PS: Having thought about it all, I have to add a small caveat here. What I wrote above does not apply to Africa where, for a number of reasons I do not want to discuss here, the historical record seems to indicate that wanton atrocities are the norm and where the very concept of "regular armed forces" is rather removed from reality.

May 11, 2013

MY LOVE-HATE RELATIONSHIP WITH MARXISTS

Let me begin by clearly spelling out that I hate most of what is considered the "moderate" left: the "NPR liberals" or the "Huffington Post progressives" who seem to be utterly oblivious to the self-evident fact that capitalism is based on growth and that infinite growth in a finite environment, something which inevitably leads to death (if you don't understand that, please ask any oncologist to explain it to you). In other words—capitalism is evil, deadly, self-defeating and there is no such thing as a form of sustainable capitalism.

Just to make one thing clear: capitalism is not the only economic system in which there can be private ownership, a relatively free market or even corporations. Real capitalism is a system in which private capital is not under the supreme control of the people. Real capitalism is, therefore, always non-democratic. The opposite of capitalism is not necessarily communism, but any economic system in which the economy is regulated; in other words, a planned economy, an economy in which the democratic majority rules always trumps private interest (by the way, these are all my own, working, definitions, not anything academic or official).

Having made this clear, I would like to share with you my love-hate relationship with Marxists. Folks like Michael Parenti or Paul Le Blanc. I love to listen to them and I deeply admire their sharp analytical minds. Yet, they also regularly make me howl in frustration. Here is why:

First, here is what I love in Marxists.

Their uncompromising stance on capitalism

The folks who best understand the evil of capitalism are, I think, the various Marxist schools of thought. Not only do they oppose capitalism, they have produced the best and most comprehensive analytical corpus of all the contradictions of the capitalist system and ideology.

Their focus on revolutionary change

The second quality which I love in Marxists is that, unlike the "liberals" or "progressives" I referred to above, Marxists do not believe that the system can be reformed—they want a "revolution." If we understand "revolution" not only in the sense of violent uprising but in a wider sense of a "turn around" or a "regime change" (as opposed to government change), then I fully agree with them. Something which is inherently evil cannot be reformed and capitalism is, in its very essence, evil. Marxists were the first ones to understand that.

Their understanding of class struggle

Lastly, I think that mankind owe a big debt to Marxists for having thoroughly analyzed the topic of class interest and class struggle. Living the modern USA in which the top 1% is richer than the bottom 95% gives the Marxist analysis of class war a totally new dimension, does it not? And who are the allies of this top 1% of US plutocrats in the rest of the world? Why—the millionaire and billionaire "class comrades" in Colombia, in Russia, in Nigeria, in Japan or Iran! There is an undeniable class consciousness and class solidarity among the rich of the world who did a much better job uniting than the "proletarians of all countries" ever could.

And yet, the Marxists also drive me crazy with frustration. Here is how:

Their futile attempts at explaining, justifying or even denying the crimes of Marxist mass murderers.

The other day, I was listening to a podcast of Paul Le Blanc on Socialism and Democracy[484] on Seeing Red Radio. Le Blanc is a brilliant speaker and his lecture is most informative. And then, suddenly, Le Blanc embarks upon what I can only call a mind-boggling lunacy: he states that Lenin and Trotsky were, of all things, real democrats. And he is not the only Marxist parroting that kind of nonsense. Somehow, the Marxists seems to believe that a brilliant mind (as both Lenin and Trotsky most definitely had) necessarily implies a pure heart. This reminds me of the slogan by the founder of the Soviet terror police (the ChK or ЧК) that a real "Chekist" must have a "cool head, burning heart and clean hands." Clean hands?! That coming from the folks who butchered entire classes of people in Russia and whose hands where so soaked in the blood of millions innocent people that no amount of propaganda could ever clean them again. Yes, Lenin and Trotsky were brilliant people. But they were also ghoulish mass murderers who founded the secret police only one month after the Bolshevik revolution and who personally approved of hostage taking, summary executions, mass murder, tortures and who created the infamous Soviet Gulags.[485] Lenin personally send out telegrams urging "mass terror"[486] and while Trotsky even authored a very interesting book entitled "Terrorism and Communism"[487] which I recommend to anyone who has any doubts about where Trotsky stood on this issue. Yet, Le Blanc and other Marxists speak of a "bureaucratic" terror in Russia, and they systematically point their finger at Stalin as The Sole Evil Culprit (all in caps) for all the horrors of Bolshevik rule in Russia. I have already written about the Jewish myth about "Stalinism" else-

---

[484] Paul Le Blanc on Socialism and Democracy 2.9 http://seeingredradio.org/2010/06/27/paul-le-blanc-on-socialism-and-democracy-2-9/

[485] The Gulag Archipelago https://en.wikipedia.org/wiki/The_Gulag_Archipelago

[486] Red Terror https://en.wikipedia.org/wiki/Red_Terror

[487] Leon Trotsky; Terrorism and Communism https://www.marxists.org/archive/trotsky/1920/terrcomm/index.htm

where[488] and I will not repeat it all here other than say that there never was such a thing as "Stalinism" and that the ONLY difference between Lenin and Trotsky on one hand and Stalin on the other is that Stalin also directed his terror at the Party apparatchiks who themselves had terrorized Russia under Lenin and Trotsky. Think of it as something not unlike the mass elimination of the SA by the SS under Hitler. Hardly a reason to sob in sympathy for the poor SA brown shirts killed by the SS.

Their narrow-minded hostility toward religions

Marxism was born in Europe, the continent which produced the Papacy with its endless list of crimes against humanity, its collaboration with the ruling classes, its justification of every conceivable abomination *ad majorem Dei gloriam*. So I understand that any European revolutionary faced with the oppression and exploitation of the feudal or bourgeois order in Europe would end up fighting "the Church." But, come on! The religious phenomenon in history can hardly be reduced to the crimes of the Papacy, now can it?! Look at the history of Orthodox Christianity, of Islam, or even Hinduism. Do you find the same systematic use of terror as in the Papacy? Sure, Ivan the Terrible did commit mass murder against the Muslims of Kazan, and the Ottomans did forcibly convert many Bosnians to Islam, and even today Hindu fanatics massacre Muslims with vicious glee. But if you take a closer looks at these events, you will realize that these are the actions of "ruling elites" who a) hide behind religious motives and b) who act in direct contradiction with the religious imperatives and ethos of the religion they claim to struggle for.

Furthermore, I would argue than in history organized religions were most often engines for progress and civilization and that tyrants and plutocrats saw them as enemies and not "opium for the people" which they could use to exploit the poor. Lastly, considering the millions of people

---

[488] How a medieval concept of ethnicity makes NATO commit yet another a dangerous blunder http://thesaker.is/how-a-medieval-concept-of-ethnicity-makes-nato-commit-yet-another-a-dangerous-blunder/

killed word-wide by various Marxists, who are they to blame organized religions? According to the best estimate in just the 20th century communist governments have killed about 110,000,000 people.[489] That's one hundred and ten million people. With a tally like that, no amount of whitewash and denial will do. Marxists need to accept history for what it was, not for what they wish it had been.

The Marxists are still unable to understand the role of religion today

In that sin, they are not the only ones, of course. Most Western "progressives" are equally guilty of this one. Still, I have heard pro-Hezbollah Arabs declaring that the Shia ethos and piety have really very little to do with Hezbollah's stunning success and that when Hezbollah Secretary-General Hassan Nasrallah praises Ayatollah Ali Khamenei, the Supreme Leader of Iran, its only out of "political necessity." Many Marxists simply fail to understand something which Hassan Nasrallah repeats over and over and over again in every single one of his speeches: the power of Hezbollah comes from its faith which is the existential core of the entire Hezbollah phenomenon. And we are not talking about just some vague amorphous "I believe" à la Hollywood movies. Hezbollah are the spiritual followers of Ayatollah Ali Khamenei whom they chose as their spiritual leader over the recently deceased Grand Ayatollah Mohammed Hussein Fadlallah (who never was the "spiritual leader of Hezbollah" as the corporate media claims). So what is at the core of Hezbollah is not just Islam, but Shia Islam, and not just any Shia Islam, but the Shia Islam personified by the guidance of Ayatollah Ali Khamenei. And it is precisely this expression of Shia Islam which achieved that which all the progressive, Marxist and socialist Lebanese political parties could not: free Lebanon and beat back the Zionists. Is that a coincidence? I don't believe so and, more importantly, neither does Hassan Nasrallah.

---

[489] HOW MANY DID COMMUNIST REGIMES MURDER?* By R.J. Rummel http://www.hawaii.edu/powerkills/COM.ART.HTM

Many Marxists have also supported the "Gucci Revolution" in Iran only because they perceived the power of "the mullahs" (as they would put it) as being "reactionary" and "theocratic" (hence—very bad). Such Marxists have never read Ayatollah Khamenei, they know nothing of the progressive reforms introduced by the Islamic Revolution in Iran and they are oblivious to the fact that the leaders of the "Gucci Revolution" were representing the reactionary multi-millionaire and bourgeois classes of Tehran. For some mysterious reason, most Marxists when looking at Iran completely forgot about class interest and class warfare. That is what ideological blindness does to them. If religion is reactionary, then the mullahs are bad, and any movement which attempts to overthrow the Islamic Republic (which is what he "Gucci Revolution" was all about, of course) is worthy of support, even if it is CIA sponsored.

In all fairness, I have to admit that the new generation of Marxists is changing, at least in Latin America where leaders like Chavez or even Castro have considerably toned down their opposition to religion. I have some very real hope that the new "Bolivarian Socialism" or "Bolivarianism" will resolutely turn away from the deep errors of 20th century "classical" Marxism and, in the words of Hugo Chavez,[490] create *"a new type of socialism, a humanist one, which puts humans and not machines or the state ahead of everything."* Hopefully, this new type of socialism will, unlike Leninism and Trotskyism, value each individual life and never use terror. And hopefully this new type of socialism will accept and embrace the diversity of human spirituality and not designate any religion as the class enemy. Such a new socialism will be able to fully integrate the Marxist, Leninist and Trotskyist analysis and critique of the capitalist system and ideology, but will reject their methods and prescriptions. After all, a

---

[490] Venezuela's Chavez Closes World Social Forum with Call to Transcend Capitalism http://venezuelanalysis.com/news/907

"progressive" must—by definition—learn from past mistakes and yearn for a new, better, way.

July 14, 2010

APPENDIX: Q&A WITH A CHINESE FRIEND, BY MR. UNKNOWN AND THE SAKER

Foreword by the Saker: For centuries, the paramount geostrategic goal of the British Empire was to maintain or, as needed, to create a state of war in continental Europe. The top priority was to prevent any form of alliance between Russia and Germany. This policy enabled the British Empire to become a world power by dominating the seas. The successor empire to the British Empire, the Anglo-Zionist Empire, has basically pursued the same policy and is still using all its power to prevent any co-operation or alliance between Russia and the European Union. In both cases, the geostrategic goals of these empires were developed within the framework of Halford Mackinder's Heartland versus Rimland paradigm.

The crucial mistake that the Anglo-Zionist Empire committed in our times was to focus solely on Europe. As a result, Western strategists failed to foresee that Russia would turn to a far more capable and advantageous ally: China. Vladimir Putin and Xi Jinping have done something unprecedented in history: they have decided to create a symbiotic relationship between two superpowers, each one depending on the other for its very survival. The relationship is by far the most important development since the Second World War and it will change the very nature of our planet. Needless to say, the AngloZionists are horrified by this process and clueless as to how to prevent or delay it. But it is already too late. Still, we can expect the Empire to use all its economic, political and propagandistic power to try to implement the age-old maxim *divide et impera* (divide and rule). A key element of that effort will be to try to reinforce anti-Chinese propaganda in Russia and anti-Russian propaganda in China.

That is why "Mister Unknown" and I decided to engage in a Q&A in which we ask each other **deliberately hostile and even silly questions**. We wanted to give each other the opportunity to debunk the imperial propaganda and to counter the various clichés it uses to try to turn Russians and Chinese against one another, mostly by creating fear.

Please be assured that these questions do **not** reflect our views in the least. We are both deeply convinced that our two nations are natural allies that desperately need each other to survive and we both strongly support Xi and Putin in their efforts to build a different cooperative order for the Eurasian landmass and the rest of our planet: a multipolar, multi-ethnic, multi-confessional cooperative realm made up of truly sovereign nations, peacefully and freely cooperating with one another, without any hegemonic master setting the rules or violently enforcing its will. We believe that BRICS (the Brazil, Russia, India, China, and South Africa) and the SCO represent an alternative to the current US/NATO/IMF/WB system, and that the symbiosis between China and Russia is vital to the success of this alternative.

The authors' thanks are expressed for helping with the editing and translation of the texts to the following wonderful and dedicated people:

- Alena Scarecrow
- Alex
- Bing
- Eugenia
- Ian
- Lizen
- Matt
- Ms. Newmoon
- Robin

- The Heavy Anglo-Orthodox
- Zheng Yiping

MISTER UNKNOWN'S QUESTIONS FOR THE SAKER

QUESTION 1. Why should China engage today in a strategic partnership with Russia, given that Czarist Russia robbed the Qing Dynasty of more than a million square kilometers of territory under the Treaty of Aigun—the Qing Empire's largest territorial loss under all the humiliating and unequal treaties with European imperialists?

ANSWER: When we say "Russia," we should distinguish between the following categories:

- Pre-1917 Russia, which officially became an Empire under Peter I in 1721;
- Post-1917 Soviet Russia;
- Post-1991 "Democratic Russia"; and
- Post-2000 "Putin's New Russia."

These four phases are fundamentally different from one another, especially in that each phase marked a deliberate and strong repudiation of the preceding one. There is simply no continuity in the worldview and policies of Czarist Russia, Soviet Russia, Democratic Russia and New Russia. True, the geostrategic interests of any entity in the territory occupied by New Russia can show evidence of continuity, but the way in which these interests are defended and promoted changes.

One of the single most important features of modern Russian political thought is that Russia paid a huge price for being an empire, and there is simply **no** constituency in Russia for any kind of imperial project, not for a Czarist one, not for a communist one, and most definitely not for a New Russian one. Yes, from time to time Vladimir Zhirinovsky says something crazy, but the reality is that Russians suffer from a huge case of empire fatigue; when they look at the United States today, they do not want to emulate it in any way.

Consider this: Russia was the first Soviet republic to secede from the Soviet Union, and very few Russians objected when immense territories, such as the Ukraine and Kazakhstan, also declared their national independence and sovereignty. And even though Ukrainian politics eventually soured Russian-Ukrainian relations, look at Kazakhstan, with which Russia has superb relations. Nobody in Russia is suggesting that Kazakhstan be conquered anew. The notion that Russians have any territorial ambitions aimed at China, or that they are inclined to renege on the territorial agreements signed with China, is ludicrous. In fact, if anything, Russians are afraid that the Chinese might have a change of heart and consider taking parts of Siberia.

But here is the most important aspect of this question: there is no denying that Russia during her long history did commit imperialist actions. Russians were no better than other people in this regard, and neither were her rulers. But it is crucial to note that imperialism is not an integral part of the Russian culture and civilization, and in the history of Russia imperialist wars of occupation are the exception rather than the norm. Modern Russia wants China as an ally, a partner and a civilizational brother, and Russians want to be judged on their actions, not the sins of their forefathers.

QUESTION 2. How can China trust Russia as a partner, when Russia sells arms to India and Vietnam, both of which have border disputes with China and have fought wars against China over such matters?

ANSWER: I understand that such sales can be a problem for China, but only if one assumes that China, India and Vietnam are still potential military enemies. Frankly, I think the main reason for these arms sales is that Russia needs the money pretty badly (energy and weapons are what Russia can export right now), and the Russians believe, probably correctly, that China doesn't really object.

The solution is also obvious: the BRICS. I'm quite sure Russia sees improved relations between India and China as a strategic priority. Ideally, Russia, China and India should develop weapons systems together, such as the Perspektivny Aviatsionny Kompleks Frontovoy Aviatsii, "Prospective Airborne Complex of Frontline Aviation" (PAK FA) fighter aircraft program. To the best of my knowledge, China has never objected to Russia's weapons sales to India or Vietnam. Pragmatic politics and the need for money are the reasons for these sales. But, yes, as long as there are tensions between China and India, or China and Vietnam, this issue will be delicate. The solution isn't a suspension of weapons sales, but a stable and mutually acceptable settlement of all the territorial disputes between all the BRICS countries, with Vietnam following suit.

QUESTION 3. Ethnically and culturally, Russians are far more European than they are Asian. How do we know Russia simply won't abandon China and curtail its economic cooperation the minute the EU and United States show some mercy and soften the sanctions, especially if someone replaces Putin? Don't all the oligarchs keep their assets in London and love everything Western? How do we know Russia won't switch sides and help the United States and Japan contain China, if given a good enough deal?

ANSWER: The notion that Russians are far more European than Asian is a fallacy supported by two factors: the external appearance of Russians, who are mostly white, and the ideology of the Russian ruling classes between the 18th and 20th centuries. Yes, most Russians are white but culturally they are most definitely not European. I won't go into a lengthy historical exposition here; I will just say that the history of Russia and the West has been one of continuous aggression from the West, combined with a deep misunderstanding between Westerners and Russians. Yes, the Russian elites have been mostly pro-Western, and that is partially true even today. The Russian elites today can be split into two groups. I call them the "Atlantic Integrationists" and the "Eurasian Sovereigntists." The former group, represented by Dmitri Medvedev, wants Russia to have an equal part in the Western Empire and wants the West to accept Russia as a partner. The latter group, represented by Putin, wants Russia to become a truly sovereign state, not a Western colony, and it wants Russia to become the center of a Eurasian space of peace, prosperity and joint development. Its disgust and disillusionment with the West is total. **So, yes, the Chinese most definitely ought to distrust the** Atlantic integrationists, who are quite capable of backstabbing China (or any other country) in the hope of pleasing the United States. But, by the same token, the Chinese ought to realize that **it is in China's strategic interests to support Russia's Eurasian Sovereigntists, who are natural allies for China.**

QUESTION 4. Why should China buy so much oil and gas from Russia, when Russia constantly uses energy as leverage against other trade partners, such as by cutting off gas to the EU over Ukrainian pipeline disputes? How do we know that similar tactics won't be used against China down the road?

ANSWER: First, it is incorrect to say that Russia used her gas leverage in a dispute with Europe. Not only has Russia always done her part in delivering gas to Europe, but she also offered the North and South Stream pipeline systems to bypass the Ukraine. It was the Europeans who decided to support the Ukraine against Russia, even though the Ukraine was literally stealing Europe's gas, and it was the EU that torpedoed South Stream. Russia would love to sell gas to Europe, but she cannot help it if the Europeans are more concerned about pleasing their U.S. colonial masters than making sure people in Europe have enough gas.

But, to answer your question, Xi and Putin will enter world history as the two men who have found the answer to this and many similar issues: instead of just signing contacts between the two countries, they have taken the unprecedented step of binding China and Russia in a **symbiotic** relationship: one of mutual interdependence. Yes, China will depend on Russia for its energy, but Russia will also depend on China for the sale of its energy and, furthermore, Russia will also depend on the Chinese economy for her own development. The two countries have basically decided to become interdependent in terms of their energy, economic and military cooperation (these are all crucial strategic programs). Once such a symbiosis is created, no short-term conjectural considerations can reverse it. In this way, a sovereign and prosperous China will become a strategic Russian objective, and a sovereign and prosperous Russia will become a strategic Chinese objective. To my knowledge, it is the first time in history that two superpowers (or two former empires) have decided to become symbionts, with each keeping its full sovereignty. What Putin and Xi have created has, I believe, no precedent.

QUESTION 5. Given the Russian invasion and occupation of Ukrainian territory, namely Crimea, how can the world be sure that Russian aggression won't be repeated in Central Asia, especially to undermine China's economic influence?

ANSWER: Here, I will have to quote the official position of the Kremlin, which I fully support. Russia did not occupy Crimea. At most, Russia can be accused of using her forces, which were in Crimea legally by treaty, to protect the Crimean population long enough for it to vote on its future, which Crimea had a right to do under both Ukrainian law and the UN Charter. By the time Russia accepted Crimea into the Russian Federation, Crimea was no longer Ukrainian. No one denies that the vast majority of the people of Crimea were in favor of this solution. Finally, what kind of occupation are we talking about if not a single person was killed during the events? Also, Crimea is truly a special case. There is no equivalent of Crimea anywhere in Central Asia—in the historical or cultural sense.

QUESTION 6. "Protection of ethnic Russians and Russian-speakers in the near abroad" is exactly the same type of excuse that Hitler used to justify Nazi aggression in Europe. Isn't Putin the next Hitler?

ANSWER: Hitler was unique. There will be no "next Hitler"—that is just Anglo-Zionist propaganda. Furthermore, Hitler made it abundantly clear in his book and speeches that he wanted to create a new European order and to give the German people the Lebensraum he thought they needed. In other words, Hitler always intended to start a world war. That is why he didn't stop at the Sudetenland. Finally, Hitler believed that the German people were racially superior to every other ethnic group. All these characteristics make the comparison with Putin ridiculous. Does anybody believe that Putin wants to start a world war? Has Putin ever claimed that the Russian people need more territory or that they are racially superior? Furthermore, why do the Baltic states fear that Russia might intervene to protect the ethnic Russians in the Baltics, but Kazakhstan has no such worries? Might that have something to do with the apartheid-like regime under which the Russian minority has to live in the Baltics, while in Kazakhstan the civil rights of ethnic Russians are protected? In the case of China, it is more relevant to ask whether there is a large persecuted Russian minority anywhere in China? I don't think so, so this is a moot point.

QUESTION 7. Russia is an expansionist parasite that has made no historical contributions to human progress, unlike the West, which propagates enlightened liberal values, scientific knowledge, and economic prosperity. Why should China be associated with an expansionist rogue state that threatens the stability of the international community and has nothing to offer the world except an oversized gas station?

ANSWER: The contributions made by Russians to human progress in the fields of science, literature, and music are well known. It is true, however, that Russia has made very little contribution to the propagation of "enlightened liberal values" for the simple reason that Russia as a civilization is neither liberal nor enlightened (in the Western sense of the word). Russia is profoundly conservative, traditionalist, and religious, and her cultural roots stem from three sources: ancient Slavic tribes (ethnic stock), the Byzantine Empire (religion), and the Tatar-Mongol occupation (state building). Furthermore, Russian culture is incompatible with the Western notion of secular humanism or individualism. Russia is profoundly collectivistic, and that is also why Western-style capitalism is alien to the Russian culture. Finally, the imperial period of Russian history, lasting roughly from the18th to the 20th century, was a reflection of the world view of the pro-Western Russian elites that ruled over the Russian masses and from which they were always separated by a deep cultural chasm. While Russia has always been multi-ethnic and multi-religious, Russian civilization has never been imperialistic, and that is why Putin's Russia truly yearns for a multipolar world. Russia's Foreign Minister Sergey Lavrov constantly stresses two concepts. The first is **collective security**: "If you don't feel safe, then I don't feel safe." The second is simple **collaboration**: "Let's make our enemies into neutrals, our neutrals into friends and our friends into allies." Does that sound like imperialist rhetoric to you?

QUESTION 8. Wouldn't the Chinese be better off if they helped the United States squeeze Russia economically, then swept in and picked up undervalued assets and resources for pennies on the dollar after Russia collapsed a second time?

ANSWER: That is exactly what Russians fear the most. But that would also be a disastrous outcome for China. Nobody can doubt that the United States wants to be a world hegemon. In contrast, Russia has no such intentions; in fact, she is putting all her efforts into creating a multipolar world through organizations such as the SCO and the BRICS. **So the choice for China is not between Russia and the United States, but between two fundamentally different world orders.**

On the one side, you have a country or a set of countries that actively supports separatist organizations that seek to have Tibet, Xinjiang, and Taiwan break away, aligns with and arms Japan, places embargoes on China to stifle its technological modernization, uses political ideology and propaganda to subvert China's domestic governance and undermine Chinese government legitimacy at every opportunity, supports every regime that escalates a territorial dispute with China, and attempts to obstruct China's attempts to reform global governance, such as its establishment of the Asian Infrastructure Investment Bank.

On the other side, you have a country that does none of the above—a country that is cautiously resolving its conflicts with China and progressively deepening its ties to China, but without intending to change or subvert China's political system, territorial integrity, culture, or economic progress.

I see this situation as the dichotomy of choices laid out before China, and the right path could not be more obvious.

I see Russia facing the same set of choices: to side with a team that actively diminishes Russia's external influence and internal governance at every opportunity or a team that does not. That is why a Sino-Russian strategic partnership is so natural and so obviously the right choice for both.

Furthermore, maybe China could join forces with the United States and turn Russia into a semi-colonial state, but that would leave China one-on-one with a triumphant United States, which is racist at its core. Look at the ECHELON countries, of which France, for example, is not a member. Neither is Japan or Germany. Why? What makes Australia or New Zealand a closer ally to the United States and the United Kingdom? The answer is obvious: it is called the Anglosphere. This is a system of power in which neither China nor Russia will ever be accepted as an equal partner. So why would China ever want to help destroy a non-racist ally such as Russia (there is no such thing as a racially pure Russian—Russians are all of mixed ethnic and cultural stock) to aid a 100% racist world empire?

For more than 200 years, the Russian ruling classes wanted to be accepted by the West as equals, and the Western elites always contemptuously rejected them—even though Russians appear physically to be white. Still, the West has always believed the quip of France's Marquis de Custine, who famously said, "Scratch a Russian and you will find a Tartar [Mongol]." And in a way he was right: Russians are much closer culturally, in their ethos, to Tartars and Mongols than to Europeans. What do the nationalists assert today in the Ukraine? That they are defending Europe against the Asiatic Russian hordes. The West has never accepted Russia; nor will it ever accept China as an equal. That is why China should cherish its alliance with Russia, and together the Russians and the Chinese should build a free, sovereign and peaceful Eurasian continent and world order.

THE SAKER'S QUESTIONS FOR MISTER UNKNOWN

Foreword by Mister Unknown: The answers to the following questions are entirely my personal opinions. I do not seek to represent anyone else, although I adopt and incorporate others' ideas into my answers. The questions cover a wide variety of topics, and my answers can be lengthy. I've put the most important points in boldface and used bullets to ensure easy reading and topic tracking for the convenience of readers who may not be interested in every issue. The key takeaway is that I'm not going to portray China as some imaginary holier-than-thou country that's 100% benign and peaceful. China is no more or less pragmatic and interest-driven than any other country (and vice versa). That being said, **China can best serve its strategic interests by pursuing a stable, progressive, long-term, cooperative relationship with Russia. For that reason alone, most existing narratives predicting and/or advocating an antagonistic Sino-Russian relationship—from China's strategic perspective—are false.** Furthermore, the world will be more peaceful and prosperous if China and Russia deepen their collaboration with each other, with the BRICS, and with other developing countries to create a truly multipolar world order.

QUESTION 1. Let's compare China and Russia using data from Wikipedia:

- China has 1,357,380,000 people living in 9,596,961 km^2 (a density of 145 people per km^2) with a GDP of $18.976 trillion;
- Russia has 143,975,923 people living in 17,098,242 km^2 (a density of 8.4 people per km^2) with a GDP of $3.458 trillion.

Do these figures not show that all China wants is to create a Lebensraum for its people and grab Siberia's vast natural resources? Russia's land mass is huge but its population and GDP are tiny compared with China's. All this talk about an alliance is really designed to conceal from the Russian people the fact that China will simply take over Russia. The most likely scenario is that the Chinese will simply buy all of Russia and turn it into a Chinese-run colony.

ANSWER: In describing why such assertions are completely false, I want to give our readers this central thesis: You do not need to believe in China's benevolence or desire for peaceful development to see that the Chinese-takeover rhetoric is based on myth and xenophobia. In fact, you can even assume that China conducts a ruthless, calculated, and power-maximizing foreign policy, and still correctly conclude that it's not in China's interests to take over Russian territory to create a "Chinese Lebensraum."

I have written two **detailed articles**[491] on the **Hidden Harmonies**[492] blog to dispel the myth of China's attempt to colonize Russia, so I will provide only a short rundown here.

Those who propagate the idea that China is a threat to Russia have never viewed the scenario from the Chinese perspective. **It is not in China's strategic interests to attempt to take over territory in Siberia or the Russian Far East. In fact, doing so would undermine China's power**, for three primary reasons:

There is no viable path toward a Chinese takeover. No one who propagates Chinese-takeover phobia inside or outside Russia has ever articulated a logical narrative as to how such a takeover could be success-

---

[491] The Myth of Chinese Mass Migration into Russia http://blog.hiddenharmonies.org/2012/08/14/the-myth-of-chinese-mass-migration-into-russia/

[492] The Myth of a Chinese takeover in Siberia – Continued http://blog.hiddenharmonies.org/2015/01/16/the-myth-of-a-chinese-takeover-in-siberia-continued/

fully carried out. But let's review a few commonly cited ways China could take over parts of Russia:

DEMOGRAPHIC: Chinese make up only about 3% of the Russian Far East's population and a negligible percentage of Siberia's. There is no mass migration of "yellow hordes."

MILITARY: Invading the world's largest nuclear power would be insane; the devastation of Russian nuclear retaliation would offset any territorial and resource gains.

POLITICAL: The Chinese have little or no political influence over the internal governance and the policy-making bodies of Russia. Translation: no Chinese-sponsored regime change.

ECONOMIC: The EU buys more Russian resources and owns far more Russian assets than the Chinese do. The real problem is not that China will simply buy all of Russia, but rather that China is currently buying too little from Russia.

Any attempt to take over Russian territory would worsen China's national security, for it would undoubtedly provoke Russian retaliation, such as Russian support for separatist movements in Tibet, Xinjiang, and Taiwan. Moreover, Russia would most likely foment insurgency among the Russian communities in the Chinese-occupied parts of Russia. Additionally, Russia would actively undermine China's strategic efforts to rebuild the Silk Road through Central Asia. This threat would be exacerbated if the United States and Russia managed to reconcile and collaborate in subverting Chinese territorial integrity.

It is cheaper for China simply to buy Russian resources. China would have more access to Russian natural resources if it didn't attempt to take over parts of Russia. Even if (and it's a big if) China succeeded in grabbing a part of Russia's territory, the rest of its vast territory would be subsequently closed to China in the ensuing hostilities. It's important to note that most of Russia's natural resources—especially its oil and gas—are not near the Chinese border.

Bottom line: Any attempt to take over Siberia or the Russian Far East would have virtually zero probability of success and would ultimately weaken China. Therefore, as long as China has a government that puts priority on its own best interests, the chances of such an occurrence are negligible.

QUESTION 2. Russia is crazy to sell its latest military technology to China, which is an aggressive power that illegally occupies Tibet, threatens Taiwan, is hostile toward Japan, and is acting in a highly provocative manner in the dispute over the Spratly Islands. India and Vietnam have both had wars with China, and Russia should heed their example instead of trusting the Chinese. China is an aggressive, militaristic country that has built thousands of missiles to strike Taiwan, regularly provokes the U.S. Navy and will not hesitate to use force against Russia. If capitalists were willing to sell Communists the rope that they would need to hang them with, then the Russians are apparently willing to sell the Chinese the weapons they need to defeat Russia.

ANSWER: If we want to use historical territorial conflicts to judge China as a military threat, let's temporarily tune out the noise and focus on some comparative history as it relates to Russia; we will return to those other issues later. Let's draw some historical contrasts between China and the Western European powers by exploring the following simple questions:

How many wars has China fought against Russia?

In comparison, how many wars have Western European powers fought against Russia?

Moreover, what are the relative sizes of those armed conflicts in terms of troops and resources committed, as well as the losses suffered by each side?

When one objectively answers these questions, the conclusion is plainly obvious: Even if Russians want to perceive China as a threat, China has never posed as much of a threat to Russia as Western Europe has and does, not even close.

Now, to explore each question:

China fought two "wars" against Russia over border disputes, if we want to exaggerate and regard the following conflicts as wars, instead of seeing them for what they really are: minor skirmishes involving fewer than 10,000 troops on each side and fewer than 1,000 deaths.

Sino-Russian border skirmishes of 1652-1689[493]: Fewer than 10,000 total troops were committed to active combat by both sides, with an estimated total of 1,000 to 2,000 casualties on both sides (not deaths, but total casualties) **over a period of 37 years.** The conflicts were ended by negotiated settlement in China's favor with the Treaty of Nerchinsk, which was later renegotiated in Russia's favor with the treaties of Aigun and Beijing.

Sino-Soviet border skirmishes of 1969[494]: Fewer than 5,000 troops were committed to active combat by both sides, with fewer than 1,000 combined casualties for both, although more than one million troops were placed on alert by both countries. The conflict ended by negotiated settlement with various Sino-Soviet/Russian agreements from 1969 to 2008.

In comparison, Russia's various Western neighbors have fought too many wars against Russia for me to count them, so I'll let Wikipedia[495] tot them up. But a few noteworthy ones include the Muscovite-Lithuanian Wars, Russo-Swedish Wars, Great Northern War, Napoleonic Wars, Crimean War, WWI, and World War II. All these wars involved far more troops in active combat, a greater commitment of national resources on both sides, and far more casualties.

---

493 Sino-Russian border conflicts https://en.wikipedia.org/wiki/Sino-Russian_border_conflicts

494 Sino-Soviet border conflict https://en.wikipedia.org/wiki/Sino-Soviet_border_conflict

495 List of wars involving Russia https://en.wikipedia.org/wiki/List_of_wars_involving_Russia

The combatants in **all** historical Sino-Russian/Soviet conflicts total fewer than 50,000.

The total Chinese and Russian casualties from these conflicts were fewer than 5,000. The total combatants in historical conflicts between Russia and Western Europe were many millions.

The total Russian and European casualties from these conflicts were 20 million to 40 million, at a minimum.

One more comparison just to help these figures all sink in: Let's not even try to compare the Sino-Russian conflicts to the World Wars or the Crimean War. In terms of total combatants committed and casualties, all conflicts in the entirety of Sino-Russian history cannot even compare to the **Russo-Swedish War**[496] of 1788-1790. That said, you hardly hear about the imminent Swedish threat to Russia, but somehow Russians are frequently reminded that China is the historical boogieman hell-bent on war with Russia, whereas Western Europe is the eternal friend and brother. In what world is that logical?

Finally, I want to address these other territorial disputes China has with India, the Philippines, Vietnam, etc. In the post-colonial/post-imperial age, it's inevitable that newly independent states will have unresolved border issues. I have neither the patience nor the expertise to articulate who is right and who is wrong in each case, or to predict how each will be resolved. What I can do is point out what China has and hasn't done in the past.

In all cases, China has pursued diplomacy as a means of resolving or forestalling conflict, and it continues to do so today. In all cases, China expanded cooperation in other areas (such as trade) despite unresolved disputes. In all cases, China successfully prevented armed disputes from escalating to sustained, full-scale interstate warfare, despite having significant military superiority in most circumstances. In no case did China

---

[496] Russo-Swedish War (1788–90) https://en.wikipedia.org/wiki/Russo-Swedish_War_%281788%E2%80%9390%29

ever pursue all-out invasion/conquest, protracted military occupation, or regime change/color revolutions as a means of resolving conflicts.

In sum, I'm not going to portray China as a pacifist country that will never use force to protect its sovereignty and strategic interests; but history clearly shows that China is far more restrained than most major powers—especially the Western countries—when it comes to armed conflict.

This restraint applies even to **Taiwan—a territory that all nations unequivocally recognize as a part of China**, even those that recognize Taipei instead of Beijing. Even in Taiwan, where Mainland China has a legal right to use force or execute a regime change it is pursuing a strategy of peaceful reunification if possible, and forceful reunification only if necessary.

Finally, as for the so-called illegal occupation of Tibet—the same thing applies: **No country in the world, regardless of whether it recognizes Beijing or Taipei as China's legitimate government, recognizes Tibet as an independent nation-state**. There are some people who do not like[497] this reality, but disliking it does not make it illegal.

The other anti-Chinese accusation I often hear about Tibet is one of cultural genocide. There is a reason that China-bashers use the term cultural genocide: **even the most skillful propagandists cannot accuse China of actual genocide**. The ethnic Tibetan population hovered around 2.5 million to three million back in the 1950s; today the population has tripled to more than 7.5 million, with about 50% of ethnic Tibetans living in the rest of China—outside the Tibet Autonomous Region.

For those who claim that China is polluting Tibetan culture, here is another reference point: before the communist revolution, Tibetan-language literacy among ethnic Tibetans was about 4% to 6% because education was largely limited to the ruling theocracy. Today this number is more than 60%. In other words, **a greater percentage of Tibetans can**

[497] CIA Tibetan program https://en.wikipedia.org/wiki/CIA_Tibetan_program

now read and write their own language than ever before in the entire history of the Tibetan people, yet somehow the "evil ChiComs" are conducting cultural genocide. What is a more important foundation for culture than language?

QUESTION 3. Russia's overtures to China just go to prove that birds of a feather flock together. Russia is ruled by an authoritarian former Communist who tries to suppress dissent, and China is ruled by actual Communists who have never apologized for the Tiananmen massacre, the repression in Tibet, or censorship of the Internet. Both countries are also run by pseudo-capitalists who in reality are ruthless Mafia dons, and the alliance of two such ruthless and non-democratic powers as China and Russia is a major threat to the civilized world. As for the friendship between Xi and Putin, it is a disaster for the freedom-loving people of China and Russia.

ANSWER: At the root of this statement lies a false narrative of democracy versus authoritarianism, **the blind faith that democracy is superior to all other forms of governance,**[498] and the ideological dogma that you are civilized and deserving of prosperity and success only if you believe in democracy. These are the biggest myths in our world today. I've written about them extensively on the Hidden Harmonies Blog; here are some commonly held myths about liberal democratic institutions and values, relative to their non-democratic counterparts. It would take too long to explain each in detail, but I have provided associated links.

Myth 1:[499] Democratically elected governments are better able to prevent unaccountable abuse of power.

Myth 2:[500] Participatory governance is more capable of preventing violent civil unrest, since freedom of expression and the vote are pressure

---

[498] The Aspen Institute: China and Democracy https://www.youtube.com/watch?v=G-YSiWJ9WP0

[499] Three Common Myths about Democratic Institutions http://blog.hiddenharmonies.org/2012/08/03/three-common-myths-about-democratic-institutions/

valves that give disenfranchised individuals and communities some non-violent means of redressing grievances.

Myth 3:[501] Transparency and rule of law give everyone a fair voice and equal opportunity in the democratic decision-making process.

Myth 4:[502] Free societies (as the West defines freedom) are more capable of scientific and technological innovation than their so-called non-free counterparts.

Myth 5:[503] Democracy + capitalism = prosperity. All wealthy, developed countries got rich primarily because they embraced liberal democratic values along with free-market economic policies.

I would add one more myth here that I haven't discussed before:

Myth 6: Democratic societies govern more humanely than their non-democratic counterparts.

How can one measure "humanity" in this context? I say a good start would be the state's ability to preserve its citizens' lives. After all, without life, one cannot have liberty or the pursuit of happiness. I'll let the data do the talking on which countries do this better.

Thus far in 2015, U.S. law enforcement agencies have **killed more than 650 individuals,**[504] and they killed **more than 1,000 individuals in 2014.**[505] But that is nothing new. Since 2001, **U.S. law enforcement has**

---

[500] same

[501] same

[502] Rethinking the Freedom-Innovation Nexus http://blog.hiddenharmonies.org/2012/09/15/rethinking-the-freedom-innovation-nexus/

[503] Yet another myth about democracy: "democracy+capitalism = prosperity" http://blog.hiddenharmonies.org/2014/03/15/yet-another-myth-about-democracy-democracycapitalism-prosperity/

[504] Killed By Police 2015 http://www.killedbypolice.net/

[505] Killed By Police 2014 (1105) http://www.killedbypolice.net/month/14year.html

killed 500 to 1,000 civilians a year.[506] If you think they were all violent and dangerous individuals who deserved to be killed, **think again.**[507]

In comparison, China had twelve police-related deaths[508] (including legitimate incidents where the suspect was caught on camera committing violent acts) **in 2014, and has had nine deaths so far in 2015.** Even if you want to believe that police killings are simply covered up in repressive Russia and China, the scale of such secret police killings would have to be 50 to 100 times greater than those officially recorded, in order to even come close to that of the United States.

Say what you will about repression in Russia and China, statistically speaking a person is a lot less likely to die as a result of Russian or Chinese law enforcement than U.S. law enforcement.

You brought up Tiananmen Square, and I think that's a useful reference point. I think the government acted in a harsh and heavy-handed manner, and I will not sugar-coat the fact that Deng Xiaoping sent in the army to regain control of the capital, and hundreds of civilians died in the ensuing clashes. **Tiananmen was a bad outcome, but a far better one for the Chinese than allowing China to end up like the Soviet Union.**

That said, judging by the number of fatalities, U.S. law enforcement commits the equivalent of a "Tiananmen Square massacre" every one to two years. U.S. citizens are routinely killed by police, not to preserve stability or to prevent a coup d'état, but rather for such heinous crimes as

---

[506] Katie Rucke: US Police Have Killed Over 5,000 Civilians Since 9/11 http://www.mintpressnews.com/us-police-murdered-5000-innocent-civilians-since-911/172029/

[507] Matt Agorist: Police in the US Kill Citizens at Over 70 Times the Rate of Other First-World Nations http://www.globalresearch.ca/police-in-the-us-kill-citizens-at-over-70-times-the-rate-of-other-first-world-nations/5438391

[508] List of killings by law enforcement officers in China, 2014 https://en.wikipedia.org/wiki/List_of_killings_by_law_enforcement_officers_in_China#2014

talking back to a cop,[509] selling cigarettes on the street,[510] or drunk driving.[511] U.S. police brutality has reached the point where it's necessary to publish guides[512] and hold seminars[513] on how to stay alive during police encounters.[514] Yet somehow we're supposed to believe that democracy equals humanity, and authoritarianism equals brutality.

I'm not arguing that authoritarianism is superior to democracy, for there are authoritarian states that are highly effective (Singapore and the United Arab Emirates) and highly dysfunctional (North Korea), just as there are democratic states that are highly effective (Sweden and Norway) and highly dysfunctional (Kenya and India). **But the notion that the process of governance alone determines the legitimacy and quality of governance is a myth.**[515]

QUESTION 4. The new Chinese assertiveness in the international arena is a disaster for poor and developing countries; Chinese entrepreneurs show up with big money in their pockets only to promote the worst kind of exploitation of labor and natural resources. For all their alleged communism, the Chinese are ruthless capitalists who are as least as bad as the notorious robber barons. Nobody in China cares about socialism or communism. All they care about is money.

---

[509] Death of Sandra Bland https://en.wikipedia.org/wiki/Death_of_Sandra_Bland#Dashcam_footage

[510] 'I can't breathe': Eric Garner put in chokehold by NYPD officer – video http://www.theguardian.com/us-news/video/2014/dec/04/i-cant-breathe-eric-garner-chokehold-death-video

[511] Texas Soldier Killed In Police Custody [Graphic Video] https://www.youtube.com/watch?v=KzdinvzfAiY

[512] How To Survive A Crazy Cop https://www.youtube.com/watch?v=TmIzDJDEJVg

[513] Stops & Cops: A Youth's Survival Guide for Police Encounters https://www.youtube.com/watch?v=F4DuZocOQdU

[514] Stops & Cops: A Youth's Survival Guide for Police Encounters https://search.yahoo.com/yhs/search?p=Stops+%26+Cops%3A+A+Youth%27s+Survival+Guide+for+Police+Encounters&ei=UTF-8&hspart=mozilla&hsimp=yhs-002

[515] Eric X. Li: A tale of two political systems https://www.youtube.com/watch?v=s0YjL9rZyR0

ANSWER: I believe all humans are tempted by the same broad range of vices and virtues, and I will not pretend that the Chinese are any different. Chinese entrepreneurs are no less profit-driven than their counterparts in Europe, Africa, the United States, or elsewhere. That said, even if one believes that Chinese businesses are exploitative capitalists, China's increasing global economic presence is one of the best things that has happened for poor and developing countries.

For developing economies, China has become an alternative source of development capital and expertise, and this trend will become more prevalent now that other countries are joining China in alternative multilateral institutions, such as the Asian Infrastructure Investment Bank and the BRICS New Development Bank. China offers investment and trade opportunities without the stringent, unrealistic preconditions imposed by traditional Washington-dominated institutions such as the IMF and the World Bank.

China passes no judgment on how a society governs itself or its way of life, nor does China pretend to know how to govern local communities better than the locals. Furthermore, economic engagement with China is entirely voluntary. No sovereign country in the world has ever been invaded, occupied, or politically subverted (through color revolutions) in any way by the People's Republic of China because of the country's refusal or reluctance to trade with China or to use the Chinese currency.

Another positive byproduct of Chinese economic engagement in poor and developing regions is the attention that these regions now get from other economic powers. Countries such as Japan and Russia are now competing to offer trade and development opportunities to Africa. Increased competition means more choices for poor and developing societies, as long as this competition is carried out without malicious means, such as color revolutions, proxy wars, or invasions.

I will not elaborate further on this topic. I'd rather let international development experts such as Dambisa Moyo[516] and Deborah Brautigam[517] do the talking. **But suffice to say, because of trade and investment opportunities offered by China, poor societies now have more choices about their path toward development and more say about trade preferences.**

QUESTION 5. The Russians should not trust the Chinese because the Chinese are in bed with the Americans. Just look at the Walmart economy binding the United States and China. What can Russia offer to compete? Nothing. The first priority for the Chinese will always be to sell to the Americans, not to the Russians, and that, in turn, means that the Russians cannot count on the Chinese to back them in any way in case of a surge of tensions or even hostilities between Russia and the United States.

ANSWER: The most recent Ukrainian crisis has already proved that surging hostilities between the United States and Russia do not hinder Sino-Russian cooperation. On the contrary, the size and scope of Sino-Russian collaboration have expanded at an accelerated pace in the post-Maidan environment.

It is true that Sino-U.S. trade volumes are larger than Sino-Russian trade, and will likely remain so in the foreseeable future. That does not mean China will reduce or deemphasize trade from Russia if coerced by the United States. In fact, since the start of the Ukrainian crisis, **Sino-Russian relations have expanded in some ways that defy the conventional narrative that is depicted in both Russian and Western media.**

Traditionally, China's efforts to expand trade with Russia have often been portrayed as a sinister ploy to turn Russia into a Chinese resource appendage; China will import only Russia's natural resources, while

---

[516] Economist Dambisa Moyo on China's Pursuit of Resources https://www.youtube.com/watch?v=bf8-5QBbzmU

[517] The Dragon's Gift: The Real Story of China in Africa https://www.youtube.com/watch?v=JNx5DvTIbQE

flooding the Russian market with Chinese consumer goods. This theme is repeated non-stop in the U.S. and European media, and is frequently echoed by some of the Russian media.

Contrary to the media hype, recent (post-Maidan) joint efforts—more so than ever before—emphasize collaboration in the form of Chinese imports of Russian high-tech manufactured goods and projects conducive to Russia's industrial advancement and modernization beyond primary materials extraction.

Examples include the leasing of 100 Sukhoi-100 Superjets,[518] joint R&D of wide-body passenger aircraft,[519] joint development and manufacturing of heavy transport helicopters,[520] joint use of ground stations for navigation satellites,[521] Russian exports of cutting-edge industrial manufacturing equipment,[522] to China, Chinese investment in Russian high-tech entrepreneurship,[523] Chinese participation in Russia's high-speed rail development,[524] China's renewed purchase of advanced Russian air-

---

[518] Alexander Korolkov: Sukhoi enters lucrative Chinese civil aircraft market http://rbth.com/business/2015/07/17/sukhoi_enters_lucrative_chinese_civil_aircraft_market_47833.html

[519] Vladimir Karnozov: Russia and China Push for Next-Gen Widebody https://www.ainonline.com/aviation-news/aerospace/2015-06-11/russia-and-china-push-next-gen-widebody

[520] Russia, China to develop massive heavy-lift helicopter https://www.flightglobal.com/news/articles/russia-china-to-develop-massive-heavy-lift-helicopter-412140/

[521] Russia, China can host each other's ground navigation stations http://rbth.com/news/2014/06/30/russia_china_can_host_each_others_ground_navigation_stations_37796.html

[522] Optogard Nanotech blazes a trail for Skolkovo in China http://sk.ru/news/b/articles/archive/2015/04/06/optogard-nanotech-blazes-a-trail-for-skolkovo-in-china.aspx

[523] Hallie Siegel: Sino-Russian robotics boosted as Skolkovo signs $200M deal with Chinese investment fund http://robohub.org/skolkovo-signs-200m-deal-with-chinese-investment-fund/

[524] China to Design New Russian High-Speed Railway http://www.wsj.com/articles/china-to-design-new-russian-high-speed-railway-1434729400

defense equipment[525] and China's increasing role as a substitute supplier of microelectronics for the Russian defense industry[526]—all since the anti-Russian sanctions were imposed.

Other endeavors that are not related to raw materials and that got under way before Maidan include China's purchase of Russian nuclear reactors[527] as well as the expansion of tourism[528] and educational exchanges.[529]

All these examples are not meant to prove that China is some kind of angel that is helping Russia solely out of charity or friendship, but rather that **it is in China's strategic interest to cooperate with Russia in all fields, not just natural resource extraction.**

One final note on this issue, as I pointed out in a previous opinion piece on this blog: it seems to me that Russians, and Chinese also to some extent, place excessive emphasis on the U.S. factor in Sino-Russian relations. **There are many areas where China and Russia can benefit from long-term cooperation, regardless of each country's relationship status with the West. The sole criterion for the Sino-Russian collaborative roadmap should be bilateral mutual benefit, and it should be independent of their relationships with third parties, be they the United States, the European Union, or anyone else.**

---

[525] Catherine Putz: Sold: Russian S-400 Missile Defense Systems to China http://thediplomat.com/2015/04/sold-russian-s-400-missile-defense-systems-to-china/

[526] Chinese microelectronics will replace U.S. microelectronics in Russian space, defense industries - newspaper

http://rbth.com/news/2014/08/06/chinese_microelectronics_will_replace_us_microelectronics_in_russian_spa_38790.html http://rbth.com/news/2014/08/06/chinese_microelectronics_will_replace_us_microelectronics_in_russian_spa_38790.html

[527] Russia's Rosatom to build new units in China's Tianwan nuclear power plant http://www.power-technology.com/news/newsrussias-rosatom-to-build-new-units-in-chinas-tianwan-nuclear-power-plant-4548529

[528] Russia to see more tourism revenue from Chinese tourists http://www.shanghaidaily.com/article/article_xinhua.aspx?id=293694

[529] Russia, China create joint university in Shenzhen free economic zone http://www.rt.com/news/179536-china-russia-joint-university/

QUESTION 6. If Russia expands trade with China, won't Russia just become China's resource appendage? After all, Russia only exports raw materials to China, while China only exports manufactured goods to Russia.

ANSWER: Here's my short answer to this misleading line of logic: If Russia does not expand its trade with China, it will continue to be a resource appendage of Europe and it will have fewer opportunities to climb the global economic value chain in the long term.

Those who think Russia is becoming a resource appendage to China should consider the following data:

- Russia sells 140 billion to 160 billion cubic meters (BCM) of natural gas to the EU each year.
- In comparison, Russia sells less than 10 BCM a year to China today and will sell no more than 70 BCM a year even if both the eastern and western export routes become operational.
- Russia sells two million barrels per day (bpd) of oil to the EU.
- In comparison, Russia sold 700,000 bpd to China in 2013 and may reach one million bpd this year (May 2015 data show 900,000 bpd).

The tough reality for Russia is that, even though it is striving to diversify its economy into areas other than the primary materials sector, natural resources will still make up the majority of its export value for the next 10 to15 years, if not longer. **Given this reality, the ideal way for Russia to make the best of this difficult situation is to sell its natural resources to as many trade partners as possible, and use the revenue to transform Russia into an industrial and knowledge-based economy.**

During this process, having multiple partners compete for its natural resources means Russia has relatively more leverage to extract technology transfers and favorable terms. Diversification of trade partnerships also means that if one partner goes into a recession or an economic downturn, other trade partners can soften the impact. Therefore, **even if the**

structure of Sino-Russian trade is currently sub-optimal for Russia, it's still a net benefit, given the alternative of continued dependency solely on the West.

Moreover, as stated above, China's trade with Russia has advanced into many areas outside the raw materials sector, which will be conducive to Russia's technological advancement.

Finally, if Russia can successfully modernize its infrastructure in the Russian Far East (a project that China can participate in and accelerate), its trade with other Asian economies, such as South Korea, Japan, and India, will inevitably be stimulated. In this way, Russia could further diversify its trade relationships.

QUESTION 7. China's behavior at the United Nations Security Council is lopsided, especially when compared with Russia's. Typically, when the Russians veto, the Chinese abstain. Why? If China is really a partner for Russia, why isn't that apparent at the Security Council? And did China not take a highly ambiguous position on the Crimean referendum?

ANSWER: China's political stances have indeed not been aligned 100% with those of Russia, but that does not mean China isn't Russia's committed strategic partner. I tend not to focus too much on symbolism in the world of geopolitics, but rather action. And, as outlined above, China has accelerated its strategic partnership with Russia in just about every sphere. **Full political alignment at all times shouldn't be a criterion for partnership. One can hardly find two individuals who have the same opinion about every issue, let alone two massive and diverse countries. No two countries in the world—not even the United States and the United Kingdom[530]—agree on everything all the time.**

[530] Clint Gray: US Condemns UK For Supporting China's Asian Infrastructure Investment [AIIB] Bank Move http://monitorgraph.com/2015/06/13/us-condemns-uk-for-supporting-china-s-asian-infrastructure/

Even as Russo-Chinese collaboration expands and deepens, we should still expect these two independent powers to have differing opinions, we should still expect competition with each other in some areas, and we should even expect failure to accomplish our goals at times.

We should not expect the Sino-Russian strategic partnership to tread an easy path, even though it's clearly the best path. The key to maintaining a stable and progressive relationship is to take the right approach when difficulties arise. China and Russia have both chosen dialog, compromise, mutual value creation, and trust building as the way to handle their differences. These methods are more practical and ethical than are military confrontation, proxy wars, economic sabotage, and regime change.

September 28, 2015

CPSIA information can be obtained
at www.ICGtesting.com
Printed in the USA
LVOW04*0507211115
463581LV00015B/300/P